HORIZONS IN HERMENEUTICS

Horizons in Hermeneutics

A Festschrift in Honor of
ANTHONY C. THISELTON

Edited by

Stanley E. Porter & Matthew R. Malcolm

WILLIAM B. EERDMANS PUBLISHING COMPANY
GRAND RAPIDS, MICHIGAN / CAMBRIDGE, U.K.

© 2013 Wm. B. Eerdmans Publishing Co.
All rights reserved

Published 2013 by
Wm. B. Eerdmans Publishing Co.
2140 Oak Industrial Drive N.E., Grand Rapids, Michigan 49505 /
P.O. Box 163, Cambridge CB3 9PU U.K.

Library of Congress Cataloging-in-Publication Data

Horizons in hermeneutics: a festschrift in honor of Anthony C. Thiselton /
   edited by Stanley E. Porter & Matthew R. Malcolm.
      p.   cm.
   Includes bibliographical references and index.
   ISBN 978-0-8028-6927-2 (pbk.: alk. paper)
   1. Bible — Hermeneutics.   2. Bible — Criticism, interpretation, etc.
   3. Thiselton, Anthony C.   I. Thiselton, Anthony C.
   II. Porter, Stanley E., 1956-   III. Malcolm, Matthew R., 1975-

BS476.H63   2013
220.601 — dc23

                                              2012032134

www.eerdmans.com

Contents

CONTRIBUTORS	vii
Thiselton and Hermeneutics: An Introduction to a Celebratory Contribution *Stanley E. Porter and Matthew R. Malcolm*	ix
The Life and Work of Anthony Charles Thiselton *Stanley E. Porter and Matthew R. Malcolm*	1

FACING THE OTHER

Poetry and Theology in Isaiah 56–66 *John Goldingay*	15
Thiselton on Bultmann's *Sachkritik* *Robert Morgan*	32
Experience and the Transfiguration of Tradition in Paul's Hermeneutical Christology *Mark L. Y. Chan*	51
Kerygmatic Rhetoric in New Testament Epistles *Matthew R. Malcolm*	69
"The Rock Was Christ": Paul's Reading of Numbers and the Significance of the Old Testament for Theological Hermeneutics *Richard S. Briggs*	90

CONTENTS

ENGAGING THE OTHER

The Earliest Interpreters of the Jesus Tradition:
A Study in Early Hermeneutics   119
    James D. G. Dunn

Metaphors, Cognitive Theory, and Jesus' Shortest Parable   148
    David Parris

"But We Have the Mind of Christ": Some Theological
and Anthropological Reflections on 1 Corinthians 2:16   175
    Richard H. Bell

PROJECTING POSSIBILITIES

Reading Scripture in a Pluralist World:
A Path to Discovering the Hermeneutics of *Agape*   201
    Tom Greggs

Scripture and the Divided Church   217
    Stephen Fowl

What Exactly Is Theological Interpretation of Scripture,
and Is It Hermeneutically Robust Enough for the Task
to Which It Has Been Appointed?   234
    Stanley E. Porter

"Let Us Cook You Your Tea, Vicar!" Church, Hermeneutics,
and Postmodernity in the Work of Anthony Thiselton
and Stanley Hauerwas   268
    John B. Thomson

INDEX OF MODERN AUTHORS   286

INDEX OF ANCIENT SOURCES   292

Contributors

RICHARD H. BELL, Department of Theology and Religious Studies, University of Nottingham, UK

RICHARD S. BRIGGS, Cranmer Hall Theological College, Durham, UK

MARK L. Y. CHAN, Trinity Theological College, Singapore

STEPHEN FOWL, Department of Theology, Loyola University, Baltimore, Maryland

JAMES D. G. DUNN, Department of Theology, University of Durham, UK

JOHN GOLDINGAY, Fuller Theological Seminary, Pasadena, California

TOM GREGGS, King's College, University of Aberdeen, Scotland

MATTHEW R. MALCOLM, Trinity Theological College, Perth, Western Australia

ROBERT MORGAN, Faculty of Theology, University of Oxford, UK

DAVID PARRIS, Fuller Theological Seminary, Colorado Springs, Colorado

STANLEY E. PORTER, McMaster Divinity College, Hamilton, Ontario, Canada

JOHN B. THOMSON, Diocese of Sheffield, Rotherham, UK

Thiselton and Hermeneutics:
An Introduction to a Celebratory Contribution

Stanley E. Porter and Matthew R. Malcolm

The title of this volume is *Horizons in Hermeneutics*. By selection of this title, we are making an explicit allusion to the important contribution to the field of hermeneutics by Professor Anthony C. Thiselton, and using terminology that has come to be identified with him and his work.[1] The title is not so simple as it may at first seem, as it utilizes one of the dominant metaphors in the field of hermeneutics as a means of extending the field itself. Indeed, this volume is intended to honor Professor Thiselton for his significant influence and impact upon the fields of hermeneutics, biblical studies, and their complex relationship. As editors of this volume, however, our intention has gone beyond that of simply feting the honoree, but we have attempted to honor Professor Thiselton by making this book a contribution in its own right to this complex of topics. Rather than gathering a vaguely-related group of essays as a *Festschrift*, we have asked contributors to reflect on the impact of Professor Thiselton's work, and thereby to contribute to an exemplification, extension, or critical adjustment to his and related approaches.

For this reason, there will be some value in introducing these contributions at the same time as we reflect on Professor Thiselton's approach to biblical hermeneutics. To return to the imagery of the title, Thiselton's

---

1. In particular, see Anthony C. Thiselton, *The Two Horizons: New Testament Hermeneutics and Philosophical Description with Special Reference to Heidegger, Bultmann, Gadamer, and Wittgenstein* (Grand Rapids: Eerdmans; Carlisle: Paternoster, 1980); *New Horizons in Hermeneutics: The Theory and Practice of Transforming Biblical Reading* (Grand Rapids: Zondervan; Glasgow: Marshall Pickering, 1992). See the following chapter, which includes Professor Thiselton's bibliography, to see other ways in which he has engaged the metaphor of horizons.

contribution may be briefly — though recognizably inadequately — summarized as the attempt to illuminate the transforming engagement of the horizon of the interpreter with the horizon of the biblical text.[2]

Such a horizonal engagement must begin with the primary acknowledgment that the text to be interpreted is genuinely "other."[3] Whether in lectures or in writing, Professor Thiselton is fond of quoting Dietrich Bonhoeffer's striking theological encapsulation of the basic hermeneutical principle that the text is an "other" subject to be encountered, rather than an object to be mastered: "If it is I who say where God will be, I will always find there a [false] God who in some way corresponds to me, is agreeable to me, fits in with my nature. But if it is God who says where he will be . . . that place is the cross of Christ."[4]

Doing justice to the otherness of the biblical text involves attention to the entextualized "directedness" that the varied scriptural texts exhibit as products of real authors living in a real (ancient) world.[5] For this reason, Professor Thiselton's justly famous commentary on First Corinthians involves "close attention to the sociohistorical background since it clarifies many issues."[6] With a similar conviction, the present volume of essays begins with the section *Facing the Other*. The essays in this section reflect on elements of this engagement with a plurality of variously "directed" texts that come to us from a horizon that is different from our own.

The section begins with John Goldingay's essay, "Poetry and Theology in Isaiah 56–66," in which Goldingay reflects on the way in which poetry is utilized in Isaiah as a tool by which the "unsayable" may be suggestively expressed. Goldingay's essay is a fine exemplification of Professor Thiselton's

---

2. Professor Thiselton introduces *The Two Horizons* by explaining: "The goal of biblical hermeneutics is to bring about an active and meaningful engagement between the interpreter and text, in such a way that the interpreter's own horizon is re-shaped and enlarged" (xix). In a later reflection on his subsequent work *New Horizons*, Thiselton comments: "Whereas my earlier major volume concerned *engagement* between two horizons, the theme of this still larger volume was that of *transformation*" ("Situating the Explorations," in *Thiselton on Hermeneutics: Collected Works with New Essays* [Grand Rapids: Eerdmans, 2006], 11).

3. Thiselton identifies this as the "heart of hermeneutical endeavour." Thiselton, "Resituating Hermeneutics in the Twenty-First Century," in *Thiselton on Hermeneutics*, 37.

4. Cited in "Resituating Hermeneutics," 45; cf. *New Horizons*, 619.

5. Thiselton is clear that such "directedness" is internal to the text itself, and should not be mistaken for the naïve pursuit of "psychological hypotheses." See *New Horizons*, 559-60.

6. *The First Epistle to the Corinthians* (NIGTC; Grand Rapids: Eerdmans, 2000), xvii.

conviction that the culturally sensitive analysis of compositional devices need not be pejoratively seen as a naïve attempt to master the psychological intentions of a dead author, but rather may be understood as careful attention to the entextualization of performative force.

Following this is Robert Morgan's essay, "Thiselton on Bultmann's *Sachkritik*." Morgan appreciatively and critically engages with Professor Thiselton's work on Rudolf Bultmann in his *The Two Horizons*. In the light of Professor Thiselton's commitment to honoring the "otherness" of the biblical text, Morgan explores the possibility that Bultmann's *Sachkritik* may be retrieved as a way of doing just that. Rather than necessarily exerting a domineering control over the text, Bultmann's approach may be regarded as an attempt to do justice to the (entextualized) intentions of the biblical authors.

The following three essays, while fitting within this section of *Facing the Other*, begin to mark a transition within this volume to the subsequent section, as they consider both features of "directedness" in Paul, and ways in which Paul himself was part of a tradition that passed on "lived readings" of ancient texts.

Mark Chan's essay, "Experience and the Transfiguration of Tradition in Paul's Hermeneutical Christology," examines "the embodiment of understanding in the life of the interpreter." Bearing witness to Professor Thiselton's long interest in embodied discipleship,[7] Chan considers the way in which Paul may be seen as an exemplification of the embodied hermeneut, renegotiating his understanding of the Scriptures he had inherited in the light of his experience of Christ on the Road to Damascus.

The next essay, by Matthew Malcolm, pursues a somewhat parallel investigation, considering Paul as a life-affected interpreter of his scriptural tradition. This essay, "*Kerygmatic Rhetoric* in New Testament Epistles," suggests that New Testament epistles can be fruitfully analyzed as products of this sort of hermeneutical renegotiation, a renegotiation centered on the *kerygma* of messianic death and resurrection.

Professor Thiselton's work expresses the tension between Friedrich Schleiermacher's summons to interpret the biblical texts within a broader framework of *general* hermeneutics,[8] and the *special* need for the reader of the Bible to be encountered and transformed by the transcendent God of

---

7. E.g., *The Hermeneutics of Doctrine* (Grand Rapids: Eerdmans, 2007), 47, one of many places in which Thiselton affirms Ernst Käsemann's sense of embodied discipleship.

8. *New Horizons*, 197.

the cross.⁹ The final essay in this section of the book may be read as speaking to this tension. The essay is Richard Briggs' "'The Rock Was Christ': Paul's Reading of Numbers and the Significance of the Old Testament for Theological Hermeneutics." Briggs considers Paul as an interpreter of Scripture whose approach presents a stumbling block to Schleiermacher's contention.

The next section of the book moves from *Facing the Other* to *Engaging the Other*. One of Professor Thiselton's abiding concerns is that those in modern "life-worlds" might effectively engage with the biblical texts, as the interpreter's horizon moves towards fusion with the horizon of the text.¹⁰ This fusion is emphatically not a bypassing of the historical gap between the Bible and the present, but rather a meeting of genuine "others," which is mediated through a tradition of "lived readings" of the text. Today's biblical interpreter is the heir of a polyphonic plurality of such lived readings, which suggest "horizons of expectation" that may be confirmed or surprised in subsequent readings.¹¹ The doctrines that have arisen from particular communal life-situations and have subsequently been affirmed across the history of the Church are of particular relevance, providing a provisional but coherent theological pre-understanding for those who approach the Bible.¹²

The essays in this next section of the book, then, attempt to exemplify or reflect on this interest in an engagement with ancient texts that pays attention to their reception, evaluation, and effective history.

The first of these essays is James Dunn's "The Earliest Interpreters of the Jesus Tradition: A Study in Early Hermeneutics." Dunn compares the earliest reception of the Gospel of John and the *Gospel of Thomas*, concluding that their differing canonical statuses reflect differing hermeneutical approaches: John interprets Jesus tradition from the "inside," while Thomas interprets this material from the "outside." This discerning reception by the early church sets a precedent, Dunn suggests, for the ongoing evaluation of new readings of Scripture.

Continuing the reflection on interpretation of the Gospels is David Parris's essay, "Metaphors, Cognitive Theory, and Jesus' Shortest Parable." Parris explores how insights developed in multi-disciplinary studies of re-

---

9. *New Horizons*, 615.
10. *Two Horizons*, 445; *Hermeneutics of Doctrine*, 4.
11. See "Resituating Hermeneutics," 40-45; *Hermeneutics of Doctrine*, 98-99.
12. See *Hermeneutics of Doctrine*, 125, where Thiselton characteristically points to Wolfhart Pannenberg in making this point.

cent decades may shed light on what is happening when we encounter metaphors, and, consequently, how such insights may inform our reading of Jesus' saying, "Physician, heal thyself!"

The final essay of this section is Richard Bell's contribution to the Pauline literature: "'But We Have the Mind of Christ': Some Theological and Anthropological Reflections on 1 Corinthians 2:16." Bell's essay shows full concurrence with Professor Thiselton's conviction that the text can be enlightened by attention to cultural context; but he also exemplifies Professor Thiselton's interest in how a text might move beyond the parameters of its initial (or "aesthetic") reading. Bell takes Paul to "move well beyond" the sense of the Scripture he cites; and Bell himself is interested in seeing where Paul's own words might take a theology of "mind" in the light of later philosophical discussion.

Having moved from *Facing the Other* to *Engaging the Other*, it might be thought that the interpretive task is over. However, for Professor Thiselton it is essential and inevitable that the engagement of "other" lifeworlds that occurs in a plurality of ongoing actualizations of biblical texts will project possibilities for surprising transformation, theological development, and future action. Professor Thiselton's consideration of the way in which this happens in relation to narrative texts is worth quoting:

> Narratives project *possible* worlds that engage the imagination by providing strategies of projection for *future* action. . . . In this model, narrative *stimulates the imagination,* and offers constructs which project possibilities for *future action.* They *activate* the eschatological call of Christian pilgrimage, in the sense of beckoning onwards towards new future action, or in some cases also warning readers of projected possibilities to be avoided. They provide a resource by which readers can transcend the present.[13]

The final section of the present volume, then, is *Projecting Possibilities.* It is at this point that the "goal" of hermeneutics is perhaps most explicit: the effective transformation of horizons, as, communally, we look ahead to the definitive eschatological horizon of meaning.[14] The essays in this section examine and suggest ways in which the interpretive task might provoke such transformation.

The first of these essays is by Tom Greggs, "Reading Scripture in a Plu-

---

13. *New Horizons,* 569; emphases original.
14. *Hermeneutics of Doctrine,* 541.

ralist World: A Path to Discovering the Hermeneutics of *Agape*." Greggs suggests that Scripture itself urges an ecclesial readership to interpret the Bible with an orientation of faith, hope, and love. Greggs offers an "experiment" in imagining what a hermeneutic of love might look like in a pluralist world.

From the reading of Scripture in a pluralist world, we move to the reading of Scripture in a divided church, in the essay by Stephen Fowl: "Scripture and the Divided Church." Fowl's provocative contribution explores what it means to read Scripture in a context in which a growing ecumenical outlook appears to be at odds with institutional division. Fowl illustrates Professor Thiselton's interest in considering how the horizons of the text and interpreter transform one another,[15] by attempting to freshly hear the biblical narratives about Israel as a pressing indictment of present Christian apathy over ecclesial division.

The reading of Scripture in the context of the Church has prompted development of a form of biblical interpretation related to and in some ways derived from Professor Thiselton's theological hermeneutics. In a wide-ranging article Stanley Porter asks the question "What Exactly Is Theological Interpretation of Scripture, and Is It Hermeneutically Robust Enough for the Task to Which It Has Been Appointed?" By examining five recent summative works on theological interpretation and their proposals, he notes that their shortcomings leave such an approach without the kind of basis that is demanded of a biblical hermeneutic that seeks to serve both the academy and Church.

Following this note of warning, the final section of the book ends on a note of hope, with John Thomson's essay, "'Let Us Cook You Your Tea, Vicar!' Church, Hermeneutics and Postmodernity in the work of Anthony Thiselton and Stanley Hauerwas." Thomson seeks to demonstrate the necessity of embodied ecclesial "performances on the Scriptural script" for the actualization of the goal of biblical hermeneutics. Thomson finds reasons for hope in the Christian communities of Sheffield, where Professor Thiselton himself lived for nearly fifteen years.

This volume moves, then, from *Facing the Other*, through *Engaging the Other*, to *Projecting Possibilities* of transformation. We believe that in many ways this movement captures the impetus of Professor Thiselton's scholarly and ecclesial work through the years. He himself has attempted to embody these emphases in both his own abundant and significant scholarship, and

---

15. *New Horizons*, 31.

the life that he has led as a person of the academy, the church, and the surrounding culture. Living such a life of complex interactions has, no doubt, not always been easy to maintain and to persevere in, as both church and academy have themselves been transformed through their various engagements during the last nearly half century. As a result, and in honour of his efforts, we offer this volume to Professor Thiselton in gratitude for his impact upon us personally and professionally, and in hope that this represents a positive contribution to his work's history of effects.

The Life and Work of Anthony Charles Thiselton

Stanley E. Porter and Matthew R. Malcolm

Professor Anthony C. ("Tony") Thiselton was born on 13 July 1937 in Woking, a town in west Surrey, about twenty-five miles southwest of the heart of London, and within the Greater London urban region. Thiselton's education at the City of London School followed the rigorous classical curriculum of the day just before its modernization, so he was given thorough exposure to the classical languages. He then entered the University of London, where he completed the B.D. in 1959 and the M.Th. in 1964 at King's College.

A life-long Anglican, Thiselton was ordained in the Church of England, so that, before graduating with the M.Th., he took up a position as Chaplain and Lecturer in Theology at Tyndale Hall Theological College in Bristol (now Trinity College Bristol), along with being a Recognized Teacher in Theology in the University of Bristol. Thiselton stayed in this position in Bristol from 1963 to 1970. During this time, he helped John Wenham with his well-known elementary Greek grammar, and continued to teach Greek at various points in his academic career. In 1970, not only did he publish his first scholarly article (of many), but Thiselton was appointed Sir Henry Stephenson Fellow at the University of Sheffield, a research fellowship reserved for Anglican priests engaged in theological research. After only one year of the fellowship, in 1971 he was appointed to the position of Lecturer in Biblical Studies at the University of Sheffield, and then was promoted to Senior Lecturer in 1979, a position he held until 1985. Thiselton was appointed to his position in Sheffield under the departmental headship of Professor James Atkinson, a renowned Luther scholar with wide-ranging interests that also included the Bible. Thiselton appreciated the collegial and ecclesial atmosphere of the department under Atkinson's leadership. While at Sheffield, Thiselton completed his thesis as a staff candidate for the Ph.D., which was accepted in 1977 for the degree (externally examined by James Torrance and John Macquarrie) and subsequently published as *The Two Horizons: New Testament Hermeneutics and Philosophical Description with Special Reference to Heidegger, Bultmann, Gadamer and Wittgenstein* (1980). During this time, Thiselton regularly taught a course on hermeneutics, one of the few such courses offered in the United Kingdom at the time, and began the supervision of a long list of successful research students. Atkinson was succeeded by Professor John Rogerson, under whose guidance the Department of Biblical Studies rose to pre-eminence in the English-speaking world. Thiselton was invited during the 1982-1983 academic year to serve as Visiting Professor and Fellow at Calvin College in Grand Rapids, Michigan, where he collaborated with two literary scholars, Roger Lundin and Clare Walhout, on a volume subsequently published as *The Responsibility of Hermeneutics* (1985). This volume was later revised and expanded by all three authors and published as *The Promise of Hermeneutics* (1999).

Thiselton left Sheffield in 1985 to take up the position of Principal of St. John's College Nottingham, along with being a Special Lecturer in Theology in the University of Nottingham. St. John's at the time was one of the largest Anglican theological colleges in the United Kingdom, as well as being one of the leading evangelical theological institutions. Thiselton looked forward to the opportunity to be involved in the training of ordinands for Christian ministry, something that he had not been able to be involved in while teaching in Sheffield. In 1988, Thiselton took up the equivalent position of Principal of St. John's College in the University of Durham, the evangelical theological college within the university. Coincidental with his departure in 1992, Thiselton was made Honorary Professor of Theology in the University of Durham. In 1992, Thiselton published his second major work, *New Horizons in Hermeneutics: The Theory and Practice of Transforming Biblical Reading*, adding to his already significant reputation as a major thinker in the area of hermeneutics and biblical interpretation.

In 1992, Thiselton was appointed to the position of Professor of Christian Theology and Head of the Department of Theology in the University of Nottingham. His appointment to a professorship was considered by many to be long overdue, due to his service to scholarship, the academy, and the church. During his tenure at the University of Nottingham, Thiselton took an already well-established and strong department and strengthened it further, especially in his area of internationally recognized expertise, hermeneutics. Thiselton continued in this position until 2001, when he was appointed Emeritus Professor of Christian Theology at Nottingham. In high demand for his academic expertise, as well as his work with postgraduate students, Thiselton was made Research Professor of Christian Theology in the University of Chester from 2003 to 2008, and then resumed the position of Professor of Christian Theology (though not head of department) in the University of Nottingham from 2006 to 2011, when he again and finally retired as Emeritus Professor. Thiselton's time at Nottingham was incredibly productive for him in all ways. He continued his New Testament and hermeneutics teaching, supervised a large number of research postgraduates as this volume attests, and published a number of major works in the area of hermeneutics, New Testament studies, and cognate areas.

In 1995, Thiselton confronted head-on the question of postmodernity in his *Interpreting God and the Postmodern Self: On Meaning, Manipulation and Promise*, based upon his Scottish Journal of Theology Lectures delivered at the University of Aberdeen. In 2000, Thiselton finally, after years of dedicated research and writing beginning in his days in Sheffield, published his major commentary on Paul's first letter to the Corinthians, *The First Epistle to the Corinthians: A Commentary on the Greek Text*, a 1500-page tome on the Greek text that incorporates his distinctive positions regarding interpretation. He published a shorter, more pastoral commentary on the same book in 2006, entitled *First Corinthians: A Shorter Exegetical and Pastoral Commentary*. Thiselton followed his major commentary on 1 Corinthians in 2002 with *A Concise Encyclopaedia of the Philosophy of Religion*, which at 344 pages is a substantial resource in the field. In conjunction with his work at Chester, he published the concise *Can the Bible Mean Whatever We Want It to Mean?* (2004), addressing a question that inevitably arises in contemporary biblical studies, especially for those influenced by hermeneutics. In 2006, Thiselton gathered together a huge number of his previously published essays, dating from 1970 to the present, as well as including a number of new essays, in a volume published as *Thiselton on Hermeneutics: Collected Works and New Essays*.

Thiselton unfortunately suffered a major stroke in 2007, but he fully recovered from this major medical event and continued his productive scholarship. When he suffered the stroke, he was just completing his *The Hermeneutics of Doctrine* (2007), his last and arguably most significant major work (to date) in constructive hermeneutics, here addressed to important questions of doctrine. Nevertheless, he has continued to publish important works in New Testament and related areas. He published in 2009 a more popular introduction to hermeneutics, entitled *Hermeneutics: An Introduction*, at over 400 pages offering a substantial and up-to-date treatment of the subject. One of the areas explored earlier in Thiselton's work was that of reception history, which he himself practiced and exemplified in *1 & 2 Thessalonians through the Centuries* (2011). In that same year, he also published *Life after Death: A New Approach to the Last Things* (2011), in Britain titled *A New Approach to the Last Things*. A recent manuscript, entitled *The Holy Spirit — In Biblical Teaching, through the Centuries, and Today*, is scheduled for release in 2013. These last two works bring Thiselton's deep experience in hermeneutics and biblical interpretation to bear on subjects that have often caused confusion because of issues related to language, understanding, and prior theological commitments.

In the course of his long and productive career, Thiselton has received various types of significant recognition for his important and valuable scholarship and contribution to academia. This has included a volume in the Scripture and Hermeneutics series that he edits being published in his honor, entitled *After Pentecost: Language and Biblical Interpretation* (ed. Craig Bartholomew, Colin Greene, and Karl Möller; 2001). He also has been awarded the D.D. by the University of Durham in 1993, the Lambeth D.D. by the Archbishop of Canterbury in 2002, and the honorary D.Theol. from the University of Chester in 2012. The highpoint of his career in terms of professional recognition by his peers occurred in 2010, when Thiselton was elected as a Fellow of the British Academy.

As might be expected, Thiselton has been active throughout his career in various professional societies and ecclesial organizations, as well as serving as a visiting professor and lecturer at other institutions. From 1994 to 2010, he served as Canon Theologian of Leicester Cathedral, and since then as Emeritus, and from 2000 to 2007 as Canon Theologian of Southwell and Nottingham, and since then as Emeritus. Thiselton has traveled widely as a visiting scholar, teaching in twelve countries on four different continents. Besides the year-long appointment at Calvin College in Grand Rapids, Michigan, USA, mentioned above, he was Visiting Professor at Fuller Theological Seminary in Pasadena, California, USA, on three occasions, Visiting Professor at Regent College in Vancouver, British Columbia, Canada, Visiting Professor at North Park University in Chicago, Illinois, USA twice, Visiting Professor at the University of Utrecht in the Netherlands, Visiting Professor at Oradea University in Romania, Lecturer at the University of Natal in South Africa, and Visiting Professor and speaker at five different seminaries in South Korea. Thiselton was President of the Society for the Study of Theology from 1998 to 2000, and has been a member of the Society of Biblical Literature, the American Academy of Religion, and from 1976 the *Studiorum Novi Testamenti Societas*. He has served on the editorial boards or as an editorial consultant for *Ex Auditu*, the journal *Biblical Interpretation*, the *International Journal of Systematic Theology*, and *Ecclesiology*. Thiselton is also Fellow of St. John's College, Durham, from 1995 and Fellow of King's College, London, from 2010.

As noted above, Thiselton's academic work has always gone hand in hand with his service to the church. As a result, he has served in a variety of capacities within the Church of England, besides regularly functioning in various local parishes. These include serving on the Church of England Doctrine Commission from 1976 to 1990 and again from 1996 to 2006 and as acting chairman in 1987, functioning as a member of the Church of England Committee for Theological Education from 1989 to 1992 and from 1997 to 2005, serving as a member of the Crown Nomination Commission from 2000 to 2008, being on the House of Bishops Clergy Discipline (Doctrine) Group as a consultant, serving on the House of Bishops Working Party on Women in the Episcopate from 2001 to 2005, being on the Anglican Communion Working Party on Theological Education from 2004 to 2009, and serving on the Church of England Board of Education from 2005 to 2010. Thiselton has also been a member appointed by the Minister of Health to the Human Fertilisation and Embryology Authority, and was vice-chairman for the Board of Theological Studies of the Council for National Academic Awards from 1984 to 1989.

Having observed Thiselton at both the beginning and nearing the end of his professional career, the editors of this volume are pleased to be able to note the way in which he has practiced an exemplary form of Christian scholarship that has benefited both the church and the academy. This has been a consistent pattern throughout his career, and has served as an example to many who have studied with him and have been edified through his many significant publications.

STANLEY E. PORTER AND MATTHEW R. MALCOLM

List of Publications

Books

1980   *The Two Horizons: New Testament Hermeneutics and Philosophical Description with Special Reference to Heidegger, Bultmann, Gadamer and Wittgenstein* (Exeter: Paternoster Press; Grand Rapids: Eerdmans), xx + 484 pages. Translated into Korean: Seoul: Chongshin, 1990.

1985   *The Responsibility of Hermeneutics* (with Roger Lundin and Clare Walhout; Grand Rapids: Eerdmans; Exeter: Paternoster Press), xi + 129 pages.

1992   *New Horizons in Hermeneutics: The Theory and Practice of Transforming Biblical Reading* (London: HarperCollins; Grand Rapids: Zondervan; reprinted: Carlisle: Paternoster Press), 703 pages.

1995   *Interpreting God and the Postmodern Self: On Meaning, Manipulation, and Promise* (Scottish Journal of Theology Lectures, University of Aberdeen; Edinburgh: T&T Clark; Grand Rapids: Eerdmans), xii + 180 pages.

1999   *The Promise of Hermeneutics* (with Roger Lundin and Clare Walhout; Grand Rapids: Eerdmans; Carlisle: Paternoster Press), xii + 260 pages.

2000   *The First Epistle to the Corinthians: A Commentary on the Greek Text* (New International Greek Testament Commentary; Grand Rapids: Eerdmans; Carlisle: Paternoster Press), xxxiii + 1,447 pages.

2002   *A Concise Encyclopaedia of the Philosophy of Religion* (Oxford: Oneworld; Grand Rapids: Baker Academic), viii + 344 pages.

2004   *Can the Bible Mean Whatever We Want It to Mean?* (Chester: Chester Academic Press).

2005   (Joint Editor with Craig G. Bartholomew and Joel B. Green) *Reading Luke: Interpretation, Reflection, Formation* (Carlisle: Paternoster Press), xxii + 484 pages.

2006   *Thiselton on Hermeneutics: Collected Works with New Essays* (Ashgate Contemporary Thinkers on Religion Series; Aldershot, UK: Ashgate; Grand Rapids: Eerdmans), xvi + 827 pages.

2006   *First Corinthians: A Shorter Exegetical and Pastoral Commentary* (Grand Rapids and Cambridge, UK: Eerdmans), xvi + 325 pages.

2007   *The Hermeneutics of Doctrine* (Grand Rapids and Cambridge, UK: Eerdmans), xxii + 649 pages.

2009   *Hermeneutics: An Introduction* (Grand Rapids and Cambridge, UK: Eerdmans), xiv + 409 pages.

2009	*The Living Paul: An Introduction to the Apostle and His Thought* (London: SPCK; Downers Grove, IL: InterVarsity), x + 190 pages.
2011	*1 & 2 Thessalonians through the Centuries* (Blackwell's Biblical Commentaries; Oxford: Wiley-Blackwell), xvi + 317 pages.
2011	*Life after Death: A New Approach to the Last Things* (Grand Rapids: Eerdmans); British edition: *A New Approach to the Last Things* (London: SPCK, 2011).
2013	*The Holy Spirit — In Biblical Teaching, through the Centuries, and Today* (Grand Rapids: Eerdmans).

Research Articles, Chapters, and Booklets

1970	"The Parables as Language-Event: Some Comments on Fuchs's Hermeneutics in the Light of Linguistic Philosophy," *Scottish Journal of Theology* 23: 437-68.
1973a	"The Meaning of *Sarx* in 1 Corinthians 5.5: A Fresh Approach in the Light of Logical and Semantic Factors," *Scottish Journal of Theology* 26: 204-28.
1973b	"The Use of Philosophical Categories in New Testament Hermeneutics," *Churchman* 87: 87-100.
1974a	"The Supposed Power of Words in the Biblical Writings," *Journal of Theological Studies* 25: 282-99.
1974b	"The Ministry and Church Union: Some Logical and Semantic Factors," *Faith and Unity* 18: 288-92.
1974c	"The Theology of Paul Tillich," *Churchman* 88: 86-107.
1975a	*Language, Liturgy and Meaning* (Nottingham: Grove Liturgical Studies 2) (second edition 1986).
1975b	"Explain, Interpret," in *New International Dictionary of New Testament Theology* (ed. Colin Brown; Grand Rapids: Zondervan), vol. 1: 573-84.
1975c	"Flesh," in *New International Dictionary of New Testament Theology* (ed. Colin Brown; Grand Rapids: Zondervan), vol. 1: 678-82.
1975d	"Kierkegaard and the Nature of Truth," *Churchman* 89, no. 2: 85-107.
1976a	"The Semantics of Biblical Language as an Aspect of Hermeneutics," *Faith and Thought* 103: 108-20.
1976b	"The Parousia in Modern Theology: Some Questions and Comments," *Tyndale Bulletin* 27: 27-54.
1977a	"Semantics and New Testament Interpretation," in *New Testament Inter-*

	pretation: Essays on Principles and Methods (ed. I. H. Marshall; Exeter: Paternoster Press; Grand Rapids: Eerdmans), 74-104.
1977b	"The New Hermeneutic," in *New Testament Interpretation: Essays on Principles and Methods* (ed. I. H. Marshall; Exeter: Paternoster Press; Grand Rapids: Eerdmans), 308-33.
1977c	"Myth, Paradigm, and the Status of Biblical Imagery," in *Using the Bible in Liturgy* (Nottingham: Grove), 4-12.
1978a	"Realized Eschatology at Corinth," *New Testament Studies* 24: 510-25.
1978b	"Truth," in *New International Dictionary of New Testament Theology* (ed. Colin Brown; Grand Rapids: Zondervan), vol. 3: 874-902.
1978c	"Language and Meaning in Religion," in *New International Dictionary of New Testament Theology* (ed. Colin Brown; Grand Rapids: Zondervan), vol. 3: 123-46.
1978d	"Structuralism and Biblical Studies: Method or Ideology?" *The Expository Times* 89: 329-35.
1979a	"The 'Interpretation' of Tongues? A New Suggestion in the Light of Greek Usage in Philo and Josephus," *Journal of Theological Studies* 30: 15-36.
1979b	"Schweitzer's Interpretation of Paul," *The Expository Times* 90: 132-37.
1981	"Knowledge, Myth and Corporate Memory," in *Believing in the Church: Essays by Members of the Church of England Doctrine Commission* (London: SPCK), 45-78.
1982a	"On the Logical Grammar of Justification in Paul," *Studia Evangelica* VII (Berlin: Berlin Academy), 491-95.
1982b	"Academic Freedom, Religious Tradition, and the Morality of Christian Scholarship," in *Their Lord and Ours: Essays Commissioned and Introduced by the Archbishop of Canterbury* (ed. Mark Santer; London: SPCK), 45-78.
1986a	"Sign, Symbol," in *New Dictionary of Liturgy and Worship* (ed. J. G. Davies; London: SCM), 491-92.
1986b	"Hermeneutics and Theology," in *A Guide to Contemporary Hermeneutics* (ed. Donald K. McKim; Grand Rapids: Eerdmans), 78-107.
1986c	"The New Hermeneutic," in *A Guide to Contemporary Hermeneutics* (ed. Donald K. McKim; Grand Rapids: Eerdmans), 142-74.
1986d	"La Nouvelle Herméneutique," *Hokhma* 33: 1-36 (translation of 1977b).
1987	*We Believe in God: A Report of the Church of England Doctrine Commission* (London: Church House Publishing), 168 pages (contributor).
1988a	"Hermeneutics," in *New Dictionary of Theology* (ed. Sinclair B. Ferguson et al.; Leicester: IVP), 293-97.

1988b "Kierkegaard," in *New Dictionary of Theology* (ed. Sinclair B. Ferguson et al.; Leicester: IVP), 365-67.

1988c "Tillich," in *New Dictionary of Theology* (ed. Sinclair B. Ferguson et al.; Leicester: IVP), 687-88.

1988d "Wittgenstein," in *New Dictionary of Theology* (ed. Sinclair B. Ferguson et al.; Leicester: IVP), 726-28.

1990a "Meaning," in *A Dictionary of Biblical Interpretation* (ed. R. J. Coggins and J. L. Houlden; London: SCM), 435-38.

1990b "On Models and Methods: A Conversation with Robert Morgan," in *The Bible in Three Dimensions: Essays in Celebration of Forty Years of Biblical Studies in the University of Sheffield* (ed. David J. A. Clines, Stephen E. Fowl, and Stanley E. Porter; JSOT Supplement Series 87; Sheffield: JSOT Press), 337-56.

1990c "Religious Language and Symbolism, Psychology of," in *Dictionary of Pastoral Care and Counseling* (ed. Rodney J. Hunter; Nashville: Abingdon Press), 1066-68.

1991a "The Spirit of Truth," in *We Believe in the Holy Spirit: A Report by the Doctrine Commission of the General Synod of the Church of England* (ed. Alec Graham, as Bishop of Newcastle; London: Church House Publishing), 112-33.

1991b "The Holy Spirit and the Future," in *We Believe in the Holy Spirit: A Report by the Doctrine Commission of the General Synod of the Church of England* (ed. Alec Graham, as Bishop of Newcastle; London: Church House Publishing), 170-86.

1993a "Language, Religious," in *Blackwell's Encyclopaedia of Modern Christian Thought* (ed. A. E McGrath; Oxford: Blackwell), 315-19.

1993b "Hermeneutics," in *The Oxford Companion to the Bible* (ed. Bruce Metzger; New York and Oxford: Oxford University Press), 279-80.

1994a "Luke's Christology, Speech-Act Theory and the Problem of Dualism in Christology after Kant," in *Jesus of Nazareth: Lord and Christ* (Essays in Honour of I. H. Marshall; ed. Joel B. Green and Max Turner; Grand Rapids: Eerdmans; Carlisle: Paternoster), 453-72.

1994b "The Logical Role of the Liar Paradox in Titus 1:12, 13: A Dissent from the Commentaries in the Light of Philosophical and Logical Analysis," *Biblical Interpretation* 2: 207-23.

1994c "Authority and Hermeneutics: Some Proposals for a More Creative Agenda," in *A Pathway into the Holy Scripture* (ed. Philip Satterthwaite and David F. Wright; Grand Rapids: Eerdmans), 107-42.

1994d "Barr on Barth and Natural Theology: A Plea for Hermeneutics in Historical Theology," *Scottish Journal of Theology* 47: 519-28.

1995a "James Atkinson: Theologian, Professor, and Churchman," in *The Bible, the Reformation, and the Church: Studies in Honour of James Atkinson* (ed. W. P. Stephens; Sheffield: Sheffield Academic Press), 11-35.

1995b "Luther and Barth on 1 Corinthians 15: Six Theses for Theology in Relation to Recent Interpretation," in *The Bible, the Reformation, and the Church: Studies in Honour of James Atkinson* (ed. W. P. Stephens; Sheffield: Sheffield Academic Press), 258-89.

1995c "New Testament Interpretation in Historical Perspective," in *Hearing the New Testament: Strategies for Interpretation* (ed. Joel B. Green; Carlisle: Paternoster; Grand Rapids: Eerdmans), 10-36.

1997a "Speech-Act Theory and the Claim That God Speaks," review article of *Divine Discourse* by Nicholas Wolterstorff, *Scottish Journal of Theology* 50: 97-111.

1997b "Biblical Theology and Hermeneutics," in *The Modern Theologians* (ed. David F. Ford; Oxford: Blackwell), 520-37.

1998a "Human Being, Relationality, and Time in Hebrews, 1 Corinthians and Western Traditions," *Ex Auditu* 13: 76-95.

1998b "Thirty Years of Hermeneutics: Retrospect and Prospect," in *International Symposium on the Interpretation of the Bible* (ed. J. Krasovec; Ljubljana: Slovenian Academy of Sciences and Arts; Sheffield: Sheffield Academic Press), 1559-74.

1998c "Biblical Studies and Theoretical Hermeneutics," in *The Cambridge Companion to Biblical Interpretation* (ed. John Barton; Cambridge: Cambridge University Press), 95-113.

1998d "Hermeneutics, Biblical," in *Routledge Encyclopaedia of Philosophy* (ed. Edward Craig; London: Routledge), vol. 4, 389-95.

2000a "Signs of the Times: Towards a Theology for the Year 2000 as a Grammar of Grace, Truth, and Eschatology in Contexts of So-Called Postmodernity," in *The Future as God's Gift: Explorations in Christian Eschatology* (ed. David Fergusson and Marcel Sarot; Edinburgh: T&T Clark), 9-39 (Presidential Paper of the Society for the Study of Theology, 1999-2000).

2000b "1 Corinthians," in *New Dictionary of Biblical Theology* (ed. T. Desmond Alexander and Brian S. Rosner; Leicester: IVP), 297-306.

2000c "Postmodernity," in *The Dictionary of Historical Theology* (ed. Trevor A. Hart; Grand Rapids: Eerdmans; Carlisle: Paternoster), 434-37.

2001 "'Behind' and 'in Front of' the Text: Language, Reference and Indeterminacy," in *After Pentecost: Language and Biblical Interpretation* (Scripture and Hermeneutics 2; ed. Craig Bartholomew, Colin Green, and Karl Moeller; Grand Rapids: Zondervan; Carlisle: Paternoster), 97-120.

2003a "Can a Pre-Modern Bible Address a Post-Modern Mind?" in *2000 Years and Beyond: Faith, Identity, and the Common Era* (ed. Paul Gifford et al.; London: Routledge), 127-46.

2003b "The Epistle to the Hebrews," in *Eerdmans Commentary on the Bible* (ed. John W. Rogerson and James D. G. Dunn; Grand Rapids and Cambridge: Eerdmans), 1431-62.

2004 "The Holy Spirit in 1 Corinthians: Exegesis and Reception-History in the Patristic Era," in *The Holy Spirit in the New Testament: Studies in Honour of James D. G. Dunn* (ed. Graham N. Stanton, Bruce Longenecker, and Stephen Barton; Grand Rapids and Cambridge: Eerdmans), 207-28.

2005a "Biblical Interpretation," in *The Modern Theologians* (ed. David F. Ford; 3rd ed.; Oxford: Blackwell), 287-304.

2005b "Hermeneutical Circle," in *Dictionary for Theological Interpretation of Scripture* (ed. Kevin J. Vanhoozer et al.; Grand Rapids: Baker; London: SPCK), 281-82.

2005c "Hermeneutics," in *Dictionary for Theological Interpretation of Scripture* (ed. Kevin J. Vanhoozer et al.; Grand Rapids: Baker; London: SPCK), 283-87.

2005d "The Hermeneutical Dynamics of 'Reading Luke' as Interpretation, Reflection, and Formation," in *Reading Luke: Interpretation, Reflection, Formation* (ed. Craig G. Bartholomew, Joel B. Green, and Anthony C. Thiselton; Carlisle: Paternoster), 3-53.

2006a "Richardson, Alan," in *The Dictionary of Twentieth-Century British Philosophers* (ed. Stuart C. Brown and Alan Sell; Bristol: Thoemmes Press).

2006b "The Significance of Recent Research on 1 Corinthians for Hermeneutical Appropriation of This Epistle Today," *Neotestamentica* 40 (2): 320-52.

2006c "Introduction: Canon, Community, and Theological Construction," in *Canon and Biblical Interpretation* (ed. Craig G. Bartholomew et al.; Carlisle: Paternoster; Grand Rapids: Zondervan), 1-30.

2006d "Corinthians, First Letter to," in *The New Interpreter's Dictionary of the Bible* (ed. Katherine Doob Sakenfeld; Nashville: Abingdon Press), vol. 1, 735-44.

2007a "Devoted," in *The New Interpreter's Dictionary of the Bible* (ed. Katherine Doob Sakenfeld; Nashville: Abingdon Press), vol. 2, 118.

2007b "Bultmann, Rudolf (1884-1976)," in *Dictionary of Biblical Criticism and Interpretation* (ed. Stanley E. Porter; London: Routledge), 42-43.

2007c   "Schleiermacher, Friedrich D. E. (1768-1834)," in *Dictionary of Biblical Criticism and Interpretation* (ed. Stanley E. Porter; London: Routledge), 329-30.
2011a   "Wisdom in the Old Testament and Judaism," *Theology* 114, no. 3: 163-72.
2011b   "Wisdom in the New Testament," *Theology* 114, no. 4: 1-9.
2011c   "Paul's Missionary Preaching in 1 Thess. 2:1-16, with an Apocalyptic Addition from 2 Thessalonians," in *New Testament Theology in Light of the Church's Mission: Essays in Honor of I. Howard Marshall* (ed. Jon C. Laansma, Grant R. Osborne, and Ray Van Neste; Paternoster Biblical Monographs; Milton Keynes: Paternoster), 365-75.
2011d   "Reception Theory, H. R. Jauss, and the Formative Power of Scripture," *Scottish Journal of Theology* 65, no. 3: 289-308.
2011e   "The Holy Spirit in the Latin Fathers with Special Reference to Their Use of 1 Corinthians 12 and This Chapter in Modern Scholarship," *Communio Viatorum* (Prague) 53, no. 3: 7-24.

Not included are some 300 reviews.

FACING THE OTHER

Poetry and Theology in Isaiah 56–66

John Goldingay

In *The Hermeneutics of Doctrine,* Anthony Thiselton remarks that "We cannot generalize about the role of propositions, metaphors, or poetry in the Biblical writings as a whole. The issues depend on what genre the writer is using, the purpose of the passage in question, and whether a 'closed' or 'open' text is under consideration."[1] In the Old Testament, poetry is the dominant form of speech in the Wisdom writings, the Psalms, and the Prophets. What is the theological significance of that fact? In light of Tony's comment, in this paper I consider the question in relation to a particular textual unit within the Prophets, Isaiah 56–66.

In modern Hebrew and English Bibles, most of Isaiah 56–66 is printed as verse while some of the closing verses and a few others are printed as prose, yet there is difference between editions and translations over distinguishing verse and prose. NJPS and BHS lay out 66:22-24 as verse, TNIV lays it out as prose, while NRSV lays out just 66:22-23 as verse and 66:24 as prose. These differences may reflect the fact that distinguishing between prose and verse is a Western practice, going back to Hellenistic writers[2] but then encouraged by the invention of the printing press. Further, the two are ideal types. The distinction between them is real, but fuzzy; poetry can be prosaic and prose can be poetic. Hortatory sentences and poetic prophecies occupy different places on a spectrum that includes both prose and

---

1. *The Hermeneutics of Doctrine* (Grand Rapids/Cambridge: Eerdmans, 2007), /8. An open text invites various interpretations on the part of readers. A closed text invites readers to a particular interpretation.

2. Jed D. Wyrick notes that they distinguish two categories of authors, poets *(poiētai)* and prose writers *(sungrapheis):* see *The Ascension of Authorship* (Cambridge, MA/London: Harvard University Press, 2004), 17.

verse. It can therefore be a judgment call whether one sees particular units or verses as one or the other.

As ideal types, one could say that Old Testament prose regularly incorporates longer and more complex sentences, uses more straightforward and literal description, and provides more aids to understanding such as the relative particle *'ăšer*, suffixes, and the object marker *'et*. Poetry makes more use of imagery such as simile, metaphor and symbol, which enable it to say things that cannot be said by means of straightforward statements and are indispensable to our being able to make statements about God. It often omits those syntactical and grammatical aids to understanding; this contributes to its being characterized by greater denseness, by a capacity to use fewer words yet to say more than prose. Its making less use of *w*-consecutive often leaves the relationship between clauses less clear. Whereas prose seeks to make things as easy as possible for its listeners and appeals to the left side of the brain, poetry focuses more on making its listeners think and feel, and appeals to the right side of the brain. It has to be read slowly and attentively, and it involves its readers in discerning its meaning and significance at several levels and not just the analytical.

English poetry and Old Testament poetry share the characteristics of denseness and the use of imagery. Old Testament poetry has a third key characteristic that is more distinctive. It commonly expresses itself in units or lines that are shorter than regular prose sentences, comprising about six words, and that divide roughly into two halves in which the second repeats, intensifies, clarifies, contrasts with, or simply completes the first. These two-part lines or bicola often constitute complete short sentences, though it is also possible for one or more lines to be syntactically subordinate to a preceding or following line. While "parallelism" is not a very accurate term to describe the interrelationship of the two-part lines that characterize Old Testament poetry, it is a useful shorthand expression.[3] Parallelism compares and links with the device of hendiadys, in which two terms form a single compound expression. An example I shall come back to is *mišpāṭ ûṣĕdāqâ* or *ṣĕdāqâ ûmišpāṭ*, conventionally "justice and righteousness." Parallelism also compares with the way larger textual units can form chiasms, concentric structures in which the second half of the unit mirrors the first half. Like the use of imagery, parallelism in general and hendiadys in particular can feature in prose, but they find their natural

---

3. See further James Kugel, *The Idea of Biblical Poetry* (New Haven: Yale University Press, 1981).

The Binary Nature of Old Testament Theological Ideas

I begin from the theological significance of parallelism, a characteristic of Old Testament poetry that features in the opening verse of Isaiah 56–66.

> Guard *mišpāṭ*, act in *ṣĕdāqâ*,
>   Because my *yĕšû'â* is near to coming, my *ṣĕdāqâ* to appearing.
> (Isa 56:1)

Each of these lines is a bicolon (2-2 and 3-2 in MT).[4] Each is characterized by parallelism. The combination of the terms *mišpāṭ* and *ṣĕdāqâ* in the first line recurs in 58:2; 59:4, 9, 14. The fact that these two nouns appearing in parallel cola can elsewhere form a hendiadys encourages us to take them as a compound expression, which serves to articulate a complex theological and ethical idea. *Mišpāṭ* suggests the making of decisions by the exercise of legitimate power. *Ṣĕdāqâ* suggests people doing right by one another in light of the relationships between them; it connotes doing the right thing by people. I thus translate the two words as "authority" and "faithfulness." The compound expression associates power with right relationships in the community. Utilized in the context of poetic parallelism, it illustrates how poetic form facilitates the expression of compound theological ideas. If it is an overstatement to see hendiadys as an implicitly poetic device, the way parallelism encourages the separation of the elements in the hendiadys highlights the separate yet related nature of the two expressions.

The second line in Isaiah 56:1 points to the related link between my *yĕšû'â* and *ṣĕdāqâ*, deliverance and faithfulness (cf. 59:16, 17; 61:10; 62:1; 63:1) and thus offers another instance of parallelism's capacity to express the binary relationship of ideas. Faithfulness suggests the basis for Yhwh's acts, which lies in Yhwh's relationship with Israel; deliverance suggests the nature of the action.

In Isaiah 57:15, Yhwh goes on to declare,

> I dwell on high and holy, and with the crushed and low in spirit.

---

4. I treat the opening "Yhwh has said this" as extra-metrical.

On one hand, Yhwh is on high and is holy; the transcendent God dwells in a heavenly realm, as a king lives in a palace to which ordinary people do not have access. On the other hand, whereas the king may not make a habit of visiting people in their ordinary homes in the city, Yhwh does go walkabout with ordinary people, especially with people who are hurt.[5] Parallelism compares with and facilitates the expression of Yhwh's two-sided nature as both holy and involved. Perhaps parallelism thus has intrinsic theological significance: the very existence of parallelism points to the binary (not dualistic) nature of reality (e.g., divine and human, creator and creation, corporate and individual).

Subsequently, the prophet testifies to a commission,

> To proclaim the year of acceptance by Yhwh, the day of redress by
> our God. (61:2)

Whereas Isaiah 49:8 referred to "a time of acceptance" and "a day of deliverance," in Isaiah 61:2 "deliverance" becomes "redress." The two terms "acceptance" and "redress" recognize the twofold significance of Yhwh's act. The line's parallelism reflects the fact that its cola offer two ways of describing the same occasion: a year becomes a day, Yhwh becomes our God, and acceptance becomes redress. Yhwh later similarly declares,

> A day of redress was in my mind, my year of restoration had come.
> (63:4)

Here "day of redress" is balanced by "year of restoration," the "negative" and "positive" phrases appearing in the reverse order compared with 61:2.

The phrase "day of redress" recalls the expression "day of Yhwh." Traditionally people had expected Yhwh's day to be an occasion when they would experience blessing and when redress would be exacted of their enemies; this is the expectation that Amos 5:18-20 subverts. Isaiah 61:2 and 63:4 reverse the expectation again, reaffirming the traditional assumption about the day. As Isaiah 47:3 has already promised God's redress on Babylon, and as Jesus will speak of God's redress on his people's adversaries, presumably the Romans (Luke 18:7-8), and also on the peo-

---

5. *Dakkâ* is conventionally translated "contrite" rather than "crushed" with the implication that *šāpāl* then denotes humble or lowly in a subjective sense, but I do not think there is etymological or contextual basis for these understandings. Here and elsewhere in this paper I assume exegetical positions I have come to in working on a commentary on Isaiah 56–66, a draft of which is posted at www.fuller.edu/sot/faculty/goldingay.

ple themselves (Luke 21:22), so Isaiah 61:2 promises God's redress on Judah's current overlords.

So both acceptance/restoration and redress will be realities when God acts. Jesus' quoting of Isaiah 61:1-2 in Luke 4:18-19 stops after the reference to "acceptance," and he might be thought to be deliberately distinguishing the year of acceptance from the day of redress; this understanding would cohere with modern dislike for the idea of redress.[6] Yet in Luke 21:22 he does also refer to the days of redress.[7] A Christian expositor of Isaiah 61 such as Theodoret of Cyrrhus thus comments on the Lord's not only promising deliverance but warning of just judgment.[8] The promise of deliverance presupposes the logic that the freedom of the people depends on the putting down of their overlords, but its specific talk of "redress" *(nāqām)* as opposed to mere putting down implies Yhwh's recognition that punishment is appropriate in light of the overlords' wrongdoing (hence the common translation "vengeance" is also misleading). Acceptance/restoration and redress are complementary aspects of the meaning of Yhwh's act, though it may be significant that the prophet speaks of a *year* of acceptance/restoration and only a *day* of redress. One might compare this with the way the Old Testament sees the dominant side of Yhwh's moral character as love and mercy; while wrath and a willingness to exact judgment are also part of that character, they are less central to it.

As well as facilitating expression of the binary of aspects of reality, parallelism also facilitates expression of the more complex nature of other key theological realities. In Isaiah 58:1 Yhwh bids the prophet,

> Tell my people about their rebellion, the household of Jacob about their shortcomings.

One might say that the Old Testament has a range of ways of talking about sin, but formulating the point in that way implies that there is something that we can adequately term "sin." While it is convenient to have a summarizing expression of this kind, the Old Testament does not imply the view that one term such as "sin" can adequately convey the nature of the reality to which it refers. The Old Testament rather uses a variety of

---

6. Owen C. Whitehouse (*Isaiah xl–lxvi*; reprinted London: Caxton [c. 1911], 290) comments that in Isa 61:2 it "stands in contrast with the spirit of the 'Servant-songs.'"

7. The word is *ekdikēsis*, the word Symmachus uses in Isa 61:2 where LXX has *antapodosis*, though the plural "days" suggests the influence of Hos 9:7.

8. *Commentaire sur Isaïe* (3 vols.; Paris: Cerf, 1984), 3:268-69.

terms to convey this reality, and in doing so it uses a number of terms that all seem to have started off life as metaphors from everyday life (even if Old Testament writers have forgotten the metaphorical origin of some of them) — hence my translating *ḥaṭṭā't* "shortcoming" rather than "sin." In the *Symbolism of Evil*,[9] Paul Ricoeur sees defilement, sin, and guilt as the primary symbols of evil; in *The Conflict of Interpretations* he speaks of shame in these terms.[10] I do not think that the Old Testament suggests that there are primary symbols of evil, given that it has a broader range of images for evil without implying that one is primary, though it is true of this range of images that "symbol gives rise to thought."[11] All help us articulate conceptually the nature of evil or sin.

Each of the images constitutes a compressed story, as is characteristic of images. For convenience, I will express them as similes. Sin is like rebelling against a superior authority (*pāšaʿ*; e.g., 2 Kgs 3:7; cf. 1 Kgs 8:50). It is like turning one's back on one's marital relationship (*šûb*; e.g., Jer 3:6, 7, 8, 10, 11, 12, 22). It is like betraying a friendship (*bāgad*; e.g., Jer 12:1, 6; Job 6:15; cf. Jer 5:11; 9:2). It is like getting dirty (*ṭāmēʾ*; e.g., Jer 2:23). It is like wandering off the road (the noun *ʿāwôn*; e.g., Jer 3:21; 5:25; 9:5; 11:10). It is like transgressing a law (*ʿābar*; e.g., Jer 5:22; cf. 34:18). It is like failing to achieve something one should have achieved (*ḥāṭāʾ*; e.g., Jer 3:25; 8:14; 14:7, 20). It is like trespassing on someone's rights or property or honor (*māʿal*; e.g., Num 5:27; cf. Ezek 14:13; 20:27).

An adequate grasp of the significance of human wrongdoing requires the use of a variety of images. Each encapsulates an aspect of its significance; further, the body of images acts as a constraint on the narrowness of each individual image and guards against inappropriate inference from an individual image. In the parallelisms in Isaiah 56–66, rebellion and shortcoming are juxtaposed in 58:1 (also in parallel lines in 59:2), rebellion, shortcoming, and waywardness in 59:12a, rebellion and waywardness in 59:12b. Poetic parallelism encourages the juxtaposition of such images, enriches the prophet's theological statement, and safeguards against narrowness or the inference that theological statements are univocal, analytic, and conceptual.

---

9. New York: Harper, 1967; reprinted Boston: Beacon, 1969. See 1-157.
10. Evanston: Northwestern University Press, 1974. See 289.
11. *The Conflict of Interpretations*, 288; *The Symbolism of Evil*, 347.

Theological Depth and Theological Tension

The interrelationship of those opening two lines in Isaiah 56:1 points to a further theological significance of parallelism:

Guard *mišpāṭ*, act in *ṣĕdāqâ*,
Because my *yĕšû'â* is near to coming, my *ṣĕdāqâ* to appearing.

While *ṣĕdāqâ* has the same meaning each time, it has different reference; the first line alludes to human *ṣĕdāqâ*, the second to divine *ṣĕdāqâ*. What is the relationship between these two commitments to *ṣĕdāqâ*, God's and ours? This relationship is mysterious and impossible to articulate in unambiguous, univocal prose.

Poetry's freedom in omitting the link words that often clarify meaning would make it possible simply to juxtapose the lines and thus leave the question unresolved. This particular verse achieves the same end by connecting the two lines with the word "because." The particle *kî* looks as if it will clarify the cause-effect relationship between the bidding and the statement in the two lines, but actually it increases the lines' ambiguity. The prophet could mean "do what is right because then God will soon do what is right." Or it could mean "do what is right in response to the fact that God will soon do what is right." The prophet's not making clear which understanding is correct is not a weakness of thinking but a strength. Attempts to resolve the question lead either to a contractual understanding of the relationship between us and God (we do right, then God will do so) or give the impression that human responsibility is dispensable (God will deliver us whether or not we do the right thing). Actually, the relationship between God and us is neither conditional nor unconditional. When two people marry, from a legal angle they enter into a contract with one another, but they do not normally see this as the central understanding of their relationship, as if they were saying to each other, "I commit myself to you on condition that you commit yourself to me." But neither are they saying, "I commit myself to you whether or not you commit yourself to me." Both parties undertake an act of commitment that presupposes that the other is doing the same, yet do so on the basis of trust and a willingness to risk oneself to the other person. In the relationship between God and Israel, both misunderstandings are avoided and complexity is recognized by the ambiguity of the prophet's words, which poetic forms of speech facilitate.

The larger-scale concentric or chiastic structure of Isaiah 56–66 as a whole fulfills the same function of preserving mystery and ambiguity, and leaving irresolvable questions unresolved. Major sections of the book of Isaiah such as chapters 1–12 or 13–23 or 40–55 are in varying ways arranged; they do not comprise simply a series of unstructured anthologies. The same is true of chapters 56–66, but only these closing chapters have a systematically concentric structure. In this respect their rhetorical dynamic contrasts in particular with that of the preceding chapters. Isaiah 40–55 works in linear fashion; it is a little like a narrative with a plot. One cannot fully understand the significance of a passage such as 41:8-10 without considering 42:1-4, or that of 42:1-4 without considering 42:18-25, and so on. Earlier passages raise questions that later passages answer, or at least take up again. The whole section moves towards resolution. Isaiah 56–66, like virtually any text, does require a linear reading; we read Isaiah 56 before Isaiah 60. But paradoxically, a linear reading reveals that while the chapters first go somewhere, they then come back again, and the reading thus uncovers a key aspect of the chapters' burden. Here, too, individual passages need to be seen in light of the way the whole unfolds; but the linear reading reveals that this unfolding is circular rather than linear.

By its nature, a concentric structure thus has a different dynamic from a linear one. Having looked as if it is going somewhere, it turns out to be doing something more ambiguous. Its second half may indeed take the argument forward, as the second of two cola within a line characteristically goes beyond the first, and this suggests another sense in which there may be some linearity about the concentric structure; it will be more like a spiral than a circle. But formally, at least, the section ends up coming back to where it started. In Isaiah 56–66, this is then a telling indication of the thesis that emerges from the chapters. As their opening verse announces, they expound two chief convictions. One is that Jerusalem needs to face Yhwh's challenges about its life (see 56:9–59:8; 65:1–66:17). The other is that Yhwh is committed to the city's glorious restoration (see 60:1–62:12). But like their opening verse, the chapters do not establish the relationship between these two convictions. They simply juxtapose them. They, too, imply that it is an oversimplification to say that the vital thing is for Jerusalem to clean up its act, and that its restoration will then follow. But neither is it the case that Yhwh's act of restoration will take place irrespective of Jerusalem's stance in relation to Yhwh.

As the genius of Isaiah 40–55 is to expound theological issues by means of a linear argument, the genius of Isaiah 56–66 is to expound theological issues by means of a chiasm. These strategies are contextual and not interchangeable. The thrust of Isaiah 40–55 could hardly be expressed as a chiasm, whereas the thrust of Isaiah 56–66 could hardly be expressed by a linear sequence. It expounds the irresolvable tensions between challenge and promise, and also between prayer and promise, between judgment and restoration, and between an interest in the nations that focuses on their blessing and one that focuses on Israel's blessing.

Such significance in a chiasm emerges when one contrasts it with a text open to deconstruction. There are texts that emphasize either divine action or human action, and it is not then surprising if readers can see the other emphasis lurking somewhere beneath the surface of the text. This is so in Isaiah 40–55.[12] The genius of a chiasm (or is it the cowardice of a chiasm?) is to avoid deconstruction by being upfront with the two assertions that stand in tension with each other. To put it another way, while Isaiah 40–55 is amenable to deconstruction without inviting it, Isaiah 56–66 wears its deconstruction on its sleeve. It thereby engages its audience in reflecting on the relationship between its affirmations and in forming an attitude to the questions they raise.

Points of Connection and Saying the Unsayable

One of the significances of metaphor is to suggest points of connection between things. Isaiah 60:1-3 urges,

> Get up, be alight, because your light has come; Yhwh's splendor has shone forth upon you.
> Because there: darkness will cover the earth, pitch dark the peoples,
> But upon you Yhwh will shine forth, his splendor will appear upon you.
> Nations will walk to your light, kings to your shining brightness.

Prosaically put, at present Judah and other peoples live under the oppressive domination of an imperial power, but God intends to bless and restore Jerusalem; its task and privilege is to let that blessing and restoration be seen by the other peoples so as to draw them to Jerusalem to share in the

---

12. See John Goldingay, "Isaiah xl–lv in the 1990s: Among Other Things, Deconstructing, Mystifying, Intertextual, Socio-critical, and Hearer-involving," *Biblical Interpretation* 5 (1997): 226-46.

blessing and restoration. Working with the image of light and darkness not only makes the prophet's message express that prospect with greater rhetorical force. It fulfills a theological function by suggesting a link between the nations' calamity, Yhwh's blessing, Jerusalem's vocation, and the nations' response.

In isolation, the bidding to Jerusalem to shine could constitute an exhortation to the city to take action to bring light, analogous to Jesus' exhortation to let our light shine so that people may see our good deeds (Matt 5:16). The prophets would affirm that idea, but this is not a way the Old Testament uses the image of light. The only other occasion where it uses the qal of 'ôr in a metaphorical sense is 1 Samuel 14:27, 29 to describe Jonathan's eyes brightening, and this idea fits well here following on the exhortation or invitation to rise from a position of humiliation and subjection.[13] "What the prophet has in mind is a beaming look on the face."[14] It implies enjoying the brightness of restoration and blessing.[15] "Be alight" is the kind of imperative that actually constitutes a promise (cf. Isa 54:14),[16] "not a mere admonition but a word of power which puts new life into her limbs."[17]

Whereas darkness suggests the gloom of defeat, loss, oppression, and disaster, light suggests deliverance, healing, restoration, and blessing: see for instance, Isaiah 9:1 [2], an earlier passage that talks about darkness, light, and about this light being bright (the related noun "brightness" comes in 60:3).[18] In 60:1, the city will be able to shine out its light because its light will have dawned upon it. The verse's second colon heightens and sharpens the point of the first. "God's splendor" suggestively heightens "your light." The light that dawns will be no ordinary light but something supernaturally bright, and this is because it is not natural light but divine

---

13. Cf. Ernst F. C. Rosenmüller, *Scholia in Jesajae Vaticinia* (2nd ed.; Leipzig: Barth, 1835), 747.

14. Claus Westermann, *Das Buch Jesaja Kapitel 40–66* (Göttingen: Vandenhoeck, 1966), 284 (ET *Isaiah 40–66* [London: SCM/Philadelphia: Westminster, 1969], 357).

15. See the discussion in Birgit Langer, *Gott als 'Licht' in Israel und Mesopotamien. Eine Studie zu Jes 60,1-3.19f.* (Klosterneuburg: Österreichisches Kathologisches Verlag, 1989), 22-24.

16. See GK 110c; *IBHS* 34.4c.

17. Franz Delitzsch, *Biblischer Commentar über den Propheten Jesaia* (2nd ed.; Leipzig: Döffling und Franke, 1869), 607 (ET from the 3rd ed., *Isaiah* [2 vols. in 1; reprinted Grand Rapids: Eerdmans, 1975], 2:409).

18. Cf. J. Vermeylen, *Du prophète Isaïe à l'apocalyptique* (2 vols.; Paris: Gabalda, 1977 and 1978), 2:472.

light. The city will mirror Yhwh's own shining brilliance. Its restoration will not be something that can be humanly generated but something that issues from and reflects divine action. The city's being able to "lighten up" will be a response to light having shone out on it. A paronomasia is involved,[19] but the paronomasia is not simply a literary device; it implies a theological point.

Isaiah 60:4-22 demonstrates how the prevalence of metaphor in prophetic poetry also relates to the fact that prophecy often speaks about the ultimate future. By the ultimate future I mean not so much an event such as the fall of Jerusalem that was imminent in the time of Jeremiah and Ezekiel (though they also use metaphor to convey its significance, not least the way it anticipates the ultimate future) but the coming consummation of God's purpose, which may or may not be imminent, but which either way may be less amenable to literal description.

> Lift your eyes around and look: all of them have gathered, they have come to you.
> Your sons will come from afar, your daughters will support themselves on the hip.
> Then you will revere and glow, your heart will be in awe and swell.
> Because the sea's multitude will turn over to you, the might of the nations will come to you.
> A multitude of camels will cover you, dromedaries of Midian and Ephah; all of them will come from Sheba.
> They will carry gold and frankincense and bring news of the great praise of Yhwh.
>
> All the flocks of Kedar will gather to you; the rams of Nebaioth will minister to you.
> They will come up for acceptance on my altar and I will glorify my glorious house.
> Who are these that fly like a cloud, like doves to their hatches?
> Because for me far shores wait, Tarshish ships at the first,
> To bring your children from afar, their silver and gold with them,
> For the name of Yhwh your God, for Israel's holy one, because he has glorified you.

---

19. Cf. Wolfgang Lau, *Schriftgelehrte Prophetie in Jes 56–66* (Berlin/New York: de Gruyter, 1994), 27.

Foreigners will build your walls, their kings will minister to you,
Because in my fury I struck you down, but in acceptance I have had compassion on you.
Your gates will open continuously; day and night they will not shut,
For they bring to you the might of the nations, with their kings also being led along.
Because the nation and the kingdom that will not serve you: they will perish, and the nations will become a total waste.
The splendor of Lebanon will come to you, juniper, fir, and cypress together,
To glorify the place of my sanctuary; I will make splendid the place for my feet.

The children of those who humbled you will walk to you bending low, all those who despised you will bow low at the soles of your feet.
They will call you "Yhwh's city, Zion of Israel's holy one."
Instead of your being abandoned, rejected with no one passing through,
I will make you an object of pride forever, a joy from generation to generation.
You will suck the milk of nations, suck the breast of kings.
You will acknowledge that I am Yhwh; I am your deliverer, I, Jacob's champion, am your restorer.

Instead of the bronze I will bring gold, instead of the iron I will bring silver;
Instead of the wood, bronze, instead of the stones, iron.
I will make well-being your oversight, faithfulness your bosses.
Violence will not make itself heard any more in your country, destroying or smashing in your borders;
You will call deliverance your walls, praise your gates.

The sun will no longer be light for you by day, for brightness the moon will not be a light for you.
Yhwh will be for you perpetual light, your God your glory.
Your sun will no longer set, your moon will not withdraw,
Because Yhwh — he will be for you perpetual light; your days of grief will end.
Your people, all of them, are the faithful ones who will possess the

country forever.
They are the shoot I planted, the work of my hands, to manifest glory.
The smallest will become a clan, the least a strong nation.
I am Yhwh; in its time I will speed it.

Prophecies commonly stand somewhere on a line between promising or warning of a concrete event whose fulfillment can be seen on the earthly plane (see e.g., Jer 28:16-17) and promising or warning of an event whose fulfillment requires or presupposes the introduction of a new world order, such as has not yet come about even two and a half millennia after the prophet's day (see e.g., Rev 21). Isaiah 40–55 and Isaiah 60–62 stand on that line, the former nearer the former end, the latter nearer the latter end. Isaiah 60 speaks of the actual city of Jerusalem and its actual temple, of actual Judahite exiles and contemporary peoples, but it describes events in terms that are figurative and larger than life. The rebuilding of temple and city and the return of many exiles form a partial fulfillment of its promises, but the figurative and larger-than-life form of the promises is one reason why they stand open to reformulation in later contexts, as still instructive statements of God's ultimate intent. Isaiah 60 thus resembles the prophecy of Ezekiel 40–48 (prose, but not prosaic) in being imaginative and visionary without this implying that the prophets have no hopes or expectations regarding something to happen in the community's experience. Poetry makes it possible to describe the indescribable. The Bible thus characteristically speaks poetically when speaking of the Beginning (creation) as well as the End (it is the failure to recognize that Genesis 1, though formally prose, is poetry-like that leads to a mistaken literalism in approaching the Bible's first creation account).[20]

Christian lectionaries set the beginning of Isaiah 60 for Epiphany and thus link the chapter with the story of eastern sages bringing Jesus gold, incense, and myrrh (Matt 2:1-12). While the recurrence of reference to gold and incense constitutes a formal link between the two passages, there is insufficient correspondence between prophecy and event to make it possible to see Isaiah 60 as a "prediction" of which that event is the "fulfillment."

---

20. I here take up a comment by Patrick D. Miller at the session during the Society of Biblical Literature 2010 Annual Meeting at Atlanta, Georgia, at which I read a shorter form of this paper; the paper has profited from other comments by participants in the session, by participants in a biblical colloquium at Fuller Theological Seminary in October 2010, and by my wife Kathleen Scott.

The New Testament itself does not explicitly relate the prophecy and the event; it rather links the sages' coming with Micah 5:1-3 [ET 2-4]. Yet the subsequent explicit Christian juxtaposing of Isaiah 60 and Matthew 2 does better justice to the nature of Isaiah 60 than does a reading that envisages Isaiah 60 as essentially describing the way a prophet expects political events to unfold at the end of the sixth century or in the fifth. The chapter is poetic, lyrical, and hyperbolic in its language, not prosaic.

Isaiah 60 is typical of Isaiah 56–66 in not relating its promises to specific political contexts or events. It does link with a particular historical context in the sense that it emerges from such a context and reflects it. But both the attempt to see it as envisaging fulfillment in such a context and the understanding of it as a prediction of a particular event six centuries later miss the significance of its poetic nature. It is questionable whether establishing its precise historical context "does very much at all to explain its character and intention."[21]

Its character and intention do relate to the broad context of the Second Temple period rather than the period of the exile or the monarchy or an earlier time. Patrick D. Miller does argue that decontextualization is a characteristic feature of biblical poetry, as of poetry in general. "Poetry in nearly all instances stands in some fashion on its own."[22] With regard to the Old Testament, while this comment is appropriate to the Psalms and the Wisdom Books, I do not think it applies to biblical poetry generally, and specifically to the Prophets. Within Isaiah, the prose material does not seem to be more overtly contextual than the poetic material; indeed, a prose section such as 30:19-26 is harder to position contextually than the poetic material earlier in that chapter. The point applies more broadly to Jeremiah. Isaiah 56–66 is indeed the least overtly contextual of the major sections in the book of Isaiah in the sense that it makes no reference to concrete historical events or people, as is reflected in scholarly disagreement about its dating. But this again links with the theological message reflected in its concentric structure. It sees the tension between promise and challenge as a dominant feature of the relationship between God and Israel

---

21. Ronald E. Clements, "'Arise, Shine; for Your Light Has Come,'" in Craig C. Broyles and Craig A. Evans, eds., *Writing and Reading the Scroll of Isaiah* (2 vols.; Leiden/New York: Brill, 1997) 1:441-54 (446).

22. "The Theological Significance of Biblical Poetry," in Samuel E. Balentine and John Barton, eds., *Language, Theology, and the Bible* (James Barr Festschrift; Oxford/New York: Oxford University Press, 1994), 213-30 (224); reprinted in Miller, *Israelite Religion and Biblical Theology* (Sheffield: Sheffield Academic Press, 2000), 233-49 (244-45).

in the period following that to which Isaiah 40–55 overtly belongs, when Cyrus is on his way to throwing down the Babylonian empire and making it possible for Judahites in Babylon to go home. To put it another way, the decontextualization of the poetry of Isaiah 56–66 reflects the theological significance of the period. Decontextualization is not of the essence of biblical poetry. This conclusion coheres with the remark by Anthony Thiselton from which I started. Closed texts are more likely to derive their significance from contextual considerations; open texts are less likely to do so. Isaiah 60 is not an open text in the way that the Psalms are.

Indirectness and Obscurity

The genius of prose is a capacity to make things clear. The genius of poetry is a capacity to obscure them. Why would prophets want to obscure their statements? Sometimes their delivering of their message is designed as an act of punishment; it utilizes, confirms, and deepens the people's willful stupidity (see Isa 6:9-10, taken up by Jesus in Mark 4:11-12). But in addition, their enigmatic poetic utterances have the potential to make people think and (in combination with their use of imagery) even to get them to yield to their message before they quite understand the nature of this message (as might also be true of Jesus' parables). Poetry attacks the mind not frontally (like prose) but indirectly and subversively.

At one level this is a point about rhetoric rather than about theology, but these two are closely related. The use of rhetoric presupposes a theology. This aspect of the use of poetry implies the assumption that the prophets' message will not be welcome and that its hearers will need to be won.[23] That is so whether the prophet is critiquing people who think they are in the right or seeking to encourage people who think there is no hope. Prophetic poetry draws attention to humanity's resistance to God. It presupposes that the people of God are inherently resistant to listening to God's word through a prophet.

Isaiah 56:9-11 speaks of the community's leaders:

> All you animals of the wild, come on and eat, all you animals in the forest!
> Its lookouts are blind, all of them; they do not know.

---

23. Cf. Yehoshua Gitay's discussion of "Why Metaphors? A Study of the Texture of Isaiah," in Broyles and Evans, eds., *Writing and Reading the Scroll of Isaiah*, 1:57-65.

> All of them are dumb dogs, they cannot bark.
> They are snoozing, bedding down, loving to doze.
> But the dogs — they are mighty in appetite; they do not know "enough."
> Those people — they are shepherds who do not know how to be discerning.
> All of them have directed themselves to their own way, each one to his own ill-gotten gain, every last part of him.

With whom is the prophet seeking to communicate? The intended audience might be the leaders themselves, or might be the people who follow them, or might be the community as a whole. At one level the answer becomes clearer in the material that follows, in Isaiah 57, where the prophet directly addresses the segment of the community that engages in religious observances that the prophet disdains, such as sacrificing children and making these or other offerings in connection with seeking to contact dead family members. Yet the difference in the prophets between the audience on the stage and the audience in the house may mean that the prophet's own direct audience is the segment of the community that does not engage in such practices. Either way, in 56:9-11 the prophet seeks to get the audience to look at the leadership in a new way, and it does so by means of a series of metaphors. Prosaically put, the prophet declares that the community's leaders do not recognize the danger that threatens it and thus do not warn the community, and that they are failing in this respect because of their self-indulgence. The poetic imagery presupposes that the community does not recognize that this is so. The people with whom the prophet identifies do not see it, the other members of the community do not see it, and the leaders themselves do not see it.

Many aspects of a passage such as Isaiah 56:9–57:13 now raise difficulties of understanding. Our exegetical study often implies we assume that these difficulties would disappear if we possessed better information on the meaning of the passage's words or could gain access to a version of the text that was closer to the original. While this assumption is no doubt appropriate to a number of the passage's difficulties, other difficulties were likely inherent in the text from the beginning. While some might reflect the prophet's unintentional failure to be clear and using words and formulating sentences that were obscure only by accident, others might reflect a deliberate desire to be compressed and dense so as to compel listeners to wrestle with the prophecy in order to come to an understanding. That very process requires listeners to engage with its content in a more self-involving way than is necessary if the prophecy has the immediate clarity that more commonly attaches to prose. At the same time it gives listeners the opportunity to avoid engaging with the prophecy, and thereby to avoid their last state being worse than their first by virtue of the fact that they have had God's message made clear to them and have rejected it. In both respects the theological significance of using poetry includes its drawing attention to the way the people of God characteristically resist God's message.

In varying ways, then, parallelism, hendiadys, paronomasia, chiasm, imagery, ambiguity, and obscurity in the poetry in Isaiah 56–66 suggest the complexity, depth, interrelatedness, intelligibility, and unacceptability of the theological ideas that run through the chapters.

Thiselton on Bultmann's *Sachkritik*

Robert Morgan

Anthony Thiselton's revised PhD thesis *The Two Horizons* (1980) is one of the best theological works of its day and remains worthy of careful study.[1] Its most creative contribution was to show the potential of Wittgenstein's later philosophy for biblical interpretation, teaching students to consider the "logical grammar" of a passage, not merely its vocabulary, grammar and syntax. It also introduced the continental hermeneutical tradition from Schleiermacher and Dilthey to Gadamer and Ricoeur, and persuaded some that this might be more fruitful for theology and biblical interpretation than they had recognized. Thiselton's range of philosophical and literary resources was greatly expanded in his magisterial *New Horizons in Hermeneutics* (1992)[2] and some of this theory was then applied in a major commentary on 1 Corinthians (2000).[3] The same determination to combine theory and practice can be traced through the retrospective *Thiselton on Hermeneutics* (2006), and is especially visible in *Hermeneutics of Doctrine* (2007).[4] *Hermeneutics: An Introduction* (2009)[5] is equally successful in communicating the importance of the sub-discipline for theology.

---

1. Thiselton, *The Two Horizons: New Testament Hermeneutics and Philosophical Description with Special Reference to Heidegger, Bultmann, Gadamer, and Wittgenstein* (Exeter: Paternoster, 1980).

2. Thiselton, *New Horizons in Hermeneutics: The Theory and Practice of Transforming Biblical Reading* (London: HarperCollins, 1992).

3. Thiselton, *The First Epistle to the Corinthians: A Commentary on the Greek Text* (New International Greek Testament Commentary; Carlisle: Paternoster Press, 2000).

4. Thiselton, *Thiselton on Hermeneutics: Collected Works with New Essays* (Ashgate Contemporary Thinkers on Religion Series; Aldershot, UK: Ashgate, 2006); *The Hermeneutics of Doctrine* (Grand Rapids: Eerdmans, 2007).

5. Thiselton, *Hermeneutics: An Introduction* (Grand Rapids: Eerdmans, 2009).

Thiselton on Bultmann's Sachkritik

A further significant achievement of the first big book was to change some evangelicals' perceptions of Bultmann from a bogey-man to a Christian theologian who shared many of their own evangelistic concerns. His theology was no doubt open to criticism but there was evidently much to be learned from him, as Thiselton showed by taking up Dennis Nineham's challenge to attend to "the modern end of the problem" in biblical interpretation.[6] Bultmann was the only professional theologian among the four major thinkers discussed at length in that book. He was also a New Testament scholar who had shared Thiselton's own belief "that God speaks through the Bible today," and that "viewed from this theological perspective, the Bible is seen neither as the mere past record of the religious beliefs and aspirations of men [sic] in the ancient world, nor as a trigger designed to spark off premature 'applications' of men's own devising. To hear the Bible speak in its own right and with its due authority, the distinctive horizon of the text must be respected and differentiated in the first place from the horizon of the interpreter."[7] Bultmann had observed that his historical "reconstruction stands in the service of the interpretation of the New Testament writings under the presupposition that they have something to say to the present,"[8] but both biblical scholars gave priority to critical historical exegesis while addressing "the modern end of the problem."

The distance between Thiselton's evangelical and Bultmann's kerygmatic theology is considerable, but their hermeneutical aims to communicate the gospel in their own day are similar and Thiselton's early expositions of Heidegger and Bultmann served them nearly as well as his ongoing engagement with Gadamer and Wittgenstein. Bultmann's relevance for Thiselton's project lay not only in his drawing on modern philosophy to help him communicate the message of the New Testament but also in his wanting to do this without compromising his critical historical exegesis. That intention, whether or not achieved, unites them against some re-

---

6. Thiselton, *Two Horizons*, xx.
7 Thiselton, *Two Horizons*, xx.
8. Rudolf Bultmann, *Theology of the New Testament*, vol. 2 (London: SCM Press, 1955), 251. See also his 1925 essay "The Problem of a Theological Exegesis of the New Testament," ET J. M. Robinson, ed., *The Beginnings of Dialectic Theology* (Richmond, VA: John Knox, 1968), 236-56 at 239: "When we give up a neutral attitude toward the text the question of truth can dominate the exegesis. So in the final analysis the exegete is not interested in the question, 'What is the meaning of what was said (as merely said) at its historical *(zeitgeschichtlichen)* location, in its original context?' He asks rather in the last analysis, 'What kind of matters *(Sachen)* is this talking about, to what realities does it lead?'" (translation modified).

cent theological interpreters of Scripture. Several of Bultmann's conclusions are so uncongenial to Thiselton that he might easily have seen here merely a negative example, a warning of the dangers of allowing a modern philosophy to determine the content of one's Christian theology rather than simply providing tools to assist in reading the texts. Others have dismissed Bultmann in this way, but Thiselton provides an accurate and in many ways sympathetic account of the theologian once so distrusted by conservatives. In doing so he raised not only the standards but also the self-confidence of evangelical theology in England, and put us all in his debt.

His presentation of Bultmann is inevitably briefer than some and directed to the argument of the book, but his aims are so close to Bultmann's own that a balanced assessment of some central issues emerges from a quite narrow sampling of Bultmann's biblical interpretation. Thiselton builds on the work of Roger Johnson and others to provide a syllabus of "the ingredients of Bultmann's hermeneutical concerns prior to Heidegger's philosophy" and "further philosophical ingredients in Bultmann's hermeneutics" (chapters 8 and 9). The following chapter distils "Bultmann's hermeneutics and the New Testament" to manageable proportions by focussing on his hermeneutical manifesto of 1941, "The New Testament and Mythology,"[9] and (briefly) on his use of Heidegger's conceptuality in his exposition of Paul's anthropology.

Most of the main issues in Bultmann's theology, exegesis, and hermeneutics do in fact surface in that lecture on demythologizing, and if English reception of Bultmann's theology was sometimes side-tracked by it into questions of world-view and failed to appreciate the essentials of Bultmann's thought, that was because it overlooked the essay's hinterland. This weakness is admirably remedied in Thiselton's two introductory chapters on Bultmann which highlight the importance for him of Neo-Kantian philosophy, in addition to Herrmann, Dilthey, and Heidegger. Bultmann (like Baur) had made himself a philosophical theologian and so was vulnerable to criticism by dissenting systematic theologians and philosophers of religion. But he mastered the relevant philosophy with a view to articulating Christian talk of God, and always taught and wrote primarily as a New Testament theologian. Where the character of that historical

---

9. ET *Kerygma and Myth 1*, ed. H.-W. Bartsch (London: SPCK, 1953). Revised by S. Ogden in *Rudolf Bultmann's New Testament and Mythology and Other Basic Writings* (Philadelphia: Fortress Press, 1984; London: SCM Press, 1985).

Thiselton on Bultmann's Sachkritik

and hermeneutical discipline is poorly understood Bultmann's achievement is easily misjudged. Some of the strengths of Thiselton's better grasp stem from his sharing Bultmann's focus on the theological interpretation of New Testament texts. Despite the distance between their theological positions they are both committed to modern theological interpretation and appropriation of New Testament texts. Evidently they understand some of these differently, but instead of evaluating their conflicting theologies and exegeses I want to express my admiration for Thiselton's work, and appreciation of what his career in theological research and ministerial education has meant for the Church of England, by remaining at the methodological level and exploring a point where he holds Bultmann's method responsible for their exegetical and theological disagreements. This may clarify the distance between them and in doing so underline our honorand's remarkable success in applying his own hermeneutical principles to the interpretation of a fellow-theologian and biblical scholar whose approach is more alien to his own than their agreement about the importance of philosophy in biblical interpretation might suggest.

Thiselton's case in *The Two Horizons* that "philosophical description allows the interpreter to notice certain features of New Testament thought that might otherwise be neglected" (277) is convincingly made, and his caveat that "it also tempts the interpreter to emphasize only those features that are thereby brought to his attention," encouraging "a selective or partial interpretation of the New Testament" (277), is surely right. But his own use of philosophical description is different from Bultmann's, and while a fresh angle can sharpen the critique it also makes misreading more likely. Thiselton's philosophical description stands at one remove from his systematic theology, influencing it by improving and enriching his exegesis. Bultmann's theological exegesis is more integrally related to his philosophical theology, and Thiselton is right that this carries risks as well as possibilities. He borrows some philosophical description of human existence from Heidegger to help him understand Paul and interpret him, but (as Thiselton's reference to H. Lüdemann's 1872 monograph *Die Anthropologie des Apostels Paulus* indicates) he had studied the anthropological dimensions of Paul's theology long before meeting Heidegger. The anthropological orientation of his own theology owed much to Herrmann and echoed both Luther and Schleiermacher. It was this that led him to highlight the dimensions in Paul's theology which he later articulated with help from Heidegger's analysis of human existence.

Bultmann also recognized that his (and Barth's) theological exegesis was a risky business. It does "so to speak explain away — whether it be by re-interpretation or by critical analysis" those "ideas of Paul which are at first sight the most prominent and which were certainly important to Paul (the whole 'closing scene of history,' for example)."[10] This candid quotation perhaps justifies equating Bultmann's later demythologizing with *Sachkritik*, as Thiselton does.[11] Bultmann does not himself use the word there (above, n. 9) but what in 1941 he calls *existentiale Interpretation* reaches similar conclusions to the *sachkritisch* exegesis in 1926 (below, n. 10), in accord with his lengthy theoretical discussion in 1925 (above, n. 8), and following the initial case for *Sachkritik* made in 1922.[12] There is also a difference, however. In 1926 he appealed to Paul's broader authorial intention ("a *critical standard* gained from Paul himself," below, n. 10) in criticizing some of the apostle's formulations which failed to do justice to Paul's underlying intentions in 1 Corinthians 2 and 15. That is not entirely lost in 1941 because *existentiale Interpretation*[13] is thought to correspond to Paul's and John's deepest intentions, but here, where the emphasis is on the contrast between ancient and modern world-views, that correspondence is obscured.

Bultmann's claim to authorial intention (in his 1922-26 *Sachkritik*) was abandoned when Käsemann extended the term to his theological criticism of Luke's eschatology. Here too the claim is made that certain biblical texts do not adequately represent the *Sache*, but now instead of individual texts or formulations being criticized in the light of the gospel expressed in that author's overall theology, the overall theology of some biblical authors is

---

10. From "Karl Barth, *The Resurrection of the Dead*" (1926), ET *Faith and Understanding* 1 (London: SCM Press, 1969), 66-94 at 86, translation altered. This needs to be read in the context of the essay's initial remarks on *Sachkritik* needing to find "a *critical standard* (*kritischen Maßstab*) gained from Paul himself for use in interpreting separate statements" (67).

11. Thiselton, *Two Horizons*, 266, 290, 442.

12. At the end of his review of the second edition of Barth's *Römerbrief* (ET in *Beginnings*, 100-120 at 118-20, where the word *Sache* occurs 19 times). For a fuller account of this debate see my article in *JSNT* 33, no. 2 (2010): 1-16, "*Sachkritik* in Reception History." Bultmann had understood from Barth's remark in the preface that "criticism (κρίνειν) applied to historical documents means for me the measuring of words and phrases by the standard of that about which the documents are speaking" that they were in essential agreement about this.

13. Bultmann's *existential(e)* (Heidegger's *existenzial(e)*, concerning the nature of human existence) is perhaps best left untranslated, since neither the English "existential" (Bultmann's *existentiell*) nor the French-flavoured "existentialist" refers clearly to *Existenzphilosophie*.

criticized in the light of the gospel heard more clearly in another author (Paul). Whether or not Käsemann's extension can be justified on the grounds that the aim of theological exegesis of Scripture[14] to communicate the gospel today may override not only the textual meaning of odd verses but whole writings, it is no longer exegesis of texts, as Bultmann's *Sachexegese* requiring *Sachkritik* intends to be. Käsemann's use of the term goes beyond what Bultmann justified in 1926, but Thiselton's inclusion of this extension in his criticism of Bultmann's *Sachkritik*[15] is fair, as Bultmann too was hostile to salvation-history theologies.[16]

Not even Käsemann's "canon within the canon" reduced the list of New Testament writings. His *Sachkritik* retained the whole New Testament (as even Luther's 1522 September Testament did) but identified and applied the critical norm by which he discerned authentic Christianity. The exegesis that Bultmann called *Sachkritik* in 1925 and 1926 (above, nn. 8 and 10) is more restricted in its application. It is highly contestable on historical-exegetical grounds, but can hardly be called "selective or partial interpretation." That criticism is more applicable to Bultmann when he limits his *(existentiale)* theological interpretation of the New Testament to Paul and John, but not even this selectivity and partiality is the result of his borrowing Heidegger's philosophical description or analysis of human existence. Heidegger joined Bultmann in studying Paul, Luther, Kierkegaard, Dilthey, and Herrmann in 1924-25 while working on his philosophical anthropology. Bultmann's concern, like Schleiermacher's and Otto's and (he thought) Barth's, was different: to speak intelligibly of God in a new intellectual situation where classical theism seemed to many incredible.[17] His decision to do so by speaking at the same time of human existence had

---

14. Karl Barth, *The Epistle to the Romans* (ET London: Oxford University Press, 1933), ix: "My sole aim was to interpret Scripture." Barth knew that "[n]o one can, of course, bring out the meaning of a text *(auslegen)* without at the same time adding something to it *(einlegen)*" and that he was not and is not "free from this danger . . . of in fact adding more than he extracts." He hopes his book "may perhaps lead to a fresh formulation of the problem, 'What is exegesis?'" Barth's prefaces contain the main key to Bultmann's *Sachkritik* which he sees as a necessary element in *Sachexegese* (theological exegesis).

15. Thiselton, *Two Horizons*, 265-66, 290.

16. See Thiselton's criticism of Cullmann in "History of Salvation and History" (1948) in *Existence and Faith* (London: Collins, 1964), 268-84. Acts is surrendered to "Cullmann's construction" on 283, anticipating Conzelmann.

17. On his association of Barth with Schleiermacher and Otto in 1922, see Bultmann, *Beginnings*, 100. On his basic concern, see Bultmann, "What Does It Mean to Speak of God?" (1925) in *Faith and Understanding*, 53-65.

Reformation[18] as well as modern roots and led him to focus his *Theology of the New Testament* on the two New Testament witnesses who offer some account of that. Any attempt to base one's own theology on the biblical witness is likely to highlight some, and (rightly or wrongly) marginalize other parts.

My reservations about what is only a detail in Thiselton's presentation do not imply any disagreement with his otherwise well-founded criticisms of Bultmann's theological position, nor do they deny (in fact they will confirm) that Bultmann's position raises questions about the hermeneutical method that enabled him to claim biblical warrants for it, but his *Sachkritik* seems to me to deserve closer investigation, not least on account of its attempt to do justice at some level to authorial intention. Bultmann recognizes with Thiselton that to "hear the Bible speak in its own right and with its due authority, the distinctive horizon of the text must be respected and differentiated in the first place from the horizon of the interpreter" (above, n. 7). Whether his *Sachkritik* in effect subverts the text's own horizon, allowing the interpreter to impose on it a more congenial meaning, is a fair question, and the answer may well be yes, as Barth thought, but Bultmann aimed even in his *Sachkritik* to "hear the Bible speak in its own right and with its due authority."

The first two of Thiselton's five or six references in *The Two Horizons* to Bultmann's *Sachkritik* occur in sections of chapter 10 which criticize "specific examples of (Bultmann's) re-interpretation of the New Testament," namely eschatology and the resurrection (pp. 266, 274). The third (p. 290) occurs in his "concluding comments" to that penetrating chapter on Bultmann's theology. The fourth (p. 410) occurs in the second chapter on Wittgenstein, and can be set aside as probably a mistake. It is puzzling to read that Bultmann's account of Paul on "flesh" aims "to suggest a unifying category which somehow binds these varied uses of "flesh" into a single whole . . . by applying *Sachkritik* in order to distinguish characteristic from uncharacteristic meanings." It is true that *Sachkritik* makes that distinction (for reasons to be considered) but Bultmann is not doing that here, let alone doing it by means of *Sachkritik*.

That is not, of course, to suggest that Thiselton is one of the many who do not understand what Bultmann means by *Sachkritik*. English and

---

18. "The subject of theology is God. Theology speaks of God because it speaks of man [sic] as he stands before God. That is, theology speaks out of faith" (1924) in *Faith and Understanding*, 52.

Thiselton on Bultmann's Sachkritik

American perplexity about the term is evident in the variety of unhelpful and sometimes misleading translations: objective critique, objective criticism, content criticism, content-oriented criticism, theological criticism, material criticism, material criticism of the content, critical interpretation, critical study of the content, critical theological interpretation. One difficulty is how to understand and render *Sache*, which refers to the non-objectifiable gospel, or God, but more immediately important is how to relate the *Sache* and the *Kritik*. A common mistake is to suppose that Bultmann's *Sachkritik* meant criticism *of the Sache*, and some of the English translations suggested that. "Content criticism" sounds like "criticism of the content." That is in effect not totally wrong because the "content" is then taken to mean the theological or ideational substance of a text. This is indeed criticized in *Sachkritik*. But that reversion to liberal Protestant theological criticism of Scripture in the light of modern knowledge misses the essential point of Bultmann's *Sachkritik* which is the scriptural criterion or measure *(Maßstab)* by which a text is criticized. What in fact Bultmann meant by the word was criticism of a *text* (what is *said*) in the light of the *Sache* that the New Testament author intended to speak of (what was *meant*), ultimately the truth of the gospel. A formulation in Scripture can (Bultmann insisted against Barth) be criticized in the light of the gospel Paul intended to express (see nn. 8, 10, 12).

In *The Two Horizons* Thiselton wisely avoided translating the word, but in *New Horizons* he accepts the conventional translation "content-criticism" which could be misunderstood as "criticism of the content." That misunderstanding is a real risk because the context there on p. 158 is comparing "content-criticism or *Sachkritik*, which signals an unease with what the text says as it stands," with pre-Christian allegorical interpretation. There are indeed parallels between both methods of discounting unwelcome texts in respected writings such as for the Greeks Homer, or for Christians their authoritative Scripture. But allegorical interpretation makes no claim to authorial intention and implicitly criticizes the human author's ideas or "content," whereas Bultmann's *Sachkritik* claims some authorial intention (at the level of what was really *meant*) and emphatically does not criticize the *Sache*, neither in his "theological exegesis" (n. 8) nor in his demythologizing interpretation. He is critical of some traditional understandings of the *Sache*, including perhaps Thiselton's, but his *Sachkritik* was part of his attempt to justify his own theology as more scriptural than that of his liberal Protestant teachers.

Thiselton disapproves of Bultmann's theology and blames his method of theological interpretation *(Sachkritik)* for enabling his philosophical and theological presuppositions to distort it. Rightly, for his purposes, Thiselton prioritizes the initial demythologizing essay (above, n. 9), where the word does not occur, over the detailed discussions of *Sachkritik* in 1925[19] and (with worked examples) in 1926.[20] This suggests that Thiselton's real targets are Bultmann's *existentiale Interpretation* and Käsemann's extended applications of *Sachkritik,* implicit also in Bultmann's demythologizing, rather than the *Sachkritik* discussed and applied in 1925-26.

A fuller account of Bultmann's hermeneutics would need a more detailed account of his *Sachkritik* than even most specialist expositors and critics provide.[21] Supplementing Thiselton at this point will suggest that the method Bultmann advocated and called *Sachkritik* prior to his *existentiale Interpretation* offers a theological interpretation of Scripture schooled by historical criticism (what might after Wrede be labelled "New Testament theology *properly* so-called"), a path between the Scylla of liberalism and the Charybdis of biblicism. Bultmann himself inclined to Scylla, as Thiselton does to Charybdis, but the development and further applications of the method by Bultmann and Käsemann do not discredit the original proposal. This can be judged on its own merits. Even if the method invites interpreters into those dangerous extensions, these temptations can be resisted on pragmatic grounds by theologians wanting to preserve the integrity of every biblical author's witness, as Bultmann's original proposal does. The control provided by its appeal to authorial intention cannot prevent mistaken exegesis. That is always a risk, whatever methods are used. But it can limit the damage that Thiselton alerts us to, even though Bultmann himself abandoned this appeal to authorial intention in his *Sachkritik* when he extended his criticism of myth to every New Testament writing, and was as unwilling as Käsemann to be bound by Luke's theology.

There are ambiguities in Bultmann's claim to criticize certain formulations in the light of the gospel that their author intended to communicate because "the gospel" here, being non-objectifiable, must also mean the gospel *as understood by the modern interpreter* who identifies Paul's gospel and also wants to communicate this. But because the gospel *Sache* also meant for Bultmann in 1922-26 (as for Barth) *the gospel as Paul under-*

---

19. Bultmann, *Beginnings,* 238-43, 254-56.
20. Bultmann, *Faith and Understanding,* 67-72, 81-83, 86-87, 92-93.
21. W. Schmithals, *An Introduction to the Theology of Rudolf Bultmann* (London: SCM Press, 1968; German 1966) does provide this.

stood it, his *Sachkritik* there was controlled by a historical-exegetical appeal to Paul's authorial intention. Bultmann thought that his own and Paul's understandings of the gospel were in essential agreement, not least because he had drawn his understanding of the gospel largely from Paul (with some help from Luther who was also dependent on Paul). However, an ambiguity arises because *the gospel as understood by the modern interpreter* could mean "by the modern interpreter, who is dependent on the witness of Scripture, but not necessarily on the particular New Testament writer whose statement is being subjected to *Sachkritik*." That is what the term signified when extended by Käsemann[22] to his theological criticism of Luke or "early catholicism in the New Testament" in the light of his own understanding and reception of the Pauline gospel. Like Luther, Käsemann emphasized the authentic Pauline gospel by contrasting Paul's theology with other (inferior) theologies in the New Testament which do not (in his view) provide a good criterion or "canon" (measuring-rod) of authentic Christianity. All three *Sachkritiker* were warning against misunderstandings of the gospel as they understood this, largely on the basis of their readings of Paul.

A further ambiguity is that *the gospel as understood by the modern interpreter* could mean "without any direct reference to Scripture" — though this further extension of the term to describe theological criticism of Scripture in the light of an understanding of the *Sache* not drawn directly from Scripture abandons both the tight textual control proposed by Bultmann, and the looser scriptural control presupposed by Luther and Käsemann. It need not detain us here but has to be mentioned, partly because non-specialists sometimes use the word in that older liberal sense, and partly on account of Barth's fear that Bultmann's *Sachkritik* would lead back to the old liberal Protestantism that they were both opposing by their theological exegesis. My reply to Barth (and Thiselton) is that it does not have to, and that insistence on authorial intention reduces this danger.

The dialectic between Scripture and the gospel demanded by both Bultmann's and Käsemann's forms of *Sachkritik* involves a hermeneutical circle with the interpreter moving between the particular text and its larger context or related material. However, that larger whole could be the writing in which the text stands (so Bultmann, originally), or all the author's writings (and so a view of his theology — still Bultmann), or the whole

---

22. See B. Ehler, *Die Herrschaft des Gekreuzigten. Ernst Käsemann's Frage nach der Mitte der Schrift* (Berlin: de Gruyter, 1986), 127-55.

New Testament (so Käsemann when he criticizes Luke in the light of the gospel he hears in Romans). That last possibility, a *Sachkritik* whose results are arguably true to Scripture but which no longer appeals to authorial intention, allowed Luther to criticize James and the Apocalypse in the light of an understanding of the gospel derived from Paul. It also allowed Käsemann and Schulz[23] to base their own theologies on the witness of the New Testament or its living centre, without being bound by what they considered its "early catholicism." It would also allow Bultmann himself to criticize all mythological statements of Scripture in the light of his *existentiale* understanding of the gospel, derived from an *existentiale* interpretation of Paul and John, articulated with help from Heidegger.

In one aside, Bultmann later accepted Käsemann's extension of the word *Sachkritik* to cover the kind of dialectic between Scripture and the gospel found in Luther's "canon criticism."[24] His explorations of this idea in 1922-26, on the other hand, preserved Paul's authorial intention, though at a level deeper than some of Paul's formulations. Neither Luther nor Bultmann approved of James, and Bultmann leaves the reader of his *Theology of the New Testament* in little doubt about his personal theological reservations about Acts, the Pastorals, and the Apocalypse, though he does not use the word *Sachkritik* there, nor does he explicitly apply in it in his historical presentation of "The development toward the Ancient Church." One could say that by restricting his *existentiale* theological interpretation to Paul and the Johannine theology he implicitly adopted Käsemann's extended form of *Sachkritik*, but in 1926, following his argument in 1922, he did no more than criticize some of Paul's formulations in 1 Corinthians in the light of what he judges are Paul's deepest intentions, i.e. in the light of how he thinks Paul understands the gospel (which corresponded to how he himself understood the gospel). His *Sachkritik* makes a historical and exegetical case for Paul's deepest intentions differing from what on occasion the apostle actually said. It thus implicitly defends his own claim to be biblical.

In his later demythologizing essay Bultmann takes this essential agreement between himself and Paul for granted. Anyone who does not agree with him about that may well think that he is imposing his own very different understanding of the gospel on to Paul's texts. How far he succeeded in aligning his own and Paul's and John's theology can be left open here —

---

23. S. Schulz, *Die Mitte der Schrift* (Stuttgart: Kreuz, 1976).
24. Bultmann, *Theology of the New Testament*, 2:238.

we are concerned only with the *Sachkritik* that allows his *Sachexegese* (which combines his own and Paul's theology through historical and theological exegesis) to cope with a few texts which as they stand plainly conflict with his own theology.[25] What was attempted in 1926 was also attempted in his demythologizing proposal: not the elimination of awkward texts and beliefs, but their criticism and reconsideration in the light of an understanding of the gospel based largely on other texts. The hermeneutical circle involved here guides the interpreter not only between the parts and the whole of Paul's oeuvre, but also between what is written and the gospel that this is thought to be intending to articulate.

Thiselton persuasively disputes part of the supposed correspondence between Bultmann and Paul and is dismissive of the *Sachkritik* which he rightly sees is invoked in order to defend that correspondence in the face of counter-evidence. But the method is in general terms no more than what everyone does in conversation or reading: interpreting what is said in the light of what (on that basis or the larger context) we think is intended. Whereas irony involves a conscious distinction between what is said and what is meant, we sometimes simply fail to say what we mean and depend on our hearers or readers to make the necessary adjustment. In theological interpretation disagreements are possible about the *Sache* and that means that any exegetical conclusions reached with the help of *Sachkritik* will therefore be particularly uncertain and open to dispute. This sets limits to the usefulness of the method. It offers possible readings of some troublesome texts, but cannot establish an exegetical case for a theological proposal. However, direct correlation between a problematic text and his own understanding of the gospel is not what Bultmann is aiming at. He can see what the text *says*, and builds nothing on it. His understanding of the gospel is based not on that disputed text but on his understanding of Paul's understanding of the gospel, based as this is on all Paul's available material. Some of this can be sidelined as not in accord with the general thrust of the whole corpus. His early *Sachkritik* is a way of discounting what some texts say and achieving a perception of the Pauline gospel that he himself preaches.

Anyone who disagrees with Bultmann's theology will naturally challenge its exegetical basis and will probably disagree with some of the historical judgments made in his *Sachkritik*. It is thus no surprise that Thiselton barely discusses Bultmann's *Sachkritik* of 1 Corinthians in his own

---

25. On his aim to make historical and theological exegesis coincide see Bultmann, *Beginnings* (1968, originally 1925), 253, 256.

large and excellent commentary which engages with a multitude of less gifted exegetes. He also shows little interest in the issue after *The Two Horizons*. My suggestion is that although it is easy to disagree with (and even dismiss) any historical judgments made on this basis, and adjudication is difficult to the extent that independent evidence of what the author really meant is lacking, nevertheless, the method is in principle legitimate, and perhaps even indispensable for anyone wishing to combine Barth's *Sachexegese* with historical-critical exegesis. Liberals, including some liberal evangelicals, reject this *Sachexegese,* and some conservative evangelicals reject historical criticism. In his modern development of the Reformation heritage Bultmann proposes a third way, affirming both.

Thiselton at times suggests that the difficulty in falsifying a conclusion involving a judgment for which the evidence is at best indirect, is a strong argument against the method itself.[26] But despite the *frisson* provided by the philosopher's rhetoric of "falsification" this is a cogent argument only against using the method to *establish* a historical or theological proposal. Falsifiability is desirable, but often not available in theology and exegesis. Far from being a necessary condition of the meaningfulness of theological or exegetical proposals, it is at most an indication of their relative strength. An exegetical proposal reached by means of *Sachkritik* may persuade those disposed to be persuaded, and may be judged more or less likely by anyone, but can always be rejected as speculative by those who do not like its theological consequences. Texts that Bultmann thinks are unfortunate lapses may be thought by others to be central to Paul's gospel and theology, and so the exegetical argument continues. The method's weakness lies only in the uncertainty of its conclusions. Bultmann uses it not to find an acceptable meaning for an embarrassing text but only to remove an obstacle to his claim that his understanding of Paul is on the whole correct, and his own theological proposal therefore not contrary to the witness of Scripture to the gospel. This use of *Sachkritik* has to be historically plausible to be persuasive but its conclusions do not need to be as firm as those which bear the weight of a theological claim or argument.

Those who want to say their theology is in accord with Paul or the New Testament as a whole will lose credibility if they use *Sachkritik* too often to neutralize problematical texts. They depend on Scripture for their understanding of the gospel and can prune some texts without loss, but too much theological criticism would saw off the branch they depend on.

---

26. Thiselton, *Two Horizons,* 266, 442.

However, granted the human fallibility of the biblical authors it is not unreasonable to use *Sachkritik* on occasion in attempts to understand the gospel according to Paul. That defence does not cover Luther's canon criticism, nor Käsemann's extended application of *Sachkritik*, nor even Bultmann's wholesale demythologizing. Extending Bultmann's 1925-26 theory and practice of *Sachkritik* in these ways loses the fragile rational control that Bultmann originally offered by appealing to Paul's deepest authorial intentions. It weakens the interpreter's claim to be representing the witness of Scripture.

Thiselton expresses justifiable unease with the method but without fully explaining it. Discussing Bultmann's view that contradictions in Paul justify *Sachkritik* of parts of 1 Corinthians 15, he writes that

> one of the greatest difficulties about Bultmann's hermeneutics is his use of *Sachkritik*. He is always willing to allow that *certain passages* in the New Testament may conflict with his own interpretation of Paul and John. But such passages, he always replies, conflict with the real intention or the inner logic of Pauline and Johannine thought. We have already noted that Paul's own arguments about the historical objectivity of the resurrection event are not denied, but are said to betray Paul into contradicting himself, because of his immediate apologetic purpose. The only criteria which can be invoked to test such a claim relate to beliefs about Paul's theology as a whole. However, that picture, in turn, is built up from concrete exegetical considerations. The interpreter or critic of Bultmann can only judge for himself whether the theological ingredients of Bultmann's thought allow him to construe Pauline or Johannine thought "as a whole" in a way which does full justice to Paul and John.[27]

That is well said, even though it does not explain Bultmann's dialectic between Scripture and the gospel, and perhaps reduces it to measuring one text against another. Like Käsemann, Bultmann denies that "the gospel" is "objective."[28] This means that even where his exegesis is in part guided by his own understanding of the gospel, which he believes corresponds to Paul's, in his *Sachkritik* the only public, rational criterion to which he can appeal is his understanding of the apostle's theology "as a whole." We un-

---

27. Thiselton, *Two Horizons*, 274-75.
28. Cf. E. Käsemann, "Is the Gospel Objective?" (German "Zum Thema der Nichtobjektivierbarkeit," 1953) in *Essays on New Testament Themes* (London: SCM Press, 1964).

derstand each of the parts in the light of the whole and *vice versa*, and must judge for ourselves by engaging in detailed exegesis, whether we think Bultmann has understood Paul's thought correctly. Thiselton is right about that, but when he suggests that the theological (and philosophical) "ingredients" in Bultmann's understanding of the gospel may have impeded his understanding of Paul and John, he perhaps underestimates the extent to which Bultmann's approach in principle allows his preunderstanding of what the apostle is talking about to be challenged by his historical exegesis. The interpenetration of these two factors needs further analysis. Where interpreters' modern scientific knowledge affects their understanding of the truth of the gospel, and so leads them to propose new interpretations which the author would reject, a boundary between historical and theological exegesis has been crossed. But Bultmann is arguing for an area where the author might concede that a new interpretation catches what was intended. Theological and historical exegesis might then coincide. His interpretations relate the biblical witness to his own provisional understanding of the gospel. Where historical exegesis offers alternative, equally plausible, possibilities, theologians naturally choose one that resonates with their own apprehensions of the *Sache*.

Thiselton's question "what *could have counted against*" (p. 266) Bultmann's interpretation does not substantially weaken an already questionable historical-exegetical proposal, but his claim that Bultmann assumes "on the basis of *Sachkritik* that Paul and John *must* 'really' have meant to convey an understanding of eschatology that accords with Bultmann's understanding of eschatological existence as a present reality which is not 'this-worldly'"[29] is correct, at least about Bultmann's *Sachkritik* of Paul. The argument is different in the case of the Fourth Gospel, where the evangelist is said to have himself engaged in *Sachkritik* and where most of the futurist eschatology is assigned to an "ecclesiastical redactor," but the outcome is the same: an account of eschatology is attributed to Paul and John which corresponds to Bultmann's own understanding of eschatological existence. The "closing scene of history" is "interpreted away" (see n. 10).[30] Barth in *The*

---

29. Thiselton, *Two Horizons*, 266.

30. Bultmann's view that "Paul defines the life of the believer as life characterized by faith in Christ's resurrection and hope for his own resurrection" (*Faith and Understanding*, 67) corresponds to his own view of Christian existence as open to the future, but his sense of the real temporal historical future is attenuated. Other Christians are more positive and optimistic about the future of the world and are galvanized by their faith and hope into social ethical activity. See Jürgen Moltmann, *Theology of Hope* (ET London: SCM Press, 1967), 39-69.

Resurrection of the Dead shared this view of Paul's eschatology in 1 Corinthians, gaining Bultmann's approval. Their *Sachexegese* owed much to their prior understanding of the gospel, and was historically dubious.[31] Most exegetes have agreed with Käsemann on Paul[32] and Barrett on John[33] that Bultmann underestimated the futurist aspect of their eschatologies.

Like Käsemann, Moltmann, Pannenberg, and (more equivocally) Macquarrie, Thiselton disputes both Bultmann's modern interpretation of eschatology and his understanding of the resurrection, and the exegesis by which these are justified. He rightly implies (above, n. 27) that *Sachkritik* facilitated the removal of New Testament data which conflicted with modern thought. But that may not so much discredit *Sachkritik* as alert us to the dangers of a procedure which neutralizes awkward texts without the criteria for determining what is to be neutralized and what accepted as true to the gospel, being fully transparent. Interpreters make judgments about whether a passage is true to the author's theology on historical-exegetical grounds, and even there some subjectivity is inevitable. But when the interpreter's own understanding of the non-objectifiable gospel also comes into play the scope for disagreement is much greater, and the chances of appeals to Scripture settling doctrinal disputes much reduced. One might respond that this is not how Scripture functions as a norm, but Barth's objection (echoed by Thiselton) that, by correcting what some verses say in the light of what the apostle supposedly meant, Bultmann shifted the balance of power too far from the text to the interpreter, is understandable. If the truth of the gospel depends on the truth of the scriptural witness as a whole (as it surely does — though not on the validity of every statement in it) one must ask how that witness can survive an uncontrolled *Sachkritik*.

Bultmann's 1922-26 proposal met that concern by claiming to represent Paul's authorial intention. He thought (in effect) that Paul would have accepted Barth's and his own understanding of the eschatology in 1 Corinthians, but (unlike Barth) he admitted that Paul on occasion unfortunately said something different. He thus accepted the scriptural witness in general while allowing the interpreter to challenge particular formulations. Exegetes will continue to argue about Paul's intentions, and therefore about

---

31. Moltmann criticizes their "transcendental eschatology" and bases Christian hope on God's promise of a real future. *Theology of Hope*, 39-69.

32. E.g. Ernst Käsemann, *New Questions of Today* (London: SCM Press, 1969), 10-17.

33. See Thiselton, *Two Horizons*, 265.

whether Bultmann's *Sachkritik* of a particular verse or passage contributes to a correct interpretation of Paul's theology or distorts it by discounting some of the evidence (e.g. baptism for the dead). Other theologians prefer to solve the problem of difficult texts by choosing a more acceptable meaning, one "worthy of God," as Origen put it. That may sometimes persuade, but Origen's allegorical interpretation is today less plausible than Bultmann's solution. Bultmann's *Sachkritik* allows him to reach the desired theological outcome without discounting the historical-exegetical data, even if some of his exegesis appears tendentious. His method combines historical and theological exegesis (which he sees is also Barth's aim). If we think they reach a wrong exegetical answer in a particular case, that does not necessarily discredit the method itself. No method carries guarantees. Each application has to be judged on its merits and its proposal judged probable or improbable, possible or impossible. Those who think that Barth and Bultmann caught by their *Sachexegese* something of Paul's meaning that their liberal predecessors missed can admire Bultmann's attempt to bring it into accord with his historical-exegetical judgment.

The other passages in *The Two Horizons* criticizing Bultmann's *Sachkritik* deserve brief mention. The concluding chapter 15 picks up some valid points from the earlier references, but p. 442 could mislead. The contention that "*Sachkritik* is employed in order to support a holistic view of the New Testament" could be read as attributing to Bultmann a desire to impose a theological unity on the New Testament by excising what does not fit. But Bultmann is well aware of the theological diversity in the New Testament, and that it precludes any organization of "the theological thoughts of the New Testament writings as a systematically ordered unity."[34] The unity Bultmann finds in the New Testament is at the level of its *kerygma*, not the texts or the theologies they express. If the "holistic view" attributed to him means simply that he expects the New Testament as a whole to articulate the gospel, and is dismissive of those parts which he thinks do not, that points us back to his understanding of the dialectic between Scripture and the gospel, a dialectic which his conservative critics sometimes overlook or reject.

The same issue is raised by Thiselton's claim that

> (t)he growing emphasis among New Testament scholars on the pluriformity of the New Testament, however, has backfired on Bult-

---

34. Bultmann, *Theology of the New Testament*, 2:237.

mann's method of *Sachkritik*. It is seen that his approach raises questions about a canon within the canon. Is Luke-Acts, for example, simply a betrayal of the existential perspective of Paul and John? Is Romans 9-11 a historicizing lapse after the existential perspective of chapters 1-8? Even within the Synoptic Gospels what Bultmann has accepted as axiomatic has increasingly come under criticism. . . . The work of Ebeling, Bornkamm, Käsemann, and Fuchs on the Gospels is not, as some have claimed, a step back from Bultmann's advance, but a recognition of the limitations of his holistic, even sweeping, approach to part of the New Testament.[35]

This paragraph rightly identifies some one-sidedness in Bultmann's *existentiale* theological interpretation of the New Testament, but the points touched on, including what looks like an incongruous allusion to the "new quest" of the historical Jesus, have to do with Bultmann's account of the gospel *Sache* rather than the method of *Sachkritik* (which was accepted and practised by his students listed here). Bultmann's theological objections to the so-called historical Jesus were not what led him to exclude the synoptic gospels from his *existentiale Interpretation* of the New Testament.

Thiselton's remarks rightly protest against allowing an understanding of the gospel drawn from parts of the New Testament to close an interpreter's ears to other parts of the biblical witness. Even if it is possible to hear the gospel in the witness of a single author, text, or verse, that is not a reason to discount the rest of Scripture. Bultmann and Käsemann do not in fact disregard any of the New Testament (their evaluation of the Old is another matter). They only resist allowing it all to become part of their "norm" or canon of Christian truth, as a conservative might claim it all should. Scripture is their norm only insofar as it bears witness to the gospel *Sache*, or Word incarnate who is known through the Word preached from and on the basis of the written word of Scripture.

One objection to that theology of the Word is that Bultmann and Käsemann are insufficiently biblical, suspected of ignoring the total scope of Scripture. Another is that (with Barth) they are *too* biblical in the sense of wanting *too close an alignment* between their own understanding of Christianity and that of at least one or two New Testament witnesses. Those who allow more theological space between then and now can attend to all the biblical witnesses without having to replicate those historically

---

35. Thiselton, *Two Horizons*, 290.

distant theologies. These theologians (whether liberal or catholic) have no need of the exegetical hypotheses of *Sachkritik* because they feel under no obligation to "make something of" problematic passages in Scripture.[36] But that is not a solution which many evangelicals will want to embrace. They suspect that those who do argue in this way are no longer "normed" by Scripture and often settle for a quite unbiblical view of Christianity. It is necessary to ask whether or how far being faithful to the witness of Scripture commits Christians to sharing the theology of at least some biblical witnesses. The (to some) unacceptable alternatives between an insufficiently biblical liberal Protestantism and an irrational biblicism can be avoided by a Roman Catholic doctrine of tradition. It can also be replaced by a Protestant view of the normativity of the gospel heard in Scripture where this is not tied down or "objectified" in fixed formulae but emerges (in different shapes according to local situations and needs) through the on-going conversation of Christians with one another as they listen faithfully and critically to the witness of Scripture. Bultmann's theology may be judged intolerable on account of its distance from Scripture and tradition, and Käsemann can be scolded for appearing to show too little love for the canon of Scripture (in his reaction against biblicistic pietism), but they both rose to the challenge of combining their Protestant faithfulness to Scripture with their Enlightenment-inspired historical criticism. They adumbrated the solution hinted at here, a solution which owes much to them both. This would entail biblical scholars producing an ever-increasing number of modern critical New Testament theologies properly so-called, i.e. overviews which interpret *all* the New Testament witnesses theologically and generate conversations between them,[37] and are themselves part of the conversation between these witnesses and their subsequent interpreters. Few English theologians have introduced more fresh resources into these on-going conversations than Anthony Thiselton.

---

36. See Michael Lakey, *Image and Glory of God: 1 Corinthians 11.12-16 as a Case Study in Bible, Gender and Hermeneutics* (London: T&T Clark, 2010), 181. This brilliant analysis of the problem discusses Bultmann, but barely mentions *Sachkritik*. It may be that to see the problem in terms of a gospel *Sache* which cannot be simply identified with any words of Scripture, but only with the Word himself, is already to part company with an evangelical doctrine of Scripture, or perhaps to side with the radical Reformation.

37. C. K. Barrett calls these "theological comparisons." Howard Marshall's *New Testament Theology* (Downers Grove, IL: InterVarsity Press, 2004) achieves this without sacrificing the integrity of each witness.

Experience and the Transfiguration of Tradition in Paul's Hermeneutical Christology

Mark L. Y. Chan

The development of hermeneutics as a discipline took a decisive turn with Schleiermacher's transformation of hermeneutics into a transcendental discipline. More than just an attempt to understand difficult texts, hermeneutics, in Schleiermacher's view, concerns the conditions under which the understanding of texts is possible. This led him to locate hermeneutics within the larger problem of human understanding, which in turn implicates the interpreter in the very process of interpretation. This entailment of the person of the interpreter in interpretation, so integral to Schleiermacher's philosophy of understanding, marks the beginnings of modern hermeneutics with its attentiveness to the historicality of understanding (Dilthey), the temporality of existence (Heidegger), and the rehabilitation of tradition (Gadamer).

Anthony C. Thiselton stands arguably in this same trajectory insofar as he has consistently championed a hermeneutical approach to theology that takes seriously the particularity of embodied life, the place of tradition in understanding, and the dialectic of question and answer in interpretation. Dilthey's invocation of "life" *(Leben)* as the controlling category for "understanding" *(Verstehen)*, over against an abstract rationalism that is inadequately grounded in human life as a whole, is one that Thiselton endorses heartily. He resonates with Dilthey's wry observation that "In the veins of the 'knowing subject'... no real blood flows."[1] While Dilthey's approach is not without difficulties — as critiques by Gadamer and Apel

---

1. Wilhelm Dilthey, *Gesammelte Schriften*, vol. 5: *Die Geistige Welt. Einleitung in die Philosophie des Lebens* (Leipzig and Berlin: Teubner, 1927), 4; cf. A. C. Thiselton, *The Hermeneutics of Doctrine* (Grand Rapids: Eerdmans, 2007), 56.

make clear,[2] its insistence on the embodiment of understanding in the life of the interpreter is one that Thiselton has appropriated, along with H. H. Price's *dispositional account of belief,* Wittgenstein's explorations of *forms of life, situational contexts,* and *language games,* and Gadamer's emphasis on the *historical situatedness* of both interpreter and interpretation. "The *particularity, contingency,* and *temporality* of hermeneutical inquiry," Thiselton maintains, "remain not only appropriate but also necessary for exploring the truth-claims, meaning, and life-related dimensions of Christian doctrine."[3] In this regard, he has done contemporary theology a service by issuing a clarion call to move understanding from the objectivism of solving free-floating problems to a more hermeneutical grounding in forms of life. His commitment to rooting knowledge in life is discernible not only in his oeuvre but also in the way he combines the rigors of scholarship with the everyday demands of ecclesial involvement, a fact not lost on me as a beneficiary of his doctoral supervision.

Contrary to the post-Cartesian neglect of tradition, and partly in reaction against the hegemony of the scientific method and its elevation of epistemological objectivism, there is in contemporary theology a chorus of voices calling for greater attention to tradition in theological understanding. Included in that choir is Thiselton, with his appropriation of Gadamer's notions of the rehabilitation of tradition and fusion of interpretive horizons for biblical and theological studies.[4] Following Thiselton's lead, and in gratitude to him for his guidance and friendship, I will seek in what follows to (i) look briefly at the shape and origin of Paul's Christology, and (ii) argue that Paul's encounter with the risen Christ on the road to Damascus precipitated a hermeneutical reconfiguring of his theological frame of reference. His Christology emerged from a critical and dialogical engagement with his interpretative pre-understanding or his theological and religious tradition, which provided him with the conceptual categories to reinterpret Christ. I will suggest that Paul's re-reading of the Jewish

---

2. Thiselton, *Hermeneutics of Doctrine,* 57f.
3. Thiselton, *Hermeneutics of Doctrine,* 63 (author's italics).
4. On Thiselton's engagement with Hans-Georg Gadamer's hermeneutics, see his *The Two Horizons: New Testament Hermeneutics and Philosophical Description with Special Reference to Heidegger, Bultmann, Gadamer, and Wittgenstein* (Grand Rapids: Eerdmans, 1980). Gadamer's philosophical hermeneutics is set out principally in his *Wahrheit und Methode. Grundzüge einer philosophischen Hermeneutik,* 4th ed. (Tübingen: J. C. B. Mohr, 1975), ET: *Truth and Method,* 2nd rev. ed. & translation revision by Joel Weinsheimer & Donald G. Marshall (London: Sheed & Ward, 1989).

The Transfiguration of Tradition in Paul's Hermeneutical Christology

scriptures in the light of his experience of Christ is essentially consonant with the Gadamerian insight on the historical situatedness of understanding and its entailment of self-involvement on the part of the interpreter.[5]

Contours and Origin of Paul's Christology

Much has been written about Paul's Christology,[6] and there is no need to traverse well-trodden paths again. Suffice to say that Paul's Christology is inseparably tied to his understanding of God and the outworking of God's redemptive plan in history. Despite the many references to the centrality of Christ's role in effecting God's salvation, one is hard pressed to find in the early Pauline letters a passage with Christology as its central topic. Yet, as Moo suggests, in Paul's theology, the person and work of Christ are "like the foundation of a building: it might not be seen very often, but everything rests on it."[7] There is a presuppositional Christocentrism in Paul's thought that is simultaneously theocentric and eschatologically redemptive. Paul employs a plethora of theologically loaded notions and designations to describe Christ and his salvific role — such as "Lord," "Messiah/Christ," "Adam," "Son of God," "Son of David," "image," "seed of Abraham," etc. — that together point to God's redemptive activity in history. Significantly, in expounding the interpenetrating relationship between God, salvation and Christ, Paul attributes to Christ functions and honors that are unique to God. We find for instance Christ described in 1 Corinthians 8:6 as the "Lord" who shares with God in the work of creation and providence. And it is arguable that Paul refers to Jesus as "God" in Romans 9:5,[8] which is remarkable given the strict Jewish monotheism of his upbringing. In this, Paul is doing no more than what the early Christians have done from the very beginning,

---

5. For a more detailed treatment, see Mark L. Y. Chan, *Christology from Within and Ahead: Hermeneutics, Contingency and the Quest for Transcontextual Criteria in Christology* (Leiden: Brill, 2001), 261-99.

6. See Gordon D. Fee, *Pauline Christology: An Exegetical-Theological Study* (Peabody: Hendrickson, 2007); L. W. Hurtado, "Paul's Christology," in James D. G. Dunn, ed., *The Cambridge Companion to St Paul* (Cambridge: Cambridge University Press, 2003), 185-98.

7. Douglas J. Moo, "The Christology of the Early Pauline Letters," in Richard N. Longenecker, ed., *Contours of Christology in the New Testament* (Grand Rapids: Eerdmans, 2005), 169.

8. See Murray J. Harris, *Jesus as God: The New Testament Use of Theos in Reference to Jesus* (Grand Rapids: Baker, 1992), 143-72.

namely the worship of Jesus and the inclusion of Jesus in the unique divine identity of the one God of Israel and Creator of all things.⁹

Paul's Christology cannot be determined solely by titular or linguistic considerations alone; one needs a broader interpretive framework that takes into account the story of God's redemptive work in history and how Jesus Christ fits into this. In this respect, the narrative approach of Richard Hays, N. T. Wright, Ben Witherington, and others provides a helpful way forward.¹⁰ Witherington for instance observes that there is a "narratological shape" to Paul's Christology in that the story of the historical figure of Jesus is intertwined with the story of God's dealings with Israel, and the story of God himself redeeming a world that has gone wrong.¹¹ Paul compares the human Jesus, "born of woman, born under the law" (Gal 4:4), to epochal figures from the story of Israel: Adam, Abraham, and Moses. Alongside this assumption of his humanity and Jewish identity, we find in the Pauline corpus descriptions of Christ's special relationship with the Father and the Spirit that connect the story of the historical Jesus to the story of God. Christology is thus for Paul a form of theology. And these interpenetrating stories of Jesus, Israel, and God are played out in a world that is at once sin-wrecked, presided over by dark spiritual forces, and headed for destruction (Rom 1:18-32; 1 Cor 10:21; 2 Cor 2:11; 4:4). It is against this backdrop of the need for redemption — both of humanity and creation as a whole — that Paul points to Jesus as the Christ or Messiah. This is the εὐαγγέλιον θεοῦ; and it is centered in the death and resurrection of Christ (1 Cor 2:2; 15:3; Rom 3:21-26; 4:25; 6:5), with the latter understood in terms of eschatological fulfillment.

---

9. L. W. Hurtado, *Lord Jesus Christ: Devotion to Jesus in Earliest Christianity* (Grand Rapids: Eerdmans, 2003); and Richard Bauckham's essays, "The Throne of God and the Worship of Jesus" and "Paul's Christology of Divine Identity," in his *Jesus and the God of Israel: God Crucified and Other Studies on the New Testament's Christology of Divine Identity* (Grand Rapids: Eerdmans, 2008), 152-232.

10. Richard Hays, *The Faith of Jesus Christ: An Investigation of the Narrative Substructure of Galatians 3:1–4:11* (Chico: Scholars, 1983); N. T. Wright, *The New Testament and the People of God* (London: SPCK, 1992); Ben Witherington III, *Paul's Narrative Thought-World: The Tapestry of Tragedy and Triumph* (Louisville: Westminster/John Knox, 1994); idem, *The Many Faces of the Christ: The Christologies of the New Testament and Beyond* (New York: Crossroad Publishing Company, 1998); N. R. Petersen, *Rediscovering Paul: Philemon and the Sociology of Paul's Narrative World* (Philadelphia: Fortress, 1985); and S. Fowl, *The Story of Christ in the Ethics of Paul* (Sheffield: JSOT Press, 1990). For a critical assessment of this approach, see Bruce W. Longenecker, *Narrative Dynamics in Paul: A Critical Assessment* (Louisville: Westminster John Knox, 2002).

11. Witherington, *Many Faces of the Christ*, 103-26.

The Transfiguration of Tradition in Paul's Hermeneutical Christology

There is general agreement that apocalyptic and eschatological themes figure in Paul's theology,[12] even though there is no consensus on the extent to which apocalyptic elements are present and how these relate to other key pillars in his thought. Of special interest is the eschatological dualism of two aeons in Paul's theology, where he juxtaposes "this age" (1 Cor 1:20; 2:6-8; 3:18) and the incursion of "the age to come," a new age of blessing and salvation or the "new creation" in Christ (2 Cor 5:17; Gal 6:15). The resurrection of Christ is part and parcel of the dawning of the new age of salvation, with the identity of Jesus the Son of God inextricably tied to the fact of his resurrection (Rom 1:3-4). This is evident in the almost seamless way in which Paul's exposition of the resurrection dovetails with his assertions about Christ in 1 Corinthians 15. This interpenetration between eschatology and Christology in Paul's theology owes much, as we shall see, to his hermeneutical engagement with the Jewish Scriptures, which is in turn shaped by his encounter with the risen Christ.

Paul's climactic encounter with the risen Christ on the road to Damascus is recounted both in his letters (1 Cor 9:1; 15:8-10; Gal 1:13-17; Phil 3:4-11) and in Acts (9:1-28; 22:1-21; 26:4-23). Paul's description testifies to the intensely personal and experiential nature of that encounter. It was clear to him that God had graciously revealed his Son to him (ἐν ἐμοί, Gal 1:16), having "seen" Jesus the Lord (1 Cor 9:1) and numbered himself among other eyewitnesses to the risen Christ (1 Cor 15:8-9). The Damascus Christophany was a transforming event; it turned him from a persecutor into a preacher of the Gospel, and led to a reassessment of his theology that in turn shaped his Christology.[13] How, and to what extent, that experience of the risen Christ

---

12. J. Christiaan Beker, following in the trajectory of Wrede and Schweitzer via Käsemann, has argued that apocalyptic lies at the heart of Paul's theology. See for instance his *Paul the Apostle: The Triumph of God in Life and Thought* (Edinburgh: T&T Clark, 1980); and *Paul's Apocalyptic Gospel: The Coming Triumph of God* (Philadelphia: Fortress, 1982). In recent times, D. Campbell has championed an apocalyptic interpretation of Paul's view of justification that is centered on eschatological participation in Christ; see Douglas A. Campbell, *The Deliverance of God: An Apocalyptic Rereading of Justification in Paul* (Grand Rapids: Eerdmans, 2009); and *The Quest for Paul's Gospel: A Suggested Strategy* (London & New York: T&T Clark International, 2005).

13. Seyoon Kim has consistently argued for the impact of the Damascus Christophany on the shape of Paul's Christology, as well as his soteriology and understanding of mission. See his *The Origin of Paul's Gospel* (Grand Rapids: Eerdmans, 1981); and "1 Cor. 5:11-21 and the Origin of Paul's Concept of 'Reconciliation,'" *Novum Testamentum* 39 (1997): 360-84; Kim answers his critics and reaffirms his thesis in *Paul and the New Perspective: Second Thoughts on the Origin of Paul's Gospel* (Grand Rapids: Eerdmans, 2002).

affected his theology remains a matter of debate, with opinions divided on whether the Damascus road event should be understood as a *conversion*, which entails a disjuncture between Paul's thought and his Jewish background, or a *calling*,[14] which underscores the continuity between the two. Without opting for one over the other,[15] we suggest that Paul's conversion *and* his calling to a Gentile mission are intertwined within a theological framework that allows for radical change and discernible continuity.

Paul's Damascus road encounter set in motion a reappraisal of Jesus Christ and a reconfiguration of his understanding of God and his redemptive program. In both Paul's and Luke's recounting of the event, the encounter with the risen Christ was sudden and unexpected; it came at a time when Saul was punctilious and zealous in his observance of the Law. Paul recognized that his conversion/call was the result of God's grace (Gal 1:15 — διὰ τῆς χάριτος αὐτοῦ) and that God was "pleased" (Gal 1:15-16 — ὅτε δὲ εὐδόκησεν) to reveal his Son to him (ἀποκαλύψαι τὸν υἱὸν αὐτοῦ). The description of Christ appearing in a blinding light is not unlike that of a divine epiphany in the Old Testament; and based on Paul's claim to have seen the Lord in 1 Cor 9:1, it is arguable that he understood the vision of the Christ as a manifestation of the כבוד יהוה, the *kabod* or glory of God. This association of Christ with the divine δόξα is reflected in Paul's description of Christ as τὸν κύριον τῆς δόξης (1 Cor 2:8) who was raised διὰ τῆς δόξης τοῦ πατρός (Rom 6:4; cf. Phil 2:11). This application of δόξα to Christ is significant given the fact that δόξα is frequently used in the LXX of the nature of God.[16] That revelation of the divine δόξα constitutes the

---

14. K. Stendahl famously contends that Paul was *called* and *not converted* in his essays, "Call Rather than Conversion," and "The Apostle Paul and the Introspective Conscience of the West," in *Paul Among Jews and Gentiles* (Philadelphia: Fortress, 1976), 7-23, 78-96. James D. G. Dunn argues along similar lines in "The Justice of God: A Renewed Perspective on Justification by Faith," *Journal of Theological Studies* 43 (1992): 1-22. See L. W. Hurtado, "Convert, Apostate, or Apostle to the Nations? The 'Conversion' of Paul in Recent Scholarship," *Studies in Religion/Sciences religieuses* 22 (1993): 273-84.

15. The verb καλέω (including the cognate adjective κλητός) is used to describe both God's calling of people to salvation (Rom 8:30; 1 Cor 1:9; 7:15; Gal 1:15; 5:13) and God's call to be an apostle (Rom 1:1). Paul describes himself and his converts as "called" (Rom 9:24; 1 Thess 4:7), and believers as "called ones" (Rom 1:6; 8:28; 1 Cor 1:2, 24). P. T. O'Brien, *Gospel and Mission in the Writings of Paul: An Exegetical and Theological Analysis* (Grand Rapids: Baker, 1995), 7-8.

16. See Carey C. Newman, *Paul's Glory-Christology: Tradition and Rhetoric* (Leiden: Brill, 1992), 17; and Neil Richardson, *Paul's Language about God* (Sheffield: Sheffield Academic Press, 1994), 158-59.

The Transfiguration of Tradition in Paul's Hermeneutical Christology

origin of Paul's Glory-Christology and resulted in a reinterpretation of God's messianic promises.

In all probability, the pre-conversion Saul shared the general Jewish repugnance against the idea of a crucified Messiah. Such a claim was to his mind inconceivable since a man condemned to hang on a tree is a sign of the person being cursed (Deut 21:22-23; cf. Gal 3:13; and 11QT^a 64:15-20). The aliveness of this crucified and cursed Jesus on the road to Damascus, raised no doubt to life again by God, was tantamount to an overturning by God of the verdict of the law. The Damascus encounter was in many ways a worldview-shattering experience for Paul. The once inconceivable notion of a crucified messiah became the core of his preaching (1 Cor 1:23; 2:2); and Paul, along with the other early Christians, acclaimed the crucified Jesus as κύριος, a title regularly used in the LXX in the place of the divine tetragrammaton.

Along with his transformed view of "Messiah" was a revised understanding of the outworking of God's messianic promises in history. Well versed as he undoubtedly was in the eschatological expectation of Second-Temple Judaism, Paul could not but see in the resurrection of Jesus the dawning of the Eschaton. This coming together of Messiah and eschatology, or more accurately, this eschatological interpretation of Jesus the Messiah, points already to a measure of continuity between Paul's new-found faith and his Jewish theological convictions. Significantly, Paul received God's call to preach to the Gentiles (Gal 1:16) in the eschatologically loaded revelation of God's Son to him. Paul's turn to the Gentiles was purposeful from the beginning; it was neither an afterthought nor was it a change in strategy because of the unresponsiveness of his fellow Jews. His mission to the Gentiles is inseparably linked to his revised understanding of the law vis-à-vis Christ and the place of empirical Israel and the Gentile nations in eschatological fulfillment. For our purpose, it is interesting to see how Paul's Jewish horizon of understanding is expanded and transfigured while providing at the same time the categories by which Christ is interpreted. The sense of change with continuity, of articulating the new in terms of what is familiar, is precisely what is hermeneutical about Paul's Christology. And that remapping of Paul's convictional world[17] began with his encounter on the Damascus road. Despite the perceived reluc-

---

17. The notion of "convictional world" is drawn from the subtitle of Terence L. Donaldson's *Paul and the Gentiles: Remapping the Apostle's Convictional World* (Minneapolis: Fortress, 1997).

tance of New Testament scholars to attribute causative significance to religious experiences in the development of theological understanding in early Christianity, Larry Hurtado, following Philip Almond, argues that powerful religious experiences can generate creative interpretations of tradition.[18] While recognizing Paul's indebtedness to Jewish and Greek language and concepts, Dunn insists that one must not discount "the creative power of his own religious experience — a furnace which melted many concepts in its fires and poured them forth into new moulds."[19]

The Convictional Transfiguration of Paul's Theology

Given the changes that came over Paul after his Damascus road experience, it is understandable that the latter should be described as a *conversion*. Nevertheless, one could argue that Paul did not so much change religion as he did his understanding of his religion. Hagner maintains that it is incorrect to think that Paul converted to a new religion; Paul himself would not have thought of it in those terms. "Christianity, for Paul," Hagner suggests, "is nothing other than the faith of his ancestors come to an eschatological phase of fulfillment before the final consummation."[20] To be sure, the unexpected encounter with Christ threw his worldview into disarray, but this was followed by a reordering of his convictional world, which eventuated in a new appraisal of Christ. It is against this backdrop of Paul seeking to make sense of his inherited theological tradition in the light of his experience of the risen Christ that we appreciate the hermeneutical thrust of his Christology. We will argue that Paul's Christological understanding emerged through a hermeneutical process marked by change on the one hand and continuity on the other.

One of the changes rung in by Paul's conversion was the shift in his at-

---

18. Larry W. Hurtado, "Religious Experience and Religious Innovation in the New Testament," *Journal of Religion* 80 (2000): 183-205; and Philip C. Almond, *Mystical Experience and Religious Doctrine: An Investigation of the Study of Mysticism in World Religions* (Berlin: Mouton, 1982). See also Luke T. Johnson, *Religious Experience in Earliest Christianity: A Missing Dimension in New Testament Studies* (Minneapolis: Fortress, 1998).

19. James D. G. Dunn, *Jesus and the Spirit: A Study of the Religious and Charismatic Experience of Jesus and the First Christians as Reflected in the New Testament* (London: SCM, 1975), 3-4.

20. Donald A. Hagner, "Paul and Judaism: The Jesus Matrix of Early Christianity; Issues in the Current Debate," *Bulletin of Biblical Research* 3 (1993): 123.

The Transfiguration of Tradition in Paul's Hermeneutical Christology

titude towards the law vis-à-vis Jesus Christ. Prior to the Damascus road encounter, he was an ardent upholder of the law and the traditions of his fathers, a commitment that drove him to perpetrate violence against the early Christians. Different explanations have been given as motivations for Paul's prosecutorial zeal.[21] A key to understanding what spurred him on is his self-confessed "zeal" in persecuting the church of God ("extremely zealous" — Gal 1:13-14; Phil 3:6; Acts 9:1). It is likely that Paul, prior to his conversion, was party to the Shammaite form of Pharisaism, which drew inspiration from Jewish heroes of zeal like Phinehas, Elijah, and Simeon and Levi.[22] Just as these heroes acted robustly to defend and preserve the faith of the Hebrew people, so Paul, sensing the threat to the Torah in the early Christians' claim that Christ is the boundary marker for the covenant, was compelled to act against the Christians. Failure to do something about this would not only compromise the identity of God's covenantal people but also risk God's wrath (Num 25:11). Paul embarked on his persecuting campaign precisely because he recognized that the Christian message was about the *same God* that he worshipped and served. He perceived clearly that the Christ of the Christian *kerygma* represented a rival to the Torah *from within* the one tradition of Judaism. If the Christians were correct, then the basis for entry into covenantal membership had shifted from observance of the law to Christ. This would jeopardize the entire faith of the Jewish nation. To the mind of Paul the Shammaite Pharisee, this was reason enough to eliminate those guilty of such a treasonous theological idea.

In one sense, the Christ-Torah antithesis evident in Paul's epistles was already present in Paul's pre-conversion convictional frame. While he acted to uphold the Torah over against Christ prior to the Damascus Christophany, after it, it was the reverse. He came to see that salvation was to be found in Christ alone, and not under the regime of the law. To Donaldson, this amounts to "an inversion of his preconversion perceptions of the Christian message."[23] The incompatibility between Christ and

---

21. On possible reasons for Saul's persecution of the church, see Donaldson, *Paul and the Gentiles*, 284-92; and Neil Elliott, *Liberating Paul: The Justice of God and the Politics of the Apostle* (Maryknoll: Orbis, 1994), 143-49.

22. The Shammaite faction was more dominant and strident than the generally more lenient Hillelite form of Pharisaism. On Phinehas' zeal, see Num 25:7-13; cf. Sir 45:23-24; 1 Macc 2:26, 54; 4 Macc 18:12; on Elijah's zeal, see 1 Kgs 18–19; Sir 48:1-2; 1 Macc 2:58; and on Simeon and Levi, see Gen 34; *Jub.* 30:18; *T. Levi* 6:3; Jdt 9:2-4.

23. Donaldson, *Paul and the Gentiles*, 285. See also T. L. Donaldson, "Zealot and Con-

Torah is seen in "a syllogism that, on one side of the conversion experience, led to persecution of the church and, on the other, resulted in fierce resistance to the Judaizers."[24] There is thus continuity as well as change in Paul's thinking, and the commonality that links the pre- and post-conversion Paul is the concept of the covenant. In the former, membership in the covenant is via Torah-observance; in the latter, it is faith in Christ that determines one's part in God's covenantal people. Related to this is Paul's mission to the Gentiles, which is divinely announced in connection with his conversion (cf. Acts 9:15). In the Jewish eschatological-pilgrimage tradition of his time, Gentiles will *stream into* Zion one day. However, after Paul's conversion encounter, we find the direction reversed. Now we find Paul, God's messenger, moving out *from* Zion to the nations. As far as Paul is concerned, Christology and Gentile-mission go hand in hand.

The above observations fit our contention that there is a dialectic of continuity and discontinuity in the development of Paul's Christology. Paul's experience of the living Christ led to a discernible change in his interpretive and theological grid, such that one might speak, in true Gadamerian fashion, of a fusion of horizons, namely the Jewish eschatological horizon of Paul's theology prior to Damascus and the new horizon of God's revelation of his Son. Paul did not so much jettison his earlier Torah-centric convictional world as reconstruct it around Jesus Christ and the messianic/eschatological reality that he represents. As Thiselton maintains, "Paul does not separate the action of the God of the Old Testament and Israel from that of Christ."[25] While Paul remained stoutly committed to the monotheism of his Jewish faith, his exalted view of Christ as somehow ontologically related to God, along with the conjoining of the Spirit with Christ in the outworking of God's salvation, led him to what Fee describes as a "proto Trinitarian" theology.[26] This develops from the way in which "Paul's language about God has been opened up, amplified, explicated, justified, by language about Christ."[27]

Paul's reconfiguration of his Jewish theological tradition may be dis-

---

vert: The Origin of Paul's Christ-Torah Antithesis," *Catholic Biblical Quarterly* 51 (1989): 644-82.

24. Donaldson, *Paul and the Gentiles*, 289-90.

25. A. C. Thiselton, *The Living Paul: An Introduction to the Apostle's Life and Thought* (Downers Grove, IL: IVP Academic, 2009), 52-53.

26. Fee, *Pauline Christology*, 586-87.

27. Richardson, *Paul's Language about God*, 304. Richardson provides a helpful study on the fluid interchange between God and Christ references in Paul.

The Transfiguration of Tradition in Paul's Hermeneutical Christology

cerned for instance in his Adam-Christ typology in 1 Corinthians 15. While the question on what led Paul to designate Christ as the "last Adam" (1 Cor 15:45) continues to intrigue scholars, it is not inconceivable that Paul was following through on a Jewish interpretive trajectory that transferred the commission, "be fruitful and multiply" and "have dominion," originally given to Adam (Gen 1:28), to Abraham and his descendants (Gen 12:2f; 17:2f; 22:16ff). N. T. Wright suggests that Paul built upon the association already made in Jewish theology between Israel and Adam, and took the innovative step to connect Adam with Christ. Deducing from a range of Jewish sources, Wright notes that Israel's failure to embody the divine purposes for humanity set the stage for Paul to acclaim Christ as the last Adam who succeeded where both the first Adam and Israel had failed.[28] Wright's proposal finds support from Kim's suggestion that Christ's appearance on the Damascus Road led Paul to identify him as the "image of God" and thereby comparable to the first Adam who was created in the image of God.[29]

Integral to Paul's theological reconfiguration is his appropriation of the Jewish Scripture in support of his Christological affirmations. This is an area that has already attracted much scholarly interest.[30] Given Paul's undoubted commitment to the teachings of the Hebrew Scripture, it is not surprising to find him seeking to make sense of his experience of Christ in the light of scripture. As a hermeneutical theologian, Paul is, above all, a careful *reader* of Scripture; he considers his gospel as something foretold by and in accordance with Scripture (Rom 1:2; 3:21, 31; 10:4). His hermeneutics may be understood as an intertextual conversation that he carries out with the "scripture" or "the scriptures," which are used either in relation to spe-

---

28. N. T. Wright points to Jewish sources like *Jub.* 2:23, *1 En.* 90, and *4 Ezra* 3 in support of the contention that Israel had already been associated with Adam in Jewish theology; see his "Adam, Israel and the Messiah," in *Climax of the Covenant: Christ and the Law in Pauline Theology* (Edinburgh: T&T Clark, 1991), 18-40.

29. See Kim, *Origin of Paul's Gospel*, 162-268. Kim is critical of Wright's linkage of Adam-Christology with an Israel-Christology, though he concedes that Wright's theory is close to his construal of the origin of Paul's εἰκών-Christology and Adam-Christology from the Damascus Christophany; see S. Kim, *Paul and the New Perspectives: Second Thoughts on the Origin of Paul's Gospel* (Grand Rapids: Eerdmans, 2002), 193-94.

30. See Craig A. Evans and James A. Sanders, eds., *Paul and the Scriptures of Israel* (Sheffield: Sheffield Academic Press, 1992); Stanley E. Porter and Christopher D. Stanley, eds., *As It Is Written: Studying Paul's Use of Scripture* (Atlanta: Society of Biblical Literature, 2008); and Steve Moyise, *Paul and Scripture: Studying the New Testament Use of the Old Testament* (Grand Rapids: Baker Academic, 2010).

cific texts (e.g., Rom 4:3; 9:17; 10:11; Gal 3:8) or without specific references (e.g., 1 Cor 15:3-4; Gal 3:22). As Hays has persuasively shown, so drenched was Paul in the words of Scripture that they surfaced in all sorts of ways in his letters, sometimes as quotes and other times as allusions or echoes.[31] We see this in Paul's close reading of the Pentateuch — in concert with other contemporaneous Jewish interpreters[32] — and in his reading of Isaiah, particularly in terms of Christ as the fulfillment of Isaiah's vision of God's ultimate deliverance of Israel as a light to the nations.[33] While the Hebrew Scripture supplies the linguistic and conceptual categories for the construction of his Christology, it is his recognition that in Christ the End has arrived that in turn affects and shapes his reading of the Old Testament.

Paul's hermeneutics is Christological in orientation, and may be characterized as both retrospective and teleological vis-à-vis the fulfillment of God's covenantal promises. It is retrospective in that it entails looking at the past from the vantage point of a future consummation, a future that has already begun to be realized in Christ; and it is teleological in that it is oriented to the τέλος or purpose of the law (Rom 10:4).[34] Paul's experience of Christ led him to see Christ as the hermeneutical key to the Old Testament,[35] particularly in terms of Christ being the fulfillment of what scripture has prophesied, not in a strict one-to-one, prediction-specific fulfillment model, but more along the line of a typological correspondence. Thus Christ is regarded as the true "seed of Abraham" (Gal 3:16), with Paul reconfiguring Israel's story in the letter to the Galatians and interpreting Abraham within the eschatological framework inaugurated in Christ, espe-

---

31. Richard B. Hays, *Echoes of Scripture in the Letters of Paul* (New Haven & London: Yale University Press, 1989).

32. This is the thrust of Francis Watson's *Paul and the Hermeneutics of Faith* (London: T&T Clark, 2004).

33. J. Ross Wagner, *Heralds of the Good News: Isaiah and Paul "In Concert" in the Letter to the Romans* (Leiden: Brill, 2002); and Florian Wilk, *Die Bedeutung des Jesajabuches für Paulus* (Göttingen: Vandenhoeck & Ruprecht, 1998).

34. We follow Wright and Thielman in regarding Christ as the climax of the Old Testament covenant and take the phrase "the end of the law" to mean the *goal* rather than the *termination* of the Torah; see Wright, *Climax of the Covenant*, 241; and Frank Thielman, *Paul and the Law: A Contextual Approach* (Downers Grove, IL: InterVarsity Press, 1994), 207.

35. Morna D. Hooker avers: "Paul starts from Christian experience and expounds Scripture in the light of that experience, quarrying the Old Testament where he will." "Beyond the Things That Are Written? Saint Paul's Use of Scripture," in G. K. Beale, ed., *The Right Doctrine from the Wrong Text? Essays on the Use of the Old Testament in the New* (Grand Rapids: Baker, 1994), 291.

The Transfiguration of Tradition in Paul's Hermeneutical Christology

cially in terms of the inclusion of believing Gentiles.[36] The way in which Christians, along with Christ, are regarded as the "seed of Abraham" suggests that Paul views Christ as a corporate figure, who embodies in himself the true children of Abraham.[37] This reconfiguration of what it means to be a part of Abraham's lineage, far from being anti-Jewish, is evidence of what Francis Watson describes as a hermeneutical *rupture* within Judaism,[38] a stance not unlike what is found in early Christian biblical interpretation in general. This hermeneutical reinterpretation is, in Paul, inextricably linked to an appraisal of Christ, not "according to the flesh" (2 Cor 5:16) but from the eschatological perspective of the dawning of the new creation.

Operating with what Hays calls an "eschatological hermeneutic,"[39] Paul approaches the Scripture of Israel from the standpoint of its eschatological fulfillment. While such an interpretative stance is not unique to Paul (interpreting texts in terms of eschatological fulfillment is found for instance in the Dead Sea Scrolls), what stands out is Paul's understanding that this fulfillment is centered in the person of Christ. He regards his call by the God of Israel (Gal 1:15) to bring the message of salvation to the Gentiles as indicative of the fulfillment of God's eschatological promise. In this regard, it is not inconceivable that Paul's experience of Christ as the resurrected Lord prompted him to speak of the pre-existence of the Son of God. As C. F. D. Moule suggests, it is neither difficult nor illogical to move from reflection on Christ's "post-existence" to his pre-existence. "If he is Lord of the End, is he not Lord of the Beginning also?"[40] The preexistence of Christ is precisely what Paul asserts in 1 Cor 8:6; and it is arguably presupposed in the incarnational language of Phil 2:7.

---

36. See Ian W. Scott's careful unpacking of Paul's arguments in Galatians in his book *Paul's Way of Knowing: Story, Experience, and the Spirit* (Grand Rapids: Baker Academic, 2006).

37. Moo, "Christology of the Early Pauline Letters," 172-73.

38. Francis Watson, *Text and Truth: Redefining Biblical Theology* (Edinburgh: T&T Clark, 1997), 324.

39. Richard B. Hays, *The Conversion of the Imagination: Paul as Interpreter of Israel's Scripture* (Grand Rapids: Eerdmans, 2005), 4.

40. C. F. D. Moule, *The Origin of Christology* (Cambridge: Cambridge University Press, 1977), 139, 154; S. Kim considers preexistence "an essential element in Paul's Son-Christology," *Origin*, 111, 114. Along the same line, Martin Hengel argues that eschatological considerations led to protological assertions; *Between Jesus and Paul* (Philadelphia: Fortress, 1983), 95; cf. idem, *Studies in Early Christology* (Edinburgh: T&T Clark, 1995), 73-117. See also Brendan Byrne, "Christ's Pre-existence in Pauline Soteriology," *Theological Studies* 58 (1997): 308-30.

Paul's hermeneutical horizon was informed not only by the basic tenets of his Jewish faith but also by the embryonic faith of the early Christians. Writing to the Corinthians on the resurrection, Paul appeals to a summary of the fundamentals of the Gospel, namely the death and resurrection of Christ (1 Cor 15:3-4), which he shares with his readers. This appeal to the commonality of a pre-Pauline tradition as a shared presupposition undergirds Paul's rhetorical argumentation in the Corinthians correspondence.[41] Paul's use of the rabbinic terminology of "deliver" (παραδιδόναι) and "receive" (παραλαμβάνειν) in 1 Cor 15:3 indicates that his message is consonant with the creedal beliefs of the early Christian community. There is scholarly consensus that Paul drew on what Ellis calls "preformed" theological materials in his letters, i.e. sermons, catechesis, paraenesis, confessions, hymns or other liturgical materials, household and congregational regulations, etc., dating back to the earliest strands of Christian tradition.[42] Interestingly, in drawing out the pastoral implications of Christ's salvific work in Phil 2:5-11, Paul directs his readers to the example of Christ and appeals to the incarnation of the preexistent Son of God in such a way as to suggest this was a well-established belief that he shared with the Philippians. Paul's allusion to Christ's preexistence comes across, in Hurtado's assessment, as a "passing reference," indicating that "the idea has already become disseminated among his [Paul's] churches so early that by the time he wrote his epistles he could take it for granted as known."[43] All in all, we contend that Paul's Christological assertions were worked out from within a horizon of inter-

---

41. A. Eriksson, *Traditions as Rhetorical Proof: Pauline Argumentation in 1 Corinthians* (Stockholm: Almqvist & Wiksell, 1998). John D. Moores argues pointedly that the rationality at work in Paul's epistolary appeal "presumes its addressees to have at their disposal *a code which nothing other than the experience of Christ which he and they share together . . . will suffice to supply.*" *Wrestling with Rationality in Paul: Romans 1–8 in a New Perspective* (Cambridge: Cambridge University Press, 1995), 21; emphasis added.

42. How much of these "preformed" materials are incorporated varies from letter to letter, with the role they play in Paul's epistolary arguments determined largely by the pastoral or theological questions being addressed. Ellis provides a summary of the percentage of probable or highly possible preformed traditions in the New Testament: E. Earle Ellis, "Preformed Traditions and Their Implications for Pauline Christology," in David G. Horrell and Christopher M. Tuckett, eds., *Christology, Controversy and Community: New Testament Essays in Honour of David R. Catchpole* (Leiden: Brill, 2000), 310. See also Richard N. Longenecker, "Christological Materials in the Early Christian Communities," in Longenecker, ed., *Contours*, 47-76.

43. Hurtado, *Lord Jesus Christ*, 124.

pretation that was shaped in significant ways by the theological commitments of early Christianity.

We find in Paul's letters a dynamic interplay between exegesis, eschatology and experience, with the latter pointing not only to his Damascus Christophany but also his subsequent missionary and pastoral engagements. Given the necessary situatedness of understanding, one can see Paul's reading of Scripture being impacted by his engagement with Gentile Christianity. It is not inconceivable that his experience of fellowship with Gentile believers in his missionary journeys played a part in reorienting his thinking on the law. Paul may well have witnessed in the years between the beginning of his ministry and his letter writing clear manifestations of the Spirit's presence among Gentile believers, which undoubtedly would have reinforced for him the reality of eschatological fulfillment. The experience of oneness in Christ, whereby ethnic, gender and social distinctions are transcended, may well have influenced his Christological interpretation of God's election in Abraham in Gal 3:7-9 (cf. Gen 12:3; 22:18). The impact of Paul's mission experiences on the development of his theology should not be underestimated. Adding to this, we find Paul working out his Christology in the context of pastoral controversy with those who preached different "gospels," especially in the way he appealed to Israel's scriptures to authenticate his message. His Adam and First Fruits Christology in 1 Corinthians 15 was arguably formulated as a corrective to the over-realized eschatological enthusiasm of some within the Corinthian church.[44] Paul's hermeneutics operates within the reciprocity that exists between Christ, scriptures, and contingent situations.

Notwithstanding the contingency of the various pastoral situations addressed in his letters, Paul does operate with a coherent center, the fundamentals of which were already in place in the kerygma of the church. Paul's theology may not be systematic in the sense of having all its parts neatly arranged in a hierarchical and interconnected manner, but he is nevertheless "a coherent thinker,"[45] with his coherent Gospel functioning as an interpretive framework. Without going into the details of the debate

---

44. Note Thiselton's caution against either attributing the over-realized eschatology to the influence of Gnosticism or over-stressing it as a problem at Corinth. See A. C. Thiselton, "Realized Eschatology at Corinth," *New Testament Studies* 24 (1977): 510-26; and his *The First Epistle to the Corinthians*, NIGTC (Grand Rapids: Eerdmans, 2000), 1173-74 and 1285.

45. E. P. Sanders, "Did Paul's Theology Develop?" in J. Ross Wagner, C. Kavin Rowe, and A. Katherine Grieb, eds., *The Word Leaps the Gap: Essays on Scripture and Theology in Honor of Richard B. Hays* (Grand Rapids: Eerdmans, 2008), 329-30.

on what constitutes the heart of Paul's theology, what is of interest to us is the relationship between coherence and contingency in his theology. Particularly helpful in this regard is Christiaan Beker's suggestion that Paul's thought is best understood as a hermeneutical interaction that goes on between the contingency of his letters and the coherence of his theology. Beker distinguishes between on the one hand the deep symbolic structure of Paul's thought, which is the apocalyptic triumph of God inaugurated in Christ, a triumph that will only be fully realized at the Parousia, and on the other hand, the contingent expressions which are Paul's epistolary responses to particular pastoral situations.[46] He contends that "the *character* of Paul's contingent hermeneutic is shaped by his apocalyptic core in that in nearly all cases the contingent interpretation of the gospel points — whether implicitly or explicitly — to the imminent cosmic triumph of God."[47] Coherence for Paul is not a "frozen text or a creedal sacred formula but a symbolic structure," a field of meaning or a network of symbolic relations. It expresses the convictional basis of Paul's proclamation of the gospel. Contingency is the variable element and has to do with the particularity of situations that Paul encounters in his churches and on the mission field. Coherence as symbolic structure is always interacting with contingent events.[48] The dialectic between coherence and contingency in Paul is not unlike the hermeneutical interaction between text (coherence) and context (contingency).

In the same vein, Witherington argues that there is a coherent "narrative thought world" discernible in Paul's letters. Parsing this grand multilayered narrative, Witherington sees four interrelated stories that together comprise the one large drama: (i) the story of a world gone wrong; (ii) the story of Israel; (iii) the story of Christ; and (iv) the story of Christians, which includes Paul himself. The last of these arises from the previous

---

46. To demonstrate the contingent nature of Paul's letters, Beker focuses on Romans and Galatians — two epistles widely regarded as the most systematic and least occasional of his letters — and shows that the former is primarily a situational missive targeted at the Jewish-Gentile congregation of Rome while the latter is an exposition of the Abraham story given in debate with Judaizers in the Galatian church; see Beker, *Paul*, 71-74.

47. Beker, *Paul*, 19.

48. Beker, *Paul*, 351. In a later article, Beker argues that "coherence" is to be preferred to "core," since the latter suggests a fixed and non-pliable substance whereas the former allows for fluidity and flexibility; see J. C. Beker, "Recasting Pauline Theology: The Coherence-Contingency Scheme as Interpretive Model," in Jouette M. Bassler, ed., *Pauline Theology*, vol. 1: *Thessalonians, Philippians, Galatians, Philemon* (Minneapolis: Fortress, 1991), 17.

The Transfiguration of Tradition in Paul's Hermeneutical Christology

three, and is the "first full installment of the story of a world set right again." The story of Christ, Witherington maintains, "is the hinge, crucial turning point, and climax of the entire larger drama, which more than anything else affects how *the* Story will ultimately turn out."[49] Paul's coherent theology as a web of interconnecting convictions may be understood in terms of the grand narrative of God's salvific work in history coming to climactic fulfillment in the history of Jesus Christ.

Paul's multi-tiered narrative world may be compared to H. H. Price's notion of belief as *disposition*, which refers to a certain orientation or attitudinal stance in the midst of varying circumstances.[50] Paul's Christology is dispositional in that it is at once rooted in tradition and responsive to different pastoral situations. This understanding of his coherent theology as something that is not "closed" in advance of contingent engagement is, I submit, a fundamentally Gadamerian insight. On both poles of this dispositional dialectic between fidelity to tradition and contextual openness, Paul, in articulating his Christology, is personally involved in reconfiguring his Jewish theological tradition, appropriating to himself the beliefs of the early Christian communities, and applying the gospel to the many pastoral contingencies confronting him. There is thus a subjective dimension alongside the necessary inter-subjectivity of Paul's engagement with tradition, scripture, fellow Christians, converts, and even detractors. In a sense these existential entailments are not surprising, considering that it was through an experiential encounter with the risen Lord that Paul became a follower and apostle of Christ.

Drawing attention to the self-involving character of experience in Paul's Christology does not mean jettisoning metaphysical claims about God in Christ in favor of a Bultmannian form of self-involving existentialism. Thiselton laments the "disastrous dichotomy between an existential approach which perceives *only* a confession of *personal faith* here and a conservative counterreaction which sometimes perceives *only* a statement of *bare fact* here."[51] Proclamation or kerygma that makes truth claims, he suggests, is closely related to confession or self-involvement that declares a personal stake in what is asserted. Part of the problem, Thiselton maintains, is a failure to understand that the authenticity of the call of God through Jesus of Nazareth is not dependent simply on "a voluntarist ac-

---

49. Witherington, *Paul's Narrative Thought-World*, 5.
50. H. H. Price, *Belief* (London: George Allen & Unwin, 1969), 243-44.
51. Thiselton, *First Epistle to the Corinthians*, 1188 (author's italics).

count of language, but *on the promise that certain states of affairs are the case, or are true.*"[52] In other words, the existential or experiential in Christology is never just a subjective sensation of pure interiority cut off from its moorings within an interpretive tradition and unhinged from events in time and space. Paul's experience of Christ on the Damascus road was not an uninterpreted experience; it depended on the covenantal and messianic categories of Paul's Jewish background. Nevertheless, that encounter was transformative in that it precipitated a radical reconfiguration of his convictional or narrative world. It soon became clear to Paul that the eschatological salvation promised by the God of Israel had in fact arrived in Jesus Christ. In Paul's Christology, we find a convergence of experience, scripture, tradition, and eschatological fulfillment.

---

52. Thiselton, *Hermeneutics of Doctrine*, 382 (author's italics).

Kerygmatic Rhetoric in New Testament Epistles

Matthew R. Malcolm

It was my pleasure to research 1 Corinthians under the supervision of Professor Thiselton at the University of Nottingham from 2007 to 2010. I sought to account for the arrangement of the letter, and in this pursuit I found it was necessary to move beyond the scope of classical (Greco-Roman) epistolary or rhetorical analysis, to include Jewish and Christian resources. In the present paper I seek to apply that interpretive approach to the analysis of the letters of Paul and the New Testament more generally.[1]

Although there has been fruitful development in the study of (especially Pauline) New Testament argumentation in recent decades, the tendency to utilize generic Greco-Roman oratorical categories in describing

---

1. Such a broadening of scope has been called for by many involved in the study of Pauline rhetoric for some time. Peter Lampe has recently urged, "When comparing ancient rhetoric with early Christian literature, we need to have in mind not only the pagan Greco-Roman culture, but also the *Jewish* rhetorical (and epistolary) practice, both in its Hellenistically influenced and its apocalyptic specifications. . . . [W]e mainly need to observe the Jewish rhetorical and epistolary *praxis*, trying to systematize it and then compare it with the New Testament. . . . There might still be a lot to discover." Peter Lampe, "Rhetorical Analysis of Pauline Texts — Quo Vadit? Methodological Reflections," in *Paul and Rhetoric* (ed. J. Paul Sampley and Peter Lampe; New York: T&T Clark, 2010), 3-21, here 19; emphasis original. Fifteen years earlier, Khiok-Khng Yeo commented, "In rhetorical study of the NT, the traditional, predominant approach is to read the NT in the light of the Greco-Roman tradition. So far, few have employed the Jewish rhetorical tradition to study the NT. That shortcoming may be attributed to the following two conditions: (a) The absence of Jewish rhetorical handbooks; and (b) the tendency to see the disjunction or opposition between Hellenism and Hebraism, or generally between Greco-Roman and Jewish cultures." Khiok-Khng Yeo, *Rhetorical Interaction in 1 Corinthians 8 and 10: A Formal Analysis with Preliminary Suggestions for a Chinese, Cross-Cultural Hermeneutic* (Leiden: Brill, 1995), 64.

rhetorical movement has meant that Jewish or creatively Christian modes of argumentation have been relatively under-examined and unappreciated. One feature of New Testament argumentation that has eluded significant illumination from classical Rhetorical Criticism, for example, is the well-known broad movement from indicative to imperative in certain epistles of the New Testament. Regardless of the application of oratorical (or epistolary) categories to sections of the letter, the interpreter is left with the question: *why* is the material arranged so as to move from a general (but not exclusive) emphasis on the theological establishment of identity to a general emphasis on the hortatory treatment of conduct — and what does this movement represent in terms of communication?[2]

My suggestion is that this movement of argumentation represents one expression of creative Christian rhetoric, or *kerygmatic rhetoric*,[3] which arose from early Christian conceptual negotiation of Jesus Christ and his significance for Christian identity and conduct.

Rhetorical Resources

Most of the New Testament documents are genuine letters to churches that reflect at length on scriptural themes and historical situations, with a view to influencing conduct. It is conceivable, then, that numerous epistolary and broadly rhetorical resources were drawn upon in their formation, whether consciously or unconsciously. Two broad rhetorical backgrounds are worth mentioning here, before exploring in more detail the idea of *kerygmatic rhetoric*.

---

2. Victor Paul Furnish argues that there is by no means a clear-cut division between "theological" and "hortatory" sections in Paul. Rather, "Romans has, almost from the beginning, a hortatory aspect of which chs 12–15 are only, so to speak, the denouement." Furnish, *Theology and Ethics in Paul* (2nd ed.; Louisville: Westminster John Knox Press, 2009), 101; cf. 208-26. The question remains, however: Why does Romans flow in such a way as to have a denouement in which overt exhortation is more heavily featured?

3. There is a sense in which what I am describing does not fit into the field of Rhetorical Criticism. My identification of *"kerygmatic rhetoric"* does not assume an ancient oratorical practice with flexible rules, but rather the creative literary issue of early conceptual imagery concerning Jesus Christ. It is, then, "rhetoric" in the broader sense of the word. On the other hand, this approach does attempt to account for New Testament literary movement in relation to its first century environment, so it is different from the "new rhetoric."

Covenant Conformity: The Hebrew Scriptures

One motif of the Hebrew Scriptures that may have partially influenced the arrangement of certain New Testament letters is the logical link between the establishment of identity and the summons to conduct, notable at certain crucial points:[4]

> **Exodus 20:1-3 (NRSV)**
> Then God spoke all these words: I am the LORD your God, who brought you out of the land of Egypt, out of the house of slavery; you shall have no other gods before me.

> **Leviticus 19:2-3 (NRSV)**
> You shall be holy to me; for I the LORD your God am holy. You shall each revere your mother and father, and you shall keep my Sabbaths: I am the LORD your God.

That this logic of conformity to covenant identity is influential for argumentation patterns of the New Testament is evident from 1 Peter 1:14–2:3, in which four images of familial belonging (arising from the theme of rebirth introduced in 1:3) issue in four general imperatives: As obedient children, be holy; as callers on a Father, be fearful; as brotherly-lovers, love; as newborn infants, crave milk. Indeed, Leviticus 19:2 is cited in this very context.

Moral Formation: Plutarch and the Twelve Patriarchs

It is well known that Plutarch is interested in the way in which essential character[5] is worked out in the histories of significant figures. Christoph F. Konrad rightly points out that Plutarch's interest is "moral, not

---

4. Andrew T. Lincoln makes this point in his examination of Ephesians: "The two basic parts of this written discourse and their functions may . . . reflect general patterns familiar from Jewish tradition. One example is the 'covenant speech' pattern in which a reminder of what God had done of behalf of his people was followed by a call to keep his commandments." Andrew T. Lincoln, *Ephesians* (Word Biblical Commentary; Dallas: Word, 1990), xl.

5. This is not to claim that for Plutarch character is completely inflexible. On this topic see especially Christopher Gill, "The Question of Character-Development: Plutarch and Tacitus," *The Classical Quarterly* 33, no. 2 (1983): 469-87; and Simon Swain, "Character Change in Plutarch," *Phoenix* 43, no. 1 (1989): 62-68.

political,"[6] and that his concern is the way in which the figures' behaviour in good or bad fortune "could reveal their nature."[7] This hortatory interest in the factors behind human conduct provides insight into first-century assumptions about the nature and development of human moral expression, and may further illuminate patterns of argumentation in the New Testament.

The *Life of Sertorius* is instructive. When the fundamentally noble Sertorius acts successfully or honourably, it is presented by Plutarch as the manifestation or proof of his essential virtue (particularly, that of his mind):

> And in the rest of the campaign he did many things that evidenced both understanding and daring. (3.3)

> And the lofty-mindedness of Sertorius was evident firstly in relation to the Roman councillors who fled from Rome. (22.3)

> And the negotiations with Mithridates also show his lofty-mindedness. (23.1)

> For to a noble man victory is desirable if it comes with honour, but not if it comes with shame. (23.5)

Pompey, similarly, is able to act in accordance with a noble *mind*:

> So Pompey did not act as one with a youthful mind, but as one whose mind was well matured and disciplined. (27.3)

When Sertorius is unsuccessful, on the other hand, it is frequently explained with reference to "misfortune":

> In understanding he was inferior to none of these people, but in fortune he was inferior to all. (1.5)

> And they experienced a fortune that was harsh and unjust in their deaths. (1.6)

---

6. Christoph F. Konrad, *Plutarch's Sertorius: A Historical Commentary* (Chapel Hill: The University of North Carolina Press, 1994), xxvi.

7. Konrad, *Sertorius*, xxvi.

Kerygmatic Rhetoric *in New Testament Epistles*

When Sertorius finally acts with unconscionable severity, it is seen as fortune's[8] misshaping of his essentially virtuous character:

> To me it seems that virtue which is established by sincerity and reason is not able to be turned into its contrary by any sort of fortune; although it is not impossible for good principles and natures, when unworthily oppressed by great calamities, to have their character changed in spirit. And this is what, it seems to me, was suffered by Sertorius when fortune had abandoned him. (10.4)

Plutarch's estimation of human morality seems to involve, on the one hand, the idea that one's character has a particular orientation from the outset; and on the other hand, the idea that this character may respond flexibly to the winds of fortune. This flexibility demands genuine responsibility of Plutarch's characters, and by extension, of his readers who must learn from their stories. The minds (or souls) of Plutarch's readers, one may reflect, are being instructed such that they might face the uncertainties of fortune with the resolve to express and develop the best of their own character.

Sharing Plutarch's concern that readers might learn from the examples of key figures, the *Testaments of the Twelve Patriarchs* illustrate the significance of a rightly-oriented mind or soul for one's moral conduct. The first episode, indeed, is headed "Concerning Thoughts," and summons hearers to learn from the example of Reuben. Reuben warns in chapters 1–2 that young men perish by having darkened minds. He laments that his own mind had been captivated by sexual thoughts, and urges his descendents to align their character with that of Joseph, who had purged fornication from his mind.

Whereas in Plutarch the conduct of readers is addressed by an implicit summons to develop the best of their own character by comparison with that of famous figures, the hortatory character of the *Testaments* is clearly more overt (as one might expect of testamentary literature). The assumption that conduct will flow from character or mind, however, is common to both, as is the didactic method of providing exemplars.

The necessity of a rightly directed mind is similarly evident at crucial

---

8. At times, such as in the events following the death of Eumenes (with whom Sertorius is compared by Plutarch), it is "divine providence" rather than fortune that is explicitly in view. On this topic see Simon Swain, "Plutarch: Chance, Providence, and History," *American Journal of Philology* 110, no. 2 (1989): 272-302.

turning points in numerous New Testament letters. When Romans moves from doxology to exhortation, it begins: "Be transformed by the renewal of the mind" (Rom. 12:2). When Philippians introduces the central paradigm of the suffering and vindication of Jesus Christ, it begins, "Let this mindset be among you, which was also in Christ Jesus" (Phil. 2:5). When 1 Peter moves from doxological narrative to general imperative, it begins, "Therefore, girding up the loins of your minds, being completely sober, set your hope on the grace" (1 Pet. 1:13). Clearly there is a similar assumption that conduct will arise from the orientation of the mind.

Reception of the Messiah and the Development of *Kerygmatic Rhetoric*

My contention, however, is that conceptualizations inherent in early Christian liturgical declaration and celebration of the Messiah gave birth to a new type of epistolary rhetoric, drawing on but going beyond the assumptions and patterns explored above (among others).[9] In this new type of rhetoric the conceptual imagery of the *kerygma* influences the arrangement and formulation of Christian communication for a liturgical context.[10] I therefore refer to it as *kerygmatic rhetoric*.

Before exploring this in more detail it is important to clarify two points. First, I do not mean to imply that such a rhetorical approach is the only approach adopted in the letters of the New Testament, or that it is entirely distinct from other epistolary or rhetorical approaches. Second, I am not claiming that the New Testament proclaims *rather than* persuades.[11]

---

9. Other rhetorical resources include the motif of divinely initiated dual reversal (as in the Psalms of Lament), as well as the numerous modes of "religious mantic . . . , philosophical, and ritual discourse in the Mediterranean world" identified by Vernon K. Robbins, recently summarised in "Socio-Rhetorical Interpretation," in *The Blackwell Companion to the New Testament* (ed. David E. Aune; Chichester: Wiley-Blackwell, 2010), 192-219, here 193.

10. That is, for public reading at ecclesial gatherings. Larry Hurtado rightly notes that "New Testament epistles seem to have been composed for liturgical reading and incorporate liturgical formulae (e.g. the 'grace and peace' salutation and grace-benediction, the 'amen' and 'Abba, Father' prayer expressions, the 'maranatha' of 1 Cor. 16:22)." Larry Hurtado, *At the Origins of Christian Worship: The Context and Character of Earliest Christian Devotion* (Carlisle: Paternoster Press, 1999), 42.

11. This might be implied by G. A. Kennedy's reflection on rhetoric in Christianity: "The message is proclaimed, not proved; it is persuasive to those who are called or chosen by

Rather, I am suggesting that various structures and formulations of New Testament persuasion distinctively arise from the *kerygma* of Messianic death and resurrection — and that this fundamental characteristic is sufficiently different to the fundamental characteristics of other rhetorical or argumentative approaches to constitute a broad explanatory category in its own right. While *deliberative rhetoric* aims to persuade the political assembly to action by demonstrating an advisable way forward, and *exemplary argumentation* aims to promote moral progress by inspiring emulation, *kerygmatic rhetoric* aims to effect the adoption of a new mindset and code of conduct by proclaiming the died-and-risen Messiah.

Kerygma and Conceptualization

I suggest that early Christian negotiation of Jesus in the liturgical activities of declaration and celebration (and the communally maintained traditions associated with these liturgical activities)[12] formed the environment in which this new type of rhetoric arose.[13] In declaration of Jesus as the embodied fulfilment of the Scriptures of Israel, and in celebration of Jesus in baptism and the Lord's Supper, Jesus was conceptualized among early believers as God's Messianic answer to the hope of Israel, and the archetype of Christian identity. And this was no accident, but arose from the cooperative effort of apostolic leaders, who recognized that they shared a common "faith," a common "word," a common "gospel," focused on the Messiah who suffered and was vindicated.[14]

God." G. A. Kennedy, *Classical Rhetoric and Its Christian and Secular Tradition from Ancient to Modern Times* (2nd ed.; Chapel Hill: University of North Carolina Press, 1999), 150.

12. By which I mean the oral and written schematic summaries developed for catechetical purposes. Birger Gerhardsson argues, "[T]he early Church possessed an elementary sense of history, relatively firm memories from the time 'when the Spirit was still not given' and relatively fixed traditions from that time; this applies at least to those circles of early Christianity, in which the Synoptic tradition was preserved and edited." Birger Gerhardsson, *Tradition and Transmission in Early Christianity* (Coniectanea Neotestamentica 20, combined ed.; trans. Eric J. Sharpe; Grand Rapids: Eerdmans, 1998 [original 1964]), 44.

13. Hurtado rightly comments, "At the risk of severe understatement, one of the characteristic things early Christians did was to worship.... If, therefore, we want to analyse major phenomena of early Christianity, Christians' devotional practices are clearly key matters for attention." Hurtado, *At the Origins*, 1.

14. It may be that the use of such singular nouns to label the Christian message (occurring in NT writings attributed to Paul, Peter, James, and John) was at least partially intended

Indeed, it is significant that both of these modes of liturgical attention — liturgical *declaration* and liturgical *celebration* — centre on Jesus' death and exaltation.

Hints provided by a cross-section of the New Testament concerning the earliest traditions of Christian Messianic *declaration* commonly focus on Jesus as the one who suffered, died and rose to glory as God's answer to Israel's scriptural hopes. As this answer, moreover, he carries significance for "you" or "us":

1 Corinthians 15:3-5
For I passed on to you, as of foremost importance, that which I also received: that the Messiah *died* for our sins according to the Scriptures, and that he was buried, and that he was *raised* on the third day according to the Scriptures, and that he appeared to Peter, then to the Twelve.[15]

1 Peter 1:10-11
Concerning this salvation the prophets searched and investigated the grace that was prophesied for you, investigating as to what manner or time the Spirit of the Messiah in them was declaring, as it bore witness to the *sufferings* of the Messiah and his *subsequent glories*.[16]

Luke 24:25-26
And Jesus said to them, "O how ignorant and slow in heart you are to believe all that the prophets have declared! Was it not necessary for the Messiah to *suffer* these things and enter into his *glory*?"[17]

---

to indicate the unity of a common singular cooperative Christian movement, whether in Rome, Greece, Jerusalem, or Asia Minor. Indeed, the use of the singular noun *euangelion* is almost without parallel in contemporary usage, and may have been one way of drawing attention to the universal commonality of a singular Christian proclamation.

15. Thiselton expresses the consensus that this passage utilizes preformed traditional material: "Paul does . . . refer to a continuity of **handing on** and **receiving** which constitutes, in effect, an early *creed which declares the absolute fundamentals of Christian faith and on which Christian identity* (and the experience of salvation) *is built*." Anthony C. Thiselton, *The First Epistle to the Corinthians* (New International Greek Testament Commentary; Grand Rapids: Eerdmans, 2000), 1186; emphases original.

16. Paul J. Achtemeier acknowledges the author's use of traditional "rudiments of salvation" here: "Its use here reflects part of the early kerygma, understood to be rooted in Jesus' teaching (e.g., Luke 24:25-26)." Paul J. Achtemeier, *1 Peter: A Commentary on First Peter* (Hermeneia; Minneapolis: Fortress Press, 1996), 105, n. 5.

17. John Nolland reflects on the likely traditional formulation lying behind this passage: "Despite the Lukan links, the wording is probably more traditional than Lukan, since

Kerygmatic Rhetoric *in New Testament Epistles*

In all three of these passages, the identity of the Messiah as one who fulfils prophecy by dying and rising (or suffering and being glorified) is presented as a traditional summary that ought to be known by contemporary hearers.

Hints provided by the New Testament concerning early liturgical traditions of Christian Messianic *celebration* (or sacrament) likewise focus on Jesus as the one who died and rose to a position that awaits cosmic manifestation. Again, this identity bears direct significance for "you" or "us":

1 Corinthians 11:23-26
For I received from the Lord that which I also passed onto you: that on the night he was betrayed, the Lord Jesus took a loaf of bread and, having given thanks, broke it and said, "*This is my body,* which is for you. Do this in remembrance of me." Similarly he took the cup after the supper, saying, "This cup is the new covenant *in my blood.* Do this as often as you drink it, in remembrance of me." For as often as you eat this bread and drink from the cup, *you proclaim the death* of the Lord *until he comes.*[18]

Romans 6:3-4
Do you not know that as many of us as were baptised into Christ Jesus were baptised *into his death?* So we were buried with him through baptism into death, so that, just as Christ was *raised from the dead* through the glory of the Father, we also might walk in newness of life.[19]

(i) the thought development of the account requires something equivalent at this stage (after v. 25, vv. 26-27 need to mention the suffering of the redemptive figure [the actual word 'Christ' may be Lukan] and the outcome of the suffering, as well as the interpretation of Scripture); and *(ii)* 'glory' is not the word that Luke would most naturally have penned at this point." John Nolland, *Luke 18:35–24:53* (Word Biblical Commentary; Dallas: Word, 1993), 1204.

18. Joseph A. Fitzmyer rightly acknowledges that this passage is "derived from an early liturgical tradition." Joseph A. Fitzmyer, *First Corinthians: A New Translation with Introduction and Commentary* (Anchor Yale Bible 32; New Haven: Yale University Press, 2008), 436.

19. Hurtado describes the importance of the logic evidenced in this passage for liturgical formation in early Christian identity: "Their initiation ritual, baptism, was invested with enormous significance. . . . It was not simply an act of individual obedience, but was to be seen as signifying a powerful connection of believers with Jesus' death and resurrection that was to issue in an eschatological 'newness of life' expressed in the present in moral transformation (Rom. 6:1-4), and ultimately in the full resurrection life of the age to come." Hurtado, *At the Origins,* 53.

Mark 14:22-25

While they were eating, he took the loaf of bread, gave thanks for it, broke it, and gave it to them, saying, "Take it; *this is my body*." And taking the cup, he gave thanks and gave it to them, and all of them drank from it. And he said to them, "This is *my blood* of the covenant, which has been poured out for many. Truly I say to you that I will certainly not drink from the fruit of the vine until *that day when I drink anew* in the kingdom of God."[20]

1 Peter 3:18-21

For Christ also *suffered once for sins*, the just for the unjust, to bring you to God. Being put to *death in the flesh*, he was made *alive by the Spirit*.... And now baptism, which [Noah's flood] prefigured, saves you, not by putting away filthy flesh, but by the appeal of a good conscience before God, *through the resurrection* of Jesus Christ.[21]

In these passages the Messiah is presented as one whose benefits are appropriated by the reception of his death and/or resurrection, in anticipation of his coming.[22] Again, this is presented as a traditional summary that ought to be known.

It seems, then, that in the environment that gave birth to the New Testament letters, the notion of the died-and-exalted Jesus as *Messiah* and *archetype* is inherent in liturgical declaration and celebration. Those who lead or belong to this environment declare that the Messiah has come in fulfilment of the Scriptures of Israel, effecting a change for *us*. They celebrate and identify with this died-and-risen Messiah in baptism, and in the corporate sharing of bread and wine. For these people, the identity of Jesus as the died-and-risen Messiah of God, and their own identity as partakers in him, are fundamental in their experience of worship.

---

20. Hurtado comments on the established liturgical tradition underlying this passage: "Presuming readers who are baptized and participate in the Eucharist as a sacred meal (the latter practice directly reflected in 14:22-25), the author calls them to be prepared for the full consequences of their profession and ritual practice." Larry Hurtado, *Lord Jesus Christ: Devotion to Jesus in Earliest Christianity* (Grand Rapids: Eerdmans, 2003), 313.

21. In arguing that this section utilizes preformed traditional material, E. Earle Ellis reasons, "1 Peter 3:18-22 or, more strictly 3:18, 22 is (1) introduced by a formulaic ὅτι, (2) is hymnic in form and (3) marks a break in the context that is resumed at 4:1." E. Earle Ellis, *The Making of the New Testament Documents* (Biblical Interpretation Series 39; Leiden: Brill, 1999), 136.

22. It is often significant that the cosmic manifestation of Jesus' exaltation is deferred: the "coming" of Christ is still awaited.

Kerygmatic Rhetoric *in New Testament Epistles*

To summarise, liturgical traditions that precede the formation of the New Testament documents express and reinforce the conceptualization of *Jesus as God's died-and-exalted Messiah and archetype*.[23]

Conceptualization and Rhetorical Construction

The importance of experience-formed conceptualization for grammatical and rhetorical construction has been explored in the fields of cognitive and cultural linguistics. Farzad Sharifian and Gary B. Palmer write, "Language is shaped not only by special and general innate potentials, but also by physical and sociocultural experiences."[24]

Australian Aboriginal English is illustrative of the communicative influence of such conceptually formative sociocultural experiences: "The dominant templates used for 'packaging reality,' or schemas, in Aboriginal English are largely derived from Aboriginal culture and worldview. These schemas appear to inform all levels of language and act as the main reference frames during the process of communication."[25]

For example, the experience-formed cultural conceptualization of *intermittent travel* may be traced in the narrative structure of an Aboriginal interpretation or description of history — even in English. The experience-formed cultural conceptualization of *the stolen generation* may be evidenced in an Aboriginal retelling of a ghost-story.[26]

---

23. I argue in my dissertation that Paul in particular is gripped with the essence of this conceptualization from the time of his Damascus Road experience, becoming especially conscious of the deferred manifestation of Christ's exaltation.

24. Farzad Sharifian and Gary B. Palmer, "Applied Cultural Linguistics: An Emerging Paradigm," in *Applied Cultural Linguistics: Implications for Second Language Learning and Intercultural Communication* (ed. Farzad Sharifian and Gary B. Palmer; Amsterdam: John Benjamins, 2007), 1-14, here 1. In an earlier work, Palmer argues, "It is likely that all native knowledge of language and culture belongs to cultural schemas and that the living of culture and the speaking of language consist of schemas in action." Gary B. Palmer, *Toward a Theory of Cultural Linguistics* (Austin: University of Texas Press, 1996), 63.

25. Ian G. Malcolm and Farzad Sharifian, "Aspects of Aboriginal English Oral Discourse: An Application of Cultural Schema Theory," *Discourse Studies* 4, no. 2 (2002): 169-81, here 172-73.

26. These and other examples are explored in Ian G. Malcolm and Farzad Sharifian, "Something Old, Something New, Something Borrowed, Something Blue: Australian Aboriginal Students' Schematic Repertoire," *Journal of Multilingual and Multicultural Development* 26, no. 6 (2005): 512-32. Danièle M. Klapproth argues that distinctive cultural conceptualizations (or "schemas") among central Australian Aboriginals can be seen in distinctive

According to Sharifian, members of a cultural group renegotiate their shared conceptualizations over time, through various communicative and routine activities: "Like other complex systems, cultural cognitions have their own unique history of interactions that constantly construct and reconstruct the system. Often small changes in the interactions of cultural groups have had a remarkable influence on the future direction of their cultural cognition."[27]

If formative conceptualizations, prompted by sociocultural experiences, may be expressed in correspondingly distinctive communication, it is conceivable that this is precisely what happened in early Christianity. Indeed, I am suggesting that for the writers of the New Testament documents, the Christ event, and its experiential reception from Jerusalem to Damascus to Rome, was a culture- and language-transforming event. It demanded the renegotiation of certain existing Jewish and Greco-Roman cultural conceptualizations ("Messiah"; "apocalyptic reversal"; "growth to maturity"; "political entity as body"; "necessity of love," etc.) and resulted in new communicative manifestations.

I have argued above that, most essentially, the liturgical traditions preceding the formation of New Testament documents express the conceptualization of *Jesus as God's died-and-exalted Messiah and archetype*. My proposal is to combine this conceptual negotiation of Jesus with certain anthropological assumptions and didactic models, resulting in a flexible rhetorical resource: *kerygmatic rhetoric.*

Specifically, I suggest that this conceptualization of *Jesus as God's died-and-exalted Messiah and archetype* may be evidenced with regard to epistolary macro-structure in a literary progression of the *kerygmatic* pattern of death and resurrection (1 Corinthians, Revelation); or, similarly, the

---

rhetorical arrangement in narrative: "The story schemata underlying narrative creation in the two cultures under discussion show clear and important differences. The Anglo-Western story schema underlying the prototypical Anglo-Western narrative is protagonist-oriented and problem-solving oriented. . . . In contrast . . . traditional Pitjantjatjara-Yankunytjatjara narratives are conceptualised according to family-, nexus-, and land-oriented organisational structures." Danièle M. Klapproth, *Narrative as Social Practice: Anglo-Western and Australian Aboriginal Oral Traditions* (Berlin: Mouton de Gruyter, 2004), 383.

27. Farzad Sharifian, "Distributed, Emergent Cultural Cognition, Conceptualisation and Language," in *Body, Language, and Mind,* vol. 2: *Sociocultural Situatedness* (ed. R. M. Frank, R. Dirven, T. Ziemke, and E. Bernardez; Berlin: de Gruyter, 2008), 109-36; pre-published online version, accessed 24 November 2010: http://sites.google.com/site/professor farzadsharifian/farz/Sharifian-1.PDF; 247). See also Farzad Sharifian, "On Cultural Conceptualisations," *Journal of Cognition and Culture* 3, no. 3 (2003): 187-207.

kerygmatic pattern of present endurance and future exaltation (1 Thessalonians); or in a logical progression of *kerygmatic* identity and outworking (Romans, Galatians, Ephesians, Colossians, 1 Peter); or in recurring exemplars of a *kerygmatic* paradigm (Philippians). This same conceptualization may be traced with regard to ethical formulation in varied terms of identification with the died-and-risen Messiah, often fitting common clusters of vices or virtues into the governing imagery of the *body*, of *death-and-resurrection*, and of a *former-now dichotomy*.[28]

I will now explore some examples of *kerygmatic rhetoric* in more detail.

Kerygmatic Rhetoric in Paul

1 Corinthians

Under the warmly encouraging supervision of Professor Thiselton, I argued that the Jewish motif of dual reversal, whereby boastful rulers are destined for destruction while righteous sufferers are destined for vindication, was influential in certain early formulations of Christian *kerygma*, and consequently resourced the arrangement of 1 Corinthians. The Corinthians, who in Paul's estimation are unwittingly aligning themselves with the puffed-up "rulers of this age," are summoned to rather identify with the proclaimed Messiah who suffered and died on the cross (chapters 1–4). They are to allow this cruciform identification to affect their ethical orientation (chapters 5–14), while looking forward to sharing in the cosmic manifestation of this Messiah's resurrected glory (chapter 15):

> Chapters 1–4: Identification with the rulers of this age or with the *cross of Christ*

---

28. It seems possible to detect a common movement of concepts within Paul's discussions of sin/sanctification in particular, as follows:
   - Theme I: sanctification of the church that involves avoidance (or mortification) of "former" sexual immorality, impurity, and greed/passionate desire — often in relation to *bodies*
   - Theme II: sanctification of the church that involves the avoidance of inter-relational sin, and the promotion (or vivification) of love — particularly expressed in self-restraint/submission within the *body* of Christ

   This can be seen in the examples that follow.

Chapters 5–14: The cross applied:
Chapters 5–7: The cross and the *corporeal body:* Rejecting sexual immorality, impurity, and greed:
  A: The need to judge sexual immorality and impurity
    B: The need to judge greed
  A': Sexual immorality and marriage
Chapters 8–14: The cross and the *corporate body:* Exchanging exploitative interaction for sacrificial love:
  A: The right to eat idol food
    B: Personal rights
  A': Idol food
  A: Praise for keeping traditions
    B: I do not praise you
  A': The tradition of the Lord's Supper
  A: The gifts
    B: Love and the gifts
  A': The gifts of tongues and prophecy
Chapter 15: The destruction of rulers and powers, and the *resurrection of the dead who belong to Christ*

I suggested in my dissertation that, while the case has been made for Paul's adoption of conventional *deliberative rhetoric* here,[29] the macro-structure of 1 Corinthians is more convincingly explained by such *kerygmatic rhetoric*.

I argued that the substantial ethical section (chapters 5–14) matches the flow of Paul's ethical sections elsewhere,[30] and may represent a Pauline "christologisation" of Jewish ethics of the Hellenistic-Roman period.[31]

---

29. Margaret M. Mitchell argues that 1 Corinthians should be read as an epistolary application of deliberative rhetoric: Margaret M. Mitchell, *Paul and the Rhetoric of Reconciliation: An Exegetical Investigation of the Language and Composition of 1 Corinthians* (Louisville: Westminster John Knox, 1991).

30. See, for example, 1 Thess. 4; Gal. 5; 1 Cor. 12:20-21; Rom. 1:24-32; 12–15; Col. 3–4; and Ephesians below. I explore these and other passages in detail in my dissertation.

31. As Karl-Wilhelm Niebuhr rightly argues, Jewish ethics of this period were themselves formed by an association of behaviour directions of the Torah with popular-philosophical principles of the Hellenistic ethical tradition: "Jüdisch-hellenistisches Ethos bildet sich somit aus in der Verbindung von Verhaltensanweisungen der Tora mit popular-philosophischen Grundsätzen der hellenistischen ethischen Tradition. Es dient der Wahrung jüdischer Identität angesichts konkreter Herausforderungen im Alltag der hellenistischen Di-

Kerygmatic Rhetoric *in New Testament Epistles*

Given that in Jesus the Corinthians' *corporeal bodies* belong to God, they are to shun sexual immorality, greed and impurity (chapters 5–7).[32] Given that together they belong to the *corporate body* of Christ, they are to pursue edifying love within the one body, making use of diverse gifts (chapters 8–14).[33] The employment of this ethical pattern thus implicitly functions to continue the emphasis on dependent identification with Christ that is evidenced throughout the letter.

It seems that *kerygmatic* content, which draws on liturgical traditions, and is prepared for a church audience, has brought forth a creatively appropriate form for the main body of the letter.[34]

Ephesians

Whether or not Ephesians is taken to be authored by Paul, the letter is part of the New Testament canon and demonstrates rhetorical affinity with numerous other letters of the Pauline Corpus. It is a prime example of the

---

aspora und entfaltet sich im Rückbezug auf die eigene religiöse Überlieferung unter Heranziehung kultureller und philosophischer Traditionen der hellenistisch-römischen Welt." Karl-Wilhelm Niebuhr, "Hellenistisch-jüdisches Ethos im Spannungsfeld von Weisheit und Tora," in *Ethos und Identität: Einheit und Vielfalt des Judentums in hellenistisch-römischer Zeit* (ed. Matthias Konradt and Ulrike Steinert; Paderborn: Ferdinand Schöningh, 2002), 27-50, here 42.

32. Occurrences of terminology are illustrative: Of the twelve occurrences of the word σῶμα in this section (after no occurrences in chapters 1–4), all refer to personal bodies (5:3; 6:13 twice; 6:15, 16, 18 twice; 6:19, 20; 7:4 twice; 7:34). The words πορνεία/πόρνος occur eight times in this section (including each chapter), and nowhere else in 1 Corinthians (5:1, 9, 10, 11; 6:9, 13, 18; 7:2; the cognate verb πορνεύω occurs in two verses of 1 Corinthians: in 6:18, in relation to bodily sin; and in 10:8, in relation to the sin of Israel). The word πλεονέκτης occurs three times in chapters 5–6, and nowhere else in 1 Corinthians (5:10, 11; 6:10). The words related to purity/cleansing occur twice in these chapters (5:7: ἐκκαθάρατε; 7:14: ἀκάθαρτά), and nowhere else in 1 Corinthians.

33. The terminology of chapters 8–14 is similarly illustrative. Of the twenty-five times that the word σῶμα occurs in this section, two refer to Paul's own body (9:27; 13:3), three refer to the personal or Eucharistic body of Christ (10:16; 11:24, 27), and twenty refer to the church as the body of Christ (10:17; 11:29; 12:12 three times; 12:13, 14, 15 twice; 12:16 twice; 12:17, 18, 19, 20, 22, 23, 24, 25, 27). The word ἀγάπη, after not occurring at all in chapters 5–7, occurs eleven times in this section (8:1; 13:1, 2, 3, 4 three times; 13:8, 13 twice; 14:1).

34. This recalls the valuable work of White on the letter "body"; but what I am describing is not essentially the manipulation of an existing *form*, but the creative and flexible expression of *conceptual imagery*.

broad movement from indicative to imperative mentioned at the beginning of this essay,[35] and as such is worth considering in more detail.

Whereas the macro-structure of 1 Corinthians, according to my estimation above, follows a "chronological" progression of the death-resurrection *kerygma*, Ephesians appears to represent a more "logical" application of *kerygmatic rhetoric*. The identity and accomplishments of Jesus are "proclaimed" in the first three chapters, with a general application to the "minds" of the hearers: their identity is to be consciously shaped by this proclamation of the died-and-risen Messiah. In the latter three chapters, the ethical outflow of this identity is spelled out in familiar terms:

Chapters 1-3: The saints in Christ Jesus
    1:3-14: Blessed be God the Father who has blessed us in Christ with every Spiritual blessing
    1:15-23: I pray that you *might know* the hope, inheritance, and power
        2:1-10: In Christ you partake in resurrection from the dead, bringing freedom from *powers*
        2:11-22: In Christ you partake in reconciliation of humanity, bringing *peace*
    3:1-13: For this reason I am a servant of the gospel of Christ Jesus
    3:14-21: I pray that you might have power *to know* the love of Christ

Chapters 4-6: Therefore I beg you to live a life worthy of your calling
    4:2-16: Maintain *peace:* one body, many gifts for building up in love
        4:17-24: Put away Gentile license, greed, impurity, desires
    4:25–5:2: Love and build up one another
        5:3-18: Sexual immorality, impurity, greed (idolatry) are out of place

---

35. Ernest Best rightly captures this: "As far as content goes Ephesians contains two main elements: the first three chapters have a high theological content; the second three are largely paraenetic. 4.1 connects the two; there is a change here from a prevailing indicative to a prevailing imperative." Ernest Best, *Ephesians* (International Critical Commentary; London: T&T Clark, 1998), 64.

Kerygmatic Rhetoric *in New Testament Epistles*

5:18–6:9: Be filled with the Spirit and submit to each other as Christ's body
6:10-17: Be strong in the power of the Lord, struggling against cosmic *powers*
6:18-20: Pray in the Spirit

I do not doubt that there are (conscious or unconscious) elements of epideictic style[36] in chapters 1–3, and of deliberative style[37] in chapters 4–6; but if rhetorical analysis is going to significantly benefit interpretation, it is worth going beyond this observation to consider that the macro-structure is determined not by epideictic or deliberative governance but by a creative *kerygmatic rhetoric*.[38] The movement of the letter as a whole expresses the early Christian conceptualization in which Christian identity and conduct arise from the proclaimed Messiah, the Christian archetype.

The rhetorical identification of the conduct itself likewise lacks significant interpretive power when it is labelled generically as an *exhortatio*[39] or as *paraenesis*,[40] without recognition being given to the *kerygmatic* quality of its expression. As in 1 Corinthians (and the ethical sections of most other Pauline letters), there is a movement in the major hortatory section of Ephesians (4:2–6:9) between the "former" corporeal pursuits of sexual immorality, impurity, and greed, and the new corporate expression of gifted, edifying love within the one body, as can be seen in the structure above. Again, this ethical formulation implicitly rests on the concept of de-

---

36. Ben Witherington III holds the whole letter to be an example of epideictic rhetoric: "Ephesians . . . is basically a circular epideictic homily with only the bare minimum of epistolary elements added so that it could be sent as a written document. As a document meant to be declaimed, Ephesians partakes of the full gamut of Asiatic epideictic rhetoric." Although I disagree that the letter is an "epideictic homily," in my view Witherington is convincing in pointing to elements of style such as effusive language and long sentences. Ben Witherington III, *The Letters to Philemon, the Colossians, and the Ephesians: A Socio-Rhetorical Commentary on the Captivity Epistles* (Grand Rapids: Eerdmans, 2007), 2, cf. 7.

37. Lincoln states, "The congratulatory and the paraenetic, the reminder of the readers' calling and the appeal to live out that calling, combine the epideictic and the deliberative rhetorical genres." Lincoln, *Ephesians*, xli.

38. As Witherington rightly notes in relation to Philemon, "[T]he micro-rhetoric of Philemon contributes to and is in service of the macro-rhetoric, such that it is inadequate simply to recognize the rhetoric devices *within* Philemon. One must ask how they serve the larger rhetorical purposes of the discourse." *Socio-Rhetorical Commentary*, 51.

39. Witherington, *Socio-Rhetorical Commentary*, 20-21; Lincoln, *Ephesians*, xliii.

40. Best, *Ephesians*, 64; Lincoln, *Ephesians*, xliii.

pendent identification with Christ, the Messiah who accomplished cosmic reconciliation "in one body through the cross" (Eph. 2:16).

If early Christian communities experienced Jesus on the first day of each week as God's declared answer to Israel's hope and the celebrated archetype for Christian identity, it appears that in the rhetoric of much early Christian liturgical correspondence, a corresponding structural logic developed. In alignment with the assumption that conduct will flow from conscious identity (as seen in the "rhetorical resources" explored above), the work of the triune God in the Messianic accomplishments of death and resurrection is first proclaimed and directed to the identity of hearers via their minds, before being substantially applied to their conduct.

Kerygmatic Rhetoric Beyond Paul

1 Peter

Like Ephesians, 1 Peter appears to pursue a logical progression of *kerygmatic identity* and *outworking*. Again, the fundamental issues of the identity and accomplishments of Jesus (in his triune context) are established from 1:1 to 2:10, with a general application to the "minds" of the hearers: their identity is to be knowingly shaped by the proclamation of the died-and-risen Messiah. From 2:11 onwards, the ethical outflow of this identity is spelled out, here with special reference to suffering:

> Chapters 1–2a: Belonging to God in Jesus Christ
> 1:1-2: Elect exiles; chosen by the Father, through the Spirit, for Jesus Christ
> 1:3-12: The Father has given new birth into an imperishable inheritance, through faith in the died-and-risen Jesus Christ, attested by the Spirit
> 1:13: *Know the hope* of the grace associated with the revelation of Christ
> 1:14–2:3: Called to belong to *God's fatherly house*, rather than living with former desires
> 2:4-10: Called to belong to *God's covenantal house*, as a priesthood
> Chapters 2b–5: Good conduct despite suffering
> 2:11-12: As *exiles*, putting away *former desires*, conduct yourselves

honourably among the Gentiles *so that they might glorify God when he visits*

2:13–3:7: Accept human authority for the Lord's sake

3:8–4:11: Accept suffering for the Lord's sake, having joined him in his death in the flesh and life in the Spirit: Put away debauchery, passions, drunkenness, idolatry; rather love and serve one another with gifts

4:12–5:11: Summary and application to churches

It seems that 2:11-12 functions similarly to Eph 4:1, providing a hinge between the establishment of a christologically informed identity and the application of this identity to a socio-ethical situation. This hinge passage in 1 Peter draws together the "identity" motifs of exile (1:1-12), renounced desire (1:12–2:3) and priestly service (2:4-10), before the letter applies this calling to the societal situations of various groups.

It is noteworthy that in 4:1-11, where the hortatory character of the letter is finally broadened (in terms of target) and made most concrete, a familiar formulation is evident. Christian conduct is explicitly discussed as an expression of identification with Christ in his passion and resurrection; and once again this involves a movement from "former" passionate debauchery (in 4:1-6) to gifted love (in 4:7-11). Here especially the value of a *kerygmatic* rhetorical awareness is evident.[41] The link between 4:1-6 and 4:7-11, while abrupt, is not inexplicable, hinting at a broader tradition of christological ethical catechesis.

Reinhard Feldmeier notes the lack of consensus regarding a formal arrangement of 1 Peter, but adds, "That does not in any way mean that the author of the writing did not have a plan, that there are no steps forward in the progress of the letter. It is only that this is not demonstrable in a formal

---

41. Barth L. Campbell notices the commonality of flow between this section of 1 Peter and Pauline ethical sections, but his classical rhetorical study lacks the formal terminology to adequately express his intuitive insight that in "verse 10, the apex of ethical instruction in the *argumentatio*, and perhaps in the entire letter, has been reached." Barth L. Campbell, *Honor, Shame, and the Rhetoric of 1 Peter* (SBL Dissertation Series 160; Atlanta: Scholars Press, 1995), 196. Although I therefore appreciate Peter T. O'Brien's hesitancies about the application of Rhetorical Criticism, I do not think that the only alternative is to focus "on the apostle's own method of argument within the letter itself." Rather, what I have described as *kerygmatic rhetoric* may bring intertextual insights within and beyond the Pauline Corpus, as here. Peter T. O'Brien, *The Letter to the Ephesians* (Pillar New Testament Commentary; Leicester: Apollos, 1999), 81.

arrangement."[42] It may indeed be that for New Testament letters, the "steps forward in the progress of the letter" are often better described in terms of the flexible expression of *kerygmatic rhetoric* than in traditional terms of formal arrangement.

Kerygmatic Rhetoric, Rhetorical Criticism, and the Interpretation of Paul

Rhetorical Criticism exists with the intention of describing and evaluating processes of communication. To date it has frequently been hampered, with respect to the New Testament, by assumptions, terms, and categories that do not exactly fit the New Testament documents.[43] In this paper I have aimed to suggest ways of describing and evaluating the persuasive techniques of New Testament letters by paying attention to the distinctive environment in which they commonly arose.

The documents of the New Testament arose in an environment in which Jesus was experienced and conceptualized as died-and-exalted Messiah and archetype. This experience-formed conceptualization is evidenced in the arrangement and formulations of many New Testament letters, such that they might be characterized as exhibiting *kerygmatic rhetoric*. This is not to deny the adoption of Greco-Roman epistolary or rhetorical features in these letters; but rather to be attentive to the context in which such adoption or adaptation occurred: that of a cultural group decisively (and thus linguistically) transformed by the *kerygma* of Jesus Christ.

In congruence with developments in linguistics and the study of discourse more broadly, this conception of New Testament rhetoric empha-

---

42. Reinhard Feldmeier, *The First Letter of Peter: A Commentary on the Greek Text* (trans. Peter H. Davids; Waco: Baylor University Press, 2008); original edition *Der erste Brief des Petrus* (Theologischer Handkommentar 15, no. 1; Leipzig: Evangelische Verlagsanstalt, 2005), 23.

43. This has been recognised and lamented by scholars such as Duane Watson, Peter Lampe, and Thomas Olbricht. Olbricht suggests "church rhetoric" as an alternative conception: "The focus of 'church' rhetoric is on the present, but as informed by the past mighty acts of God (Rom 9:1-5); for Paul, more specifically on the salvific actions in Christ (Rom 5:6-11)." Clearly, this bears similarity to my conception of *kerygmatic rhetoric*. Thomas H. Olbricht, "The Foundations of the Ethos in Paul and in the Classical Rhetoricians," in *Rhetoric, Ethic, and Moral Persuasion in Biblical Discourse* (ed. Thomas H. Olbricht and Anders Eriksson; New York: T&T Clark, 2005), 138-59, here 144.

sises concept over form, and particularity rather than generality of sociocultural setting. It may be that this approach will provide useful questions and terminology for assessing the persuasion of both New Testament and early patristic writings — but especially those of Paul.[44] Without expecting a rigid form, it could be asked, "Does the macro-structure of this writing creatively evidence the conceptualization of *Jesus as God's died-and-exalted Messiah and archetype?*" Beyond the (sometimes helpful) application of generic epistolary or oratorical labels, it could be asked, "What christological conceptualizations might be inherent in the ethical formulations of this writing?" Rather than working from the assumption of a classical rhetorical situation, it could be asked, "How does this writing distinctively seek to form disciples of Jesus, the died-and-exalted Messiah?"

---

44. In terms of patristic writings, for example, 2 Clement seems to exhibit a general movement from *a call to think upon the salvation of Jesus and Fatherhood of God* to exhortation concerning *works that are fitting for those who confess Christ and make up his body.* Chapter 16 is illustrative of the writing's ethical summons from *former lusts* to *mutual love and almsgiving*. The similarity to 1 Peter and other earlier literature has not gone unnoticed: see Karl P. Donfried, *The Setting of Second Clement in Early Christianity* (Leiden: Brill, 1974), 41-48.

"The Rock Was Christ": Paul's Reading of Numbers and the Significance of the Old Testament for Theological Hermeneutics

Richard S. Briggs

The Question of "Theological" Hermeneutics

In his impressive review of a lifetime at the forefront of hermeneutical enquiry in the biblical and theological spheres, Anthony Thiselton offers a rare explicit reflection on the question of whether, or in what sense, such hermeneutics might be best thought of as "theological." He offers a significant declaration of his own view as follows:

> I have often wished that [my earlier books] had embodied a more *explicit*, rather than *implicit*, Christian theology. Yet how could I have achieved this in the face of Schleiermacher's contention, with which I fully agree, that the kind of hermeneutics that *would best serve* theology for the good of theology itself would be a transcendental, independent, critical discipline?[1]

He suggests that several issues might need attention in any avowedly theological hermeneutic, including a consideration of the effect of human fallenness on the capacities of reason, judgement, wisdom and understanding, and a consideration of the contribution of reception history after the work of Hans Robert Jauss. The theme is returned to at the very end of the collection, where perhaps the key concern is articulated thus:

> hermeneutics must resist becoming assimilated into a prior system of theology, and . . . theology must avoid compromise by being shaped by

---

1. Anthony C. Thiselton, *Thiselton on Hermeneutics: The Collected Works and New Essays of Anthony Thiselton* (Aldershot: Ashgate, 2006), 37.

"The Rock Was Christ"

an independent discipline of hermeneutics. . . . we need to find a way forward by facilitating a genuine process of dialectic between the two disciplines.[2]

The present essay is offered as a modest contribution to that way forward, in grateful thanks to Anthony Thiselton, under whose watchful supervision I pursued my own doctoral studies. Among the many things he has taught and modelled so well is attention to particular cases and texts in the midst of grand hermeneutical theorising. My proposal for the question of how best to understand hermeneutics as "theological," therefore, takes a particular text and a particular reading of it: Paul's use of the book of Numbers in 1 Corinthians 10, and asks what we might learn from attending to this example of hermeneutics in action. This case study broadens into reflections on questions of narrative mimesis, reception and canon, in an attempt to offer some fruitful questions for further exploration in the pursuit of theological hermeneutics.

Between a Rock and a Hard Place: The Dialectic between Hermeneutical and Theological Approaches

The tensions to which Anthony Thiselton alludes in the above quotes will be well understood by all who seriously wrestle with biblical texts at the present time. In contrast perhaps to the prevailing practices of a good deal of professional biblical studies through much of the twentieth century, there is today renewed attention to the nature of "theological interpretation." This must not be construed as the claim that biblical interpretation was not theological before the 1990s, to which period Daniel Treier dates the "movement" where "the quest to rediscover theological interpretation of Scripture began in earnest."[3] Clearly, no one can read von Rad on Gene-

---

2. Thiselton, *Thiselton on Hermeneutics*, 802.
3. Daniel J. Treier, *Introducing Theological Interpretation of Scripture: Recovering a Christian Practice* (Grand Rapids: Baker Academic, 2008), 11. In addition to Treier's book an ideal overview and guide to what is at stake is Stephen E. Fowl, *Theological Interpretation of Scripture* (Cascade Companions; Eugene, OR: Wipf & Stock, 2009), which adds a focus on the ecclesial location of interpretive practice as one element of theological interpretation. See also the journal issues devoted to the theme: "Theological Exegesis" in *The Princeton Theological Review* 14, no. 1, issue 38 (2008) — 8 essays — and "the theological interpretation of scripture" in *International Journal of Systematic Theology* 12, no. 2 (2010) — 6 essays.

sis (begun 1949, revised 1972), or Käsemann on Romans (1974, ET 1980), let alone such 20th century classics as Bultmann's various commentaries, and believe that these exemplars of critical commentary were not theological through and through in some sense. What then has changed in recent works self-described as "theological interpretation"? A full answer to this question cannot be given here, although any such answer might need to reflect on the significance of a focus on the final or received form of the biblical text as part of what has changed. But perhaps the heart of the matter concerns the theological self-awareness of the interpretive practice involved, alongside an openness to dialogue about the hermeneutical concerns which of necessity operate in any interpretation. Thus theological interpretation is increasingly aware of its own embodied commitments and situatedness, possibly as a result of the upheaval of scholarly norms represented by the (contestable) shift towards the postmodern in the academy generally. Such reflexive self-awareness is in itself still profoundly hermeneutical, since it entails precisely the engagement with horizons of expectation and understanding which Anthony Thiselton has shown is of the essence for hermeneutical thinking. Equally, theological interpretation today operates with a wider range of theologically sophisticated dialogue partners outside the realms of biblical studies than was perhaps common at the height of the twentieth century, in particular with an awareness of the benefits of engaging with systematic theologians and with pre-modern interpretation. This is not simply to commend a wholesale appropriation of pre-modern practice as if it represented some kind of hermeneutical Eden from which the rise of historical consciousness had banished us. It is too simplistic to affirm "the superiority of pre-critical exegesis" as David Steinmetz so memorably described it.[4] Nevertheless, that the whole of scripture serves as a constructive framing context for the interpretation of any one part of it is at least as important an insight as the recognition that the text may with profit be read in its historical or cultural particularity. Theological interpreters would want to avoid foreclosing on the relative merits of one or the other hermeneutical frame of reference as a key in any particular case.

At the very least, then, interpreters operate between the pull of two

---

4. David C. Steinmetz, "The Superiority of Pre-Critical Exegesis," *Theology Today* 37, no. 1 (1980): 27-38. It is interesting to consider how far Steinmetz's deliberately (and successfully!) polemical argument could be rearticulated without loss as "the validity of pre-critical exegesis."

contrasting frames of reference in their work with the text. On the one hand, they approach the ancient text with a disciplined and serious attention to the many historical, literary and cultural factors which helped to shape it and in part at least to provoke it into existence. These many and various dimensions to the interpretive task operate in ways that are deeply implicated in all aspects of human contingency, and trade in epistemological and hermeneutical openness to whatever may be discovered by way of such disciplined and serious attention. This is the "hard place" of various kinds of historically and critically informed scholarship, without which it is barely even possible to obtain purchase on the details of the text before us, but with which scholarship all too easily finds it possible to defer perpetually the moment of existential engagement with the text.[5] The result can be theologically thin commentary, preoccupied with free-standing or "de-contextualized 'problems'" in the interpretive tradition rather than with "a dialectical process of motivated, directed, contingent question and answer" which might engage matters of substantive enquiry regarding the theological substance of the text.[6]

The rock, on the other hand, is Jesus. Paul says as much in 1 Cor 10:4, in a hermeneutical *tour de force* which we shall consider presently. More generally, theological hermeneutics seeks to relate the claims of the text in some manner to the claims of (or for or about) Christ. Of course, how to do that well is precisely the question in discussions of theological interpretation. For much of the time under the reigning paradigms of historical-critical enquiry, there was an uneasy stand-off whereby some sort of objective analysis of the text was posited as a separable endeavour from a subsequent stage of "application," where one might (if pastoral or pietistic impulse dictated) show how the text in hand related to Christ and the Christian life. It is scarcely possible, after the magisterial discussion of "application" in Gadamer's *Truth and Method*, to sustain such a model.[7] The theological di-

---

5. An excellent study of the hermeneutical dynamics of this problem — massive detail but lack of hermeneutical judgment — remains Ben F. Meyer's *Reality and Illusion in New Testament Scholarship: A Primer in Critical Realist Hermeneutics* (Collegeville, MN: Michael Glazier, Liturgical Press, 1994).

6. The citations are from Thiselton, *Thiselton on Hermeneutics*, 802, drawing upon Gadamer.

7. Gadamer devotes considerable energy in *Truth and Method* to arguing that application is not a separable and subsequent stage: "we consider application to be just as integral a part of the hermeneutical process as are understanding and interpretation" (308) and "Application does not mean first understanding a given universal in itself and then afterward

mensions of the interpretive task are bound more closely to the very act of reading the text in front of us than such a two-stage model was willing to admit. The question is how to embrace this insight without falling into the very problem which a "transcendental, independent, critical" hermeneutics was designed to counter in the first place: the methodological predisposition to reduce the text to fit "a prior system of theology."[8]

This is the point where it will be helpful to turn towards a specific example, since theoretical discussion of this matter does not always seem to make much progress beyond the accusation and counter-accusation that theological commitments do or do not serve as a distortion in interpretive practice. In fact, this discussion has some interesting parallels with current debates about the role of scripture in the theological vision (or system, or narrative) of Paul. Thus we shall consider 1 Corinthians 10 as an exemplar of a critical theological hermeneutic in practice, after first orientating ourselves to the general discussion regarding Paul's reading of scripture. It is also worth noting briefly that there are of course questions surrounding the suitability or otherwise of taking a New Testament exemplar for considering our own practices today. However I judge this to be a good deal less problematic than was once thought to be the case, not least since the goal is hardly to deduce a single correct method for reading scripture,[9] so much as to let scriptural exemplars influence our own practices of negotiating between the claims of texts and the claims of Christ.

Reading Scripture with Paul

It is clear that at no point in his letters does Paul's handling of scriptural texts look like modern exegetical study. One conclusion sometimes drawn from this rather obvious observation is that Paul is an unhelpful model of how to handle scripture. Appeal might be made to Richard Hays's delightful characterisation: "Let us not deceive ourselves about this: Paul would

---

applying it to a concrete case. It is the very understanding of the universal — the text — itself" (341). References to Hans-Georg Gadamer, *Truth and Method* (2nd rev. ET trans. Joel Weinsheimer and Donald G. Marshall; London: Sheed and Ward, 1989).

8. Thiselton, *Thiselton on Hermeneutics*, 37, 802, cf. nn. 1-2 above.

9. As in, for example, Richard N. Longenecker, "Can We Reproduce the Exegesis of the New Testament?" *Tyndale Bulletin* 21 (1970): 3-38, whose negative answer to his title question was largely a matter of concerns over method.

flunk our introductory exegesis course."[10] Hays's landmark study begins with a rehearsal of just some of the interpreters in modern times who have thereby faulted Paul for failing to make appropriate use of the Old Testament.[11] Of course, fuelled not least by Hays's own study, the tide has turned, and it is now clear that there is much to be learned from understanding Paul as an interpreter of scripture, both with respect to Paul and with respect to interpreting scripture.

Among more recent studies of this theme, Francis Watson's *Paul and the Hermeneutics of Faith* helpfully draws out this discussion in a way which allows us to articulate the dialectical understanding of the relationship between theology and hermeneutics today.[12] Watson finds a comparably dialectical understanding at work in Paul himself, as he considers the fundamental question of whether Paul appeals to scripture merely to shore up arguments he has derived from elsewhere (as much recent scholarship has averred) or whether scripture itself "exerts pressure" on Paul's theological formulations.[13] The problem is that this latter option has been reduced to a struggle over the right interpretation of the canonical (OT) text, whereby in general only one interpretive proposal can be right, and all others are thereby wrong. Since Paul is manifestly not a graduate of the kind of introductory course to which Richard Hays has referred us, he has come off badly in such comparisons. However, Watson argues that when we observe Paul's actual interpretive practice, we find a more subtle picture:

> There is for Paul a difference between a scriptural interpretation which proceeds deductively on the basis of the texts (Gal. 3.6-9), and one that proceeds inductively on the basis of the actuality of Christ (3.14a). The two approaches complement each other, and neither can exist in a pure form without the other. The deductive approach keeps the inductive one from interpretative arbitrariness by insisting that it remains accountable to the texts; the inductive approach keeps the deductive one from abstraction by insisting that it remains accountable to the actuality

---

10. Richard B. Hays, *Echoes of Scripture in the Letters of Paul* (New Haven: Yale University Press, 1989), 181.

11. Hays, *Echoes of Scripture*, 5-9 and elsewhere.

12. Francis Watson, *Paul and the Hermeneutics of Faith* (London: T&T Clark, 2004).

13. The image of exerting "pressure" is helpfully articulated in C. Kavin Rowe, "Biblical Pressure and Trinitarian Hermeneutics," *Pro Ecclesia* 11, no. 3 (2002): 295-312. On 308 Rowe attributes it in turn to Brevard Childs's *Biblical Theology of the Old and New Testaments* (London: SCM, 1992).

of Christ. Both together constitute the twofold hermeneutic whereby Paul as a Christian rereads Jewish scripture.[14]

It is significant that the texts in view in this discussion are scriptural texts: richly multivalent in ongoing significance and uniquely entwined with a complex and contested history of reception, not least the reception by those "in Christ" of texts relating to Israel's life in earlier times. These scriptural texts, especially once they function as a collection, are startlingly unlike many other sets of texts of less interesting or remarkable semantic potential. In my judgement much energy has been wasted in biblical interpretation by attempts to draw substantive conclusions from the applicability of general hermeneutical theories to everyday sample texts which bear little if any real relationship to the functioning of scriptural texts in the lives of their readers. If there does turn out to be such a thing as a "semantics of biblical language" then we can be sure, if the qualifier "biblical" is to do any significant work, that it will not look like the semantics of everyday chitchat: "the rock was big" and "the rock was Christ" are operating in language games so different that the transferable insight from one to the other will do little (if any) hermeneutical (or theological) work for us.[15] Scriptural texts generally (always?) offer many interrelated possibilities for reading; possibilities which exist in a range of dialogues with other relevant factors to those for whom the texts are scriptural. They therefore allow *readings,* which are "neither the exact reproduction of a given content nor the product of alien, non-negotiable dogmatic convictions."[16] The result is "a less confrontational and more dialogical hermeneutic" which is not held captive by "a struggle for the meaning of the [text's] own statement."[17]

Watson's own case concerning Paul is that, whatever else may be said about him, he is at minimum a reader of (scriptural) texts. What are the hermeneutical assumptions which drive Paul's concerns regarding faith,

---

14. Watson, *Paul and the Hermeneutics of Faith,* 190-91.

15. I am thus among those who find the unqualified embrace of James Barr's *The Semantics of Biblical Language* by interpreters with confessional interests slightly strange. A full analysis of this oddity must await another occasion, but for a good start with respect at least to the literary dimensions of the problem see Peter J. Leithart, *Deep Exegesis: The Mystery of Reading Scripture* (Waco, TX: Baylor University Press, 2009), 75-108. It is worth noting that Francis Watson himself earlier critiqued several confusions in Barr's work in his *Text and Truth: Redefining Biblical Theology* (London: T&T Clark, 1997), 17-29.

16. Watson, *Paul and the Hermeneutics of Faith,* 183.

17. Watson, *Paul and the Hermeneutics of Faith,* 129. Watson says "prophet" rather than "text" though it is the prophetic text which is in view.

the law, human obedience, divine action, and so forth? It is not, in the first instance, a dogmatic scheme, but "the unfolding narrative of the Pentateuch."[18] Hence the title of his work regarding "the hermeneutics of faith." So "Paul's view of the law," far from being a free-standing problem to which students might be led on an annual academic pilgrimage, required to rehearse arguments for and against such supposedly self-contained entities as "the new perspective on Paul" or "the Lutheran view of Paul," is, according to Watson, "*nothing other than his reading of Exodus, Leviticus, Numbers, and Deuteronomy.*"[19] Paul the theologian is, therefore, irreducibly, Paul the reader of scripture. But the pursuit of this Paul offers a rather interesting insight: that while it may be true that he reads scripture and Christ in a mutually illuminating hermeneutical circle, these two focal points of his enquiry are not equally significant. Watson's striking conclusion: "Paul reads the scripture in the light of Christ only *in order* to read Christ in the light of scripture; scriptural interpretation *per se* is of no interest to him."[20]

It is important, in fact hermeneutically important, to recognise that none of these observations about Paul's reading of Torah occur in the abstract. Watson's book is not the execution of a theological programme in the language of interpretive practice. His point about the priority of reading Christ occurs in an analysis of 1 Corinthians 3 for the light it sheds on Paul's reading of Exodus; while his observations about the "hermeneutical dialectic" emerge in a treatment of Paul's reading of the promise to Abraham in Genesis. Likewise he does not in turn discover a Paul who marshals scriptural texts to his own predetermined theological scheme. Thus while there clearly are theological commitments at work in Paul's reading, they do not reduce down to using the text as a mirror to reflect what he already believed. Rather, Paul's theological commitments about God, and in particular about God's being at work in the world opened up by the text, lead him to new ways of articulating his own theological understanding. The example of his reading of Numbers in 1 Corinthians 10 shall serve as a test case.

---

18. Watson, *Paul and the Hermeneutics of Faith*, 163, n. 61 — offering a clear statement of what Watson describes as "a central concern of the present work."
19. Watson, *Paul and the Hermeneutics of Faith*, 275, italics original.
20. Watson, *Paul and the Hermeneutics of Faith*, 298.

RICHARD S. BRIGGS

1 Corinthians 10: Paul's Reading of Numbers

In 1 Corinthians 8–10 Paul is considering how the congregation at Corinth should understand their responsibilities in the exercise of freedom in Christ, in particular with regard to "the everyday practical problems of social and religious life at Corinth in relation to pagan cultural or cultic backgrounds."[21] In chapter 10 the discussion turns to the spiritual danger they may be in if they persist in eating food offered to idols, and Paul explores this issue first by way of an extended set of parallels between the generations who wandered in the wilderness and those in Corinth in his own time. The chapter thus opens with a range of references to the narratives of Exodus and Numbers, and is laid out here in a manner which presumes upon the discussion which follows:

> ¹I do not want you to be unaware, brothers and sisters, that our ancestors were all under the cloud, and all passed through the sea, ²and all were baptized into Moses in the cloud and in the sea, ³and all ate the same spiritual food, ⁴and all drank the same spiritual drink. For they drank from the spiritual rock that followed them, and the rock was Christ. ⁵Nevertheless, God was not pleased with most of them, and they were struck down in the wilderness.
>
> ⁶Now THESE THINGS OCCURRED AS *EXAMPLES* FOR US, so that we might not desire evil as they did.
>
> ⁷Do not become idolaters as some of them did; as it is written, "The people sat down to eat and drink, and they rose up to play."
>
> ⁸We must not indulge in sexual immorality as some of them did, and twenty-three thousand fell in a single day.
>
> ⁹We must not put Christ to the test, as some of them did, and were destroyed by serpents.
>
> ¹⁰And do not complain as some of them did, and were destroyed by the destroyer.
>
> ¹¹THESE THINGS HAPPENED TO THEM TO SERVE AS AN *EXAMPLE*, and they were written down to instruct us, on whom the ends of the ages have come. (1 Cor 10:1-11, NRSV)

There is only one direct quote: the citation of Exod 32:6 in v. 7, but clearly there is a considerable "pressure" exerted here by the Torah narra-

---

21. Anthony C. Thiselton, *The First Epistle to the Corinthians* (NIGTC; Grand Rapids: Eerdmans, 2000), 607.

"The Rock Was Christ"

tives of Israel in the wilderness. Gary Collier offers a perceptive account of the structure of the passage,[22] and helpfully indicates its various scriptural resonances, which we can summarise as follows:

- v. 1 refers the reader to the narrative recitals of Psalms 78 and 106
- vv. 1-4 set up a 5-fold characterisation of the "all" *(pantes)* in the wilderness
- v. 5 nevertheless highlights the negative judgment passed on (most of) them (cf. Num 14:16)
- vv. 6-11 then offer a chiastic analysis of how these things serve as "examples *(typoi)* for us" (v. 6), or happened "to serve as an example" (v. 11, using the same word), bracketing four ways in which "some of them" *(tines autōn)* failed: through being idolaters, or *pornoi*, or putting Christ to the test, or complaining (vv. 7-10). The allusions informing this chiasm Collier maps thus:

v. 6 types — desiring evil	Num 11:4, 34
v. 7 some of them — idolaters ("as it is written"; *gegraptai*)	Exod 32:6
v. 8 some of them — *pornoi*	Num 25:1
v. 9 some of them — put Christ to the test	Num 21:4-7
v. 10 some of them — complained	Num 11:1
v. 11 types — to instruct us	cf. Wis 16:2-14

Collier's specific contribution to the long-running discussion of this passage is that it reflects a possibly pre-Pauline midrash on Numbers 11, drawing links between the desiring of evil (v. 6) and the ways in which the underlying OT texts relate to eating and its various ways of demonstrating failure in the wilderness, thus tying the overall discussion into Paul's main topic of food sacrificed to idols.[23] It is not my purpose here to evaluate the details of this approach to 1 Corinthians 10 in the context of Pauline studies, where one might profitably pursue questions of specific attributions of intertextual allusions or argue over which texts in particular are the bases for such midrashic development.[24] One can acknowledge

---

22. Gary D. Collier, "'That We Might Not Crave Evil': The Structure and Argument of 1 Corinthians 10.1-13," *JSNT* 55 (1994): 55-75, esp. 60-61.

23. Collier, "That We Might Not Crave Evil," 63.

24. A survey of major proposals is incorporated into the discussion of Roy E. Ciampa and Brian S. Rosner, "1 Corinthians," in G. K. Beale and D. A. Carson, eds., *Commentary on*

the dispute over such details while still affirming that some such engagement with scripture as this is at stake in 1 Corinthians 10. Likewise it is not necessary to enter the discussion of whether this passage retains pre-Pauline elements in part or even in large part, though it is perhaps worth noting that as they stand vv. 1-13 do indeed represent something of a self-contained discussion of the blessings of and judgments upon Israel in the wilderness with a view to how the Corinthians should learn from that example, before Paul returns directly to the topic of idol-worship in 10:14. This may strengthen the case for taking these verses as a focus for our own enquiry, which is to ask what 1 Corinthians 10 shows about the reading of scripture.

We start with Paul, and first we start with some straightforward observations about what Paul is not interested in with regard to Numbers. Paul is not concerned with who wrote it. This matter is largely settled in any case by his undoubted conviction that this is a book of Moses, and his assumptions regarding authorship that it pertained more to moral authority over what is affirmed in the text than to questions of who either produced or originated the text. Such background questions hold no significant interest for Paul.

Neither, secondly, do more literarily orientated questions regarding how one might set any particular text of Numbers in its literary (or even canonical) context. Such studies occupy centre stage in the study of Numbers today: witness the focus of attention on the shape of the book of Numbers in many essays in the recent Leuven colloquium.[25] This interest was given focus by Dennis Olson's influential monograph exploring the contrast between the first and second censuses of the book (in Numbers 1 and 26) as the key to an understanding of its structure and purpose.[26] When Olson writes "The central problem in the interpretation of the book of Numbers, in our judgment, is the failure to detect a convincing and meaningful structure for the book,"[27] his concern may be traced back to that of his own thesis advisor, Brevard Childs, whose brief discussion of

---

the New Testament Use of the Old Testament (Grand Rapids: Baker Academic, 2007), 695-752, on 722-27. Note also Thiselton's excursus on "Paul's Allusion to the 'Rock which went with them,'" *1 Corinthians*, 727-30.

25. Thomas Römer, ed., *The Books of Leviticus and Numbers* (BETL 215; Leuven: Peeters, 2008).

26. Dennis T. Olson, *The Death of the Old and the Birth of the New: The Framework of the Book of Numbers and the Pentateuch* (BJS 71; Chico, CA: Scholars Press, 1985).

27. Olson, *Death of the Old*, 31.

"The Rock Was Christ"

Numbers in his 1979 *Introduction* focused almost entirely on matters of the canonical shaping of the book's structure.[28]

It is not clear, however, that Paul thinks of Numbers as a literary unit at all. For him it is part of the ongoing narrative of the books of the Torah. Paul does of course recognise key transitional moments in the development of the Torah's narrative as having significance for what subsequent interpretation may or may not do: the transition from promise to law is fundamental, for example, as is the evidence of hardness of heart in the golden calf incident, or indeed the persistent narratives of desire and death in the wilderness which we find in the book of Numbers.[29] But on the whole these transitional moments do not correspond to the demarcations between the five books of the Torah. Arguably Childs's own interest in this question betrays more Childs's form-critical concerns with literary units raised one level and applied to the final forms of biblical books.[30] Francis Watson's treatment of the Old Testament narrative does draw striking conclusions about separate Torah books playing different roles in Paul's thought, but it might be interesting to ask how much this argument really requires them to be separate "books" as such rather than, say, separate sections of the overall Torah narrative playing different roles. These sections may, or may not, correspond to the canonical divisions. Thus for example Numbers 1–10 could as easily be taken with Leviticus on Watson's account, since it is actually Numbers 11ff which serves as the focal text for the "death and desire" theme. In this regard it is interesting to observe that Olson's own defence of the interpretive significance of the book of Numbers as a textual unit seems to consist in an appeal to the undoubted fact that the Torah was understood as a five-fold collection, combined with some rather inconclusive observations about each book's opening and closing sentences.[31] This falls somewhat short of a demonstration that "the book of Numbers" was ever a coherent focus of interpretive interest in ancient times (as against the more modest claim that one can *read* it as a coherent whole should one choose to). Most likely, as for Paul, it makes little differ-

---

28. Brevard S. Childs, *Introduction to the Old Testament as Scripture* (London: SCM, 1979), 190-201.

29. For Watson, Numbers offers a narrative which correlates "desire and death." *Paul and the Hermeneutics of Faith*, 363; cf. 356-80.

30. See the compelling discussion of Daniel Driver, *Brevard Childs, Biblical Theologian: For the Church's One Bible* (FAT 2/46; Tübingen: Mohr Siebeck, 2010), esp. 125-36.

31. See Olson, *Death of the Old*, 43-53, entitled "The Case for the Book of Numbers as a Literary Unit."

ence how one understands the demarcation of the books either side of Numbers 1–10 (and at least arguably elsewhere in the Torah).

So what is key for Paul? It seems that the key is simply that in the text of Torah he finds the living voice of God carried through the voice of Moses, and it is the same God now known in Christ. Thus, 1 Cor 10:9, "we must not put Christ to the test, as some of them did" — Paul's point is that what it means for the Corinthians to put Christ to the test is to be understood in terms of how the Israelites put God to the test. This need not be read as a complex claim about the presence of the second person of the Trinity in the wilderness, although clearly it *could* be read that way. Indeed the textual history of 10:9 betrays the fact that there was some confusion on this point, since there is MS attestation of "the Lord" rather than "Christ" in this text, in part because it was thought too problematic to have Paul affirming some kind of christological presence in the events narrated in Numbers.[32] But, as vv. 6 and 11 say explicitly, these things serve as *typoi*, "examples" or "types" for us (i.e. for the Corinthians and Paul). Hence, one can receive all the blessings of God, as the Israelites did in the wilderness (vv. 1-4), but still earn God's displeasure. And this is true of the Corinthians. Equally one can, in the midst of such blessing, "desire evil as they did" (v. 6, illustrated in vv. 7-10), though the purpose of recognising this is that it might not happen among us. And if one might suggest that there are basic differences between the experiences of the Israelites in the wilderness and the Corinthians in the meat markets, Paul's use of *"typoi"* seems designed to draw those two contexts into a fairly strong relationship, such that the blessings experienced back then are now understood as comparable to the blessings of Christ.

What aspects of Numbers are in view here? As theological interpreters like to say (rightly), what is the *Sache* of the text which is at issue in Paul's appeal to it? He seems to draw upon Numbers (and Exodus) in order to highlight the warning which awaits the faithful and blessed people should they stumble as the Israelites in the wilderness did. Theological interpretation of Numbers today should perhaps be particularly alert to this point. For present purposes, however, it is a slightly different angle I want to pursue. Part of Paul's concern is with specific textual details which he can now see illuminate the reality he wishes to describe. It is precise points in the text which serve to shape his understanding. 1 Corinthians 10:4 offers an illuminating case study of this more focused phenomenon.

---

32. The issues are admirably summarised in Thiselton, *1 Corinthians*, 740.

"The Rock Was Christ": Paul among Jewish Readings of Numbers

In his reference to "the spiritual rock that followed them" in 1 Cor 10:4, Paul is assuming the broad contours of a well-established midrashic tradition about the rock in the wilderness, as Peter Enns among others has shown.[33] Two key texts are *Targum Neofiti* 21:1, which speaks of the Canaanite king of Arad hearing "that Aaron, the pious man for whose merits the clouds of glory used to lead Israel forth, had been removed; and that Miriam the prophetess, for whose merits the well used to come up for them, had been removed . . ."; and Pseudo-Philo, who picks up on this:

> And after Moses died, the manna stopped descending upon the sons of Israel, and then they began to eat from the fruits of the land. And these are the three things that God gave to his people on account of three persons; that is, the well of the water of Marah for Miriam and the pillar of cloud for Aaron and the manna for Moses. And when these came to their end, these three things were taken away from them. (*LAB* 20:8)

The assumption at work here is that the death notices of the three main figures can all be correlated with the cessation of some of the remarkable phenomena encountered in the wilderness trek:

	Death Notice	Cessation of . . .
Miriam	20:1	Water — 20:2
Aaron	20:24-29	Pillar of cloud — (last noted in 14:14, or 16:42?)
Moses	Deut 34	Manna — cf. Josh 5:12

The logic of the midrashic claim is straightforward, but it is the "scriptural logic" of which Jewish interpreters such as Peter Ochs have spoken,[34] rather than the logic of most-plausible-historical-reconstruction. It is, as we shall see, the reading of the details of the text to see where they exert their own pressure upon the interpreter. How does it work in this case?

---

33. Peter Enns, "The 'Moveable Well' in 1 Cor 10:4: An Extrabiblical Tradition in an Apostolic Text," *Bulletin for Biblical Research* 6 (1996): 23-38. The basic data is gathered in James L. Kugel, *Traditions of the Bible: A Guide to the Bible As It Was at the Start of the Common Era* (Cambridge, MA: Harvard University Press, 1998), 620-21, supporting Enns's account.

34. Peter Ochs, *Peirce, Pragmatism and the Logic of Scripture* (Cambridge: Cambridge University Press, 1998), 286-325.

The Israelites are in the desert, following the exodus, and they find themselves without water (Exod 17:1ff). Provision is made for them by Moses' striking the rock (17:6) so that water comes out from it. In an obscure detail, we read that Yhwh says to Moses "I will be standing there in front of you on the rock at Horeb." It is unclear whether this is to suggest a theophany on the rock, or an invisible presence, or some sort of personification of this rock, such that God could be understood as a rock. This tradition is apparently evoked in Deuteronomy 32: God is "the rock" whose work is perfect (v. 4), who is the people's ("Jeshurun's") salvation (v. 15), and who is described as "the Rock that bore you" (v. 18). God the Rock — in the wilderness — provides water for the people. But, on reflection, if the people are moving around, then the rock must be as well. For the rabbis (and presumably also for Paul, although we do not have any record of his view of this matter) this is confirmed by careful attention to the next occasion when the Israelites are described as being without water, in Num 20:2. Here, notoriously, Moses strikes a rock and water comes out for all the people, and indeed their livestock (v. 11), but this time Moses' action disqualifies him from the promised land, on the grounds that, somehow, Moses had thereby "failed to show Yhwh's holiness before the eyes of all the Israelites" (v. 12). Exegetes have long been exercised by what precisely Moses did wrong here: "Moses our Teacher committed one sin, but the exegetes have loaded upon him thirteen sins and more, since each of them has invented a new sin."[35] In a thorough treatment of this topic, Jacob Milgrom reviews ten options canvassed by medieval Jewish commentators and relating to Moses' character or his actions or his words here, and adds an eleventh: the modern view that the sin of Moses has been removed from this passage in the interests of preserving Moses' reputation.[36] Milgrom's own view is that the problem lies in Moses' question, "shall *we* draw forth water from this rock . . ." (v. 10), since he argues that a silent miracle would have underlined the distinction between this divine provision and the kind of miracles known from Egyptian magic practices from before the exodus, where the magician's incantation would have been understood to be efficacious.

[35]. This widely quoted comment is always attributed to the eighteenth-century rabbi Shmuel David Luzzato (e.g., as cited by Stephen K. Sherwood, *Leviticus, Numbers, Deuteronomy* [Berit Olam; Collegeville, MN: Liturgical Press, 2002], 171) though I have been unable to trace a clear source for it.

[36]. Jacob Milgrom, *Numbers* (JPS; Philadelphia and New York: Jewish Publication Society, 1990), 448-56.

"The Rock Was Christ"

That is plausible, as is his "modern" theory that the text deliberately does not tell us, as are a range of other interpretive options. What is clear in the text, however, is that it is the death of Miriam (in v. 1) which appears to result in the absence of water, and from this juxtaposition comes the targumic interest in "Miriam's well," thought to have travelled with the Israelites rather as the rock did.[37] The topic of water in the wilderness is next broached by Yhwh in Num 21:16, where the Israelites are urged to sing "Spring up, O well" (the singular reference to "well" here being understood as indicating that it is the same well that they have been used to). In the past Miriam's merits secured the water supply, but with Miriam gone they need these further divine interventions — which as we saw was how Pseudo-Philo read it.

How does Paul's reading compare with the "matrix" of Jewish interpretations sketched here? First, Paul does indeed see the provision of water (and also food) in the wilderness as a spiritual reality: note the repeated "spiritual" in vv. 3-4. Secondly, he works with the midrashic assumption that the rock "followed" the Israelites in the wilderness. This does not look like an assertion of Paul's (cf. v. 4) so much as an identification of the rock he is talking about which he takes to be uncontroversial, for the more controversial part of the identification follows: "and the rock was Christ." Thirdly, he seems to presuppose the midrashic understandings that the narratives of the wilderness in Numbers are occupied with matters of divine testing and provision, in particular with the provision of life-giving water. The notion that the rock followed the Israelites in the wilderness, which is not so much explicit in Numbers as deduced by a plain reading of the literal sense of the text, already invites the consideration that something miraculous occurs in the way in which God is present to the Israelites in the rock (and perhaps lends weight to a certain reading of Exod 17:6a). Paul now sees that this divine presence is what he, from his own vantage point this side of the resurrection, would call the presence of Christ. Just as God's presence in Numbers brought about both blessing and a mixture of testing and punishment for failure (with Numbers 11 standing as an immediate and obvious example of the inseparability of narratives emphasising these two factors), so God's presence in Christ to the Corinthians can be narrated as a presence of blessings (10:1-4) and/or testing and potential punishment (10:5-11). Numbers, written about the Is-

---

37. See the fascinating study of Germain Bienaimé, *Moïse et le don de l'eau dans la tradition juive ancienne. Targum et midrash* (AB98; Rome: Biblical Institute Press, 1984).

raelites, is written for the Corinthians. When reality is mapped this way, the rock is Christ.[38]

In terms of method, Paul's reading could be characterised as offering a christological twist on familiar Jewish frames of reference for reading Numbers. Certainly it is hard to see that much sense could be made of it removed from the midrashic tradition upon which he draws. In this connection it is appropriate to recall Jon Levenson's pertinent observation that "the rough functional equivalent in Christianity for the Oral Torah of Judaism is the New Testament."[39] Paul's reading of Numbers, therefore, draws some of its key conceptualities from the Jewish tradition in which it operates: in particular in seeing the voice of the text speaking to an ongoing living tradition in his time. In other respects, it makes a bold new theological move in understanding the tradition in view in connection with Christ. There is no neutral option, as if one could ask how the text speaks to no tradition in particular: it can only speak to a particular listener (or listening tradition).[40]

Some Aspects of a Theological Hermeneutic in Light of Paul's Reading of Numbers

How might we today best articulate the categories at work in Paul's reading of scripture? Such an articulation, I suggest, will offer us one valuable way of describing how our hermeneutics might best be understood as theological. A key issue, in my judgment, is that the reading of the Numbers text is framed for Paul by the twin poles of the text's ongoing life in the interpretive tradition (the midrash) and the reality of Christ which is

---

38. The claim is that the rock was "literally" Christ, but in a sense of "literal" to be discussed below. It is not that historically Christ was present in the wilderness — he was not. As theological interpreters have begun to note, one does need to beware of losing the particularity of the incarnation in positing the presence of Christ in the Old Testament: one implication of the doctrine of the incarnation is that Christ is *not* indiscriminately present everywhere; cf. Rowe, "Biblical Pressure," 297.

39. Jon D. Levenson, "The Exodus and Biblical Theology: A Rejoinder to John J. Collins," in Alice Ogden Bellis and Joel S. Kaminsky, eds., *Jews, Christians, and the Theology of the Hebrew Scriptures* (SBLSS 8; Atlanta: Society of Biblical Literature, 2000), 263-75, here 268.

40. This is the burden of much of Levenson's own work: to demonstrate that supposedly neutral biblical scholarship is effectively a "historicist evasion" of the claims of the text. Jon D. Levenson, *The Hebrew Bible, the Old Testament, and Historical Criticism* (Louisville: Westminster John Knox Press, 1993), esp. 1-32 and 82-105.

now known through the experience of Christ's life, death and resurrection. If one were to focus on the first of these poles, it might lead to an interesting discussion of the constructive role of questions of reception theory and interpretive tradition in interpretation.[41] However in regard to our present concerns, it is to the second pole that we turn our attention: the new reality brought about in Christ. This new reality sets up a hermeneutical tension in the reading of any scripture which comes from before that time, a tension which persists today whenever Christians read "Old Testament texts." To put the point most simply: in addition to all the general hermeneutical concerns which rightly occupy any careful reader of scriptural (and other) texts as they are passed down any interpretive tradition, there is a particular additional stumbling block which lies between general and theological hermeneutics in biblical interpretation — the nature of the Old Testament as Christian scripture. Several aspects of this argument deserve fuller articulation, and here I offer brief clarification of four of them, all interrelated, conscious that in each case a far longer discussion would be needed to do justice to what is at stake.

First, and most simply, the prevalence of the word "type" *(typos)* twice in the Corinthians passage seems inevitably to urge the interpreter to take up a notion of "typological" reading as if it were the name of a particular kind of hermeneutical approach.[42] In one sense this intuition is helpful: it highlights the unique old/new relationship which pertains between scriptural texts from the two testaments. The problem, however, as Frances Young has clearly demonstrated, is that most accounts of "typology" describe modern constructs, where an unhelpful view of historical particularity is used to separate out such a supposed "typological approach" from the more general characteristics of allegorical interpretation.[43] But the notion that types in the text required some sort of historical reference "behind them" almost certainly obscures the categories with which ancient

---

41. Rather along the lines indicated by Thiselton in his discussion of Jauss and others, *Thiselton on Hermeneutics*, 39-45, in relation to the points cited at the beginning of the present article.

42. Such as is explored in the key study of Leonhard Goppelt, *Typos: The Typological Interpretation of the Old Testament in the New* (ET Grand Rapids: Eerdmans, 1982; German original 1939).

43. See Frances Young, *Biblical Exegesis and the Formation of Christian Culture* (Cambridge: Cambridge University Press, 1997), esp. 152-60 and 192-201. She dates the earliest accounts of "typology" as such to 1840, and notes the argument that typology is only distinguished from allegory in the wake of post-Reformation rejection of allegory (193, n. 20).

texts operated. In Young's account, allegory and typology are both basically concerned with a kind of mimetic resonance from one account to another: "a 'type' is a mimetic 'impress' or figure in the narrative or action described.... It is not its character as historical event which makes a 'type'; what matters is its mimetic quality."[44] Allegory and typology are therefore in the same business, but what that business is requires careful attention to what texts were about in ancient times, which could be called their "literal sense" were it not for the fact that this term has been hijacked to historicist concerns.

Secondly, therefore, the "literal sense" in view is to be understood as the sense to which the text points; a reading *ad litteram*, as several scholars have suggested in recent years.[45] It is to be taken in the traditional manner eloquently defended by Hans Frei in his work on the history of hermeneutics: as realistic but ascriptive rather than historicist and descriptive.[46] In essence this means that Numbers would have been understood, by Paul, as a realistic narrative describing the way one was expected to understand the world. The confusion which arose in the modern period, as mapped by Frei, was to conflate this realistic ascription with historical description, leading to the familiar stand-off between those who criticised the biblical account for being historically inaccurate and thus untrustworthy (as in some liberal critique) and those who defended the biblical account as being historically accurate and thus trustworthy (the standard conservative manoeuvre). Frei's position effectively advocates that the biblical account is trustworthy because it is the biblical account, and although there is clearly still a historical dimension to the text, it is not a *historicist* one,[47] and thus questions of its historical accuracy or otherwise are largely a secondary issue.[48] Paul reads

---

44. Young, *Biblical Exegesis*, 153.

45. See most notably K. E. Greene-McCreight, *Ad Litteram: How Augustine, Calvin, and Barth Read the "Plain Sense" of Genesis 1–3* (New York: Peter Lang, 1999).

46. Cf. Hans Frei, *The Eclipse of Biblical Narrative* (New Haven: Yale University Press, 1974), 10-12.

47. On "historical" but not "historicist" see the fine discussion of C. Clinton Black, "Trinity and Exegesis," *Pro Ecclesia* 19, no. 2 (2010): 151-80, esp. 166-70, noting Greene-McCreight's work, *Ad Litteram*.

48. A great deal hangs on the "largely" — especially with respect to Jesus' resurrection according to Frei's 1975 work *The Identity of Jesus Christ: The Hermeneutical Bases of Dogmatic Theology* (Philadelphia: Fortress Press) — but this is not the place to explore that matter. I have offered an account of Frei's work under the rubric of trust in my *The Virtuous Reader: Old Testament Narrative and Interpretive Virtue* (Studies in Theological Interpretation; Grand Rapids: Baker Academic, 2010), 106-13.

"The Rock Was Christ"

Numbers literally, if we understand "literal sense" in this traditional way. In this ascriptive sense the rock is "literally" Christ: in other words the mimetic impress of the Numbers text is the same as that of Christ.

Such concerns do of course take one a long way from modern concerns with author's meaning and so forth; concerns motivated at least in part by an awareness of the pitfalls of being overly beholden to interpretive traditions of various sorts. One should certainly accept that in the modern era the notion of "literal" has largely been put to use within the modern project of rendering a factual or historicist *descriptive* account of matters (and hence the arrival of a label such as "literalistic" to describe what might be happening in interpretation). In a significant review of the history of the term, Childs suggested that the Reformers briefly managed to hold the two together, but that — once unleashed — the historical questions broke apart the consensus reading: "The Reformers' achievement was to offer an interpretation of the literal sense which, at least for a short time, held together the historical and the theological meaning, but shortly this unity of interpretation also broke apart."[49] In Frei's terms, the literal sense would only "break" under the pressure of the modern approach, and for there to be any hope of its "stretching" to function meaningfully today it was necessary to return to the kinds of Jewish and Christian communal reading practices which sustained scripture as identity-forming for specific communities.[50] It is too easy to see the alternatives as polar opposites here: to postulate an interpreter who must either pursue theological or historical interests. Childs, for one, resisted such a polarisation, as may be seen by comparing his interest in traditional theological interests with the kind of claims he made, as we saw earlier, for the significance of form-critical analysis of the shape of biblical literature. One should not press for an either/or in describing best hermeneutical practice in the reading of scripture. At minimum, though, theological hermeneutics is likely to want to be attentive to traditional reading practices, and to find its norms for

---

49. Brevard S. Childs, "The Sensus Literalis of Scripture: An Ancient and Modern Problem," in Herbert Donner, Robert Hanhart, and Rudolf Smend, eds., *Beiträge zur Alttestamentlichen Theologie. Festschrift für Walter Zimmerli zum 70 Geburtstag* (Göttingen: Vandenhoeck & Ruprecht, 1977), 80-93; here 87.

50. Hans W. Frei, "The 'Literal Reading' of the Biblical Narrative in the Christian Tradition: Does It Stretch or Will It Break?" in his *Theology and Narrative: Selected Essays* (ed. George Hunsinger and William C. Placher; New Haven and Oxford: Oxford University Press, 1992), 117-52. It is noteworthy how much of the positive part of Frei's article is given to the significance of readings of Old Testament texts.

critique from within them, at least as often as it might import them from elsewhere.[51]

Thirdly, and perhaps most importantly, the word "new." It is central to the above argument that the hermeneutical and theological resonances of the word "new" are understood as distinct, even if they do in practice overlap from time to time. The Numbers text is caught up in a theological understanding that human history is now uniquely divided into two distinct (though not entirely discontinuous) periods: the "old," before Christ, and the "new" (or perhaps better "renewed") in Christ. God's revelation, in and through the written texts of old, is therefore open to being understood in new ways which are fundamentally to do with Christ rather than with a general theory of "newness." By this last phrase I mean to indicate all those hermeneutical theories which rightly emphasise that texts are open to new readings with the passing of time, or the changing of context, or the development of new horizons of reception, or the progress (or otherwise) of human thought and experience. All that is true, and biblical texts, like any other texts, give themselves up to new readings in such ways every time an advocate of some new perspective or construal comes along. But the newness which pertains to being newly in Christ is a once-for-all newness which is only hermeneutically similar in some limited formal ways (since it is after all a kind of newness), but which is driven by a set of theological convictions about divine presence and divine revelation, now newly understood in Christ.

In particular, too general a hermeneutical account lacks theological traction on what makes the Old Testament unique: this is a text (or set of texts) which is sprung into a new and theologically determined tension by what takes place in Christ. Hebrews 1:1-2 structures its understanding of revelation and time around this basic polarity: "in the past"/"now in these last days." The Old Testament, in its many and various voices, is set in tension with the new revelation: "God has spoken in Christ." Understood in this theologically determined way, "old" and "new" remain essential to an adequate description of the nature of the Christian Bible, which is of course a constructed entity, but is primarily *theologically* constructed. This leads directly to reflection upon the nature of the "Old Testament as

---

51. A helpful example of the kind of practice being described here is offered by Garrett Green in his discussion of a hermeneutic of suspicion which is driven more by the cross than by modern philosophy. See Garrett Green, *Theology, Hermeneutics, and Imagination: The Crisis of Interpretation at the End of Modernity* (Cambridge: Cambridge University Press, 2000), 187-93, in a book much indebted to Frei's analysis.

[Christian] scripture," in Childs's profound book title,[52] in which its specificity as the Scripture of Israel is taken up and recast in the new theological understanding brought into being by the existence of the *new* testament.

On a hermeneutical level, by way of contrast, newness works through such categories as reception history or literary notions of "canon" wherein any new work or interpretation may be added in at the end of the chain of texts, which is in principle open-ended and capable of ongoing revision. One sees plenty of attempts to make theological capital out of this hermeneutical phenomenon in cases where appeal is made to the New Testament's relativisation of the Old as a mandate for our own relativisation of the New, usually, it might be said, in ways which seem suspiciously conformed to the culture in which we live. Now it is of course true that the hermeneutical phenomena of canon and reception can illuminate many and diverse aspects of biblical texts. I have always enjoyed the comment of Frank McConnell in his editorial introduction to *The Bible and the Narrative Tradition:* "you can make a movie called *Star Wars,* and it will be a good or a bad film. But, then, what if you make a sequel? Are you continuing the story, or are you, in fact, reinterpreting the story by extending it?"[53] In some ways this illuminates the position of the Old Testament in our time. But it does not illuminate it in a manner sufficient to the theological significance of Old and New in Christian Scripture.[54]

One of the most evident corollaries of this line of thinking is that those more traditional modes of interpretation which were deeply influenced by the biblical figuration of time into old and new, such as the allegorical/typological approaches characteristic of a former age, continue to offer profound insights into the tasks of biblical interpretation, alongside newer approaches which are somewhat bereft of any sort of reflection on

---

52. Childs, *Introduction to the Old Testament as Scripture.*

53. Frank McConnell, "Introduction," in Frank McConnell, ed., *The Bible and the Narrative Tradition* (New York: Oxford University Press, 1986), 3-18, here 6, in dialogue with Frank Kermode's contribution to the volume which also, it may be noted, contained Frei's article on "Literal Reading."

54. Can *any* "sequel" furnish a theologically adequate example of the OT/NT relationship? According to Walter Moberly, there is one such instance: the way in which the El-related ancestral narratives of Genesis are taken up in the Yahwistic rereading offered in the Old Testament, whereby Genesis becomes, in his book's title, *The Old Testament of the Old Testament* (subtitled *Patriarchal Narratives and Mosaic Yahwism* [OBT; Minneapolis: Fortress, 1992], esp. 105-46). Moberly's account of the logic of "old" and "new" here, however, makes it clear that this is precisely a reflection on "the theological significance of Old and New in Christian Scripture" rather than any more general sense.

the significance of time. Matthew Levering makes this point in his call for a mode of interpretation which acknowledges "participation" in Christ as a way of transcending the non-christological, linear understandings of time which have predominated in the modern era.[55] And Christopher Seitz puts the point sharply: modern or late-modern approaches to Scripture can leave us lost in time, adrift from any meaningful doctrine of providence, and susceptible to whatever "new" theological vision captures the day. The two-testament Christian scripture, in contrast, figures our own time into the scriptural narrative.[56]

Fourthly, and lest the above argument should be misunderstood, does this mean that it should not be possible to interpret the book of Numbers, say, without reference to Christ? By no means! Clearly one would have to nuance the presenting question here in any case: perhaps it is whether one can interpret Numbers "well," or "correctly," or "as a Christian," without reference to Christ, and the answers to these questions might not all be the same. But it is not just empirical observations about the evident wisdom of much Jewish interpretation which should give the enthusiastic Christian interpreter pause here. If what we have said about the "mimetic impress" of the texts is right, then the Christian theological perception of that same impress in Christ is not the only way of describing the Old Testament text *ad litteram*. Ellen Davis puts the matter helpfully in a discussion of Christian preaching of the Old Testament, which may be especially germane to our reading of Paul reading Numbers: "The freedom to preach Old Testament texts christologically is, in my judgment, just that: a freedom that the Christian preacher may exercise at any time and should exercise sometimes, not a requirement for preaching any particular text responsibly."[57] In point of fact, the New Testament itself pursues this interpretive path only occasionally. Certain key texts in the tradition have brought attention to the christological dimensions of reading Old Testament texts: 1 Corinthians 10 is one, and Galatians 4 and arguably Ephesians 5 (esp. vv. 31-32) are others. In general, such texts pursued allegorical means of linking the ancient text and the present theological reality under discussion. Indeed, Robert Wilken suggests that "the term allegory is used so loosely today that

---

55. See Matthew Levering, *Participatory Biblical Exegesis: A Theology of Biblical Interpretation* (Notre Dame, IN: University of Notre Dame Press, 2008).

56. Christopher R. Seitz, *Figured Out: Typology and Providence in Christian Scripture* (Louisville: Westminster John Knox Press, 2001), esp. 195-96.

57. Ellen F. Davis, *Wondrous Depth: Preaching the Old Testament* (Louisville: Westminster John Knox Press, 2005), 72.

"The Rock Was Christ"

it is sometimes forgotten that it is primarily a technique for interpreting the Old Testament, the Jewish Scriptures that the early Christian community made its own."[58] Notably, Wilken thinks that it is precisely the specificity of our two-testament scripture which requires a recovery of allegory today in the church as "indispensable for a genuinely Christian interpretation of the Old Testament."[59] Again this underlines our point that, for any theological interpretation to take place, the Old Testament is not so much a generic "text" to which any hermeneutical approach might be applied, as a specific case requiring its own unique set of hermeneutical moves.

One might also wish to point out that, on balance, the book of Numbers has not been well-served with careful allegorical (or figural or christological) interpretation in recent times. For a rare example one might consider Nathan MacDonald's striking reading of the *sotah* text of Num 5:11-31 in terms of "the relationship between Yhwh and Israel and, within the context of a Christian two testament canon, between God and the church."[60] MacDonald's article offers exactly the combination of attention to the text and to the theological dimensions of the literal sense which we have been discussing. It would be a pity if the rhetoric of a supposed need to "liberate" the biblical text from over-zealous Christian allegorical interpretation obscured the fact that all of one article represented the counter-voice in recent scholarly discussion.[61]

General Hermeneutics Reconsidered

I have suggested that the basic limitation of general hermeneutical theory with respect to its usefulness for reading Christian scripture is its insufficient attention to the particularities introduced by the unique two-testament structure of the text at hand. Now on one level this may be put

---

58. Robert Louis Wilken, "Allegory and Old Testament Interpretation," *Letter & Spirit* 1 (2005): 11-21, here 12.

59. Wilken, "Allegory and Old Testament Interpretation," 21.

60. Nathan MacDonald, "'Gone Astray': Dealing with the *Sotah* (Num 5:11-31)," in Stanley D. Walters, ed., *Go Figure! Figuration in Biblical Interpretation* (Princeton Theological Monograph Series 81; Eugene, OR: Pickwick Publications, 2008), 48-64, here 60.

61. One may sample the very different profile of allegorical interpretation of Numbers in patristic times via the helpful survey article of Hendrik F. Stander, "The Patristic Exegesis of Moses Striking the Rock (Ex 17.1-7 & Num 20.1-13)," *Coptic Church Review* 12, no. 3 (1991): 67-77.

(at least to some small degree) in a positive sense. It is a hermeneutical observation that we need to pay sufficient attention to the text at hand. But to make such a general point is not the same as allowing one's interpretation to be substantively shaped by the specifics of Christian scripture as a frame of reference for interpreting biblical texts.

A further example may clarify the point at issue. Congruent with this discussion of the importance of the unique nature of the text which confronts us, we may consider the sophisticated treatment of textuality in the hermeneutical work of Werner Jeanrond.[62] "Text," says Jeanrond, "is a category of theological thinking." More specifically: "Every theory of interpretation postulates a theory of text," and if we do not develop a theological theory of text then we cede the ground to other disciplines. Jeanrond thus proceeds to "outline a theologically adequate theory of textuality."[63] All this is helpful, but it is then striking that the discussion which follows focuses on text-linguistics, genre, and reading theory in the light of the non-theological work of Iser and Fish.[64] At no point does the specific nature of the Old Testament as the text canonically bound to its redefining partner, the New Testament, make any difference to the discussion. So in the end much of Jeanrond's *general* discussion is entirely fine within its general frame of reference, but does not in fact indicate how the prime pressing issues of the nature and function of Old Testament texts may be addressed.

Schleiermacher, not insignificantly, developed his hermeneutical thinking with respect to the New Testament, and much of the subsequent pull of hermeneutical thinking, towards the so-called "universality of hermeneutics,"[65] derives its logic from the ways of thinking he set in motion. Now clearly there is a tremendously valuable sense in which such thinking challenges any easy over-assimilation of the New Testament text at hand into prior dogmatic theological systems. The present argument is not an attempt to contest the gains of hermeneutics, nor suggest that its insights into interpretive tasks are not worthwhile. But all that said, my contention is that there was an alternative route to the same challenge to dogmatic

62. In particular Werner G. Jeanrond, *Text and Interpretation as Categories of Theological Thinking* (New York: Crossroad, 1988).

63. Jeanrond, *Text and Interpretation*, 73.

64. Jeanrond, *Text and Interpretation*, 73-128.

65. Hans-Georg Gadamer, "The Universality of the Hermeneutical Problem," in his *Philosophical Hermeneutics* (trans. and ed. David E. Linge; Berkeley: University of California Press, 1976), 3-17.

"The Rock Was Christ"

foreclosure on New Testament interpretation, and that it lay nearer to hand than hermeneutical philosophy: the route of taking seriously the status and function of the Old Testament as Christian scripture. The conclusion I would like to draw from this, and propose for further consideration in the work of other New Testament interpreters in particular, is as follows: the Old Testament is a stumbling block for the application of general hermeneutical understanding to the tasks of reading biblical texts well, and in particular with respect to their theological voice.

How then does hermeneutical theorising work?[66] It offers at best a *via negativa*, ideal for showing up the problems of unexamined frameworks and assumptions. It successfully demonstrates that there can be no simple "objectivity" in the reading of texts. It forces productive reflection on the nature of embodied assumptions and commitments in the reading of the texts before us. On these terms, the New Testament may then be able to take care of itself.[67] The Old Testament, however, is a stumbling block to the application of general hermeneutical thinking to the tasks of biblical interpretation. It is intriguing to recall Origen's comment on the divine provision of problems which require the reader to take roads less travelled:

> the divine wisdom has arranged for certain stumbling blocks and interruptions of the historical sense to be found therein, by inserting in the midst a number of impossibilities and incongruities, in order that the very interruption of the narrative might as it were present a barrier to the reader and lead him to refuse to proceed along the pathway of the ordinary meaning. (*On First Principles*, 4.2.9)

Perhaps the Old Testament itself is the great stumbling block to the generalised hermeneutical projects of modern theology. It is I think no coincidence that Schleiermacher found little constructive role for the Old Testament in his work. Neither is it coincidence, I suggest, that a resurgence of interest in the interpretation of the Old Testament as Christian Scripture (after Childs and others) propels us to a place where theological interpretation becomes a major concern of Christian interpreters, and where the hermeneutical thinking in play may thus become appropriately theological.

---

66. See here more generally my "What Does Hermeneutics Have to Do with Biblical Interpretation?" *Heythrop Journal* 47, no. 1 (2006): 55-74.
67. Cf. Wilken's striking citation of a medieval Spanish exegete that "the New Testament stands on its own; it does not need allegory"; "Allegory and Old Testament Interpretation," 12.

RICHARD S. BRIGGS

Theological Interpretation and the Limits of Hermeneutical Theory: A Concluding Unscientific Allegory

What then should we say? That general hermeneutical theory is a waste of time? By no means! For without hermeneutical theory I would not have known what it meant to read scripture more probingly than by way of reflecting back my own assumptions and theological preferences. But hermeneutics, seizing an opportunity in the consideration of method, produced in me all kinds of proliferating prolegomena. I was once a happy reader apart from hermeneutics . . .

Or again:

Why then hermeneutics? It was added because of inadequate readings. Is it then opposed to the promises of God? Certainly not! Hermeneutics was our disciplinarian until Christ is revealed in the impress of the text . . .

And so:

A proper theological understanding of general hermeneutical theory may be as simple as grasping Paul's view of the law, which is to say, not simple at all. Which would befit an account of the dynamics of reading a text which is playing its part in the mysterious divine economy of action, presence, judgment and blessing. Against such things there is no law.

ENGAGING THE OTHER

The Earliest Interpreters of the Jesus Tradition: A Study in Early Hermeneutics

James D. G. Dunn

There was never a time when the teaching of Jesus was not being interpreted. To receive and respond to his teaching was already to interpret it, or to let it interpret the hearer and responder. To pass on that teaching inevitably involved grouping and adapting it — more interpretation. And to show its continuing relevance to the changing situations of the first disciples of Jesus inevitably involved elaboration, explanation, addition — still more interpretation. This is the teaching as it comes down to later centuries — already in the Synoptic tradition used by the first three Evangelists. It would be most accurate to speak of the Synoptic tradition itself as the earliest interpretation, including the tradition on which Mark drew, the Q material on which Matthew and Luke drew, as well as other Jesus tradition accessible to them. For the purposes of this essay, however, I treat the Synoptic tradition as the base material for the early Christian churches, and so can refer to the interpretation of that base material as the earliest interpretation.

The obvious first main candidates for the title "earliest interpreters" are, of course, Mark, Matthew, and Luke. And since the emergence of redaction criticism and narrative or composition criticism there has been no end to the attempts to analyse the interpretation imposed on the Jesus tradition by the first three Evangelists. Here I want to do something different: to examine and compare the interpretations imposed on the Jesus tradition by John and Thomas,[1] that is, to examine the hermeneutic they used in developing and presenting the Jesus tradition as they did. Whether John

---

1. As with Mark, Matthew, and Luke, I use the names John and Thomas to refer to the Gospels to which their names are attached. For this essay there is no need to go into the question of authorship in each case.

and Thomas should be included in the title "earliest interpreters" is a fair question, and I do not propose to mount any argument on the subject. But I do acknowledge the strong bodies of opinion which argue that the tradition used by both Gospels is early: that John was drawing on early Jesus tradition, whether in direct dependence on one or more of the Synoptic Gospels, or, as I prefer, was drawing on oral Jesus tradition, Synoptic-like in character;[2] and that Thomas too is evidence for Jesus tradition in several cases at least arguably earlier than the Synoptic tradition.[3] So I beg for some tolerance in my inclusion of John and Thomas among "the earliest interpreters of the Jesus tradition." I was prompted to this subject — the comparison of John's and Thomas's "take" on the Jesus tradition — by the thought that Tony Thiselton, the prince of present-day hermeneuts, might find this exploration of some of the earliest heremeneutical treatments of the Jesus tradition of particular interest.

Why Compare John and Thomas?

The reason is simple. Both John and Thomas draw (but differently) on the early Jesus tradition as attested in the Synoptic tradition. But they also diverge markedly from that tradition in the content and the character of their material; the diversity in the use they make of the earlier tradition is so different from the diversity evident in Mark, Matthew and Luke, that they might legitimately be regarded as different species from that of the Synoptics. For those familiar with the New Testament, and with both the *canonical* status of John and the *non*-canonical status of Thomas, this may be a very questionable comment to make. But a dispassionate judgment of these Gospels is likely to be surprised both by the *divergence* of John's treatment of Jesus from that of the other canonical Gospels, and by the *closeness* of much of Thomas's account to the Synoptic tradition. This is why a treatment of them rather than of the Synoptics, and a comparison of their interpretation of the Jesus tradition, is such a fascinating study in hermeneutics. Not least such a study may help clarify why one of the two

---

2. See particularly P. N. Anderson, *The Fourth Gospel and the Quest for Jesus* (London: T&T Clark, 2006).

3. E.g. S. J. Patterson suggests the possibility that *Thomas* "has its own roots, which reach deeply into the fertile soil of early Christian tradition" (*The Gospel of Thomas and Jesus* [Sonoma: Polebridge, 1993], 9), cited by R. Uro, ed., Thomas *at the Crossroads: Essays on the Gospel of Thomas* (Edinburgh: T&T Clark, 1998) in his Introduction (1-2).

The Earliest Interpreters of the Jesus Tradition

hermeneutical tacks prospered within the New Testament canon, and the other was deemed to have gone astray.

I begin with a reminder of how much dependence on Synoptic or Synoptic-like tradition is evident in John and Thomas, and how diverse is that dependence.

John's Dependence on Synoptic-like Tradition

The differences between John and the Synoptics are so extensive that it is quite difficult to classify them in the same category — though a decisive factor is that like Mark, and Matthew and Luke who followed Mark, John has retained the character of the account of Jesus' mission as "a passion narrative with an extended introduction."[4]

The differences between the Synoptics and John are especially clear in their accounts of Jesus' teaching:

Synoptics	John
Jesus speaks little of himself — nothing quite like John's "I am's"	Jesus speaks much of himself — notably the "I am" statements[5]
Jesus looks for faith in God[6]	Jesus looks for faith in himself

---

4. The famous description given to Mark by M. Kähler, *The So-Called Historical Jesus and the Historic Biblical Christ* (1896; Philadelphia: Fortress, 1964), 80 n. 11.

5. John 6:35, 48 — "I am the bread of life"
    6:41 — "I am the bread that came down from heaven"
    6:51 — "I am the living bread that came down from heaven"
    8:12 — "I am the light of the world"
    8:24, 28 — "I am"
    8:58 — "Before Abraham was, I am"
    10:7, 9 — "I am the gate for the sheep"
    10:11, 14 — "I am the good shepherd"
    11:25 — "I am the resurrection and the life"
    13:19 — "I am"
    14:6 — "I am the way, and the truth, and the life"
    15:1, 5 — "I am the true vine"

"Practically all the words of Jesus in John are *assertions about himself*" (R. Bultmann, *Theology of the New Testament*, vol. 2 [London: SCM, 1955], 2:63).

6. Explicit in Mark 11:22 par., but implicit in the other Synoptic references (Mark 2:5 pars.; 4:40 par.; 5:34 pars.; 10:52 pars.; Matt 8:10/Luke 7:9; Matt 17:20/Luke 17:6; Matt 15:28; Luke 7:50; 17:5, 19; 18:8; 22:32); see further my *Jesus Remembered* (Grand Rapids: Eerdmans,

The central theme of Jesus' preaching is the kingdom of God	The kingdom of God barely features in Jesus' speech[7]
Jesus speaks of repentance and forgiveness quite often	Jesus never speaks of repentance, and of forgiveness only in 20:23
Jesus speaks typically in aphorisms and parables	Jesus engages in lengthy dialogues and circuitous discussion
Jesus speaks only occasionally of eternal life	Jesus speaks regularly of eternal life[8]

However, the contrast between on the one hand the Synoptics' aphoristic sayings and parables, and on the other hand the Johannine discourses can be overdrawn. For, as we shall see, Jesus' teaching in John includes some parabolic material. And, most intriguing, the Johannine discourses often seem to grow out of or to be based on more aphoristic teaching of Jesus as evidenced by the Synoptic tradition.[9]

- 3:5 — "Very truly I tell you, unless a person is born from water and Spirit he cannot enter into the kingdom of God"; Matt 18:3 — "Truly I tell you, unless you turn and become like children, you will never enter into the kingdom of heaven." This is the only passage in which John has retained a Synoptic-like reference to "the kingdom of God" (Matthew — "of heaven"). In John the entry-requirement is stated in similar but more radical terms and is the base point for the more extended teaching of 3:3-15, 21.[10]

2003), 500-503. John does not speak of "faith," but talk of "believing in" Jesus is common (John 2:11; 3:15-16, 18; 4:39; 6:29, 35, 40; etc.).

7. Matt 47x; Mark 18x; Luke 37x; John 5x in only two passages (John 3:3-5; 18:36).

8. Mark 10:30 pars.; Matt 25:46; John 3:15-16, 36; 4:14, 36; 5:24, 39; 6:27, 40, 47, 54, (68); 10:28; 12:25, 50; 17:2-3.

9. See further C. H. Dodd, *Historical Tradition in the Fourth Gospel* (Cambridge: Cambridge University Press, 1963), 335-65 (particularly 347, 349, 360-61); and my "John and the Oral Gospel Tradition," in H. Wansbrough, ed., *Jesus and the Oral Gospel Tradition* (JSNTS 64; Sheffield: Sheffield Academic, 1991), 351-79, particularly 356-58. See also C. M. Tuckett, "The Fourth Gospel and Q," and E. K. Broadhead, "The Fourth Gospel and the Synoptic Sayings Source," in R. T. Fortna & T. Thatcher, eds., *Jesus in the Johannine Tradition* (Louisville: Westminster John Knox, 2001), 280-90 and 291-301 respectively; R. J. Bauckham, *Jesus and the Eyewitnesses: The Gospels as Eyewitness Testimony* (Grand Rapids: Eerdmans, 2006), 106-12. About 70 verses in the Johannine discourses can be said to have Synoptic parallels.

10. See also C. C. Caragounis, "The Kingdom of God: Common and Distinct Elements Between John and the Synoptics," in Fortna and Thatcher, eds., *Jesus in the Johannine Tradition*, 125-34.

- 3:29 — likening Jesus' presence to the presence of the bridegroom, as marking the difference between Jesus and the Baptist, echoes Mark 2:19 pars. (also Mark 2:19-20 pars.).
- 5:19-30 — the exposition of the close relationship between the Father and the Son and of the authority given by the Father to the Son may well have grown out of teaching like Matt 11:27/Luke 10:22 (cf. also John 3:35).
- 6:20 — the close similarity with Mark 6:50 suggests that John's distinctive "I am" sayings may have been suggested to him by the story of Jesus' epiphanic appearance walking on the water.[11]
- 6:26-58 — the great bread of life discourse reads like an extensive reflection on Jesus' words at his last supper with his disciples — "This is my body," "This is my blood" (Mark 14:22, 24 pars.).
- 8:31-58 — the lengthy discussion on the significance of Jewish descent from Abraham could have grown out of the Baptist's warning to his fellow Jews not to rely on having Abraham as their ancestor (Matt 3:7-10/Luke 3:7-9).
- 10:1-18 — Jesus' elaborated claim to be the good shepherd is most simply explained as growing out of Jesus' use of the imagery of sheep, particularly his parable of the lost sheep.[12]
- 12:24-26 — perhaps a slight elaboration of Jesus' own teaching, as in Mark 8:35, about the cost of discipleship.
- 13:13-16 — and perhaps the account of Jesus washing his disciples' feet (13:1-11), could well be an extension and "visual aid" to illustrate teaching like Matt 10:24-25.
- 14:16-17; 15:26-27; 16:4-15 — the repeated promise that the Holy Spirit would teach the disciples probably began with the elsewhere remembered assurance of Jesus that the Spirit would inspire what they should say (Mark 13:11 pars.).
- We should add that the *"Amen, Amen"* introductory formula so regularly used by John[13] is obviously drawn from the tradition, well-known in the Synoptics, of Jesus' introducing a saying with "Amen."[14]

---

11. Cf. Anderson, *Fourth Gospel*, 56-8.
12. Matt 18:12-13/Luke 15:4-7; also Mark 6:34; Matt 10:6; 15:24; Luke 12:32.
13. John 1:51; 3:3, 5, 11; 5:19, 24, 25; etc.
14. *Jesus Remembered*, 700-701 and n. 418. See further R. A. Culpepper, "The Origin of the 'Amen, Amen' Sayings in the Gospel of John," in Fortna and Thatcher, eds., *Jesus in the Johannine Tradition*, 253-62.

- Note also that several enriched versions of Synoptic-like exhortations pepper chs. 13–16:
  13:16 — Matt 10:24/Luke 6:40;
  13:20 — Matt 10:40/Luke 10:16;
  13:34-35 — Mark 12:28-31 pars.;
  15:14-15 — cf. Mark 3:35 pars.;
  15:16 — Mark 11:23-24 pars.;
  15:18-21 — Mark 13:13 pars.;
  16:1-4 — Mark 13:9, 12-13 pars./Matt 10:17-18, 21-22;
  16:23-24 — Matt 7:7/Luke 11:9;
  16:32 — Mark 14:27 par.[15]

It should also be noted that the discourses contain a number of parables not dissimilar to the more characteristic Synoptic form,[16] and three sequences of sayings again closer to the Synoptic pattern.[17] Not least of significance is the fact that the overlap with the Synoptic tradition at point after point indicates an independent awareness of the teaching which the early churches all remembered as Jesus' teaching.[18] The relative lack of reworking by John at these points is both what allows us to recognize the parallel (the shared memory of the same teaching) and what enables us to say with confidence that John's discourses are rooted in the memories of what Jesus taught during his mission, in Galilee or in Judea.

---

15. J. Beutler, "Synoptic Jesus Tradition in the Johannine Farewell Discourse," in Fortna and Thatcher, eds., *Jesus in Johannine Tradition*, 165-73, boldly concludes "that John 13–17 is pervaded by early Jesus tradition, mostly tradition of a synoptic character and perhaps even derived from the Synoptics themselves," though "no single coherent discourse source can be uncovered. Rather, there has been creative use of the traditional material, forging it into a new form that expresses F(ourth)E(vangelist)'s peculiar view of Jesus . . ." (173).

16. John 3:29; 5:19-21; 8:35; 10:1-5; 11:9-10; 12:24; 16:21; see Dodd, *Historical Tradition*, 366-87. J. A. T. Robinson, *The Priority of John* (London: SCM, 1985) notes 13 or 14 Johannine parables (319-20).

17. John 4:31-38; 12:20-26; 13:1-20; see Dodd, *Historical Tradition*, 388-405. Tom Thatcher, "The Riddles of Jesus in the Johannine Dialogues," in Fortna and Thatcher, eds., *Jesus in Johannine Tradition*, 263-77, notes the substantial body of riddles in the Johannine dialogues. Since riddles are a widely attested oral form, he suggests that at least some of these sayings circulated orally in Johannine circles before the Fourth Gospel was written, and that some of the larger dialogues may also have circulated orally as riddling sessions (he refers particularly to John 8:12-58).

18. See further R. Schnackenburg, *The Gospel according to St John*, vol. 1 (1965; ET New York: Herder & Herder, 1968), 26-43.

The Earliest Interpreters of the Jesus Tradition

In short, for all their difference in style, and the elaboration and enrichment of individual sayings and motifs, it would appear that several of the discourses of John's Gospel are deeply rooted in Synoptic-like tradition. In addition, the possibility should not be excluded that John knew other Synoptic-like tradition, not picked up in the Synoptic tradition itself, and treated it in similar manner — as a theme to be developed and elaborated in similar discourse style. Are the Johannine discourses then simply an example of how radically and extensively the Jesus tradition could be elaborated within the churches of the emerging Christianity of the late first century?[19]

Thomas and the Synoptic Tradition

The contrast with John's dependence on the Synoptic tradition is very striking. For with John, the surprise is that the Johannine presentation of Jesus is so different from that of the Synoptics. In contrast, with Thomas we seem to move back from the substantially developed Jesus tradition of John, to material much closer in form to that of the Synoptics. As just indicated, the case for seeing John's presentation of Jesus' teaching as rooted in Synoptic-like Jesus tradition is not self-evident and has to be demonstrated with some care. In contrast, even a brief consultation of Thomas can hardly fail to observe that the links between Thomas and the Synoptic Jesus tradition are clear and substantial.[20] This indeed is the paradox of John and Thomas, and why they make for such an interesting comparison: that John is part of the NT canon, but Thomas is regularly closer to the Synoptic tradition than John! In the following list I include only the close parallels.[21]

---

19. "The formation of the sayings of Jesus into the Johannine discourses represented a profound theological synthesis" (R. E. Brown, *The Gospel according to John* [AB 29; 2 vols.; New York: Doubleday, 1966], 1:xlix).

20. As observed also, e.g., by I. Dunderberg, "*Thomas'* I-sayings and the Gospel of John," in Uro, ed., Thomas *at the Crossroads*, 33-64, here 33.

21. By "close parallels" I indicate a verbal similarity indicating a variation of the same saying. The most useful listing of *Thomas* and Synoptic interdependence is A. D. DeConick, *The Original Gospel of Thomas in Translation* (LNTS 287; London: T&T Clark, 2006) with an Appendix on "Verbal Similarities between *Thomas* and the Synoptics" (299-316). Here I usually follow DeConick's translation and sub-verse division of the Thomas logia.

GThomas	Close Synoptic parallels
4:2-3	Mark 10:31 pars.
6:4-5	Mark 4:22 (Matt 10:26/Luke 8:17)
8:4; 21:11; 24:2; 63:4; 65:8; 96:3	Mark 4:9 + Matt (3x), Luke (3x)
9:1-5	Mark 4:3-8 pars.
14:5	Mark 7:15 (Matt 15:11)
16:1-2	Luke 12:51/Matt 10:34
16:3	Luke 12:52-53 (Matt 10:35-36)
20:1-4	Mark 4:30-32 pars.
21:5	Matt 24:43 (Luke 12:39)
21:10	Mark 4:29
26:1-2	Matt 7:3-5/Luke 6:41-42
31:1-2	Luke 4:23-24 (Mark 6:4 par.)
33:1	Matt 10:27 (Luke 12:3)
33:2-3	Luke 11:33; 8:16 (Matt 5:15; Mark 4:21)
34	Matt 15:14 (Luke 6:39)
35:1-2	Mark 3:27 (Matt 12:29; Luke 11:21-22)
36:1-3	Matt 6:25-30/Luke 12:22, 27-30
39:1-2	Matt 23:13/Luke 11:52
39:3	Matt 10:16
41:1-2	Mark 4:25 pars.
44:1-3	Matt 12:31-32/Luke 12:10 (Mark 3:28-30)
45:1-4	Luke 6:44-45/Matt 7:16; 12:34-35
47:3-4	Mark 2:22 pars.
47:5	Mark 2:21 pars.
54	Luke 6:20 (Matt 5:3)
55:1-2; cf. 101:1	Luke 14:26-27/Matt 10:37-38
57:1-4	Matt 13:24-30
63:1-3	Luke 12:16-21
64:1-11	Matt 22:2-10/Luke 14:16-24
65:1-7	Mark 12:1-9 pars.
66	Mark 12:10 pars.
68:1	Luke 6:22 (Matt 5:10-11)
69:2	Luke 6:21 (Matt 5:6)
71	Mark 14:58 par.
73	Matt 9:37-38/Luke 10:2
76:1-2	Matt 13:45-46
76:3	Luke 12:33/Matt 6:19-20

The Earliest Interpreters of the Jesus Tradition

78:1-3	Matt 11:7-8/Luke 7:24-25
79:1-3	Luke 11:27-28 and 23:29
86:1-2	Matt 8:20/Luke 9:58
89:1-2	Luke 11:39-40 (Matt 23:25-26)
90:1-2	Matt 11:28-30
93:1-2	Matt 7:6
94:1-2	Matt 7:7-8/Luke 11:9-10
96:1-2	Matt 13:33/Luke 13:20-21
99:1-3	Luke 8:19-21 (Mark 3:31-35 par.)
100:1-4	Mark 12:13-17
107:1-3	Matt 18:12-13/Luke 15:4-7

The findings are striking.

1. Of the 114 Thomas logia, 42 contain close parallel material — that is, 36.8%. The percentage is misleading, since the Thomas logia vary in length, and in some cases only part of the whole logion has closely parallel material (e.g., Thomas 21, 61, 68). I have not counted the multiple occurrences of "Whoever has ears should listen" (8:4, etc.).
2. When the less-close parallels are included, the figure goes up to about 63, that is, 56.2% (with the same qualification).[22] This assuredly indicates that Thomas shared a great deal of the Jesus tradition known to us from the Synoptics. And if the Synoptic tradition has the best claim to express the impact made by Jesus himself and the way he was remembered by the earliest Christian disciples, then it follows that Thomas is also a witness to that impact and to the way Jesus was remembered.
3. The parallels with Q material (that is, the non-Marcan tradition shared by Matthew and Luke) are particularly notable, 29 in all (25.4%).[23] But it is also notable that at other times Thomas seems to share the tradition with only one of the Synoptics — Mark (21:10),[24]

---

22. R. Cameron maintains that "no fewer than 68 of the 114 sayings in the text have biblical parallels" ("Thomas, Gospel of," ADD 6:536).

23. Q parallels — Thomas 2; 16; 21:5; 26:1-2; 33:1, 2-3; 34; 36:1-3; 39:1-2; 44; 45:1-4; 46:1-2; 47:2; 54; 55:1-2; 61:1; 64:1-11; 68:1; 69:2; 73; 76:3; 78:1-3; 86:1-2; 89:1-2; 91:1-2; 92:1-2; 94:1-2; 96:1-2; 107:1-3. H. Koester, *Ancient Christian Gospels* (London: SCM, 1990) reckons that of 79 sayings of Thomas with Synoptic parallels, 46 have parallels in Q; he includes Thomas 5; 6:3; 10; 17; 24:3; 43; 61:3; 69; 79:1; 95; 103 (87-89); but assignation of most of these to Q is highly disputable.

24. But perhaps the parallels noted as Mark par(s). should be included, since it is quite

Matthew (11 in all, 9.6%),[25] and Luke (9 in all, 7.9%).[26] The extent of the parallels certainly confirms that Thomas shared much of the Q material, but gives no support to the possibility that Thomas knew the Q material in a document the sequence of whose sayings Luke may have preserved.[27] Even if there was a distinctive Q collection (or a Q document), Thomas's knowledge of the Jesus tradition as represented by the Synoptic tradition was much broader than Q.

The first point of comparison between John and Thomas is thus clear: *both* were familiar with/dependent on the early Jesus tradition as attested in the Synoptic tradition; but whereas Thomas retained the early tradition in similar form, John developed aphoristic and parabolic teaching of Jesus into lengthy dialogues and discourses. The question for us is: What does this tell us about the hermeneutical strategies of John and Thomas? What is the hermeneutical significance of the very different use made of the Jesus tradition?

The Difference between John and Thomas — an Initial Probe

The difference between John and Thomas seems to be straightforward: that John has developed and elaborated the Jesus tradition, so much so that to discern the earlier Jesus tradition is not easy; whereas Thomas has been content to follow the Jesus tradition, in a way similar to the Synoptists, that is, with the sort of variation which we find also in the Synoptists. It is for this reason that Thomas has presented itself to several scholars as a source for the teaching of Jesus similar or superior to the Synoptics as preserving original content and forms.[28] At first glance Thomas seems to have been

---

possible that the other Synoptists were dependent on Mark at these points, which would add another 10 or so to the list (notably Thomas 9; 20; 41).

25. Specifically Matthean parallels — Thomas 8:1-3; 32; 39:3; 40:1-2; 57:1-4; 62:2; 76:1-2; 90:1-2; 93:1-2; 109:1-3.

26. Specifically Lukan parallels — Thomas 3:1-3; 10; 14:4; 63:1-3; 72:1-3; 79:1-3; 95:1-2; 101:1; 113:1-4. Surprisingly, Koester thinks that special Lukan material occurs only once in Thomas (*Ancient Christian Gospels*, 107).

27. It is generally recognized that Luke's form and ordering more fully reflect the form and order of Q, whereas Matthew has grouped the Q material according to his own editorial strategy.

28. As in R. W. Funk and R. W. Hoover, eds., *The Five Gospels* (New York: Macmillan,

The Earliest Interpreters of the Jesus Tradition

more responsible, and John much more adventuresome in his use of the Jesus tradition. However, a little deeper digging begins to challenge such a provisional verdict and to raise important questions.

The issue can be posed by noting that while in some cases both John and Thomas seem to have been content to recall and reuse a saying of Jesus without significant elaboration, other cases reveal their hermeneutical strategy more clearly. There are several cases where both John and Thomas show awareness of the same Synoptic teaching, and where Thomas in particular seems to have been content to reproduce the earlier tradition without much variation.

	John	Synoptics	Thomas
Prophet	4:44	Luke 4:23-24 (Mark 6:4 par)	31
Temple saying	2:19	Mark 14:58; 15:29	71
The bridegroom	3:29	Mark 2:19-20 pars.	104:2
Shepherd	10:1-18	Matt 18:12-13/Luke 15:4-7	107:1-3

In other cases, however, it would seem that John has developed a saying of Jesus in the manner of his dialogue and discourse style, where the development has been along the line of the saying's earlier meaning, an elaboration of the earlier saying itself. In contrast, Thomas, while retaining the same earlier saying in its earlier form, has added fresh material which alters the character of the imagery and its meaning.

- The shared saying is Matt 18:3/Mark 10:15 (to enter the kingdom one must become as a little child). As already noted, John 3:3-8 seems to sharpen it (to enter the kingdom of God one must be born again/from above); and in answer to the question which arises, John elaborates the metaphor in terms of being born of the Spirit. In contrast, in Thomas 22, when the disciples ask the equivalent question in response to a more Synoptic-like version (22:1-3), Jesus replies, "When you make the two one, and make the outside like the inside, and the above like the below. And when you make the male and the female into a single being, with the result that the male is not male nor the female female.

1993). Passages where arguably Thomas preserves a form earlier than that used by the Synoptics include Thomas 9 (Mark 4:3-8 pars.); Thomas 20:1-4 (Mark 4:30-32 pars.); Thomas 26:1-2 (Matt 7:3-5/Luke 6:41-42); Thomas 55:1-2 (Luke 14:26-27/Matt 10:37-38); Thomas 93:1-2 (Matt 7:6).

When you make eyes in place of an eye, and a hand in place of a hand, and a foot in place of a foot, and an image in place of an image, then you will enter (the kingdom)" (22:4-7).
- The pericope where Jesus asks who his disciples think he is and where he silences Peter's confession that Jesus is the Messiah (Mark 8:27-30 pars.) is transformed in John throughout his Gospel by a sequence of open confessions and self-confessions (e.g., John 1:49; 4:25-26; 5:46; 6:41, 69; 8:12, 58; etc.). In contrast, in Thomas the responses of Peter ("You are like a righteous angel") and Matthew ("You are like a sage") (13:2-3) are climaxed by Thomas being given special revelation secretly which was too dangerous for him to pass on (13:6-8).
- Jesus' encouragement to ask, seek, and knock (Matt 7:7/Luke 11:9) is taken up by John in Jesus' encouragement to the disciples to ask after he has left them (John 16:12-24). Thomas also draws on the Synoptic tradition but adds a quite different theme: "Jesus said, 'He who seeks should not stop (seeking until) he finds; and when he finds, he will be amazed; and when he is amazed, he will marvel, and will be king over all/he will rest'" (Thomas 2).

These differences provide a clue to what is probably the principal difference between John's and Thomas's use of the Jesus tradition. Both draw on that tradition heavily, and both add their own slant to that earlier material. But John does so by elaborating the tradition itself, by drawing out its deeper/fuller significance through question and answer, dialogue and discourse. Thomas, on the other hand, draws in other material which is quite distinct in character from the earlier Synoptic-like tradition. John we may say builds as it were *from the inside* expanding the meaning of the inherited Synoptic tradition. In contrast, Thomas introduces fresh and often unrelated material as it were *from the outside*.

This different hermeneutical strategy is what is suggested by the initial probe into the same Synoptic tradition which both John and Thomas use and use differently. Does a wider probe confirm and clarify the initial suggestion, or point in another direction? The most obvious procedure is a wider probe into what can be discerned of the major objectives of John and Thomas, and into how they attempted to fulfil these objectives. We will look first at their respective christologies and at the good news which they sought to convey.

The Christologies of John and Thomas

John's Christology

As John 20:31 indicates, Jesus as Messiah, the Son of God, was the central thrust of his christology. For John it was (still) important that Jesus was *Messiah*. John in fact is the only NT writer who refers to Jesus as "Messiah" *(Messias)* (John 1:41; 4:25). The claim that Jesus was indeed Israel's Messiah was foundational for earliest Christianity, as indicated by the fact that "Christos" had become so established as an appellation for Jesus that it functioned largely as a proper name already in Paul. The same was true in the Jesus tradition in the Synoptics, where the confession of Peter that Jesus was the Christ played a central role (Mark 8:29 pars.) and his crucifixion for claiming to be the Christ was central to the climax of the passion narrative (Mark 14:61; 15:32 pars.). For John the claim remained central: to win belief that Jesus was indeed the Messiah was the principal aim of the Gospel (John 20:31), and unlike the Synoptics ("the messianic secret") the claim is broadcast openly from the first (John 1:41; 4:25-26).

Particularly striking is the way John adapted the traditions regarding John the Baptist to reinforce the messianic claim regarding Jesus. He does this by presenting the Baptist *as witness par excellence* to Jesus, and does so by *narrowing* the Baptist tradition so that it focuses almost exclusively on that role (already signalled in John 1:6-8).[29] So,

- John was not the light but came only to testify to the light (1:6-7, 31);
- the Messiah always ranked before him (1:15, 30);
- he was not the Messiah, as he himself triply confessed (1:20; 3:28);
- he had to decrease while Jesus increased (3:30);
- he came from the earth, whereas Jesus came from above, from heaven (3:31).

This we should note comes in typically Johannine language, so that we can certainly speak of the Johannine elaboration of the earlier tradition, whether that elaboration is to be traced to the Evangelist himself or to the (elaborated) traditions on which he drew. But we should also note that *the*

---

29. John 1:7-8, 15, 19, 32, 34; 3:26, 28; 5:33-34, 36. The point was made very effectively by W. Wink, *John the Baptist in the Gospel Tradition* (SNTSMS 7; Cambridge: Cambridge University Press, 1968), 87-106.

distinctive Johannine emphasis is rooted in the earlier tradition — of the Baptist speaking of the one to come as of a far higher status than his own ("I am not worthy to untie the thong of his sandals" — Mark 1:7 pars.).

Another intriguing feature is the way John represents the (still continuing?) dispute among Jews as to whether Jesus was Messiah. The issue is a major structural motif in the middle of the Gospel, particularly in ch. 7 (7:26-27, 31, 41-42), and the debate continues through the rest of the Book of Signs, with some believing and confessing Jesus as the Christ (9:22; 11:27), but others still swithering in uncertainty (10:24; 12:34). This motif, we may fairly infer, was well rooted in the earliest memories of Jesus' mission. For the question whether Jesus was Messiah was almost certainly a live issue during Jesus' mission. The impact he made would naturally have aroused the hopes of many (and suspicions of others).[30] So John is again drawing on good tradition, and his dramatization of the issue in this way is wholly understandable and should be uncontroversial.

Equally, probably more important for John was the claim that Jesus was the *Son of God;* in 20:31, "the Son of God" is an explanatory addition to the primary assertion, "Jesus is the Christ." That Jesus is God's Son indeed is John's principal means of identifying Jesus and his significance. Although the title was important for the Synoptics, it does not feature much in their Gospels. Only in Matthew is the Father-Son language extended. But in John the imagery becomes a cascade:[31] for example,

- the confessions of John 1:34, 49 and 11:27;
- the claim enhanced, Jesus as "the one and only *(monogenēs)* Son" (1:14; 3:16, 18; also 1:18);
- the Son commissioned by the Father (3:17; 5:22, 27; also 3:35; 5:19, 26);
- "The Father who sent me" becomes the most regular way in which Jesus speaks of and identifies God.[32]
- An interesting aspect is that John aligns "the Son of Man" motif with that of the Son of God; the apocalyptic Son of Man "coming on the clouds of heaven" disappears from view, and the Son of Man "de-

---

30. Dunn, *Jesus Remembered* §15.3.

31. J. Jeremias, *The Prayers of Jesus* (London: SCM, 1967), 30, 36 noted the tremendous expansion of references to God as "Father" in the words of Jesus within the Jesus tradition — Mark 3, Q 4, special Luke 4, special Matthew 31, John 100.

32. John 4:34; 5:23, 24, 30, 37; 6:38, 39, 44; 7:16, 18, 28, 33; 8:16, 18, 26, 29; 9:4; 12:44, 45, 49; 13:20; 14:24; 15:21; 16:5; also 3:17, 34; 5:36, 38; 6:29, 57; 7:29; 8:42; 10:36; 11:42; 17:3, 8, 18, 21, 23, 25; 20:21.

scending from heaven" (3:13) complements the Son of God sent by the Father.[33]

This Son of God/Son of Man christology of John's Gospel has certainly to be regarded as a substantial development within the Jesus tradition. But here not least the roots of the development are still very clear: in the early memory of Jesus' praying to God as "Abba," perhaps already elaborated in the Synoptic tradition;[34] in the similarly early memory of Jesus' occasional self-reference as one "sent" (by God);[35] it could even be claimed that the thought of Jesus as God's *only (monogenēs)* Son was an elaboration of the Synoptic tradition of Jesus as God's beloved (only?) son (Mark 1:11; 9:7; 12:6 pars.); and the familiarity of Jesus as "the Son of Man" in the Synoptics is too well known to require comment.[36]

The most distinctive feature of John's christology, of course, is his portrayal of Jesus as the divine *Logos* incarnate (John 1:1-18). Since the Logos-christology of John is not explicit in the rest of the Gospel, it is important to recognize that the prologue could be more accurately described as *Wisdom*-christology.[37]

- 1:1 — With you is wisdom, who knows your works and was present when you made the world (Wis 9:9; Prov 8:23, 27, 30);
- 1:3 — The Lord by wisdom founded the earth (Prov 3:19);
- 1:4 — Whoever finds wisdom finds life (Prov 8:35);
- 1:4 — All light comes from her (wisdom) (Aristobulus in Eusebius, *Praep. Evang.* 13.12.10; Bar 4:2);
- 1:5 — Wisdom's light prevails over the night and evil (Wis 7:29-30);

---

33. See also 6:33, 38-42, 50-51, 58, 62; cf. 1:51. The somewhat surprising assertion of 3:13 — "No one has ascended into heaven, except the one who descended from heaven" — may be directed against the characterization of the patriarchs and prophets as those who in effect ascended into heaven to hear (first hand) what God said, as suggested originally by H. Odeberg, *The Fourth Gospel* (Stockholm: Almqvist & Wiksells, 1929), 72-98.

34. Dunn, *Jesus Remembered*, 711-24.

35. Mark 9:37 pars.; 12:6 pars; Matt 15:24; Luke 4:18; 10:16.

36. Dunn, *Jesus Remembered* §§16.4-5.

37. There is a wide consensus on the point; see particularly C. A. Evans, *Word and Glory: On the Exegetical and Theological Background of John's Prologue* (JSNTS 89; Sheffield: JSOT, 1993), 83-94 (with bibliography in 83 n. 1); on parallels with Philo (100-13); J. F. McGrath, *John's Apologetic Christology: Legitimation and Development in Johannine Christology* (SNTSMS 111; Cambridge: Cambridge University Press, 2001), 136-43.

- 1:11 — Wisdom went forth to make her dwelling place among the children of men (Wis 9:10; Bar 3:37), but found none (*1 Enoch* 42:2);
- 1:14 — The one who created me assigned a place for my tent *(skēnēn)*. And he said, "Make your dwelling place *(kataskēnōson)* in Jacob" (Sir 24:8).

And it is equally important to realize that the Wisdom tradition seems to have provided much of the inspiration for the way John crafted his christology.[38] For example:

- 3:13 — Wisdom sent from heaven (Wis 9:16-17; Bar 3:29);
- 3:16-17 — Wisdom sent into the world to bring eternal life and salvation (Wis 8:13; 9:10, 17-18);
- 4:10, 14 — living water as especially the gift of Sophia (Sir 15:3; 24:21, 30-31; Bar 3:12);
- 6:30-58 — Sophia as the provider of both bread and drink (Prov 9:5; Sir 15:3);[39]
- 7:25-36 — Sophia's origins as a matter of speculation (Job 28:12-28; Bar 3:14-15);
- The "I am"s echo the kind of imagery and self-presentation characteristic of Wisdom (Proverbs 8; Sirach 24),[40] but also as elaborations of John 1:18 — Jesus as the exposition of the "I am" of Exod 3:14.[41]

---

38. "The fourth evangelist saw in Jesus the culmination of a tradition that runs through the Wisdom Literature of the OT; . . . in John, Jesus is personified Wisdom" (Brown, *John* 1:cxxii-cxxv). See also particularly J. M. C. Scott, *Sophia and the Johannine Jesus* (JSNTS 71; Sheffield: JSOT, 1992); M. E. Willett, *Wisdom Christology in the Fourth Gospel* (San Francisco: Mellen, 1992); B. Witherington, *John's Wisdom* (Louisville: Westminster John Knox, 1995), 18-27.

39. See also McGrath, *John's Apologetic Christology*, ch. 11.

40. "All of them [the I ams] except the 'good shepherd' are explicitly associated with Wisdom ('bread' in Sir. 24:21; the 'vine' in Sir. 24:17, 19; the 'way' in Prov. 3:17; 8:32; Sir. 6:26; 'light' in Wisd. Sol. 7:26; . . . ; 'truth' in Prov. 8:7; Wisd. Sol. 6:22; 'life' in Prov. 3:18; 8:35; and even 'gate of the sheep' . . . in Prov. 8:34-35)" — S. H. Ringe, *Wisdom's Friends: Community and Christology in the Fourth Gospel* (Louisville: Westminster John Knox, 1999), 61.

41. Note also Isa 41:4; 43:10, 25; 45:18-19; 46:4; 51:12; 52:6. See also C. H. Williams, "'I Am' or 'I Am He'? Self-Declaratory Pronouncements in the Fourth Gospel and Rabbinic Tradition," in Fortna and Thatcher, eds., *Jesus in Johannine Tradition*, 343-52; McGrath, *John's Apologetic Christology*, 109-15; H. Hübner, "EN ARCHĒ EGŌ EIMI," in M. Labahn et al., eds., *Israel und seine Heilstraditionen im Johannesevangelium* (Paderborn: Schöningh, 2004), 107-22.

The Earliest Interpreters of the Jesus Tradition

It cannot, should not, and need not be denied that in thus developing his presentation of Jesus, Messiah and Son of God, John has moved far beyond the Jesus tradition as most clearly attested in the Synoptic Gospels. Yet even here we can see the seeds out of which John grew the more exotic expressions of his christology.

- Jesus as the "word" is in a degree foreshadowed by Luke's prologue, where he speaks of "those who from the beginning were eyewitnesses and servants of the word" (Luke 1:2). Here Luke was no doubt thinking in terms of his regular reference to the gospel (Acts 2:41; 4:4, 29, 31; etc.), but the thought of Jesus as embodying that word is not far distant.
- The thought of Jesus as child of and spokesman for Wisdom is rooted in the Synoptic tradition (Luke 7:35; Jesus' aphoristic teaching); the link between Jesus as teacher of wisdom and Son of the Father is already made in the most Johannine statement of the Synoptics (Matt 11:25-27/Luke 10:21-22); and Matthew had already taken the step of identifying Jesus the teacher of wisdom with Wisdom herself.[42]
- Even the "I am"s are rooted in the earlier Synoptic tradition of Jesus walking on the water, and his numinous self-identification, "I am; do not be afraid" (Mark 6:50 par.), which John also records (John 6:20).

It is quite possible, then, to envisage how the Johannine Word/Wisdom christology is the product of long reflection on such features of the earlier Jesus tradition. In the light of Jesus' resurrection and exaltation to the right hand of God, as they believed, it was natural to see fuller and deeper significance in such features, and natural to develop a richer expression of them within the Gospel framework already established by the Synoptic Gospels.[43] The point is that John's developed christology can fairly be said to grow out of the earlier forms of the Jesus tradition attested in the Synoptic tradition, more an unfolding than an evolutionary mutation.

In a famous *bon mot* Rudolf Bultmann highlighted the role in John's Gospel of Jesus as the *revealer;* but all that he reveals is that he is the

---

42. Matt 11:19, 27-30; 23:34, 37-38. See M. J. Suggs, *Wisdom, Christology and Law in Matthew's Gospel* (Cambridge, MA: Harvard University Press, 1970), 67; and my *Christology in the Making* (London: SCM, 1980, ²1989), 202-4.

43. McGrath's thesis is that "the Fourth Evangelist adapted and developed the traditions which he inherited as part of a defence of his (and his community's) beliefs against objections raised by Jewish opponents" (*John's Apologetic Christology*, 230).

revealer!⁴⁴ That was an inadequate summary of John's purpose. For the significance of Jesus as the divine revealer for John was that he revealed *God*, the Son revealed *the Father*, the uttered Word revealed the one who uttered the word. To know this was to know the reality which Jesus was, and thus to know God, the Father. "This is eternal life that they know you, the only true God, and the one you sent, Jesus Christ" (17:3). So the revelation of God (1:18) was essentially salvific in effect — that is, it was also the conveyor of the life promised, as a process of revelation still continuing in the work of the *paraklētos* (John 16:12-15).

The same claim could be expressed in terms of illumination, the opening of blind eyes, the contrast between light and darkness (John 1:4-9; 3:19-21; 8:12; ch. 9); the link between life and light in 1:4 should not be missed. The thought here is probably a development of the theme of light which comes to expression several times in the Q material (Matt 5:14-16/Luke 8:16; Matt 6:22-23/Luke 11:33-35; Matt 10:27/Luke 12:3) — a theme taken up by Matthew and Luke in their own ways (Matt 4:16; Luke 22:56) — and John 9 represents a category of healing of the blind well known in the Synoptic tradition (Matt 11:5/Luke 7:22). Alternatively the same message could be given in terms of the *truth* which Jesus brought and embodied (as in 1:14, 17; 8:31-32; 18:37). Again the link between truth and life should be noted (14:6), as also that the *paraklētos* is "the Spirit of truth" (14:17; 15:26; 16:13). Somewhat curiously, the "truth" theme is not common in the Synoptic tradition, except that Jesus is acknowledged by opponents and admirers as a truth-teller (Mark 12:14 pars.; 12:32). So here again it can be said that John develops motifs and themes which were already present in the earlier Jesus tradition.

But here we have already moved into the second half of the deeper probe — into the good news as John saw it — so we return to a comparison with Thomas on the way Jesus is presented.

Thomas's Christology

The most immediate feature for any comparison on this point with the canonical Gospels is the absence of titles and names for Jesus familiar from

---

44. Bultmann, *Theology*, 2:66 — "Jesus as the Revealer of God *reveals nothing but that he is the Revealer*" (his emphasis); "in his Gospel (John) presents only the fact *(das Dass)* of the Revelation without describing its content *(ihr Was)*."

The Earliest Interpreters of the Jesus Tradition

these other Gospels. Jesus is never spoken of as Messiah or Christ.[45] The issue of whether he was Israel's Messiah, crucial for earliest Christianity, is never even alluded to. There is one reference to "the son of man" (Thomas 86), but it is not even very clear whether the phrase is a title referring to Jesus, or simply a reference to "the human being," who lacks any sense of belonging to this world, in contrast to foxes and birds.[46] Jesus is referred to only once as God's "Son" (Thomas 37) and never as "Lord." The curiosity of this fact should not be bypassed. For the strength of Thomas's claim to provide a witness to Jesus' mission and to the earliest positive response to that mission, a witness of value equal to or greater than the witness of the Synoptics, is that Thomas retains much of the content and character of Jesus' teaching and of the initial response to him. But the omission or ignorance of such key features of Jesus' mission and of the impact he made (as attested by the Synoptic tradition) inevitably poses the question of how deeply rooted the Thomas material actually was in the earliest traditions regarding Jesus. Had the earlier Jesus tradition that Thomas has retained become detached from its initial context and floated away in different currents within the religio-philosophical reflection of the period?

For Thomas the most characteristic way of referring to Jesus is as "the Living One" (Thomas Incipit, 52, 59, 111), though also as "the Son of the Living One" (37). The significance of Jesus is not dissimilar from John's christology, except that there is no sense of the limitations of Jesus as incarnate. Jesus is presented as the embodiment of "the light which is above all things. I am everything" (77). He is everywhere in the world: "Lift the stone and you will find me there. Split the wood and I am there" (30:3-4). To be far from him is to be far from the kingdom (82). And Jesus is presented as a model for those for whom Thomas was writing: "Jesus said, 'Whoever drinks from my mouth will become as I am. I myself will become that person, and what is hidden will be revealed to him'" (108).

In one of the most interesting logia, Thomas 13, already referred to, Thomas's equivalent of Peter's confession in Mark 8:29 pars., no attempt is made to correct or clarify the confessions (Peter — Jesus is "like a righteous angel"; Matthew — Jesus is "like a sage"). Instead Thomas is given secret knowledge which he is unable or unwilling to indulge. The implication may be that the revelation given secretly to Thomas is that Jesus shares

---

45. Though Thomas 52:1 reports the disciples saying to Jesus, "Twenty-four prophets have spoken in Israel, and all of them spoke about you."
46. DeConick, *Thomas*, 251-52.

the divine name.[47] In other words, the Thomas logion may have been trading on the speculation regarding the angel in whom God put his name (Exod 23:21) and correlated it with the Johannine elaboration of the same speculation (John 17:11). This would tie in also with Thomas 15,[48] where again John and Thomas seem to be close to each other: Jesus can be identified with the Father (cf. John 10:30; 14:9). Also with Thomas 61:2-5:[49] Jesus as equal with the Father (cf. John 5:18).

This brings us to what is probably the main distinctive of Thomas's christology: that Jesus is valued and reverenced in the Thomas tradition, not because of his mission in Galilee and Judea, and not because of his death and resurrection. He is the Living One because he represents the Father so completely. His significance for Thomas is primarily that he has brought the (saving) revelation.[50] Like the Johannine Christ he is the Revealer. But whereas John takes pains to correlate Jesus' role as Revealer with the story of Jesus' mission and the gospel of his death and resurrection, Thomas focuses almost exclusively on the revelation — "the secret words which the living Jesus spoke and which Didymus Judas Thomas wrote down" (Incipit).

So we turn to the second half of the deeper probe.

The Good News of John and Thomas

John's Good News

John's purpose is also clear from 20:31 — "that through believing you may have life in his (Jesus') name." John sums up the promise of his Gospel in terms of "life," another characteristically Johannine term.[51]

---

47. As DeConick notes, the *Acts of Thomas* alludes to Thomas 13 in ch. 47, and in ch. 133 states that the Name given to Jesus is "the exalted Name that is hidden from all" (Thomas 85).

48. Jesus said, "When you see the one who was not born of woman, fall on your face and worship him. That one is your Father."

49. Salome said, "Who are you, sir? That is, from (whom)? You have reclined on my couch and eaten at my table." Jesus said to her, "I am he who comes from the one who is an equal. I was given some who belong to my Father." "I am your disciple." "Therefore I say, when a person becomes (equal) (with me), he will be filled with light. But if he becomes separated (from me), he will be filled with darkness."

50. See also J. Schröter, "Die Herausforderung einer theologischen Interpretation des *Thomasevangeliums*," in J. Frey, et al., eds., *Das Thomasevangelium: Entstehung — Rezeption — Theologie* (BZNW 157; Berlin: de Gruyter, 2008), 435-59 (here 444-53).

51. *Zōē* ("life") — John 36x; other NT Gospels 16x. *Zaō* ("live") — John 17x; rest of Gospels 18x. "Eternal life" — John 17x; other Gospels 8x (see above n. 8).

The Earliest Interpreters of the Jesus Tradition

- 3:15, 16, 36 — "Whoever believes in him has eternal life" (also 6:40, 47);
- 4:10, 14 — the living water that Jesus gives will be a spring welling up to eternal life;
- 6:27, 33, 35, 48, 53, 54 — Jesus as the bread of life; those who eat his flesh and drink his blood have eternal life;
- 8:51-52 — "Whoever keeps my word will never see/taste death";
- 10:10 — "I came that they might have life and have it abundantly";
- 11:25 — "I am the resurrection and the life";
- 14:6 — "I am the way, the truth, and the life";
- 17:3 — "This is eternal life, that they may know you, the only true God, and Jesus Christ whom you have sent."

Typical of John is the thought that this eternal life is something which can be enjoyed now, something which the believer already *has* — John's typical way of speaking on the subject.[52] "Whoever keeps my word will never see/taste death" (8:51-52). Also characteristic of John is the way he ties in the thought of the Spirit of God as the instrument of life: the mystery of new birth is attributed to the Spirit (3:5-8); the "living water" (4:10, 14) is explicitly identified with the Spirit which those who believed in him were to receive (7:39); the Spirit is identified as "the life-giver" (6:63); and on the evening of Jesus' resurrection Jesus says, "Receive the Holy Spirit," and breathes *(enephysēsen)* on his disciples in an act of new creation (20:22, echoing the language of Gen 2:7 and Ezek 37:9). John also no doubt related this to the promise of the Spirit *(paraklētos)* in the farewell discourses (John 14:25-26; 15:26; 16:7-14) and makes a point of linking the gift of the Spirit and the life-giving water as part of the single event of Jesus' glorification in death, resurrection and ascension (John 19:30, 34; 20:22).

Here again we can see that John has developed the talk and promise of (eternal) life as it appears in the Synoptic tradition (Mark 9:43, 45 par.; 10:17, 30 pars.; Matt 7:14; 25:46). It was natural also to develop the promise of the Spirit in the Synoptic tradition (Mark 1:8 pars.; 13:11 pars.; Luke 11:13), and as the life-giver, to link the Spirit with the promise of life.

The way to receive this life is to *believe:* ". . . and that through believing you may have life in his name" (John 20:31). Curiously, John never uses the word "faith." But he uses the verb "believe" far more than any other NT writer.[53] His summons to believe is more insistent than any other NT Evan-

---

52. ". . . has eternal life" — 3:15, 16, 36; 5:24, 40; 6:40, 47, 53, 54; 10:10; 20:31.
53. Matthew 11x; Mark 14x; Luke 9x; Acts 37x; Paul 54x; John 98x.

gelist. For example: to bring about belief was the point of the Baptist's witness (1:7, 12); the signs Jesus did prompted people to believe in him (also 2:11, 23; 4:53; 7:31; 10:38, 41-42; 11:45; 12:11, 42; 14:11-12); the Son of Man would be lifted up "in order that everyone who believes in him might have eternal life" (also 3:15, 16, 36; 5:24; 6:40, 47); "This is the work of God, to believe in the one he has sent" (6:29); in the bread of life discourse it becomes clear that eating the bread/Jesus' flesh and drinking his blood are images for coming to and believing in him (6:37, 44-45, 51, 53);[54] "I am the resurrection and the life; he who believes in me will never die" (11:25-26); and so on.

Here again it is evident that John has developed a prominent strand in the earlier Synoptic tradition — even if he preferred the verb *(pisteuein)* to the noun *(pistis)*.[55] It is also noticeable that the call to believe is the only demand that John makes, the only response his Gospel seeks for. A call to "repent" or for "repentance" never crosses his lips, not even in describing the Baptist's mission — a central feature in the equivalent references to the Baptist in the Synoptics.[56] This is characteristic of John's reworking of the Jesus tradition: that he focuses on and enlarges elements and aspects that he wanted to emphasize, while ignoring or setting aside elements and aspects which did not advance the portrayal that he wanted to highlight.

Another interesting aspect of John's message, particularly when comparing with Thomas, is John's presentation of *the world as hostile*. *Kosmos* ("world") in fact is one of the most frequently used terms in the Johannine literature.[57] The "world" in John is where humankind live their lives (John 1:9), a realm of darkness (1:5; 3:19) in which those who belong to the world dwell (12:35-36). Satan is the ruler of this world.[58] The world hates Jesus' disciples as it hated him (15:18-19; 17:14); in the world they must expect persecution (16:33). But, rather astonishingly, it is just this world that God loves (John 3:16); he has sent his Son to save the world,[59] to give his life for

---

54. C. R. Koester, *Symbolism in the Fourth Gospel* (Minneapolis: Fortress, [2]2003), 99-104, 301-9. "To 'come' to Jesus means neither more nor less than to believe in him (5:40; 6:37, 44f., 65)" (Bultmann, *Theology* 2.70).

55. See above, n. 6.

56. Mark 1:4 par.; Matt 3:8/Luke 3:8; also Acts 13:24; 19:4.

57. Brown provides the following statistics (*John* 1:508):

Synoptics	John	1-3 John	Revelation	Total Johannine	Total NT
14	78	24	3	105	185

58. John 12:31; 14:30; 16:11.

59. John 3:17; 4:42; 12:47.

The Earliest Interpreters of the Jesus Tradition

the world (6:33, 51); Jesus is not of this world (8:23; 17:16; 18:36), but he is the lamb of God who takes away the sin of the world (1:29), the light of the world (8:12; 9:5; 12:46). Here again John has sharpened and deepened a sense both of the hostility of the world and of responsibility towards it which is present in the Synoptic tradition but in a much more limited way (Mark 4:19 pars.; 14:9 par.; Matt 5:14; 18:7; 24:14).

In each case, then, John has developed and in most cases substantially elaborated motifs and themes which were part of the early Jesus tradition, indicative of the impact that Jesus made as that was expressed in the Synoptic tradition. In no case was there an imposition of themes and motifs which were strange to the earlier tradition, or a diverting of the tradition into wholly divergent paths. In each case the paths, which did take readers and auditors well beyond the Synoptic tradition, can be traced back into the earlier Jesus tradition itself. This is what I mean by describing the Johannine development and elaboration of the Jesus tradition as a growth from within, an unexpected flowering for many, no doubt, but not an attempt to grow figs on olive trees.

Thomas's Good News

So far, particularly in the theme of Jesus as revealer, John and Thomas run on parallel lines. However, it is in the message which is revealed in Thomas that the ways have clearly parted between the two developments of the early Jesus tradition.

A strong underlying assumption is that those for whom Thomas has been written and circulated were people who believed that their *true nature and spiritual home is different from their existence in this world*. For example,[60]

- 3:3-4 — "The kingdom is within you. When you know yourselves, then you will be known; and you will know that you are sons of the living Father."
- 19:1 — Jesus said, "Blessed is he who was before he was born."
- 49 — Jesus said, "Blessed are the celibate people, the chosen ones, because you will find the kingdom. For you are from it. You will return there again."

60. See also Thomas 18, 67, 83, 111:2-3.

- 50 — Jesus said, "If they say to you, 'Where did you come from?,' say to them, 'we came from the light' — the place where the light came into being of its own accord and established (itself) and became manifest through their image. If they say to you, 'Is it you?,' say, 'We are its children, and we are the chosen people of the living Father.' If they ask you, 'What is the sign of your Father in you?,' say to them, 'It is movement and rest.'"
- 84 — Jesus said, "When you see the likeness of yourselves, you are delighted. But when you see the images of yourselves which came into being before you — which neither die nor are visible — how much you will suffer."[61]

Such people may be ignorant of their true nature and origin, and *unaware* of, *lacking knowledge* of the real contrast between their true nature and their present existence. For example,[62]

- 3:5 — When you know yourselves, you will know that you are sons of the living Father. But if you do not know yourselves, then you are in poverty, and you are poverty.
- 28 — Jesus said, "I stood in the midst of the world, and I appeared to them in flesh. I found all of them drunk. I found none of them thirsty. And my soul suffered pain for the sons of men, because they are blind in their hearts and do not see that they have come into the world empty, seeking to go out of the world empty again. But now they are drunk. When they shake off (the effects of) their wine, then they will repent."
- 29 — Jesus said, "If the flesh existed for the sake of the Spirit, it would be a miracle. If the Spirit (existed) for the sake of the body, it would be a miracle of miracles! But I marvel at how this great wealth settled in this poverty."

Bound up with this is what seems to be a form of Adam theology (Thomas 85), that the *original divine image was androgynous* (a way of reconciling the two creation stories — Gen 1:26-27 and 2:7, 22), so that resto-

---

61. On *Thomas* 83 and 84 see particularly E. E. Popkes, "The Image Character of Human Existence: *GThom* 83 and *GThom* 84 as Core Texts of the Anthropology of the *Gospel of Thomas*," in Frey, ed., *Das Thomasevangelium*, 416-34.

62. See also Thomas 56 = 80, 70, 87, 112.

ration to primal purity was a return from the two to the one, and women becoming men. For example,

- 11:3-4 — When you are in the light, what will you become? On the day when you were one, you became two. But when you are two, what will you become?
- 22:4-7 — Jesus said to them, "When you make the two one, and make the outside like the inside, and the above like the below. And when you make the male and the female into a single being, with the result that the male is not male nor the female female. When you make eyes in place of an eye, and a hand in place of a hand, and a foot in place of a foot, and an image in place of an image, then you will enter (the kingdom)."[63]
- 106:1 — Jesus said, "When you make the two one, you will become sons of man."
- 114 — Simon Peter said to them, "Mary should leave us because women are not worthy of life." Jesus said, "Look, I shall lead her, in order to make her male, so that she too may become a living spirit, resembling you males. For every woman who will make herself male will enter the kingdom of heaven."[64]

Unlike John, there is no call for belief. The solution to the human plight is not to believe in Jesus, but to accept the revelation he has brought, and to live accordingly. The good news is that by ascetic discipline the one to whom the revelation is given will enter the kingdom. The ethical corollary seems to have been a *strongly ascetic* code of practice, including a high regard for celibacy. In consequence, Thomas is frequently regarded as emanating from encratite circles,[65] but notably lacking in

---

63. Discussion in R. Uro, "Is *Thomas* an Encratite Gospel?," in Uro, ed., Thomas *at the Crossroads*, 140-62 (here 149-56), with reference to the parallels in 2 Clem 12:2, 6 and the *Gospel of Egyptians*, cited by Clement of Alexandria in his *Stromateis* 3.13.92.

64. A. Marjanen, "Women Disciples in the *Gospel of Thomas*," in Uro, ed., Thomas *at the Crossroads*, 89-106, suggests that the saying reflects a tendency towards a more rigid lifestyle among some Thomasine Christians, and perhaps a conflict between two strongly ascetic positions, one insisting on the complete exclusion of women, the other maintaining that the hope of salvation included women.

65. "Encratite" was "a title applied to several groups of early Christians who carried their ascetic practice and doctrine to extremes"; referred to by Irenaeus, Clement of Alexandria and Hippolytus, but without precision, and including Gnostic, Ebionite and Docetic sects (*ODCC* 545). Uro notes that "*Thomas* praises those who have broken with their fami-

community or ecclesiastical concerns.⁶⁶ The hostility to the world is far more dualistic than John's, and wholly lacks the Johannine concern for the world. For example,⁶⁷

- 21:1-4 — Mary said to Jesus, "What are your disciples like?" He said, "They are like little children who dwell in a field which does not belong to them. When the owners of the field come, they will say, 'Leave our field to us!' In front of them, they strip naked in order to abandon it, returning their field to them."
- 37 — His disciples said, "When will you appear to us? When will we see you?" Jesus said, "When you strip naked without shame, take your garments, put them under your feet like little children, and trample on them. Then (you will see) the son of the Living One, and you will not be afraid."
- 75 — Jesus said, "Many are standing at the door, but those who are celibate are the (only) ones who will enter the bridal chamber."

The narrative underlying all this is fairly clear, familiar particularly from Gnostic literature. It is of individuals who perceive their real selves and true home to be other than this world, of a spirituality entirely uncomfortable with existence in the material world. Not all for whom this is the case are aware of their true spiritual selves, their true spiritual origin and home. The good news is that Jesus came from there, the kingdom of the Father, his teaching bringing the secret wisdom which is the revelation of their true being and counsel on how to act now to ensure return to that kingdom.⁶⁸ Whether this should be described as "gnostic" depends on one's

---

lies and have become 'solitary,' but never directly rejects marriage and sexual intercourse"; he concludes that *Thomas* does not derive from a strictly encratite sect as such, "even though encratite tendencies must have occurred in *Thomas'* environment" ("Is *Thomas* an Encratite Gospel?" 161).

66. B. Blatz, "The Coptic Gospel of Thomas," in W. Schneemelcher, ed., *New Testament Apocrypha* (2 vols. ET Cambridge: James Clarke, 1991), 1:114.

67. See also Thomas 4:2-4; 16:4; 23:2; 105.

68. Cf. J. M. Robinson, ed., *The Nag Hammadi Library* (Leiden: Brill, 1988), 1-10; Koester, *Ancient Christian Gospels,* 124-28. A. D. DeConick, *Voices of the Mystics: Early Christian Discourse in the Gospels of John and Thomas and Other Ancient Christian Literature* (JSNTS 157; Sheffield Academic, 2001) argues that "the Thomasine Christians were mystics seeking visions of God for the purpose of immortalization"; the encratite lifestyle was "the way to be in a state of continual purification and sinlessness, a state of readiness for the dangerous journey" (107-8).

definition of Gnosticism.[69] But if "gnostic" can properly be used for a widespread spirituality which assumed a basic dualism between spirit and matter, which felt itself to be not at home in and at odds with the world, and which looked for an answer which resolved the paradox of human existence (in terms of knowledge of their true identity and an accordingly ascetic lifestyle), then Thomas can be described as "gnostic."[70]

Two Different Hermeneutical Strategies

In John's Gospel we see a presentation of Jesus' mission and of Jesus' teaching whose roots can readily be traced back to the earliest impact made by Jesus as attested in the Synoptic tradition. The early tradition has evidently been reflected on for many years. The Gospel of John is the fruit of that reflection. In effect John has stripped that tradition down to what he regarded as its principal features, and these have been the focus of that reflection. In what stands as the final stage of that reflection, we see these principal features of the earlier tradition expanded and elaborated, well beyond what the Synoptic Evangelists allowed themselves to do in their Gospels. We see elements which were present but not prominent in the earlier tradition brought into the spotlight and their significance brought out at length. We see elements which one or more of the earlier Gospels had already reflected on and developed, even if modestly, similarly brought to centre stage and given a prominence which showed how much more light could be shed on the significance of Jesus' mission and teaching. This I characterize as a development of the earlier Jesus tradition *from within*.

In contrast, whatever the label we attach to Thomas's gospel, the essential point is that the basic narrative which holds the Thomas tradition together is distinctly other than what we find in the Synoptic and even the

---

69. Like "the pre-Christian Gnostic Redeemer myth," and the "divine man" — important reference points in twentieth-century NT study — "Gnosticism" is more a modern construct than a historical phenomenon; see particularly M. A. Williams, *Rethinking "Gnosticism": An Argument for Dismantling a Dubious Category* (Princeton: Princeton University Press, 1996).

70. See also Cameron, *ABD* 6:539; Popkes, "Image Character," 431-33. Although a similar argument could be made for calling John's Gospel "gnostic" (Uro, *Thomas at the Crossroads*, 5), unlike the distinctive *Thomas* tradition, the distinctive features of John's Gospel are firmly rooted in the earlier Jesus tradition. See further A. Marjanen, "Is *Thomas* a Gnostic Gospel?," in Uro, ed., *Thomas at the Crossroads*, 107-39.

Johannine traditions.[71] The distinctive message of Thomas comes from a source and an explanation of the human condition which is not to be found elsewhere in the Jesus tradition. It is an import into that tradition. There are sufficient elements in the Synoptic tradition which Thomas was able to use and to blend into its underlying narrative. But it is hard to see the distinctive Thomas message as drawn from the Jesus tradition as attested in the Synoptic tradition. Thomas has a very different "take" on human existence, even though Jesus, drawn into that milieu, was evidently believed to be the one whose teaching brought them the message which the Thomas community needed. Quite a number of Jesus' sayings could be heard as speaking to their situation.[72] But the recognizable Jesus tradition was essentially a bolt-on addition to a framework which originated in a different perception of reality from that of the Jewish scriptures and of the Jesus tradition known to us from the Synoptic tradition.

There are various parallels between John and Thomas, notably in the presentation of Jesus as a revealer, who can be identified with God. But the content of the good news revealed is very different; the attitude to the world is very different; the response called for is very different; the degree of rootedness in the earlier Jesus tradition is very different. It can certainly be argued that the Thomas community, or its direct predecessors, were influenced by the Synoptic tradition known to them, but not because they could unfold it to bring out its message, as did John, not because they could draw out their distinctive message from it, as did John. Rather the Thomas people found the earlier Jesus tradition attractive because it helped to fill out their own instinctive narrative, because it spoke to a self-understanding which they derived from elsewhere than Jesus. Not entirely unlike John, Thomas people found in the Jesus tradition a figure whose teaching contained revelation which they could add to their own instinctive insights. But in effect, the Jesus tradition which appealed to them was simply tacked on to their basic "gnostic" world-view and spirituality.

In short, John developed the Synoptic Jesus tradition *from the inside*, expanding the meaning of the inherited Synoptic tradition, with a message still rooted in the Old Testament and still of immediate relevance to "the Jews." In contrast, Thomas worked on the early Jesus tradition *from the*

---

71. Cf. the analysis of Thomas's characteristic and distinctive vocabulary and themes by A. D. DeConick, *Recovering the Original* Gospel of Thomas: *A History of the Gospel and Its Growth* (LNTS 286; London: T&T Clark, 2005), 71-76.

72. E.g., Thomas 3, 5, 39, 76, 86, 92.

The Earliest Interpreters of the Jesus Tradition

outside: it addresses a different constituency of humankind, with a very different understanding of the human situation and a very different understanding of the good news which it needed; by tacking on a range of early Jesus tradition, which could be read in the light of that other philosophy, presumably Thomas hoped to enlarge the appeal of his message. But Thomas's use of the early Jesus tradition is more like a hostile takeover, whereas John's is like an heir exploring the richness of the inheritance which had come to him from Jesus through the Jesus tradition.

All this makes clearer why John was preserved within the canon of the New Testament by the great church, and why Thomas was rejected. The different hermeneutical strategies made the difference. And the corollary for church tradition — and for translating scripture into other languages — should not be ignored. If John is a precedent and model, then the acceptable hermeneutic is one which draws out from within the earlier tradition (scripture) what it sees to be of continuing or newly perceived significance. If Thomas is the warning precedent, then the hermeneutic which should be regarded with suspicion is one which makes a philosophy with different roots the key to understanding the earlier tradition (scripture), or which simply attaches elements from scripture on to a frame or narrative drawn from elsewhere.

Metaphors, Cognitive Theory, and Jesus' Shortest Parable

David Parris

Metaphor plays a central role in Paul Ricoeur's hermeneutical theory. According to Ricoeur, metaphor has its feet firmly planted in both poetry and rhetoric, *poiesis* and *mimesis*. Metaphors imitate reality in some manner, *mimesis*, but this is not a mere copying but rather a re-presentation of its subject that results in a new perception of the subject, *poiesis*. Metaphors are not mere linguistic ornamentation, but allow us to creatively see the referent(s) of the metaphor in new ways. As a result, metaphors cannot be reduced to description but always possess a surplus of meaning that can "give rise to thought."[1] This chapter will not explore how metaphors accomplish this through *poiesis* and *mimesis* as Ricoeur claims and Anthony Thiselton has covered in other locations. Rather, I will take a different line of questioning, and ask how resources within Cognitive Theory complement Ricoeur's work and shed insight into how metaphors "give rise to thought."

Cognitive Theory is a multidisciplinary field studying how the mind and intelligence function that dates its inception to the late 1970s with the formation of the Cognitive Science Society and the publication of the journal *Cognitive Science* (1980). Its contributors come from the fields of

---

1. Paul Ricoeur, *The Rule of Metaphor* (Toronto: University of Toronto Press, 1977), 6; idem, *Hermeneutics and the Human Sciences* (Cambridge: Cambridge University Press, 1981), 287-334.

This chapter represents a condensation of two papers that were originally presented as: "Cognitive Metaphors and Parables," Rocky Mountain and Great Plains Regional Meeting (Denver, CO, March 28-29, 2008), and "Cognitive Theory, Parables and Luke 4:23," Use of Cognitive Linguistics in Biblical Interpretation Consultation, Annual SBL Conference (Boston, MA, November, 2008).

Metaphors, Cognitive Theory, and Jesus' Shortest Parable

psychology, neuroscience, anthropology, linguistics, philosophy, and literary theory. A core tenet to Cognitive Theory is that human thought operates by means of representational structures on which we can perform a number of different procedures. Even though every human being shares certain basic mental operations, how these operations are carried out lead to very different cultural manifestations. These representational structures and the computational procedures can be investigated by means of theory and experimentation. Due to the diversity of fields participating in Cognitive Theory this paper will primarily concentrate on the contributions from the linguistic and literary sides of the field.

Cognitive Metaphor Theory

George Lakoff and Mark Johnson are often credited with initiating this line of thought with the publication of *Metaphors We Live By* in 1980. They argued that metaphorical thought is one of the most basic and powerful mental procedures. Metaphors are not merely linguistic flourish but structure our most basic understandings of the world.[2]

The *Oxford Concise Dictionary* defines metaphor as a figure of speech in which a descriptive term or phrase is figuratively applied to another object or concept.[3] Aspects of the meaning or connotations from the source (often referred to as the vehicle) are applied to the target (the tenor) in a fairly straightforward manner. We could diagram this conception of a metaphor in the following manner:

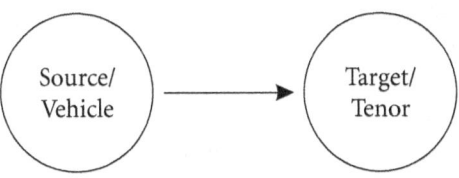

FIGURE 1   *Traditional view of metaphors*

---

2. It is significant to note that Lakoff and Johnson acknowledge that they have been "significantly influenced by Paul Ricoeur" in the acknowledgments to their work. George Lakoff and Mark Johnson, *Metaphors We Live By* (Chicago and London: University of Chicago Press, 1980), xii.

3. "Metaphor," in *Concise Oxford Dictionary,* ed. Robert Allen (New York and Oxford: Oxford University Press, 1990).

This definition contains five assumptions that Cognitive Theorists reject: (1) that metaphor is a matter of word usage, (2) it is based on a similarity between the two terms, (3) that concepts and truth are based on literal not metaphorical language, (4) it does not take into consideration how our bodies and brains shape our thoughts, and (5) this view primarily conceives of metaphor in terms of individual instances of figurative uses of language and not in terms of connections made at the conceptual level that form many of our basic patterns of thought.[4] Ricoeur would add that one of the greatest weaknesses to the traditional view is that it fails to grasp a metaphor's ability to tell us something new.[5]

Metaphors are based not so much on similarity between two concepts but operate by means of inferences and blending. Basic conceptual metaphors draw inferences from our physical experience of the world (the sensory-motor domains — space and objects) and apply them to other fields such as emotions, intimacy and so on.[6] These proto-metaphors are like cognitive blue-prints that form patterns that we employ to organize how we understand the world. Because metaphors are pervasive in our everyday lives, thought, and communication, they tend to structure and give coherence to how we understand our world and live our lives.[7] Thus, the title of their book: *Metaphors We Live By*.

Conceptual Metaphors and Blending

Metaphors are the primary vehicle we cognitively employ when we integrate two mental ideas, notions, or thoughts. "Mental spaces," or "domains," "are small conceptual packets constructed as we think and talk, for purposes of local understanding and action."[8] A metaphor is the result of a "blend" that draws from both source and target mental spaces. A metaphor is not just un-

---

4. Lakoff and Johnson, *Metaphors We Live By*, 244; Joseph E. Grady, "Metaphor," in *The Oxford Handbook of Cognitive Linguistics*, ed. Dirk Geeraerts and Hubert Cuyckens (Oxford: Oxford University Press, 2007), 188-89, 191; Mark Turner, *Death Is the Mother of Beauty: Mind, Metaphor, Criticism* (Christchurch, NZ: Cybereditions, 2000), 18-21.

5. Ricoeur, *Hermeneutics and the Human Sciences*, 12.

6. Lakoff and Johnson, *Metaphors We Live By*, 14-32; Sandra Blakeslee and Matthew Blakeslee, *The Body Has a Mind of Its Own: How Body Maps in Your Brain Help You Do (Almost) Everything Better* (New York: Random House, 2008), 4-14.

7. Lakoff and Johnson, *Metaphors We Live By*, 4-6, 194.

8. Gilles Fauconnier and Mark Turner, "Conceptual Integration Networks," *Cognitive Science* 22, no. 2 (2001): 133-87; Grady, "Metaphor," 199.

Metaphors, Cognitive Theory, and Jesus' Shortest Parable

derstanding one thing in terms of another but is the result of a new, blended mental space that selectively incorporates elements from both the source and target spaces and possesses its own unique structure, organization, and meaning. As Ricoeur wrote, "If the essence of metaphor is to 'present an idea under the sign of another idea that is more striking or better known,' *does not the procedure consist as much in combining as in substituting?*"[9]

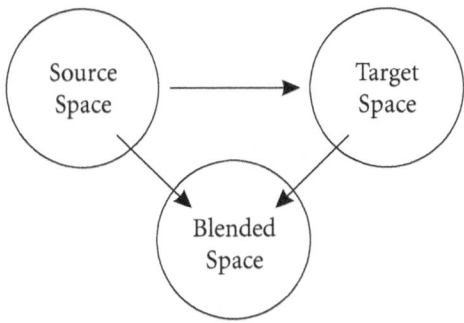

FIGURE 2   *Three Space Model*

Mark Turner uses the following visual example to explain conceptual blending. In a German advertisement for Toblerone chocolate, the pyramids of Giza are depicted in the background with pieces of Toblerone arranged in a similar configuration in the foreground. The top of the page reads *"Antiker Tobleronismus?"* This advertisement creates a blended space between two mental spaces: the ancient pyramids of Giza and the contemporary chocolate. The only similarity the two mental spaces share is the triangular profile of the pyramids and the chocolate bar. However, this advertisement achieves a lot more than bringing that similarity to the reader's attention. The time frames between the modern and ancient are compressed into one time frame in the image and, in fact, they are even reversed. The inspiration for the ancient pyramids was Toblerone chocolate, as the tag line at the bottom reads *"Inspiration ist Alles."*[10]

---

9. Ricouer, *Rule of Metaphor*, 179-80 (emphasis mine).

10. Turner in his interview with Underhill. Toblerone is a metaphorical blend on several levels. At the lexical level the name "Toblerone" is a blend of Theodore Tobler's family name and the Italian word for nougat, *"torrone."* But contrary to the idea that the Matterhorn or the pyramids were the inspiration for Toblerone's unique shape, his sons confess that it has a sexier origin. Theodore was paying homage to the dancers at the Folies Bergères who would form human pyramids at the conclusion to their performances. "Toblerone,

This graphical advertisement foregrounds how metaphorical blending operates, often in subconscious ways, in our daily lives. "We encounter such an ad as we are flipping negligently through a magazine and we absorb it in a second. The conceptual work involved in absorbing it is exceptionally difficult, but it seems to us entirely easy, even enjoyable."[11]

Cross-Space Mapping

One of the tools employed to elucidate how metaphors and conceptual blending operates is that of cross-space mapping. Consider the following example that Fauconnier and Turner cite:

> As we went to press, Rich Wilson and Bill Biewenga were barely maintaining a 4.5 day lead over the clipper Northern Light, whose record run from San Francisco to Boston they're trying to beat. In 1853, the clipper made the passage in 76 days, 8 hours. — "Great America II," *Latitude* 38, volume 190, April 1993, page 100.[12]

In order to understand this passage the reader must construct four different mental spaces. One for the clipper ship, the *Northern Light*, making its record-setting run in 1853. The second for the contemporary racing catamaran, *Great America II*. Third, a blended space in which both ships are competing against each other over a set course. This blend allows us to conceptually compare the relative positions of the two ships by mapping them simultaneously on the same route. A fourth mental space is constructed as well, that of a generic middle space (see figure 3). The generic space contains what the source spaces have in common and a skeletal structure that is appropriate to both spaces. The generic space also gives rise to a structural topography that shapes how the blend is construed.[13] In this instance, the generic space would include boats, path (with start and stop points), and the time to traverse the path.

Chocolate, Our Secret," Kraft Foods, 2009 [online] http://www.toblerone.co.uk/toblerone1/page?siteid=toblerone1-prd&locale=uken1&PagecRef=586. January, 2010.

11. Underhill, "Interview," 707.

12. Cited in Fauconnier and Turner, "Conceptual Projection and Middle Spaces," *UCSD Department of Cognitive Science*, report 9401 (1994): 7; citing "Great America II," *Latitude* 38 (April 1993): 100.

13. Mark Turner, *The Literary Mind* (New York and Oxford: Oxford University Press, 1996), 86-93.

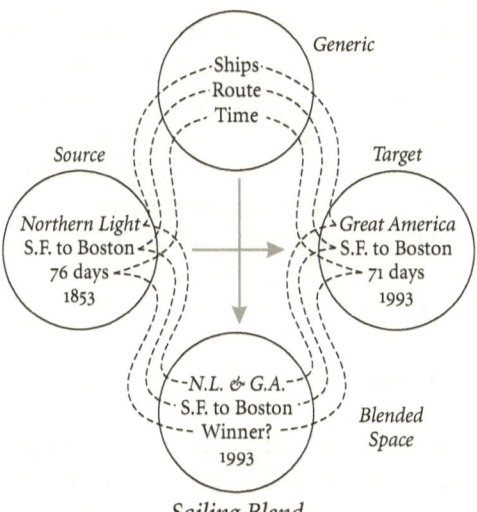

FIGURE 3   *Sailing Blend*

This blend achieves far more than allowing us to compare the relative positions of the two ships. The primary structure that this blended space employs is that of a *race*, something completely absent from either of the two source domains. The structure of a *race* is consonant with what is being appropriated from the two source spaces: two boats, a course, and time keeping. As a result, the blended space creates a richer structure and inferencing than is found in either of the source spaces.[14] Not only does it allow us to compare the position of the two boats (which in reality are separated by more than 100 years), the chance of breaking the record, but it also creates an image of the *Great America*'s crew running on adrenaline trying to maintain their lead, their determination and anxiety, and the possibility of some form of celebration in Boston harbor if they beat the *Northern Light*.

Blending is always selective and partial. The blended space created in regard to these two ships conceals and reveals features from both source spaces.[15] In this instance, the blend does not incorporate the time of year,

14. Blends allow us to make predictions and evaluations, plan, explain, categorize events and objects, make projections, and incorporate image schemas. Turner, *Literary Mind*, 9-11.

15. This aspect of metaphorical blending has parallels with Heidegger's concept of truth as ἀλήθεια, "unconcealment." In every disclosure of truth not only is something revealed but something is concealed as well. Martin Heidegger, *Being and Time* (Oxford: Blackwell, 1962, 1992 reprint), 261-65; David Parris, *Reception Theory and Biblical Hermeneutics* (Eugene, OR: Pickwick, 2009), 76-80.

weather, number of crew members, or that one was a commercial clipper ship and the other a custom racing yacht. It also contains more than either of the input spaces possessed in that two boats are present in the same mental space. And the relationship between the two boats is structured by their racing each other. The purpose of this blend is to project a mental space where we can arrive at conclusions about the possible success of *Great America*'s attempt to set a new record time and the drama involved in their endeavor.

Case Study: "Physician, heal thyself!" Luke 4:23

While blends about Swiss chocolates and racing catamarans may be interesting in their own right, we need to turn our attention to metaphorical blending in the biblical text. In this regard, I have chosen Jesus' statement in Luke 4:23 as a case study for two reasons. First, the parable that Jesus utters in this verse, "Physician, heal thyself!" is the shortest parable in the New Testament. The brevity of this parable presents a challenge: *How much thought can arise* in just three words? Second, this parable is based on an established metaphorical blend between doctors and teachers. The conventional nature of this parable opens the door for hermeneutical inquiry into how speakers employed statements analogous to that recorded in Luke. Rather than being isolated linguistic flourishes, metaphors often depend on culturally established patterns and conceptual associations.[16] By diachronically and synchronically examining the frames that stand behind proverbs comparable to this one in Greek/Roman and Hebrew cultures we can arrive at a clearer understanding of how this statement is functioning in Luke.

Greco-Roman Frames

"Frames" provide us with the background knowledge, or network of beliefs, that allow us to grasp the concepts within a mental space profile. Or to put it another way, when we employ a particular word it activates a "frame" that allows us to see conceptual relationships between that word and others, and provides us with a particular perspective into that semantic frame.[17]

---

16. Grady, "Metaphor," 190.

17. Semantic Frames share similarities with Searle's concepts of network of beliefs and

Metaphors, Cognitive Theory, and Jesus' Shortest Parable

Therefore, it is essential that we understand the semantic and conceptual frames that the terms "physician" and "healing" invoked in the social institutions and structures of experience in first-century Greco-Roman and Jewish cultures.[18]

Physicians enjoyed a higher social standing in Greek culture (but were not part of the social or political elite) than Latin societies and were often considered equivalent to teachers, philosophers, or mathematicians. In both Greek and Latin literature there is an abundance of texts that skeptically recount the abuses and quackery within the medical practices because the healing rates were often so abysmal. Martial quipped that "until recently, Diaulus was a doctor; now he is an undertaker. He is still doing as an undertaker, what he used to do as a doctor."[19]

In contrast with today's practices, the boundary between medical and religious practices was very porous in Greco-Roman cultures. Often they learned and practiced their trade in conjunction with Ascelpion sanctuaries. This is clearly evidenced in the opening line of the original Hippocratic oath where the gods Apollo, Asclepius, Hygia, and Panacea were invoked even though Hippocrates is credited with attempting to turn medical understanding from supernatural causes and cures to observation and the use of diet and drugs to bring the bodily humors back into balance.[20]

Heidegger's *Vorhabe, Vorsicht,* and *Vorgriff.* John R. Searle, *Intentionality: An Essay in the Philosophy of Mind* (Cambridge: Cambridge University Press, 1983), 144-57; Martin Heidegger, *Being and Time* (repr. Oxford: Blackwell, 1992), 27-28, 191-94; for a fuller discussion see Parris, *Reception Theory and Biblical Hermeneutics,* 179-82.

18. For a fuller discussion of "frames" see Charles Fillmore's article, "Frame Semantics," in *Cognitive Linguistics: Basic Readings,* ed. Dirk Geeraerts (Berlin: Mouton de Gruyter, 2006), 373-400; Ricoeur, *Hermeneutics and the Human Sciences,* 172.

19. Martial, *Epigrams* 1.47. Evidence for the public mistrust of physicians is plentiful, including these epigrams: "Socles, promising to set Diodorus's crooked back straight, piled three solid stones, each four feet square, on the hunchback's spine. He was crushed and died, but he became straighter than a ruler." "The Convivial and Satirical Epigrams," in *Greek Anthology,* trans. W. R. Paton, Loeb Classical Library (Cambridge, MA: Harvard University Press, 1918), IV.XI.120. "Alexis the physician purged by a clyster five patients at one time, and five others by drugs; he visited five, and again he rubbed five with ointment. And for all there was one night, one medicine, one coffin-maker, one tomb, one Hades, one lamentation." *Greek Anthology,* IV.XI.122.

20. Ὄμνυμι Ἀπόλλυνα ἰητρὸν, καὶ Ἀσκληπιὸν, καὶ Ὑγιείαν, καὶ Πανάκειαν, καὶ θεοὺς πάντας τε καὶ πάσας, ἵστορας ποιεύμενος, ἐπιτελέα ποιήσειν κατὰ δύναμιν καὶ κρίσιν ἐμὴν ὅρκον τόνδε καὶ συγγραφὴν τήνδε. Hippocrates, *Opera Omnia. Texte grec avec traduction latine et commentaires,* ed. Anuce Foes (Francfort sur le Main: Wechel héritiers d'André, 1595), 1; "I swear by Apollo the Physician and by Asclepius and by Health [the god Hygieia]

One final point concerning how illness was perceived should be noted about this frame. There are three orientations toward illnesses that help us compare contemporary perspectives on illness with those found in the ancient world. First, illness then was something that impinged upon social groups collectively where we tend to view illness primarily affecting the individual today. Second, we tend to view illnesses as a loss of functionality (a blind person lacks the ability to see) whereas in the Ancient Near East illness was primarily seen as a reduced state of being (to be blind was to suffer a loss or diminution of what it meant to be a human being). And finally, our medical practices are based on the assumption that by means of science we can manipulate the natural world to restore functionality to an individual. In their worldview, they were at the mercy of the natural and supernatural realms. So an effective treatment for an illness involved restoring balance to that person's life or supplying meaning to one's suffering.[21]

In Greco-Roman culture, the Hippocratic corpus provides us with a wealth of information about physicians. The personal appearance of the physician was significant for Hippocrates. "The dignity of a physician requires that he should look healthy, and as plump as nature intended him to be; for the common crowd consider those who are not of this excellent bodily condition to be unable to take care of others."[22] As far as possible they should present themselves as clean, well-dressed, serious-minded gentlemen. The first step in the hermeneutical interaction between the sick person and the healer involves the personal appearance of the physician.[23] Not only is the physician interpreting the signs in the patient but the patient is reading a specific set of indicators off the healer, indicators which, if absent, negatively impact the interaction between physician and patient.

Toward the tail end of the classical Greek medical tradition, Galen illustrated the perseverance of Hippocrates' counsel when he admonished his students:

---

and Panacea and by all the gods as well as goddesses, making them judges [witnesses], to bring the following oath and written contract to fulfillment, in accordance with my power and judgment." Steven H. Miles, *The Hippocratic Oath and the Ethics of Medicine* (New York: Oxford University Press, 2004), xiii.

21. John J. Pilch, *Healing in the New Testament: Insights from Medical and Mediterranean Anthropology* (Minneapolis: Fortress, 2000), 3-13.

22. Hippocrates, *The Physician*, 147.2, trans. W. H. S. Jones, Loeb Classical Library (Cambridge, MA: Harvard University Press, 1923), 311.

23. "What takes place in the interaction is interpretation of symbols and signs in terms of very particular interpretive schemata." Pilch, *Healing in the New Testament*, 30.

ἐχρῆν οὖν αὐτὸν ἑαυτοῦ πρῶτον ἰᾶσθαι τὸ σύμπτωμα
καὶ οὕτως ἐπιχειρεῖν ἑτέρους θεραπεύειν.

Therefore, he (the doctor) should first heal his own symptoms and thus (in this manner) lay hands on others to heal.[24]

Galen's sage advice reiterated the conventional frames that the other authors activated in their use of the proverbs along these lines: namely, that physicians must see to their own health first before they attempt to treat others. As John Cassian wrote, "one who is himself not subject to infirmity brings remedies to one in weak health."[25] There are probably two basic metaphorical schemas that stand behind this advice. First is the concept of causation. A very prototypical understanding of causation is our experience of direct manipulation of our environment. Thus, as agents we change our environment (the patient) by our actions, plans, being the force behind an action, and being responsible for the changes that we effect.[26] This then forms a gestalt image for the physician being the source of causation in the healing encounter.[27] If healers are weak, or sick, they lack what is needed to "cause" the cure in the patient. Second is the mapping of non-physical concepts to physical ones. The internal qualities of the learning, wisdom, and skill that the healer possesses are projected onto the external manifestations in their personal well-being. A lack of health on the part of healers, then, is a visible indication that they lack this expertise.

Greco-Roman Blends

Metaphorical blends involving physicians were not uncommon in the classical world.[28] The use and application of these blends allow us to see how

---

24. Galen, *Galeni in Hippocratis sextum librum epidemiarum commentaria*, in *Corpus medicorum Graecorum*, ed. E. Wenkebach (Leipzig: Teubner, 1940), VI.152 (my translation).

25. John Cassian, "The First Conference of Abbott Joseph, On Friendship," XXIII, in *The Conferences of John Cassian*, CF-NPNF², vol. XI.

26. Lakoff and Johnson, *Metaphors We Live By*, 69-76; Turner, *Death Is the Mother of Beauty*, 120-53.

27. How can health be restored to a patient if the healer is ill? How can strength be restored if the person trying to effect this change is weak? The image schema of the source determines to a large degree how we perceive its potential for causation.

28. I am indebted to John Nolland's research in which he surveys many of the original sources that I cite in this article. I do not intend to repeat the findings of his excellent article

other authors constructed their metaphors and the frames or network of beliefs that operated as the background to these blends.

Aeschylus In *Prometheus Bound* we find our immortal protagonist chained to the cliffs by Zeus because he stole fire from Olympus and gave it to mankind. Every morning an eagle arrives to gorge on his liver, and every night it grows back in time for the following day's feast. Although his cunning has served him well in the past, Prometheus now finds himself in a helpless situation.

> Προμηθεύς
>   τοιαῦτα μηχανήματ' ἐξευρὼν τάλας βροτοῖσιν,
>   αὐτὸς οὐκ ἔχω σόφισμ' ὅτῳ
>   τῆς νῦν παρούσης πημονῆς ἀπαλλαγῶ.
> Χορός
>   πέπονθας αἰκὲς πῆμ'·
>   ἀποσφαλεὶς φρενῶν πλανᾷ,
>   κακὸς δ' ἰατρὸς ὥς τις ἐς νόσον πεσὼν ἀθυμεῖς
>   καὶ σεαυτὸν οὐκ ἔχεις εὑρεῖν ὁποίοις φαρμάκοις ἰάσιμος.

Prometheus:
   Wretched man that I am — such are the devices (machinations) I invented for mortal humans, yet have myself no skillful means to rid (deliver) me from my present suffering.
Chorus:
   You have suffered shame and humiliation.
   You have lost your mind *(phrēn)* and wander (are lost);
   and like a bad (unskilled) doctor have fallen ill, you lose heart
   and you cannot discover (do not have) what sort of medicine to
      cure yourself.[29]

In the first stanza, Prometheus bemoans his current situation suffering under the heavy wrath of Zeus. The chorus picks this up and develops the thought by use of a metaphorical blend between Prometheus and a bad doctor. The failure of his creative capabilities is connected to the chorus's

---

but use that as a springboard for exploring how cognitive metaphor theory helps us to understand those texts. John Nolland, "Classical and Rabbinic Parallels to 'Physician, Heal Yourself' (Lk 4:23)," *Novum Testamentum* 21 (1979): 193-209.

29. Aeschylus, *Prometheus Bound*, my translation based on that of Herbert Weir Smyth (Cambridge, MA: Harvard University Press, 1926), 469-75.

description that he has "lost his mind and wanders (is lost)." Aeschylus recruits the schema of a bad doctor for his source space and blends that with Prometheus who is chained to the cliffs. As such, our hero is depicted as a poorly skilled doctor who is incapable of alleviating his afflictions.[30]

Depending on which elements we perceive being selectively appropriated from the frame behind the source space for "bad physicians," there are three possible ways we could see the blended space being projected. First, Prometheus is a charlatan whose quackery has been revealed by his current helplessness which is a result of his practicing bad medicine in the past. Contextually that reading is not very strong because Prometheus has already demonstrated his cleverness and taught valuable skills to the human mortals, such as how to harness fire. On the other hand, the scenario of a doctor whose skills fail him when he encounters a particularly difficult case may be being mapped from the source space to Prometheus. John Nolland suggests, "Had he been like the really good doctor he would have known what to do in this extreme test of becoming his own patient. Here he appears as one who has failed that test."[31] If the belief that suffering and illness are the result of being at the mercy of natural and supernatural forces is projected from the source space, then a different meaning is construed in the blend. It is not that Prometheus has "failed the test" but that he has overstepped his boundaries, exceeded his reach, and now he is paying for his arrogance. In each instance though, we see that Prometheus's failure originates from his inability to remedy his current situation. He has not just failed the test, but the test is beyond his capabilities because he has committed a transgression against Olympia.

Cicero After the death of his beloved daughter, Cicero is distraught with grief. Even though friends have tried to comfort him and he has sought advice in the great philosophers, he still despairs of life.[32] One particular friend, who feels that it is time for Cicero to move on with his life, offers Cicero a different perspective on his situation.

---

30. Prometheus's plight may reflect on ancient Greek society: those who boasted about their abilities to help others but were unable to help themselves were often held up for contempt. Anitra B. Kolenkow, "Relationships between Miracle and Prophecy in the Greco-Roman World and Early Christianity," in *Aufstieg und Niedergang der Römischen Welt*, II.23.2 (Berlin: de Gruyter, 1980), 1473-74.

31. Nolland, "Classical and Rabbinic Parallels," 196.

32. Henry Joseph Haskell, *This Was Cicero* (New York: Alfred A. Knopf, 1942), 95, 248-50.

> In fine, do not forget that you are Cicero, and a man accustomed to instruct and advise others; and *do not imitate bad physicians,* who in the diseases of others profess to understand the art of healing, but are unable to prescribe for themselves. Rather suggest to yourself and bring home to your own mind the very maxims which you are accustomed to impress upon others.[33]

His friend advises him not to imitate the bad doctors who "profess to understand the art of healing" but are exposed as quacks by their negligence to treat themselves. He wants to impress upon Cicero that he is not like this. His teachings are sound, and he should apply to himself what he has taught others because his friend believes they will remedy his condition.

The source space is that of a bad doctor. The target is the person being addressed, Cicero in this instance. The generic space that stands between the source and target mental spaces contains the following: a central figure, an agent who advises others, something communicated, a subject or receiver (the sick person), and a causal relationship between the state of the agent and the state of the subject. Both the doctor and the teacher (Cicero) give advice to those who come to them. This advice should result in a beneficial result for the person who seeks their advice.

The notion that bad doctors boasted about their abilities as a healer is highlighted in this passage. However, the ineffectiveness of what they communicate to their patients is borne out in their own poor state of health. The causal relationship between their health and their prescriptions is circular: they are in a poor state of health because their prescriptions are worthless and the reason their prescriptions lack a casual effect stems from their poor health. This blend also contains an incongruity between Cicero and the worthless doctors. Implied in his friend's advice is a second source space of a good doctor who takes care of himself, whose advice has a causal effect of producing positive results in his patients. This is where the connections between the target space, Cicero and the source space of a doctor are formed.[34]

If Cicero takes his friend's advice, we can infer that he does not take such a high view of himself, he can follow another's advice, and at the same time he possesses the wisdom to meet the needs of his present situa-

---

33. M. Tullius Cicero, *Letters to His Friends*, IV.5.5. Translation by Evelyn Shuckburgh.

34. In this diagram, the source space of the "good doctor" is not strictly necessary, but does help to illustrate the blend more clearly. I am indebted to Therese Des Camp for pointing out the second source space contained in this blend.

Metaphors, Cognitive Theory, and Jesus' Shortest Parable

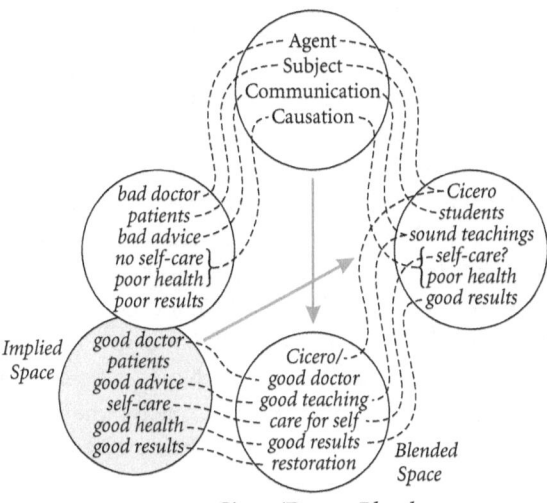

FIGURE 4   Cicero/Doctor Blend

tion.[35] As in the previous example, this blend allows us to perceive how the metaphorical blending involves systematic projections of relationships, scenarios, structures, and other conceptual properties from one or both of the mental source spaces. Included in these systematic projections are inferences that we can make based on what is selectively projected in the blend.[36] For example, when a person "simmers down" we understand that they are no longer angry. In the blend involving Cicero, we can infer that he is more like a good doctor but has fallen prey to a terrible calamity. Even though the depth of this situation is not downplayed, Cicero possesses the relevant resources to recover from this situation. What he needs to do now is appropriate these resources in a manner that will facilitate his recovery. He is like the good doctor who cares for himself and there is a causal relationship between his prescriptions and the health of those he treats, whether it be someone else or himself.[37]

---

35. Nolland, "Classical and Rabbinic Parallels," 197.

36. See also Ricoeur's discussion of mimesis. Mimesis, in this case Cicero being like a good/bad doctor, offers "a model for perceiving things differently, the paradigm of a new vision" that is an instance of productive imagination. Ricoeur, *Hermeneutics and the Human Sciences*, 292-93.

37. Nolland argues that Cicero's friend is using this particular blend to exhort Cicero that he is not a bad doctor, and that by healing himself he will avoid resembling something most unattractive. However, that does not appear in the generic space or in what is being invoked from the source spaces. Nolland, "Classical and Rabbinic Parallels," 197.

What is interesting in this blend is that Cicero would likely have been diagnosed by a physician to be suffering from melancholia, an imbalance in his black bile, not an emotional state as we would perceive it today.[38] Remarkably, his friend does not suggest a change in diet or other medical practices that were common during that day. Rather, Cicero's teachings are cross-mapped to the cure healers would prescribe for themselves and should restore balance to his life. Just as physicians' self-care served as the ground for their ability to treat others, Cicero needs to backtrack a few steps and recover his own teachings because he is a good teacher. The metaphorical blend his friend offers Cicero has the potential to disclose new perspectives and realities to Cicero. When Cicero comes to see himself as a good physician who has fallen ill and has the capacity to alleviate his illness, a new reality will take shape in his life as he now knows how to act upon it.

Both of the blends that we have discussed so far also contain emotional extrapolations that project from the source space (physician) and the target domain (teacher) to the blended space. Among them are the presuppositions that the prescription doctors offer has a causal effect in their patients. Good prescriptions produce good results; worthless advice does nothing at best and serious harm or death at worst. The efficacy and benefit of these prescriptions are grounded in the well-being of the healer, and the health of the healer is based on the effectiveness of their practices.

Plutarch In *How to Tell a Flatterer* Plutarch addresses the issue of how one should admonish a friend. Any counsel offered needs to be grounded in one's own personal virtue. If this grounding is absent, then one is like

ἄλλων ἰατρὸς αὐτὸς ἕλκεσιν βρύων

A doctor of others, running (covered) with sores.[39]

---

38. The term "melancholia" comes from the Hippocratic theory of the four humours: disease being caused by an imbalance in one or another of the four basic bodily fluids, or humours. Melancholia (also translated as "lugubriousness," "moroseness," or "wistfulness") was caused by an excess of black bile (μελαγχολία from μέλας, "black," and χολή, "bile"). Someone who tended to have an abundance of black bile had a *melancholic* disposition. Melancholia (along with other "fears and despondencies, if they last a long time") was described as a distinct disease with particular mental and physical symptoms by Hippocrates. Hippocrates, *Aphorisms*, §6.23.

39. Plutarch, *Moralia I*, "How to Tell a Flatterer," 32, trans. F. C. Babbit (Cambridge, MA: Loeb Classical Library, 1927), 71f. Plutarch's use of this proverb seems to set the trajec-

Metaphors, Cognitive Theory, and Jesus' Shortest Parable

Hippocrates' and Galen's teachings that healers should see to their own well-being if they want to effectively treat others forms a major element to the frame in the source space. The crux of this blend is based on an image schema. The visible manifestations of ill health (skin ailments, poor appearance, etc.) mirror the inner qualities of the advisor. This is most like a very basic form of metaphor in which we conceptually map the nonphysical to some form of physical entity (such as ideas are commodities, "You don't buy that idea"; or to money, "that is a valuable idea"). In this instance, vices are mapped to ill health and virtue with vigor; "we conceptualize the less clearly defined in terms of the more clearly delineated."[40] The causal relationship between their personal illness and the efficacy of their treatments is mapped to the advice given by the friend in the blended space as well. Just as a healer who is visibly ill would not be trusted (or seen as capable of effecting a cure), so also someone with a known vice would not be trusted (or seen as giving bad advice). The inference from this blend is not only that one's friend may reject the advice, but one risks possibly fracturing the relationship if the required virtues are absent in one's own life.

In the section entitled "How to Profit from Your Enemies," Plutarch employed this adage in a slightly different manner. If one corrects someone and has even a hint of that fault in one's own life, the person being admonished can whisper behind one's back, "ἄλλων ἰατρὸς αὐτὸς ἕλκεσιν βρύων." The rebuke will return to its originator and judge the speaker by his or her own words, just as skeptics spoke critically about physicians.[41] In both blends, the ability of the healer to accurately diagnose the illness is not profiled. Rather, the healer's infirmities are highlighted in the source domain and mapped to the inner moral state of the advice giver.[42] As Hippocrates and Galen noted, the well-being of the healer is critical to the healer's practice. The ability to heal, causation, and the value that others

---

tory for how some of the early church fathers interpreted Jesus' citation of the proverb in Luke 4:23. See Chrysostom, *Homilies on Matthew* XVI.5; Gregory Nazianzen, *Orations,* 10.13, who appears to be citing Plutarch's version of this proverb rather than the text in Luke 4:23.

40. Lakoff and Johnson, *Metaphors We Live By,* 59; see also 46-51, 58-60.

41. Plutarch, "How to Profit from One's Enemies," *Moralia I,* 88d. See the Greek epigrams about doctors in the section "Greco-Roman Frames" above. Kee argues that proverbs like this reflect the value that if you pointed out a problem you were responsible to resolve it. Howard Clark Kee, *Medicine, Miracles, and Magic in New Testament Times* (Cambridge: Cambridge University Press, 1986), 65.

42. "Plutarch is warning against a situation where (to retain the medical metaphor), by declaring another person ill you are drawing attention to your own sickness." Nolland, "Classical and Rabbinic Parallels," 200.

attribute to the healer's skills are compromised if this grounding is absent. Plutarch's use of this proverb creates a vivid blend in which the advice giver is visibly ill from his or her own moral deficiencies.

These two examples from Plutarch illustrate how, once a metaphorical blend gains a conventional status, it can be employed in various contexts for different purposes. The generic space that is conventionally established also constrains the flexibility one has when utilizing this metaphorical blend.[43]

Before we turn to biblical examples, it is worth summarizing some of the conventional cross-space mappings inherent in the metaphorical blend of physicians/teachers.

Physician	Teacher
agent/patient	agent/learner
personal well-being	moral character
Causal relationships between:	Causal relationships between:
well-being/expertise	virtues/character
agency/cure	agency/learning
expertise/cure	wisdom/benefit to hearer

Biblical Frames

As we shift our attention to Luke 4:23 we must consider if the frames behind "physician" and "healing" were the same in Palestine as in the wider Greco-Roman world. The predominant perspective taken regarding healing is that of miraculous restoration in biblical literature. Exceptions include Isaiah's fig paste used to treat a boil (Isa 38:21) and Paul's advice to Timothy to drink a little wine to soothe his stomach (1 Tim 5:23). Israel's perspective on illness and healing was grounded in their relationship to their Lord. In Exodus God counsels Israel at the water of Marah, "If you diligently hearken to the voice of the Lord your God . . . and give heed to God's commandments and keep all God's statutes, I will put none of these diseases upon you which I put upon the Egyptians," and closes with the most significant clause, "for I am the Lord who heals you" (Exod 15:26 RSV).

If illness was related to being at the mercy of natural and supernatural

---

43. Turner, *Literary Mind*, 86-92.

forces in the wider Ancient Near East, in Israel the scales tip in favor of supernatural causes and cures based on a person's response to the Covenant with YHWH. Fevers, for example, were considered one of the means by which God chastised those who violated his covenant (Lev. 26:16 and Deut. 28:22). The prevalence of this view is borne out by Philo, who placed fevers at the top of the list for the wages of sin and impiety.[44]

Many illnesses conveyed a state of uncleanliness on the sufferer (especially illnesses that involved skin diseases, sexual functions, and death). Uncleanliness was not viewed as contagious (like the flu) but could be transferred to others, thus rendering them unclean — not biologically sick. Like fever, illnesses that made a person unclean were often regarded as an act of divine judgment, a visible manifestation of inner corruption.[45] Unclean persons were restored to society after a priest had inspected them, they had undergone a purification rite, and the priest declared them clean. Howard Clark Kee noted that in the Jewish faith, and the Levitical laws in particular, purification, not the restoration of functionality, was the focus of the healing practices.[46]

While Greek (and other) medical and healing practices were known in Israel, three things must be noted. First, in the pseudepigraphal book of Sirach we find the only positive reference to a physician in biblical literature. However, unlike Greek medical practices, the abilities of a healer were not acquired through instruction or observation but were received through prayer and divine revelation.[47] Second, when healers from this period are mentioned in Jewish literature they were most often miracle workers who performed their ministry by means of prayer or rabbis who

---

44. Philo, *On Rewards and Divine Punishments*, §143. See also the Rabbis who argued that you could not "cure" a fever since it was a form of divine punishment, the result of cavorting in the moonlight, or demonic. *b. Berakot* 34b; *b. Gittin* 67b, 70a; *b. Nedarim* 41a and *b. Šabbat* 66b. Josephus expressed the same view when he attributed the various illnesses Herod the Great suffered from (fever, intestinal problems, gangrene of his genitals, tumors in his feet, breathing difficulties, and convulsions) to his sinful lifestyle. *Jewish War* 1:656-58.

45. Jacob Neusner, "Judaism after the Destruction of the Temple," in *Israelite and Judean History*, ed. John Hayes and Max Miller, Old Testament Library (Philadelphia: Westminster, 1977), 673-74.

46. Howard Clark Kee, *Medicine, Miracles, and Magic in New Testament Times*, ed. Graham Stanton, Society for New Testament Studies (Cambridge: Cambridge University Press, 1986), 11.

47. "There may come a time when recovery lies in the hands of physicians, for they too pray to the Lord that he grant them success in diagnosis and in healing, for the sake of preserving life." Sir 38:13-14 (NRSV).

followed a tradition of healing and exorcism attributed to Solomon.[48] Finally, in addition to their dreadful cure rate, the prohibitions against worshipping other gods or being led astray by a false teacher to follow foreign gods made Israel skeptical of the healing arts as practiced by the surrounding cultures.[49] By way of summary, the frames for physicians and healing within the Jewish community differed from the Greco-Roman frame in the following ways: illness being envisaged from the perspective of God's blessings or curses; the view of medical practitioners and how they acquired their abilities; and the focus primarily on the issue of purity. Israel's relationship to Yhwh, the covenantal nature of that relationship, and the concepts of purity/cleanliness played a central role in their network of beliefs. Therefore, we should expect that the metaphorical blends that they employed reflected those core beliefs.[50]

Biblical Blends

Job 13:3-4   οὐ μὴν δὲ ἀλλ' ἐγὼ πρὸς κύριον λαλήσω,
            ἐλέγξω δὲ ἐναντίον αὐτοῦ ἐὰν βούληται.
            ὑμεῖς δέ ἐστε ἰατροὶ ἄδικοι
            καὶ ἰαταὶ κακῶν πάντες.

But I would speak to the Almighty,
    and I desire to argue my case with God.
As for you, you whitewash with lies;
    all of you are worthless physicians. (NRSV)

48. Josephus records that Rabbi Eleazar once performed an exorcism before Vespasian's court according to the prescriptions of Solomon. *Jewish Antiquities* 8:44-49. For examples of healers see the stories of Honi, *Mishnah, Ta'anit* 3:8, or Hanina ben Dosa, *Babylonian Talmud, Berakot*, 34a.

49. For example, in Greek literature, medical practices were attributed to Asclepius, who achieved divine status in Greek mythology. His demi-goddess daughters Iaso ('Ιασώ, responsible for recuperation from illnesses), Panakea (Πανάκεια, the goddess of healing), and Hygia ('Υγιεία, who blessed humans with health and cleanliness) were all associated with and worshipped in relation to the need for healing. Two examples that relate the deplorable state of medical treatment in the ancient world are the hemorrhaging woman who suffered for 12 years under physicians only to get worse (Mark 5:25-26) and the apocryphal story of Tobit who lost his sight due to physicians treating his eyes with dung (Tobit 2:9-10).

50. This is sort of a reverse way of making Lakoff's point that "The most fundamental values in a culture will be coherent with the metaphorical structure of the most fundamental concepts in that culture." Lakoff and Johnson, *Metaphors We Live By*, 22.

Metaphors, Cognitive Theory, and Jesus' Shortest Parable

In this passage Job is replying to Zophar's counsel to Job to put his sins away and acknowledge that his sufferings are God's hand of discipline upon his life (Job 11:11-20), advice that he construes as coming from "worthless physicians." The source domain for his accusation is that of a "worthless physician."[51] Compounding this metaphorical blend is the charge that his friends are "whitewashing with lies" and they are "speaking falsely for God" (13:7).

Profiled within this blend is the concept that giving meaning to the sufferer's situation was one of the primary roles of a healer in the ancient world.[52] From Job's perspective, his friends' advice was worthless because they presumptuously misunderstood why his relationship with God had fallen into crisis. They misread the cause of his sufferings (as harboring sin in his life), and their advice (to confess his sins)[53] did not solve the question of why he was suffering in this manner. Job perceived that their counsel would do little to restore his life or relationship with God as a result. He found Zophar's advice was like that from a worthless physician who can neither diagnose nor give meaning to his patient's sufferings, contrary to his inflated claims.

In contrast to Plutarch's use of this metaphorical blend, the visible infirmity of the healer is not being mapped from the target domain. His three friends appear to be enjoying an excellent state of being compared to his condition. Nor are their personal characters being questioned. A slightly different inferencing is transpiring. The problem with Zophar's advice is not with his reading of Exodus 15 and similar passages but with its application to this particular situation. His advice is not wrong as much as it is simplistic. Zophar's exhortation not only fails to appropriately address Job's situation; his advice is portrayed as inappropriate, and he is pictured as inventing lies and speaking falsely for God (13:7).

If the tables were turned and God was to examine Zophar, he would be found wanting according to the advice he is offering Job (13:9). Job is not just rejecting his advice, but he is advising his friend to examine his own

---

51. While the Hebrew simply has the participle רֹפְאֵי, "healer," the LXX has a compound form of this idea (ἐστὲ ἰατροὶ ἄδικοι καὶ ἰαταὶ κακῶν, "you are unrighteous physicians and bad healers"), perhaps bringing even more attention to this metaphorical blend.

52. Pilch, *Healing in the New Testament*, 21-23, 34-35.

53. Job's advisors appear to be reading his sufferings as a visible manifestation of inner corruption. The unconfessed sin in his life mapped to the visible sores on his skin. We can see this in Zophar's advice, "If iniquity is in your hand, put it far off.... Surely then you will lift your face without blemish." Job 11:14-15 NRSV.

life as well. He is not rejecting his friends' help because they are sick doctors (have unconfessed sin in their lives); rather, it is their diagnosis and prescription that he objects to. Not only does he spurn their advice, but the performative force of Job's reply, "you are worthless physicians," is to warn his physician friends that they are in danger of falling under God's judgment because of their presumptuous prescriptions and should therefore keep silent and amend their ways.

Luke 4:23 We turn now to Luke 4:23. The brevity of Jesus' use of the proverb "Physician, heal thyself" creates problems, as mentioned above. On the one hand, Luke does not explicate the frames evoked in this statement; he expects his audience to possess them as part of their pre-understanding. On the other hand, because the frames are not specified, successive generations of readers may bring the wrong frames and networks of beliefs into play when reading this passage.

This pericope opens with Jesus delivering his inaugural sermon on Isaiah 61 in his hometown of Nazareth. He closes his sermon by addressing the synagogue: "Today this scripture has been fulfilled in your hearing" (4:21). His audience testifies ("speak well of," ἐμαρτύρουν) and "are amazed" or "shocked" (ἐθαύμαζον). These verbs are usually translated in a manner that indicates that Jesus' audience agreed with his sermon and was impressed by its power and eloquence. These verbs can also be translated in a manner that points to the congregation being perplexed and provoked by Jesus' message.[54] The ambiguous meaning of these verbs helps to establish the "surplus of meaning" that this passage generates. In response the congregation asks, "Is not this Joseph's son?" (4:22).

It is in this context that Jesus utters, "Doubtless you will quote to me this parable, 'Physician, heal yourself!'" It is important to note that while Jesus utters this proverbial statement and the following request, he is stating their thoughts. He has a tough audience. They are skeptical and demand that Jesus perform acts of healing in their midst as they have heard reports about his ministry in Capernaum (4:23). Jesus replies by making an analogous comparison between his ministry and that of Elijah and Elisha (4:24-27).

---

54. Θαυμάζω conveys the idea of being "extraordinarily impressed or disturbed" by someone or something. Whether this should be understood with a positive or negative is determined by context. "Θαυμάζω," in *A Greek-English Lexicon of the New Testament*, 3rd ed., ed. Frederick William Danker (Chicago: University of Chicago Press, 2000), 444.

Thus, we need to interpret this parable (4:23) in light of an audience trying to arrive at some conclusion not only about Jesus' message but about the messenger as well. And this is one of the areas in which blending carries a great deal of cognitive work. If we conceptually map this parable, we can grasp some of the conceptual dynamics taking place. The source domain is that of the physician from a Jewish perspective. On the basis of the extra-biblical sources, we know that physicians should embody what they practice; their lives should manifest a good state of health and well-being. In first-century Palestine certain elements in the source space's frame were accentuated: healers' efficacy was grounded in their relationship with God; God revealed how to heal someone; the goal of healing was the restoration of purity; and ultimately God was Israel's healer.

The target space for this metaphor is Jesus the rabbi. In understanding Jesus as a teacher or rabbi, we need to take into account additional entailments. Because of the conventional nature of this parable we can assume that the inference that teachers should practice what they preach, just as physicians should see to their own health, was an established part of this frame (see the discussion on Plutarch above). Teachings should have a causal relationship to those who practice them (enlightenment, salvation, health, or prosperity). Bad teachers' advice will be mundane or foolish, at best, and may bring the teachers and their followers under God's judgment. In Israel, someone who taught the people to worship other gods would not only have been a bad teacher but heretical as well, and deserving of death according to the Law.[55] A good teacher, in contrast, would turn the hearts of the people to their Lord and would live a lifestyle in accordance with the precepts of the scriptures.

Structure of the five blends in Luke 4:16-30
A. Isaiah 61 blended with Jesus' life and ministry (4:16-21)
  B. Jesus as Joseph's son (4:22)
    C. "Physician, heal thyself!" (4:23a)
  B'. Capernaum and Nazareth blended (4:23b)
A'. Elijah and Elisha blended with Jesus' ministry (4:24-27)
Result: Attempt to kill Jesus (4:28-30)

Jesus' statement in verse 23 stands at the chiastic center of five cognitive blends in Luke's record of Jesus' inaugural address. On the outside po-

---

55. See Deut 13:1-5; 18:9-22.

sitions (A and A') we have Jesus making two analogous appeals to the prophets. The pericope opens with Jesus reading from Isaiah 61 about the messiah who will be anointed with God's spirit, whose ministry and message will be characterized by deliverance of the oppressed and the annunciation of the year of the Lord.[56] Once he has read from the scroll, he turns to the congregation and proclaims, "Today this scripture has been fulfilled in your hearing" (4:21). Like the Toblerone advertisement, past and present are compressed into one time frame in the blended space. Isaiah is depicted as speaking about Jesus' life and ministry. Discrepancies between Isaiah's context and original references and the context for Nazareth's synagogue are concealed in this blend. What is profiled in the source and target space are an actor (Messiah/Jesus) who accomplishes certain actions (message and miracles) by means of a particular causation (the Spirit of God). The blended space will succeed only if the hearer accepts the correspondences between Isaiah's message and Jesus as matching.[57]

The pericope closes with Jesus responding to the people's request for a demonstration of his healing abilities by comparing his ministry with that of Elijah and Elisha (two messianic figures). Just as they healed outsiders (the Shunammite woman's son and Naaman the Syrian) and not those within Israel, the same holds for Jesus' ministry — he will not heal in Nazareth (4:24-27). In a manner similar to the Isaiah blend, Jesus appeals to the ancient story of Elijah and Elisha to create a blend between their ministry and his. A new perspective is also introduced in this blend. In most of the examples examined so far there was a causal relationship between the health of the physician and the physician's therapeutic abilities. In this blend a different causal relationship is established between the patient and the patient's healing. The burden is now shifted from the well-being of the healer to effect a cure to the patient's deserving to be healed. This shift from

---

56. What Jesus omitted in his reading of Isaiah is the reference to "the day of vengeance of our God" (Isa. 61:2). This illustrates how blends are selective in what they recruit from their mental spaces.

57. The blend is similar to a situation in which a contemporary philosopher might engage in a hypothetical debate with Kant in order to compare and contrast their positions. In that blend differences in time between Kant and today, as well as language, are not construed. Rather, the focus is on the two (Kant and the contemporary speaker) and their positions. Jesus' quotation of Isaiah does not juxtapose his teachings with Isaiah's but attempts to create a blend that demonstrates that Isaiah is in agreement with Jesus' life and ministry. Joseph E. Grady, Todd Oakley, and Seana Coulson, "Blending and Metaphor," in *Metaphor in Cognitive Linguistics*, ed. G. Steen and R. Gibbs (Philadelphia: John Benjamins, 1999), 114-15.

Metaphors, Cognitive Theory, and Jesus' Shortest Parable

Jesus being a sick doctor to their being sick patients (with the metaphorical implication that there is some reason for this) is the final straw that motivates them to drive Jesus out of the synagogue in order to kill him.

The congregation's responses stand one ring (levels B and B′) in from Jesus' blends that project the prophetic passages to his life and ministry (levels A and A′). The audience's questioning about Jesus being Joseph's son is a natural response to his message on Isaiah 61. "Is this not the son of Joseph?" raises questions about who Jesus is, especially in relationship to Jesus invoking Isaiah's messianic vision. The basic metaphor behind this blend is a kinship metaphor: a child resembles his parent in many ways.[58] The blend creates a space in which the people can project the possibilities and potentials for Jesus' life based on his father. The logic that "he is Joseph's son" implies that there is some degree of incongruity between what they know of Jesus and what he has just claimed. Would they "count" a local peasant's son as meeting the qualifications of Isaiah's messianic figure?[59]

The question the congregation at Nazareth is asking arises from the invariance principle, which states that the image schema from the source cannot clash with the image schema in the target space. In this instance, the invariance principle extends over two metaphorical blends. The second blend of Jesus as Joseph's son (B) encapsulated their preconceptions of who Jesus was. This allows us as readers to grasp the image schema they held about Jesus who was the target for the first blend (A). The image schema they possessed of Isaiah's portrait of the messiah clashed with their pre-understanding of Jesus. Thus, for the congregation, the first blend was not felicitous. However, as readers we possess information that the audience in Nazareth lacked. This information allows readers to apprehend the Isaiah blend as appropriate and at the same time discern clashes inherent in the blend of Jesus as Joseph's son.[60]

---

58. Turner, *Death Is the Mother of Beauty*, 28-34.

59. Wolterstorff explicates this "counting-as" function with the idea of "seeing-as." What we "count as" a trait or a correspondence involves a wider communicative situation than what is included in the text. In this instance, what we "count as" internal or external representations (Joseph or God's son) will determine how we form this blend. Nicholas Wolterstorff, *Art in Action: Toward a Christian Aesthetic* (Grand Rapids: Eerdmans, 1980), 122-55.

60. Vyvyan Evans, "Invariance Principle," in *A Glossary of Cognitive Linguistics* (Salt Lake City: University of Utah Press, 2007), 117-18. "It does not require that the image schema projected from the source already exist in the target before the projection, but instead that the result from the projection not include a contradiction of image schema." Turner, *The Literary Mind*, 31.

The congregation's second response (position B' in the diagram) — "do for us what you have done in Capernaum" — is a simple blend between two locations and Jesus' actions in those two locations. It is an appeal for consistency. If what has been rumored about Jesus in Capernaum is true, then the same miracles he performed in Capernaum should be possible in Nazareth.[61] Both the blends at positions B and B' are negative in orientation.[62] The fact that he has not performed any healings in Nazareth would only serve to validate the conceptualization of Jesus as Joseph's son.

At the center of this chiastic argument stands Jesus' quotation of the parable, "Physician, heal thyself!" The blend this statement creates is shaped by its context with the other four blends in this pericope and contains elements from those blends: messiah, personal qualifications, and healers/teachers (see the Reader's Physician Blend in figure 5). Jesus' claim to be Isaiah's messiah was preposterous because the congregation viewed him as the son of Joseph. Thus, his attempt to blend Isaiah's prophecy with his life and ministry fails, and from their perspective he is a charlatan. Like bad doctors who boast about their ability to effect cures but lack the causational grounding for these claims in their own lives, Jesus' claim that Isaiah is talking about him fails because as the son of Joseph he lacks the grounding for this claim. He is not just a charlatan making claims he cannot fill; he is also construed as in need of healing himself in this blend. The metaphorical inferences that follow are that he is ill, therefore unclean, and by extension a sinner under God's judgment. He has fallen into the error that Job warned his friend about: he has spoken lies about God. As such, he is a false teacher who is attempting to lead Israel astray by claiming to be the messiah. The blend produces a strong religious and emotional response that is metaphorically embodied in the audience. They drive him *out* of the congregation and attempt to throw him *down* a cliff.[63]

---

61. Mark 6 records that Jesus was unable to perform any miracles in Nazareth. Luke omits this in his account but it is implied in this blend (4:23b). Audrey Dawson, *Healing, Weakness, and Power: Perspectives on Healing in the Writings of Mark, Luke, and Paul* (Eugene, OR: Wipf and Stock, 2008), 123.

62. The negative quality of "Joseph's son" is clear in the text. But the blend between Capernaum and Nazareth only takes on a negative quality based on its location in the text. First, while the crowd do not directly state it but Jesus is stating their thoughts, it is directly linked to "Physician, heal thyself!" Second, it stands parallel to the question about being Joseph's son in that both reflect their reasoning about Jesus' claims.

63. For a fuller discussion of gestures and movements as metaphorically motivated, see David McNeill, *Hand and Mind: What Gestures Reveal about Thought* (Chicago: University of Chicago Press, 1992).

Metaphors, Cognitive Theory, and Jesus' Shortest Parable

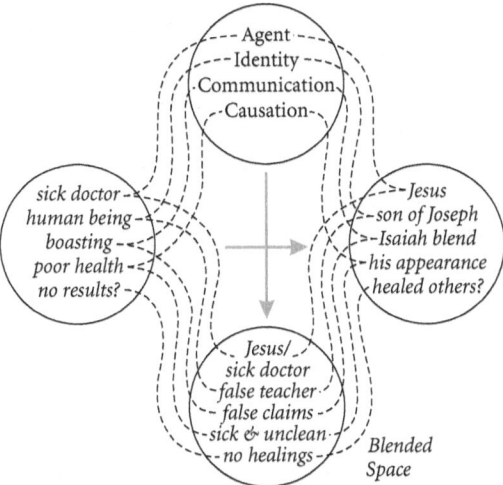

Jesus/Sick Physician Blend

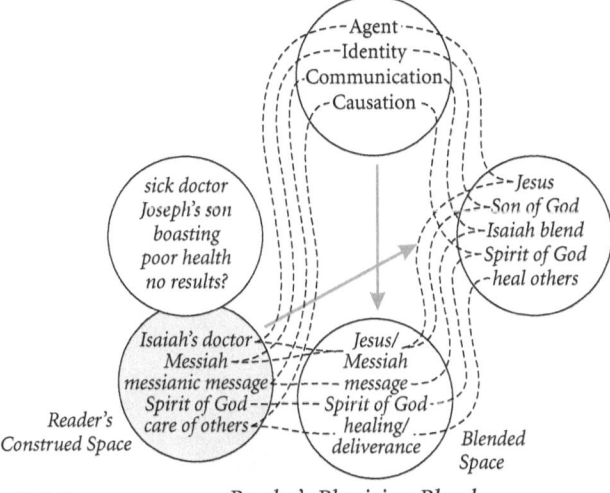

FIGURE 5   Reader's Physician Blend

While we accept the same frames as the congregation at Nazareth, as readers we possess intertextual information that enables us to construct a different blended space than they did. First, we know from the previous chapters that Jesus' birth fulfills a number of the messianic aspirations in the Old Testament (Luke 1:46-55; 2:29-32; 3:2-6, 16-17). Second, we have been given insiders' information that Jesus is only supposedly the son of Joseph (1:26-38; 3:22, 23; 4:3, 9). And third, we shall see as Luke continues with his narrative that Jesus will perform many acts of healing. The audience in the synagogue reached their conclusions by performing a blend between Jesus and the sick doctor, but as readers we reject that blend and construct one that sees Jesus as the fulfillment of Isaiah 61, the messianic healer. Thus, we as readers accept the two outer blends (A and A′) that Jesus makes and find the middle three (B, C, and B′) infelicitous — they misfire in certain aspects for Luke's readers. However, by cognitively performing the blends in this passage we must either follow or reject the logic of these successive blends. Returning to Paul Ricoeur's idea that "metaphors give rise to thought," these metaphorical blends in Luke 4 invite us to participate with the congregation at Nazareth in reasoning about who Jesus is.

It is my hope that this exploration of metaphorical blends involving physicians and teachers in classical and biblical literature has demonstrated the incredible amount of cognitive load a short conventional proverb can carry — how, with only slight variations in context or selection from the input spaces, these blends can perform various rhetorical/cognitive functions. In Luke 4:23 we have an incredible amount of cognitive cargo which is compressed into and carried in three words, "Physician, heal thyself!"

"But We Have the Mind of Christ": Some Theological and Anthropological Reflections on 1 Corinthians 2:16

Richard H. Bell

Anthony Thiselton has inspired many, including myself, to relate the study of the New Testament to questions of Systematic Theology. In my tribute to Anthony I will consider Paul's use of Isa 40:13 in 1 Cor 2:16 and then ask what implications this may have for a "Theology of Mind."

Isaiah 40:13 in 1 Corinthians 2:16 and Romans 11:34

Paul quotes from Isa 40:13 LXX in 1 Cor 2:16a, b:

> "For who has known the mind of the Lord
> so as to instruct him?"

> τίς γὰρ ἔγνω νοῦν κυρίου,
> ὃς συμβιβάσει αὐτόν;

He then adds the remarkable statement: "But *we* have the mind of Christ" (ἡμεῖς δὲ νοῦν Χριστοῦ ἔχομεν). In this section I am going to ask how Paul understood Isaiah's question "Who has known the mind of the Lord?"
Isaiah 40:13 LXX as given in Rahlfs' edition is as follows:

> τίς ἔγνω νοῦν κυρίου,
> καὶ τίς αὐτοῦ σύμβουλος ἐγένετο,
> ὃς συμβιβᾷ αὐτόν;

Who has known the mind of the Lord?
and who has become his counsellor,
who will instruct him?

Paul quotes from the first and third lines of Isa 40:13 LXX.[1] He clearly knew all three lines since he quotes (with minor changes) the first two in Rom 11:34. It is not entirely clear why he omitted the second line in 1 Cor 2:16 yet included the third;[2] one reason may be that a more cogent link could be made to his argument about "instruction" in v. 15;[3] another possibility is that it was a way of tightening his argument.[4]

The answer to the question "Who has known the mind of the Lord?" in Isaiah is clearly "No one!" But how does Paul understand the answer? Is Paul's essential point in quoting Isa 40:13 that God's mind[5] is unsearchable?

---

1. Paul's use of Isa 40:13 suggests that his recension of LXX belonged to the earlier "Alexandrian" text form (supported by A and Q and frequently S) rather than the later "Hexapla" text (B V). So the "attic future" συμβιβᾷ of συμβιβάζω is supported by Q^txt S* B L; the future συμβιβάσει which Paul follows is supported by A Q^mg S^c a V C (on the future of -άζω verbs, see James Hope Moulton and Wilbert Francis Howard, *A Grammar of New Testament Greek*, vol. II: *Accidence and Word-Formation* [Edinburgh: T&T Clark, 1990 (repr.)], 187). On the issue of Paul's recension of Isaiah, see Dietrich-Alex Koch, *Die Schrift als Zeuge des Evangeliums. Untersuchungen zur Verwendung und zum Verständnis der Schrift bei Paulus*, BhTh 69 (Tübingen: J. C. B. Mohr [Paul Siebeck], 1986), 48-51. See also Rom 11:34 where Paul's σύμβουλος αὐτοῦ follows A Q and not αὐτοῦ σύμβουλος of S B V L C.

2. Hans Hübner, *Biblische Theologie des Neuen Testaments*, vol. II: *Die Theologie des Paulus und ihre neutestamentliche Wirkungsgeschichte* (Göttingen: Vandenhoeck & Ruprecht, 1993), 127 n. 273: "Warum Paulus Jes 40,13b LXX weggelassen, 40,13c aber zitiert hat, kann nur ratende Spekulation beantworten."

3. See Anthony Tyrrell Hanson, "A Quasi-Gnostic Pauline Midrash: 1 Corinthians 2.6-16," in *The New Testament Interpretation of Scripture* (London: SPCK, 1980), 90: "In 1 Corinthians 2.16 Paul is mainly interested in the cognitive aspect of the citation.... He wanted to show that because Christians are in Christ they can comprehend God's revelation of himself in the events of Christ's entire career from creation to exaltation. For that purpose Isaiah 40.13ac was certainly most relevant, since these two lines express exactly what Paul wanted to prove: we can know God's mind or design because Christ has interpreted him to us."

4. Koch, *Schrift*, 115, gives this as an example of "Auslassungen als Mittel der Straffung." Note that in LXX, the relative clause ὃς συμβιβᾷ αὐτόν of v. 13c refers back to σύμβουλος of 13b. But because Paul omits 13b, his relative clause ὃς συμβιβάσει αὐτόν refers back apparently to τίς (Archibald Robertson and Alfred Plummer, *First Epistle of St Paul to the Corinthians*, ICC [Edinburgh: T&T Clark, 1955 (repr.), ²1911], 51). But ὅς is best understood as a consecutive to express contemplated result (Anthony C. Thiselton, *The First Epistle to the Corinthians*, NIGTC [Grand Rapids: Eerdmans, 2000], 274).

5. I take Paul's reference in νοῦς κυρίου to be to God's mind rather than Christ's mind (as is also the case in Paul's use of Isa 40:13 in Rom 11:34). There are, of course, in-

"But We Have the Mind of Christ"

Commentators have likened Paul's position to that of *1 En.* 93:11-14,[6] concluding that this "prophetic" tradition (where no one can "ponder his [deep] thoughts") stands in contrast to the "wisdom" tradition.[7] This "wisdom tradition" felt that the question "Who has known the mind of the Lord?" could be answered: it is through "wisdom" that one can know the mind of the Lord! Wisdom 9:17-18 is especially important here, coming at the end of a passage which alludes to Isa 40:13 and 40:12. There are also a number of links between this passage and 1 Cor 2:6-16.

> [13]For who can learn the counsel of God?
> Or who can discern what the Lord wills? (cf. Isa 40:13)
> [14]For the reasoning of mortals is worthless,
> and our designs are likely to fail;
> [15]for a perishable body weighs down the *soul,*
> and this earthly tent burdens the thoughtful *mind.* (cf. 1 Cor 2:14)
> [16]We can hardly guess at what is on earth,
> and what is at hand we find with labour;
> but who has traced out what is in the heavens? (cf. Isa 40:12)
> [17]Who has learned your counsel (βουλὴν δέ σου τίς ἔγνω)
> unless you have given *wisdom* (εἰ μὴ σὺ ἔδωκας σοφίαν) (cf. 1 Cor 2:6, 7; cf. 1:18-31)
> and sent your holy spirit from on high? (καὶ ἔπεμψας τὸ ἅγιόν σου πνεῦμα ἀπὸ ὑψίστων . . .) (cf. 1 Cor 2:10-13)
> [18]And thus the paths of those on earth were set right,
> and people were taught what pleases you,
> and were saved by wisdom.

We see that vv. 17-18 affirm that "wisdom" is God's counsellor (Isa 40:13) and this "wisdom," it appears, is identified with the holy spirit.[8] If the Book of Wisdom thinks that the question of Isa 40:13 "Who has known

---

stances where OT quotations with κύριος are "applied" to Jesus Christ (e.g., Joel 2:32 [MT 3:5] in Rom 10:13). But in 1 Cor 2:16 there is no straightforward "application" as such even though, as will become clear, there is a "trinitarian" movement of thought from v. 16a to v. 16c.

6. Wolfgang Schrage, *Der erste Brief an die Korinther (1 Kor 1,1–6.11),* EKK 7.1 (Zürich: Benziger, Neukirchener, 1991), 266 n. 269.

7. See Schrage, *Korinther I,* 266.

8. See Hanson, "1 Corinthians 2.6-16," 83. He suggests that Wis 9:18b could be seen as a Greek version of the last clause of the Targum of Isa 40:13: "To the righteous he hath made known the things of his good pleasure."

the mind of the Lord?" is both "answerable and answered"[9] and that the Lord does have a counsellor, what of Paul? Schrage believes Paul opposes such sapiential tradition.[10] To the question "Who has known the mind of the Lord?" Paul's answer must be "No one."[11] Schrage's position may seem to be confirmed by Paul's further quotation of Isa 40:13c: "so as to instruct him." However, one must recognize that the whole passage 1 Cor 2:6-16 suggests that the Christian *can indeed* know the mind of the God. The Spirit "searches everything, even the depths of God (πάντα ἐραυνᾷ, καὶ τὰ βάθη τοῦ θεοῦ)" (2:10). Christians have received the spirit of God (v. 12) such that they can understand the salvation sent by God (ἵνα εἰδῶμεν τὰ ὑπὸ τοῦ θεοῦ χαρισθέντα ἡμῖν).[12] Therefore one must conclude that Christians, those who have the Spirit, *do* know the mind of God[13] (even though *under normal circumstances* "no one" can know the mind of God). Since Paul is going well beyond the sense of Isa 40:13 (in that there are some who know the mind of God), the citation is not a "scriptural proof" in the strictest sense.[14]

I will examine the crucial *having* the mind of Christ in section 3, but for now I want to examine further *knowing* the mind of God. The double aspect of the hiddenness of God *and* the revelation of his "mind" is found not only in 1 Cor 2:6-16 but also in Romans 9–11. Romans 11:33-36 speaks of God's inscrutable ways and it is significant that this again includes a citation from Isa 40:13:

> [33]O the depth of the riches and wisdom and knowledge of God! How unsearchable are his judgements and how inscrutable his ways!

---

9. Hanson, "1 Corinthians 2.6-16," 84.

10. Schrage, *Korinther I*, 266: "Nicht von ungefähr greift Paulus hier . . . auf die Weisheitskritik der Prophetie zurück, die an der grundsätzlichen Unterschiedenheit von Gott und Mensch nie den geringsten Zweifel gelassen hat und jeden Gedanken daran ausschließt, daß angesichts der Unfaßbarkeit und Unerforschlichkeit Gottes der Mensch ihm für sein Planen und Handeln Ratschläge geben könnte."

11. Schrage, *Korinther I*, 266.

12. Hübner, *Biblische Theologie II*, 127, writes: "Wer wirklich glaubt und somit unbestritten Pneumatiker ist, *hat* Christi Geist und *weiß*, was dieser Geist über die Tiefen Gottes weiß" (his emphasis).

13. As Hübner, *Biblische Theologie II*, 127, graphically puts it: "*Wer den Geist hat, weiß, was Gott weiß!*" (his emphasis).

14. Hübner, *Biblische Theologie II*, 127: "Liegt also der Ton im abschließenden V. 16 nicht auf der Frage, sondern auf der so triumphierend klingenden Antwort, so dürfte Paulus trotz des begründenden γάρ keinen Schriftbeweis im strengen Sinne des Wortes vortragen."

³⁴"For who has known the mind of the Lord?
Or who has been his counsellor?"
³⁵"Or who has given a gift to him,
to receive a gift in return?"
³⁶For from him and through him and to him are all things. To him
be the glory (ἡ δόξα) for ever. Amen.

The quotation from Isa 40:13, this time lines 1 and 2, is supported by a quotation from Job 41:3 (a form which is close to the MT but different from the LXX).¹⁵ This section of text, taken alone, could give the impression that according to Paul no one can know the mind of God. But Romans 9–11 also reveals precisely the mystery of the salvation of Israel. Yes God's ways are unsearchable — but again God has revealed to Paul his plan to save the world in the mystery of Rom 11:25-27.

Both texts therefore have this double aspect (hiddenness and revelation). Further both 1 Cor 2:6-16 and Rom 11:33-36 share similar theological ideas. Both, in their quotation of Isa 40:13, refer κύριος to God rather than to Christ. Both passages share the theme of the depths of God; compare Rom 11:33 ('Ὦ βάθος πλούτου καὶ σοφίας καὶ γνώσεως θεοῦ) with 1 Cor 2:10 (τὰ βάθη τοῦ θεοῦ). Both passages share the vocabulary and themes of σοφία, γνῶσις and δόξα.¹⁶ Both speak of God putting to shame the wisdom of the world. As Käsemann comments on Rom 11:33: "As in 1 Cor 1:19 it is the God who acts under the opposite who is unsearchable and inscrutable. This God puts to shame the wisdom of the world by effecting the righteousness of the ungodly instead of the pious."¹⁷

Both texts point to a fundamental dialectic. God's purposes are indeed mysterious. Who can know his mind? Yet through the revelation of his mystery something can be known of God's mind. Therefore Paul is not insisting on the unknowability of God; and, of course, despite Isa 40:13, neither are the Old Testament witnesses.

Paul therefore believes that the Christian can know the mind of God. It is, I think, mistaken to contrast a "prophetic" to a "sapiential" approach.¹⁸

---

15. C. E. B. Cranfield, *The Epistle to the Romans*, vol. II, ICC (Edinburgh: T&T Clark, 1979), 591, writes that Paul either quotes the Hebrew or from a Greek version other than the LXX.
16. Note also the use of the crucial word μυστήριον in Rom 11:25 and 1 Cor 2:1, 7.
17. Ernst Käsemann, *Commentary on Romans* (ET; London: SCM, 1980), 319.
18. This I think is a problem with Schrage, *Korinther I*, 266. See also the (inappropriate)

1 Corinthians 2:6-16 has links to both traditions and to "apocalyptic."[19] Lang rightly argues that Wis 9:14-17 is an example of the wisdom tradition combined with an apocalyptic understanding of revelation which not only forms the background for a theology of revelation in 1 Cor 2:6-16 but also accounts to some extent for Paul's distinction between the "spiritual" and "unspiritual" in vv. 13-15.[20]

One of the fundamental points emerging from 1 Cor 2:6-16 is that the salvation which Christians experience is an *intelligible* salvation,[21] something perhaps taken for granted by many readers of the New Testament. But Christians not only *know* the mind of God; they *have* the mind of Christ. Paul's statement "we *have* the mind of Christ" is actually taking his argument a stage further and in fact is the crown of his argument. But how is this term "mind" to be understood? And how is *knowing* the mind of God related to *having* the mind of Christ? It is to these questions that I now turn.

The Mind of the Lord; the Mind of Christ

The answer to this particular "concept of mind" is partly to be found in the context of Isa 40:13 and the way the LXX has translated the Hebrew. Isaiah

---

polarization of views put forward by Schrage, 267, in regard to the nature of the Spirit (see below).

19. Hübner, *Biblische Theologie II*, 121, finds many theological connections between the passage and Daniel 2: "Die apokalyptische Terminologie von Dan 2 durchzieht also den hermeneutischen Exkurs 1 Kor 2,6ff." It is also worth emphasizing the links between "apocalyptic" and the "wisdom" tradition and that just as "apocalyptic" runs through 1 Cor 2:6-16 so does "wisdom."

20. Friedrich Lang, *Die Briefe an die Korinther*, NTD 7 (Göttingen: Vandenhoeck & Ruprecht, 1986), 40-41. Lang, *Korinther*, 46, also points to Gen 2:7 and Isa 31:3 to highlight the distinction between God who is "spirit" and humanity which is "flesh." In 1 Cor 2:14, Paul speaks of the "unspiritual" person (ψυχικός) who does not receive the spirit of God. Such a person is contrasted to the "spiritual" person (πνευματικός). This contrast is very unusual for Greek anthropology where "soul" (ψυχή) and "spirit" (πνεῦμα; see also νοῦς) were closely linked and which stand in contrast to the material body (σῶμα). Paul's view probably comes from Gen 2:7 LXX: "and God breathed (ἐνεφύσησεν) upon his face the breath of life (πνοὴν ζωῆς) . . . and the man became a living soul (εἰς ψυχὴν ζῶσαν)."

21. Hübner, *Biblische Theologie II*, 122: "Im Sinne des Exkurs 1 Kor 2,6ff. ist Hermeneutik essentiell *eschatologische Hermeneutik*. In diesem theologischen Zusammenhang fällt das Verstehen des Mysteriums mit dem Zustand des Heils zusammen. Verstandenes Heil ist identisch mit von Gott geschenktem Heil."

"But We Have the Mind of Christ"

40 begins with the section vv. 1-11 "Comfort my people" and a new section begins in v. 12 and runs to the end of the chapter (v. 31). Westermann entitles the section "The Creator is the Saviour."[22] There can be little doubt that this passage is concerned with God as creator. The significance of creation will, I hope, become apparent later on (although the focus is not on the *act* of creation but rather on the created order, both nature and history)[23] and is a theme which I feel has not received sufficient attention in commentaries on 1 Corinthians. For the MT of v. 13a (מִי־תִכֵּן אֶת־רוּחַ יְהוָה), most translators incorrectly render this "Who has *directed* the Spirit of God?"[24] But the MT can simply be translated "who has judged/known the Spirit of God." Exactly the same verb pi'el of תכן) has been used in the previous verse (40:12) where it means "measured."[25] If this is so, then the Septugintal translator has correctly understood the sense of the Hebrew of v. 13a: "Who has *known* the mind of God."[26] It is therefore unnecessary to argue that the LXX is based on the misreading הֵבִין.[27]

But has the LXX misrepresented the object of the verb, rendering רוּחַ not with πνεῦμα but rather with νοῦς? The term νοῦς occurs rarely in LXX. In three instances it renders "ear" אֹזֶן (Job 12:11 [B S A]; 33:16; 34:3 [A

---

22. Claus Westermann, *Isaiah 40–66: A Commentary*, OTL (London: SCM, 1969), 46-62. Note that the material in vv. 19-20 ("The Manufacture of Idols") has the same theme as 41:6-7. Westermann treats vv. 19-20 as a separate unit within chapter 40.

23. See Karl Elliger, *Deuterojesaja. 1. Teilband Jesaja 40,1–45,7*, BKAT 11.1 (Neukirchen-Vluyn: Neukirchener, 1978), 51, quoted below.

24. We have seen this in the NRSV. G. R. Driver, "Hebrew Notes," *VT* 1 (1951): 242-43, translates: "Who has set right, directed the Spirit of Yahweh." Note, however, that there are in fact cases where the root has an active sense of "setting right" (e.g., Ps 75:4[3]; see R. N. Whybray, *The Heavenly Counsellor in Isaiah xl 13-14*, SOTSMS 1 [Cambridge, London: Cambridge University Press, 1971], 14). Further, the sense of "to direct" may be the only way to translate the root in the Targum of Isa 40:13. See J. F. Stenning, ed., *The Targum of Isaiah* (Oxford: Clarendon, 1953 [repr., ¹1949]), 132: "Who hath directed (תקין) the holy spirit in the mouth of all the prophets? is it not the Lord? and to the righteous who perform his command (Memra) hath he made known the things (or *words*) of his good pleasure." See also the rendering of the Vulgate: "Who has helped the spirit of the Lord?" *(quis adiuvit spiritum Domini).*

25. As Elliger, *Deuterojesaja I*, 50, writes: "Es ist höchst unwahrscheinlich und durch nicht gefordert, das תכן in 13a eine andere Bedeutung habe als in 12ab."

26. Those who argue that this is a fitting translation include Whybray, *Heavenly Counsellor*, 16, and M. Delcor, "תכן bemessen," *THAT* 2: 1045. The only other case where תכן is rendered by γινώσκειν is Prov 24:12 (in this case the qal).

27. Cf. *BDB* 1067; Duhm J. Skinner, *The Book of the Prophet Isaiah, Chapters XL–LXVI*, CBSC (Cambridge: Cambridge University Press, 1917), 9, suggests the LXX translator read something other than תִכֵּן.

V]);[28] in six instances it renders לֵב לֵב (three of which are in Isaiah: 10:7, 12; 41:22); in one instance it renders "knowledge" דַּעַת (Prov 29:7: νοῦς ἐπιγνώμων); then in just this one instance, Isa 40:13, it renders רוּחַ. In Isa 40:13, the LXX has again faithfully translated the Hebrew for in this instance רוּחַ does have the sense of "mind." רוּחַ can be used for the mind of a human being.[29] Further, it can be used for God's mind. See Isa 30:1 where God condemns those who have "made a plan (עֵצָה, but not from me (מִנִּי); entered into an alliance, but not [sic] my Spirit (רוּחִי)."[30] One may consider also Bezalel who was filled with God's Spirit such that he was given practical intelligence (Exod 31:3; 35:31).[31] But whatever one may think of these other instances, in Isa 40:13a רוּחַ does have the sense of "mind." This is further suggested by v. 13b which speaks of intellectual formation (יוֹדִיעֶנּוּ).

Therefore in Isa 40:13a, the LXX has given a faithful translation. But what precisely is the sense of "mind" of Yahweh? The mind is not just a repository of knowledge. The "mind" of Yahweh is his executive in "creation," not just "creation" in his initial activity but also his "creation" in sustaining the world of nature and history.[32] The "mind of God" is an active entity just like the spirit and, arguing in a Kantian mode, one could say it differs from all other "minds" in that God's mind does not require spatial, temporal or linguistic categories. This is an important point to which I

---

28. Most texts of Job 12:11 and 34:3 read οὖς. David J. A. Clines, *Job 1–20*, WBC 17 (Dallas: Word Books, 1989), 295, compares Job 12:11 to Sir 36:19: "As the palate tastes the kinds of game, so an intelligent mind (καρδία συνετή) detects false words." Hence both texts concern the "mind."

29. Whybray, *Heavenly Counsellor*, 11, points to Ezek 20:32 (רוּחַ meaning the human mind) and 1 Chr 28:12 (the plan David "had in mind" for the building of the temple).

30. Whybray, *Heavenly Counsellor*, 12, argues that, although the reference may be to divine inspiration, "the context suggests that the point is rather that the plans are doomed to failure (verses 3-5) because they proceed from the defective intelligence of (rebellious) children (verse 1) rather than from the superior practical intelligence of God."

31. See Whybray, *Heavenly Counsellor*, 12, who points also to Ps 143:10: "Teach me to do your will. . . . Let your good spirit lead me."

32. Elliger, *Deuterojesaja I*, 51: "Diesen Geist nach seinen Motiven und Absichten, nach seinen Möglichkeiten und Wirkungen, und zwar nicht nur im Bestand der Schöpfung, sondern vor allem in deren Fortgang in Natur und Geschichte zu durchschauen, zu verstehen und zu begreifen, wer hat das je vermocht und vermag das überhaupt." Elliger, *Deuterojesaja I*, 50, is therefore critical of James Muilenburg, "Isaiah: Chapters 40–66," *IB* 5: 437, in writing: "God sends forth his Spirit as an active and life-giving force to do his work and achieve his purpose." In response, Elliger argues that Isaiah 40 does not concern a "Schöpfungsvorgang."

"But We Have the Mind of Christ"

shall return. Another way of understanding רוּחַ is as "heart" (לֵב). Such a רוּחַ constitutes God's personhood. In other words it could be understood precisely as his "mind."[33]

If the argument above concerning the sense of רוּחַ as "mind" is correct, then it questions an argument that has been put forward that Paul's preference for the LXX is striking in that he uses it (as in 1 Cor 2:16) even when the MT would have suited his purposes much better.[34] It is true, of course, that previously Paul has been speaking of the *Spirit* of God (vv. 10-14). By quoting the LXX it could be argued that Paul is *constrained* to switch the discussion over from the "Spirit of God" to the "mind of God" and the "mind of Christ." Or alternatively it could be argued that Paul equates "mind" and "spirit" here.

I am unconvinced by both these arguments. Regarding the first, I think that Paul is *deliberately* moving the argument on from questions of the "Spirit" to questions of the "mind." As I suggested above, his statement "But we have the mind of Christ" is the crown of his argument (and I return to this in the next section). Regarding the second argument, it is unlikely that Paul simply equates mind and spirit.[35] In fact in 1 Cor 14:14 νοῦς "is expressly opposed to πνεῦμα."[36] In 1 Cor 2:16 Paul really does mean

---

33. Elliger, *Deuterojesaja I*, 50: "Der 'Geist' ist vielmehr in einem umfassenden Sinne als לב das, was die Person Jahwes zur Person macht, das, was Duhm, wenn auch etwas zu eng, als das 'Organ des göttlichen Erkennens, Ratfindens, Beschließens' definiert und Volz in seiner Weise als 'das allumfassende und das geistige Wesen Jahwes', in dem 'vor allem die Züge des Willens und der Weisheit herausgearbeitet' sind, und wiederum etwas einseitig, aber durchaus den zentralen Punkt treffend, Westermann als 'Gottes wunderbar wirkende Kraft.'"

34. See Otto Michel, *Paulus und seine Bibel*, BFCTh 2.18 (Darmstadt: Wissenschaftliche Buchgesellschaft, ²1972 [¹1929]), 68; E. C. Blackman, "Mind, Heart," *TWBB*: 145. Some have therefore employed this argument to suggest that Paul had little or no knowledge of the Hebrew Bible.

35. Contrast Heinz-Dietrich Wendland, *Die Briefe an die Korinther*, NTD 7 (Göttingen: Vandenhoeck & Ruprecht, ⁶1954), 27, who believes Paul equates "Sinn" and "Geist." See also Gerhard Sellin, "Das 'Geheimnis' der Weisheit und das Rätsel der 'Christuspartei' (zu 1 Kor 1–4)," *ZNW* 73 (1982): 86 n. 61: "Wie πνεῦμα sozusagen Gottes νοῦς ist, so kann der menschliche νοῦς auch πνεῦμα des Menschen genannt werden. Christi νοῦς ist identisch mit dem göttlichen πνεῦμα (v. 16)." Such an identification has been rightly questioned by Christian Wolff, *Der erste Brief des Paulus an die Korinther*, ThHNT 7 (Berlin: Evangelische Verlagsanstalt, ²2000 [¹1996]), 62 n. 220. He translates νοῦς as "Sinn" (51) or "Vernunft" (62 n. 220).

36. Thiselton, *I Corinthians*, 275, quoting E. B. Allo, *Saint Paul. Première Épître aux Corinthiens* (Paris: Gabalda, ²1956), 105.

"mind" (and not "spirit") as is the case also in Rom 11:34. And rather than *equating* mind and Spirit, Spirit can be seen as the *means* by which the mind of Christ is formed in the believer.³⁷

I will return to this activity of the Spirit in the next section, but now I need to establish what Paul means by the "mind of Christ." There has been considerable debate on this and in the reading I have done, the most prevalent view is that "mind" here constitutes "not an instrument of thought" but rather "a mode of thought" or "mind-set."³⁸ I wonder though whether "mind-set" is too narrow an understanding of νοῦς. We have seen already that in the Old Testament context, "mind of God" is indeed something more like "an organ of thought." So Elliger writes that the "mind" of Yahweh is like the "heart" of Yahweh and is that which defines the *person* of Yahweh. Duhm writes that it is the organ of divine perception and decision. For Paul, such views are suggested by the context of 1 Cor 2:6-16. For v. 11 speaks of knowing the human being through his spirit and likewise knowing God through God's spirit. This is not, as many now recognize, suggesting that the human spirit is the link to the divine.³⁹ Rather Paul is simply arguing that the essence of the human being can only be known through the spirit of the human being. Likewise the essence of God can only be known through the Spirit of God.⁴⁰ Then in v. 15 he says that those who are spiri-

---

37. Cf. F. Godet, *Commentary on St. Paul's First Epistle to the Corinthians*, vol. I, CFTL 27 (Edinburgh: T&T Clark, n.d.), 163: "The Spirit is the agent by whom this mind of God is communicated to the spiritual man."

38. Thiselton, *I Corinthians*, 275. See also Hans Conzelmann, *Der erste Brief an die Korinther*, KEK 5 (Göttingen: Vandenhoeck & Ruprecht, ²1981 [¹1969]), 68: "[νοῦς] bezeichnet hier nicht das Organ des Denkens, sondern den Inhalt, seine Heilsgedanken."

39. Peter Stuhlmacher, "The Hermeneutical Significance of 1 Cor 2:6-16," in *Tradition and Interpretation in the New Testament: Essays in Honor of E. Earle Ellis*, ed. Gerald Hawthorne and Otto Betz (Grand Rapids: Eerdmans; Tübingen: J. C. B. Mohr [Paul Siebeck]), 1987), 330, points to Semler's equation of Calvin's *testimonium Spiritus Sancti internum* with "man's inner conviction of rational, moral truths" thereby eliminating "the distinction between the Holy Spirit and rational insight that was characteristic of Paul and the Reformers." Such a view was bolstered by Hegel's idealism. So Baur writes that in Christian consciousness God's Spirit and human spirit become identical. Such a view was "permanently shattered" by Hermann Gunkel's *Die Wirkungen des heiligen Geistes nach der populären Anschauung der apostolischen Zeit und nach der Lehre des Apostels Paulus* (1888), who wrote that for the early Church "the relationship between divine and human activity is that of mutually exclusive opposition. The activity of the Spirit is thus not an intensifying of what is native to all. It is the absolutely supernatural and hence divine" (ET 1979, 34).

40. Paul is therefore arguing that something can only be known through a similar entity, an ancient philosophical maxim. See, e.g., Helmut Merklein, *Der erste Brief an die*

tual discern all things, and they are themselves subject to no one else's scrutiny. This extraordinary idea is then established in v. 16. *Just as no one has known the mind of the Lord so as to instruct him (Isa 40:13c), so no one has the known the mind of the spiritual person so as to instruct him either.* Paul is speaking of the privilege of the "spiritual" Christians. They literally have the mind of Christ.[41] They have this "organ of thought."

If mind of Christ were simply taken to mean "mind-set" of Christ then there are two possible problems. First, this argument from v. 15 to v. 16 is not really appreciated. Verse 15b is established by means of the first line of the quotation from Isa 40:13. The logic from 15b-16a is therefore as follows: because no one can access God's mind, no one can make a judgement about the "spiritual person" who has received God's Spirit.[42] Or considering the logic from 15b through to 16a-c Knox writes: "No man knows the mind of the Lord, so as to be able to instruct Him; but the natural man who criticises the spiritual man is in effect trying to do so, for he is criticising the mind of Christ, as possessed by the spiritual Christian."[43]

The second problem with taking the mind of Christ as the "content of the thoughts" is that there has to be a change of meaning of νοῦς from 16a to 16c. So Schrage sees a switch from thoughts on salvation in 16a to a spiritual sense of judgement in 16c.[44] Such a change of meaning of νοῦς does not present an insuperable difficulty. But the idea of "organ of thought" seems so much more natural in the context and does not necessitate changing the meaning of νοῦς within one verse. This is because even in v. 16a we are speaking of an "organ of thought" rather than a "mind set." For Isa 40:13, as Elliger and others have argued, is speaking of something like the "heart" of Yahweh.

Korinther, Kapitel 1–4, ÖTzNT 7.1 (Gütersloh: Gütersloher Verlagshaus Gerd Mohn; Würzburg: Echter, 1992), 236-37.

41. Johannes Weiß, *Der erste Korintherbrief,* KEK 5 (Göttingen: Vandenhoeck & Ruprecht, 1977 [repr., ⁹1910]), 67: "Dem herausfordernden Satz αὐτὸς δὲ ὑπ' οὐδενὸς ἀνακρίνεται läßt P. einen noch kühneren Schriftbeweis folgen, der uns einen überraschenden Blick in das religiöse Hochgefühl des Apostels eröffnet."

42. Cf. Schrage, *Korinther I,* 266-67: "Weil kein Mensch in Gottes Denken eindringen kann, kann auch niemanden ein Urteil über die zukommen, die Gottes Geist empfangen haben."

43. Wilfred L. Knox, *St Paul and the Church of the Gentiles* (Cambridge: Cambridge University Press, 1939), 116.

44. Schrage, *Korinther I,* 267: "Offenbar ist im Anschluß an V 14f hier nicht an Gottes Heilsgedanken zu denken wie in V 16a, sondern an die pneumatische Urteilsfähigkeit, mit der die Weisheit denkerisch erfaßt und handelnd umgesetzt wird."

But are there any arguments for taking "mind" in 2:16 as "content of thought" or "mind set"? I consider two. First, one could argue that, in Rom 11:34, Isa 40:13 is simply being applied to God's plan of salvation ("Gottes Heilsgedanken"). I grant that this is the central focus here but in view of Rom 11:33-36 I am not convinced that the "mind of the Lord" is simply being reduced to this. The same goes for the "mind of Christ" in 1 Cor 2:16c. I take the point made by Lang and Wilckens that the wisdom which Paul teaches the "mature" does not *transcend* the "word concerning the cross" (1:18); but as they also suggest, it can also include things which are a *deepening* of this word.[45] Therefore the revealed wisdom of God does not have to be restricted to ideas of "salvation."[46]

A second argument for "mind set" is that νοῦς in 1 Cor 2:16 could mean precisely what it means in 1 Cor 1:10: "Now I appeal to you, brothers and sisters, by the name of our Lord Jesus Christ, that all of you should be in agreement and that there should be no divisions among you, but that you should be united in the same mind and the same purpose." Therefore Weiß argues that νοῦς in 1:10 does not means organ of judgement/thought; rather it means "mentality" ("Gesinnung"), "way of thinking" ("Denkweise").[47] But even that is not certain in 1:10. For if Paul can speak of the Church as the body of Christ perhaps he is also referring here to the mind of Christ. And even if it does mean "mind set" in 1:10, the use of "mind" in relation to "mind of *Christ*" in 2:16 could suggest a different meaning.

It is striking how many commentators wish to avoid the idea of the "organ of thought" in 2:16 even though it may be the most obvious meaning. Willis, for example, writes that "mind of Christ" in 2:16 "refers to believers having their outlook shaped by an awareness of Christ. He is the norm for the consciousness or 'outlook' of the Christian community."[48]

---

45. See Lang, *Korinther,* 41: "Der Inhalt der geheimnisvollen Weisheit, die Paulus und seine Mitarbeiter nach 2,6 unter den Vollkommenen verkündigen, ist also keine höhere Weisheit, die über den Gekreuzigten hinausführt, sondern nur 'eine vertiefende Interpretation des Wortes vom Kreuz' (U. Wilckens), die Paulus in dieser Weise den Korinthern noch nicht vorgetragen hat."

46. Hence Sellin, "Christuspartei," 88, is quite wrong to write: "Ziel der Erkenntnis ist aber nach Paulus der Plan Gottes (τὰ βάθη), das Kreuzesgeschehen."

47. Weiß, *Der erste Korintherbrief,* 14. Note that Thiselton, *I Corinthians,* 120, writes that according to Weiß νοῦς "means something *more* than an organ of thought" (my emphasis). However, I think that "organ of thought" is something more fundamental than "mind-set"; for the mind-set *emerges* from the organ of thought.

48. Wendell Willis, "The 'Mind of Christ' in 1 Corinthians 2,16," *Bib* 70 (1989): 118.

"But We Have the Mind of Christ"

He supports his view by turning to Phil 2:1-11 and believes "[t]his Philippians passage gives an important clue to correctly understanding the meaning of 'mind of Christ' in 1 Cor 2,16."[49] But Philippians 2 concerns *imitation* whereas 1 Corinthians 2 concerns *participation*.[50]

Therefore to have the mind of Christ does not simply mean to hold certain propositions to be true. Neither is it to have a certain "mind set" or to have an "outlook shaped by an awareness of Christ." Rather, as the context suggests, the Christian really does have the mind of Christ whereby he accesses the mind of God.

Theological and Anthropological Reflections

This now brings me to some theological and anthropological issues concerning the "mind." A major strand in Paul's argument in 2:6-16 is that only the Spirit of God can discern the mind of God. So in 2:10 the Spirit discerns "the depths of God" (τὰ βάθη τοῦ θεοῦ) and in 2:11 knows "the things of God" (τὰ τοῦ θεοῦ). Both these expressions, τὰ βάθη τοῦ θεοῦ and τὰ τοῦ θεοῦ, primarily connote the mind of God.[51] No one can know the mind of God. But in having the mind of Christ *we* can come to know the mind of God; *we* can plumb the depths of God.

I argued above that the "mind of God" and the "mind of Christ" are not to be understood simply as the "content" of the mind or the "mind set." Rather we are thinking of the "organ of thought" which in many respects defines the very personhood of God and of Christ. The Christian therefore knows the mind of God in that he has the mind of Christ and hence shares in his personhood. The Christian is not merely acquainted with the *saving acts of God*. He is acquainted with his *person*.

In this connection I must express some serious reservations concerning Melanchthon's idea expressed in the "theological outline" of the *Loci communes theologici* that "to know Christ means to know his benefits" *(hoc est Christum cognoscere, beneficia eius cognoscere)*.[52] This idea is reflected to some extent in Hübner's discussion of 1 Cor 2:6-16. Although it is legitimate to say that "the essence of God discloses itself in the action of God"

---

49. Willis, "Mind," 119.
50. See Weiß, *Der erste Korintherbrief,* 68-69.
51. Again see Rom 11:33-34: Ὦ βάθος πλούτου καὶ σοφίας καὶ γνώσεως θεοῦ·.... [34]Τίς γὰρ ἔγνω νοῦν κυρίου;
52. See Wilhelm Pauck, ed., *Melanchthon and Bucer,* LCC 19 (London: SCM, 1969), 21.

("Gottes *Wesen* erschließt sich in seinem *Handeln*")[53] it is certainly not correct to go on to say "Paul does not at all distinguish between Being and Doing" ("Paulus unterscheidet eben nicht zwischen Sein und Tun").[54] Hübner's approach is also reflected in his comments on Rom 8:3 where he appears to reduce Christology to soteriology.[55] The idea that God's essence and being can be reduced to his action was fundamental to theologians such as Schleiermacher,[56] Ritschl[57] and Bultmann[58] but has been rightly questioned by another Lutheran, Dietrich Bonhoeffer.[59]

Although "depths of God" does primarily refer to the "mind" of God as an "organ of thought," secondarily it could connote the "content" of the mind of God. But what precisely could "depths of God" mean here? The first point to make is that the "depths of God" are *rooted* in the crucified one, Jesus Christ. But the "depths of God" are not to be *reduced* to the cross. A superficial reading of some works of Martin Luther may suggest this.[60] And Hübner almost identifies the "depths of God" with the salvation through the word of the cross, thereby collapsing all knowledge of the "depths of God" to the cross.[61] More to the point is that the revelation of the wisdom and power of God is none other than a *deeper* understanding of the cross *and* resurrection of Christ.[62]

This now brings me to the "trinitarian" character of Paul's argument in 1 Cor 2:6-16. To a limited extent this trinitarian character is anticipated al-

53. Hübner, *Biblische Theologie II*, 125-26.
54. Hübner, *Biblische Theologie II*, 126.
55. Hübner, *Biblische Theologie II*, 298: "*Soteriologie ist Christologie*, aber *Christologie ist auch Soteriologie*" (his emphasis).
56. See, e.g., Friedrich Schleiermacher, *On Religion: Speeches to Its Cultured Despisers*, HT 36 (ET; New York: Harper & Brothers, 1958), 48.
57. See James Richmond, *Ritschl: A Reappraisal* (London: Collins, 1978), 298.
58. See John Macquarrie, *The Scope of Demythologizing: Bultmann and His Critics*, LPT (London: SCM, 1960), 117, who quotes Bultmann, *Essays — Theological and Philosophical*, 287: "The formula 'Christ is God' is false in every sense in which God is understood as an entity which can be objectivized, whether it is understood in an Arian or Nicene, an orthodox or a liberal sense. It is correct if 'God' is understood here as the event of God's acting."
59. Dietrich Bonhoeffer, *Christology* (ET; London: Fontana, 1971), 37-40.
60. See, e.g, *crux sola est nostra theologia*, WA 5:176.32-33 (on Ps 5:12).
61. Hübner, *Biblische Theologie II*, 125; Lang, *Korinther*, 79.
62. See Lang, *Korinther*, 41: "Der Inhalt der geheimnisvollen Weisheit, die Paulus und seine Mitarbeiter nach 2,6 unter den Vollkommenen verkündigen, ist also keine höhere Weisheit, die über den Gekreuzigten hinausführt, sondern nur 'eine vertiefende Interpretation des Wortes vom Kreuz' (U. Wilckens), die Paulus in dieser Weise den Korinthern noch nicht vorgetragen hat."

ready in deutero-Isaiah where God has a heavenly council. Although deutero-Isaiah denied the existence of other gods and stressed the sovereignty of Yahweh, he retained the idea of a heavenly council. As Whybray argues: "Just as the human personality was inconceivable except in the context of a society, so also was the divine."[63] The sovereign God of deutero-Isaiah is not "an isolated monad";[64] he has a heavenly council the idea of which can be discerned at the very opening of the deutero-Isaiah (Isa 40:1-8).[65]

Paul's "trinitarian theology" is related to this view of God in Isaiah but he develops it in a radical direction. For not only does he develop a "trinitarian theology"; he also argues that the Christian is incorporated into the very life of the Trinity. By sharing in the mind of Christ he has some access to the mind of God. So Paul does not speak of an *imitation* of the mind of Christ or say that information about God is simply *conveyed*. Neither is sharing in Christ's mind like a normal "learning experience." Rather Paul's point is that in some sense Christians have undergone an ontological change such that they share in Christ's mind or that the mind of Christ is formed in them. But how does this transformation occur? How can this transformation be understood in Paul's own theological framework and in the light of subsequent theological and philosophical tradition?

I think there are three possible ways of understanding how the mind of Christ is formed in the Christian. The first is through the transformative "word"; the second is through the work of the Holy Spirit; the third is through participation in Christ. These are not three hermetically sealed approaches. For sometimes Paul speaks of participation in Christ by means of the Holy Spirit (1 Cor 12:13); also "Spirit" and "word" are clearly related as are "word" and participation. Nevertheless it will help to consider these three approaches in turn.

First, the mind of Christ could be understood as formed in the Christian through the "reconciling word," in particular "the word which concerns the cross" (1:18).[66] This word of the cross (1:18) can be said to issue in,

---

63. Whybray, *Heavenly Counsellor*, 83.
64. Whybray, *Heavenly Counsellor*, 83.
65. See, e.g., H. W. Robinson, "The Council of Yahweh," *JTS* 45 (1944): 151-57; F. M. Cross, "The Council of Yahweh in Second Isaiah," *JNES* 12 (1953): 274-78; G. Ernest Wright, *The Old Testament Against Its Environment*, SBT 2 (London: SCM, 1953 [repr., ¹1950]), 37 n. 52, who acknowledges Cross.
66. The expression ὁ λόγος . . . ὁ τοῦ σταυροῦ is to be understood as an "objective genitive" (Ulrich Heckel, *Kraft in Schwachheit. Untersuchungen zu 2. Kor 10–13*, WUNT 2.56 [Tübingen: J. C. B. Mohr (Paul Siebeck), 1993], 290).

or correspond to, the preaching (1:21-23).⁶⁷ This word can have creative power "for those who are being saved" (1:18b) and it is this word which produces faith in the hearer.⁶⁸ It is a word which can be said to precede thought.⁶⁹ Paul's epistemology is therefore fundamentally anti-Cartesian. If the word produces faith in the hearer, and if it gives life to the dead (cf. Rom 4:17), if it is the word which comes to us *extra nos*,⁷⁰ could it not also form the mind of Christ in the believer? That we have the mind of Christ is something which cannot be empirically tested just as the Church being the body of Christ cannot be so tested. We are concerned with "practical knowing" as opposed to "theoretical knowing."⁷¹

67. Cf. Otfried Hofius, "Wort Gottes und Glaube bei Paulus," in *Paulusstudien*, WUNT 51 (Tübingen: J. C. B. Mohr [Paul Siebeck], 1989), 158 n. 71, who, commenting on 1 Cor 1:18, writes: "Dieser Aussage über das Evangelium korrespondiert dann die Aussage über die Predigt in 1,21."

68. Cf. Rom 10:8, where τὸ ῥῆμα τῆς πίστεως probably means the word which produces faith.

69. Cf. Eberhard Jüngel, *God as the Mystery of the World: On the Foundation of the Theology of the Crucified One in the Dispute Between Theism and Atheism* (ET; Edinburgh: T&T Clark, 1983), 155: "the place of the conceivability of God is a Word which precedes thought" (Eberhard Jüngel, *Gott als Geheimnis der Welt. Zur Begründung der Theologie des Gekreuzigten im Streit zwischen Theismus und Atheismus* [Tübingen: J. C. B. Mohr (Paul Siebeck), ⁵1985 (¹1977)], 206: "der Ort der Denkbarkeit Gottes [ist] ein dem Denken vorangehendes Wort"). John B. Webster, *Eberhard Jüngel: An Introduction to His Theology* (Cambridge: Cambridge University Press, 1986), 59, points to Jüngel's delicate balance between "revelation" and "reason." On the one hand, Jüngel, *Mystery*, 166, can write: "Thought can only begin if it begins with *something* which is already there independent of all thought" (Jüngel, *Geheimnis*, 223: "Das Denken kann nur anfangen, wenn es mit *etwas* anfängt, das unabhängig von allem Denken schon da ist"). And on the other hand, he can write: "The formation of concepts done by thought is its creative act, initiated by the object but yet derived solely from the power of reason" (167); "Die Begriffsbildung des Denkens ist dessen — am Gegenstand zwar sich entzündender, aber doch nur aus der Kraft der Vernunft entspringender — schöpferischer Akt" (223).

70. Such an external word can be related in terms of scripture to the *claritas externa*. See Friedrich Beisser, *Claritas scripturae bei Martin Luther*, FKD 18 (Göttingen: Vandenhoeck & Ruprecht, 1966), 88: "Luther betont den Vorrang der claritas externa. . . . Es liegt alles daran, daß Gott allein uns erlöst, und es liegt alles daran, daß er allein uns diese Erlösung verkündigt. Dies ist es nämlich, was im verbum externum sich vollzieht. Darum ist es selber und aus sich klar, weil Gott es spricht. Die claritas externa ist es, die das extra nos des Heiles verbürgt."

71. Commenting on 1 Cor 12:12ff., Johannes Fischer, "Über die Beziehung von Glaube und Mythos," *ZThK* 85 (1988): 306-7, writes: "Jene Sätze beziehen sich . . . auf eine Realität, welche weder empirisch festgestellt noch normativ vorgeschrieben werden kann, sondern welche aus der Glaubenserkenntnis der Korinther hervorwächst, indem diese jene indika-

"But We Have the Mind of Christ"

The second way of understanding the formation of the mind of Christ in the believer is through the work of the Holy Spirit.[72] That the Spirit forms the mind of Christ could be inferred by comparing 2:16 with 2:10-12. In 2:10-12 Paul may seem to be making a related point to that in 2:16. He does not refer to the mind but the context may suggest that "the things of the person" and "the things of God" are somehow related to the "mind" or "heart": "For what human being knows the things of the person (τὰ τοῦ ἀνθρώπου) except the spirit of the person which is within? So also, no one comprehends what is truly God's (τὰ τοῦ θεοῦ) except the Spirit of God" (2:11). Paul then takes this a stage further: not only is the Spirit the *instrument* of revelation (2:10-11); it is also the *medium* in which human beings perceive this revelation[73] for they have *received* the Spirit (2:12).

The question now is whether this receiving the Spirit (2:12) is to be equated with having the mind of Christ (2:16). Hanson simply equates Christ and Spirit.[74] Knox equates the "divine gift of the Spirit" with "the mind of the Lord"[75] and essentially equates Wisdom, Christ, and Spirit.[76] However, Paul makes a clearer distinction than Hanson or Knox allows. There may be some "Wisdom Christology" in 1 Corinthians but in our context Paul's point is that Christ has *become* our Wisdom (1 Cor 1:30). Further, Christ and Spirit are not simply equated in our passage. So rather than "receiving the Spirit" being equated with "having the mind of Christ," it is more the case that through the Spirit the mind of Christ is formed in us.[77] Hence Paul's argument in 2:16 goes beyond that of 2:10-12.

---

tivischen Sätze ihrer Erkenntnis in ihre Situation als Gemeinde abbilden.... Der Abschnitt gibt damit eine Anschauung von dem, was wir hier praktische Erkenntnis nennen, also von einer Erkenntnis, welche nicht empirische Wirklichkeit ins Wort, sondern das Wirklichkeit ansagende Wort in die Phänomene abbildet und dadurch Wahrnehmung begründet."

72. Just as the "word" can be related to the *claritas externa* of scripture, so the Holy Spirit can be related to the *claritas interna*.

73. Merklein, *1 Kor I*, 237: "Der Geist Gottes ist nicht nur das Instrument der göttlichen Offenbarung, sondern zugleich das Medium, in dem der Mensch diese wahrnehmen kann...."

74. Hanson, "1 Corinthians 2.6-16."

75. Knox, *Church of the Gentiles*, 117.

76. Knox, *Church of the Gentiles*, 118, writes that "Wisdom was the possession of the spiritual Christian, who possessed in the Spirit the mind of Christ, the Wisdom of God. Thus the purpose of God, His Wisdom hitherto concealed but now revealed in the Messianic figure of Jesus, is also the creative Wisdom which was with God in the first beginning of creation; the whole argument depends for its force on this equation of Jesus with the cosmic Wisdom, and the further equation of that Wisdom with the divine Spirit immanent in the cosmos, yet vouchsafed to the Christian, or at least to the spiritual Christian."

77. Cf. Calvin, *Institutes* 3.2.34: "It is through the Spirit that we come to grasp 'the mind

The third way of understanding the formation of the mind of Christ is through "participation." Here we have two aspects. First, there is the idea of Christ being at work in the Christian. Weiß points to this as a possible way of explaining Paul's remarkable statement that Christians have the mind of Christ. He argues that this coheres with Paul's idea that the power and personality of Christ are at work in the Christian.[78] But the second aspect of participation is that the Christian is "in Christ" as a result of having undergone certain transformations "with Christ," namely death and resurrection. This idea lies at the heart of Paul's understanding of the atonement, baptism, and the associated new creation.[79] It is this aspect of participation which now concerns me; for if the Christian is "in Christ," then it seems reasonable that he shares in the mind of Christ.

Participation is an important theme in 1 Corinthians especially in 10:16-22; 12:12-31; 15:20-58. But already we see a hint in the thanksgiving (1:4-5); it is also suggested in the discussion of baptism in 1:10-17 in that Paul denies that Christ is divided and that they were baptized into the name of Paul, implying that they have been baptized into Christ's name and are now in Christ. We see it also in 1:30: "He (God) is the source of your life in Christ Jesus, who became for us wisdom from God, and righteousness and sanctification and redemption." Although Paul does not explicitly relate the mind of Christ to participation in Christ, such a relationship does provide a possible explanation for Paul's theological logic.

I have already related this having the mind of Christ to Paul's "trinitarian" theology in 1 Cor 2:6-16. I think it is a legitimate development from this passage to say that the Christian participates not just in Christ but also in the life of the Trinity. Such participation in the Trinity is highlighted in Leonard Hodgson's Croal Lectures (1942-43). So "there is a social life in the godhead, into the current of which life the Christian is taken up, so that his life is that of a member of the divine society, *looking out on the world from within it.*"[80] Now it may be objected that although this seems an interesting theological

---

of Christ'" (John T. McNeill, ed., *Calvin: Institutes of the Christian Religion*, LCC [Philadelphia: Westminster, 1960], 2:582).

78. Weiß, *Der erste Korintherbrief*, 69, writes that for Paul it is "ein lieber und vertrauter Gedanke, daß nicht nur die Kraft (II Kor 12$_9$), sondern geradezu die Persönlichkeit Christi in ihn übergegangen sei: Christus lebt in mir (Gal 2$_{20}$), redet in mir (II Kor 13$_3$), sein Leben wirkt sich aus in meinem hinfälligen Leibe (II Kor 4$_{10}$f.). . . ."

79. See Richard H. Bell, "Sacrifice and Christology in Paul," *JTS* 53 (2002): 1-27.

80. Leonard Hodgson, *The Doctrine of the Trinity* (London: Nisbet and Co., 1946 [repr., ^{1}1943]), 49 (my emphasis).

"But We Have the Mind of Christ"

idea, it hardly corresponds to experience. Hodgson responds to this by saying that theological truth cannot be tested by experience.[81] But he develops this in a rather unfocussed way,[82] and I think something much more specific can be offered. No doubt most Christians will say that they do not really *feel* as though they are "a member of the divine society, *looking out on the world from within it.*" And certainly a process of introspection will yield little also. But if they take a moment to look inward they discover, of course, that the greater part of their personhood is unknown to them anyway, something which has been recognized by many including the Hebrew prophets,[83] Paul,[84] and the ancient Greeks.[85] By looking inward it is difficult to know whether one is looking out at the world from within the Holy Trinity.

This highlights a crucial aspect of participation. Just as the participation in Adam is not something we are conscious of, so we are not conscious of participating in Christ or in the Holy Trinity. We are not aware of dying with Christ on the first Good Friday or rising with him on the first Easter Sunday.[86] Neither are we conscious of having the mind of Christ in the sense that this can be established by looking inwards. That we have the mind of Christ is something which can only be held in faith. It is a result of participation in both the death and resurrection of Christ.[87]

---

81. Hodgson, *Trinity,* 58. However, he concedes that the experience of the Day of Pentecost suggests that experience cannot be discounted (59).

82. Hodgson, *Trinity,* 59, argues that the ultimate foundation is that "the truth of Christianity rests upon the impossibility of giving an adequate account of the appearances of the figure of Jesus Christ in the pages of history except upon the recognition of Him as God incarnate, living and dying to redeem mankind and usher in the Kingdom of God."

83. See, e.g., Jer 17:9: "The heart is devious above all else; it is perverse — who can understand it?" See also the many texts (such as Jer 17:10) which speak of God as the only one who can search the heart.

84. Even if, as is most likely, the "I" of Rom 7:14-24 is trans-subjective, it nevertheless points to the incomprehensibility of the human person.

85. The maxim γνῶθι σεαυτόν (know yourself), which goes back to the seven wise men (usually ascribed to Thales or Chilon) and is inscribed on the temple of Apollo in Delphi and quoted by Plato (*Protagoras* 343A1-B3; *Charmides* 164D3-165A7), does not so much call one to self-analysis but rather points to the severe limitations of human existence often in the light of mortality (see Dieter Zeller, "Die Worte der Sieben Weisen — ein Zeugnis volkstümlicher griechischer Ethik," in *Die Worte der Sieben Weisen,* Jochen Althoff and Dieter Zeller, TzF 89 [Darmstadt: Wissenschaftliche Buchgesellschaft, 2006], 119-22).

86. Hence the idea that participation occurs via the "soul" is so fundamental. See Richard H. Bell, *Deliver Us from Evil: Interpreting the Redemption from the Power of Satan in New Testament Theology,* WUNT 216 (Tübingen: J. C. B. Mohr [Paul Siebeck], 2007), 189-291.

87. Some have argued that the "mind of Christ" which Christians have is the mind of

So one may indeed be "looking out on the world from within [the Trinity]" without in any sense being aware of this. Descending from the heights of Paul's Christ-mythology to the more sober level of Gilbert Ryle, one can say that just as the "I" as subject is "elusive," so is the "mind." Perhaps one can say that *having* the "mind" of Christ does not entail a *consciousness* of having *that* mind.[88]

---

the *crucified* Christ. In v. 16c we have a change from κυρίου to Χριστοῦ (but note that B D* FG Ambrosiaster, Pelagius, and Augustine read νοῦν κυρίου). Paul may have used Χριστός simply to make clear that he is moving from a reference to God in 16a to Jesus Christ in 16c. However, by using Χριστός many commentators have argued that Paul is emphasizing the crucified one (see 1 Cor 1:17, 23-24, 30; 2:2) (see Ulrich Wilckens, *Weisheit und Torheit. Eine exegetisch-religionsgeschichtliche Untersuchung zu 1. Kor. 1 und 2*, BHTh 26 [Tübingen: J. C. B. Mohr (Paul Siebeck), 1959], 95; Schrage, *Korinther I*, 267). This may well be the case. But having the "mind of Christ" must also include the mind of the resurrected Christ who was crucified. If we participate in Christ, this must include the risen Christ also! Schrage, *Korinther I*, 267-68, gives false alternatives when he writes thus: "Das Pneuma, das die Christen Verstehen lehrt, ist nicht irgendein Feld-, Wald- und Wiesengeist oder eine naturhaft-magische, Enthusiasmus bewirkende Potenz, sondern das Pneuma des gekreuzigten Christus, also am Kreuz zu messen und darum unausweichlich ein Kritiker aller eigenen Weisheit und ebenso aller elitären. Letztlich ist nur der vom Geist und von Weisheit erfüllt, der im Glauben an den Gekreuzigten lebt." In this connection 1 Cor 2:16 was an important text for the doctrine of deification. Norman Russell, *The Doctrine of Deification in the Greek Patristic Tradition*, OECS (Oxford: Oxford University Press, 2004), 317, quoting Panayiotis Nellas, *Deification in Christ: Orthodox Perspectives on the Nature of the Human Person*, CGT 5 (Crestwood, NY: St. Vladimir's Seminary Press, 1987), 39: "The real anthropological meaning of deification is Christification. When he urges the faithful to show that they are attaining 'to mature manhood, to the measure of the stature of the fullness of Christ' (Eph. 4:13), and to acquire 'the mind of Christ' (1 Cor 2:16), the heart of Christ (cf. Eph 3:17), and so on, St. Paul does not do so for reasons of external piety and sentiment; he speaks ontologically. He is not advocating an external imitation or a simple ethical improvement but a real Christification. For as St. Maximos says, 'God the divine Logos wishes to effect the mystery of his incarnation always and in all things.'"

88. The relation of "consciousness" to "what it is conscious of" is mysterious even without bringing in the "mind of Christ"! Locke was the first to use the term "consciousness" consistently (Howard Caygill, *A Kant Dictionary*, BPD [Oxford: Blackwell, 1995], 126), deriving it from acts of consciousness and seeing it as the key to the "self" (see John Locke, *An Essay Concerning Human Understanding* [Harmondsworth: Penguin, 1997], 313-14 [2.27.25]). Kant subscribed to the "Wolffian school" in maintaining that "[t]he identity of the consciousness of myself at different times is . . . only a formal condition of my thoughts and their coherence, and in no way proves the numerical identity of my subject" (Immanuel Kant, *Critique of Pure Reason*, ed. Norman Kemp Smith, intro. Howard Caygill [Basingstoke/New York: Palgrave Macmillan, 2003], 342 (A 363, Third Paralogism). Caygill, *Kant Dictionary*, 127, relates this back to the "Original Synthetic Unity of Apperception" (§16).

"But We Have the Mind of Christ"

The idea of the subject as an "elusive I" is a post-Cartesian construct and despite its limitations it has proved extremely fruitful. Standing in this tradition, Schopenhauer argued that the subject of knowing can "never be known or become object or representation."[89] So what the "subject of knowing" actually comes to know is not itself but the "subject of willing." So within us "the known as such is not the knower but the willer."[90] Applying this to our enquiry, it means that by looking inward the Christian will never know whether he has the "mind of Christ." This can only be asserted "in faith."

A Concluding Philosophical Postscript on the "Theology of Mind"

The previous discussion has, I hope, highlighted the role of "mind" and of "soul" in Paul's understanding of the Christian's relationship to Christ. I argued earlier that the LXX translator may have seen the mind of God as an active entity, related to his creative activity. Such creative activity is not confined to the first moment of creation. Rather, as Elliger has rightly stressed, the creative activity of the mind of God is related to what many have called continuous creation. In particular the mind of God is related to the world of nature and of history.[91] In this final section I move on to discuss a hermeneutical question: how can we understand 1 Cor 2:16 in the light of what I consider to be some of the most profound philosophical reflection on the nature of "mind," "subject" and "object," namely that of Kant and Schopenhauer?

One of Kant's fundamental insights is the manner in which we form "representations." We are not passive receivers of sense data. What then can we say about Christians having the mind of Christ? As I have indi-

---

89. Arthur Schopenhauer, *On the Fourfold Root of the Principle of Sufficient Reason* (ET; LaSalle: Open Court, 1974), 210.

90. Schopenhauer, *Fourfold Root*, 211-12 (42), continues: "the identity of the subject of willing with that of knowing by virtue whereof (and indeed necessarily) the word 'I' includes and indicates both, is the knot of the world, and hence inexplicable. . . . whoever really grasps the inexplicable nature of this identity will call it, as I do, the miracle *par excellence*." Günter Zöller, "Schopenhauer on the Self," in *The Cambridge Companion to Schopenhauer*, ed. Christopher Janaway (Cambridge: Cambridge University Press, 1999), 26, points out: "For Schopenhauer the non-causal structural correlativity that holds between the subject of cognition and the subject of willing ultimately amounts to their identity."

91. Elliger, *Deuterojesaja I*, 51.

cated, I feel rather dissatisfied with the view that having the mind of Christ simply means sharing his "values." Paul is going much further than that. If we have the mind of Christ, then could this not entail forming the representations which Christ forms? Could it not mean that we employ the categories which Christ employs? Could it not mean that we take on the creative activity of Christ? Perhaps Christians, having the mind of Christ, form distinctive "representations" and thereby become God's "co-creators" on earth. They are not only God's hand and feet *in the world;* they are also his eyes and ears *on the boundary of the world.*[92]

But in a sense all sentient creatures could be considered God's co-creators. This can be seen in two respects. First, as I indicated earlier, the one who perceives the "thing in itself," the noumenal world, must be someone who requires no spatial, temporal and linguistic categories. And that person can only be God himself. But we, together with all other sentient creatures, who require spatial and temporal categories,[93] have the ability to "create" the world of "phenomena."

The second way in which sentient creatures are God's "co-creators" is that without them our world would essentially be "tenseless." There would be "time" but no *passage* of time. Only with a knowing subject can there be a "past," a "now," and a "future."[94] Human beings are not unique in forming representations; animals also form representations and can thereby "create" a tensed world as Schopenhauer established.[95] So what is so spe-

---

92. On the "subject" as on the boundary of the world, see Ludwig Wittgenstein, *Tractatus Logico-Philosophicus/Logisch-philosophische Abhandlung,* ILPSM (London: Routledge & Kegan Paul, 1972 [repr., ¹1921]), 150-51 (5.633): "*Where in* the world is a metaphysical subject to be noted? You say that this case is altogether like that of the eye and the field of sight. But you do *not* really see the eye. And from nothing *in the field of sight* can it be concluded that it is seen from an eye."

93. It is a moot point whether the sentient creatures of the sub-human world employ "linguistic" categories.

94. Here I am essentially taking the view of Einstein as opposed to the view of Popper (who maintained the independent reality of the passage of time). Cf. Bryan Magee, *Confessions of a Philosopher* (London: Weidenfeld & Nicolson, 1997), 566-57.

95. See the opening words of his magnum opus, Arthur Schopenhauer, *The World as Will and Representation,* vol. I (ET; New York: Dover, 1966 [repr., ¹1958]), 3 (1.1): "'The World is my representation': this is a truth valid with reference to *every living and knowing being, although man alone can bring it into reflective, abstract consciousness.* If he really does so, philosophical discernment has dawned on him. It then becomes clear and certain to him that he does not know a sun and an earth, but only an eye that sees a sun, a hand that feels an earth; that the world around him is there only as representation, in other words, only in reference to another thing, namely that which represents, and this is himself" (my

"But We Have the Mind of Christ"

cial about the human being, never mind the spiritual Christian? On the basis of 1 Cor 2:16 one can answer that spiritual Christians are co-creators in precisely this distinctive way: they form "representations of Christ" (subjective genitive!).

---

emphasis). And, in the history of the universe, animals were forming representations long before human beings. Schopenhauer, *World I*, 30 (1.7), draws attention to the significance of the first eye that opened: ". . . the existence of the whole world remains for ever dependent on that first eye that opened, were it even that of an insect."

PROJECTING POSSIBILITIES

Reading Scripture in a Pluralist World: A Path to Discovering the Hermeneutics of *Agape*

Tom Greggs

Introduction: Why Might Hermeneutics and *Agape* Belong Together?

The task of systematic theology might be considered to be the rational explication of the Christian gospel. However, the very purpose of this rational explication of the Christian gospel is to aid the reading of scripture: systematic theology might understand its goal to be the bringing together of biblical expression, to offer in turn flexible and lightweight guides for reading scripture. Systematics and hermeneutics are, therefore, deeply connected in any form of systematic theology which seeks to take the revelation of God's word in the flesh and history of Jesus Christ, and in the testimonies paid to him in scripture, seriously. In this engagement in rationally explicating the Christian gospel, there inevitably needs to be some use made of philosophy. As Barth reminds us:

> In attempting to reflect on what is said to us in the biblical text, we must first make use of the system of thought we bring with us, that is, of some philosophy or other. Fundamentally to question the legitimacy of this necessity would be to question whether sinful man as such, and therefore with such possibilities of thought as are given to him, is called to understand and interpret the Word of God which encounters us in Scripture. If we cannot and must not dispute this, if we are not to dispute the grace and finally the incarnation of the Word of God, we cannot basically contest the use of philosophy in scriptural exegesis.[1]

---

1. Karl Barth, *Church Dogmatics* (ed. G. W. Bromiley and T. F. Torrance; 4 vols.; Edinburgh: T&T Clark, 1936-77), I/2, 729-30.

This involves not only bringing philosophical categories to the engagement with the biblical text, but also thinking philosophically about the manner in which one engages with the text. However, questions immediately arise regarding how this enterprise is engaged in legitimately, or appropriately theologically. Barth establishes five points in his discussion of the legitimate use of philosophy and philosophical categories in theology: we must be aware and clear about every scheme of thought we bring to the text and how this is different from the scriptural word; philosophy can have only the fundamental character of a hypothesis; use of philosophy can claim no independent interest in itself; there are no essential reasons for preferring one particular scheme to another; and a scheme of thought is useful when it is determined and controlled by the text of scripture and the object within it.[2] While Barth rejects the idea of "replacing philosophy by a dictatorial, absolute and exclusive theology,"[3] he nevertheless cautions:

> As interpreters of Scripture, perhaps not in practice but in principle, we will be able to adopt a more friendly and understanding attitude to the various possibilities which have manifested themselves or are still manifesting themselves in the history of philosophy, and to make a more appropriate use of them, *if the object on which we reflect has put us on our guard against their particular genius.*[4]

If we are to think about the effect of the nature of the object on which biblical hermeneutics reflects, a question arises concerning the best way to think *theologically* about the use of the philosophical categories in the approach to texts. Are there ways in which the schemes of thought utilised might be determined and controlled by the text of scripture and the object within it? Put otherwise: Can we speak biblically about the task of biblical or theological hermeneutics?

One way, perhaps, of expressing *theologically* the enterprise of biblical or theological hermeneutics might be to say that it is the science of reading texts faithfully and hopefully simultaneously. The concern of hermeneutics is not only to attend to the text as authoritative source, seeking to read it *faithfully* in order to attend to what it is saying in its own terms, but also to read the text *in the hope* that it might speak to communities today or may have spoken to communities of readers who have understood the text

---

2. Barth, *Church Dogmatics*, I/2, 730-34.
3. Barth, *Church Dogmatics*, I/2, 734.
4. Barth, *Church Dogmatics*, I/2, 735 (emphasis added).

across its transmission through the years.⁵ Hermeneutics, therefore, generally attends to the necessity of both explanation *(Erklärung)*, an activity which involves the faithful reading of a text, and understanding *(Verstehen)*, which I identify as a hopeful enterprise that involves the belief that the reading of a text might offer, to use the words of Anthony Thiselton, "a more personal, intuitive, or suprarational dimension."⁶ This engagement in seeking to understand these two horizons of a text requires in its own terms, furthermore, that it is not simply a speculative theoretical engagement in *Wissenschaft*, but a genuinely formative, communal way of approaching the text, in contrast to any individualistic and (ironically) universalised approach that one might identify with the Enlightenment. For people of faith who read their texts ritualistically, ecclesially (in the broadest sense of this term), and devotionally, such a recognition of the formative and communal nature of texts needs little justification: as a Christian, I read the Bible not only to hear what Jesus said there and then, but also in the hope that I will hear what Jesus says to my community by his Spirit here and now; and clearly I do not think that there is a necessary disjuncture between those two modes of reading, but believe that the one helps to inform the other. As a preacher, the commentary work which helps me to prepare the sermon, while necessary, is nevertheless only a *preparation* and not the sermon in itself. The purpose of the sermon is to help the church to understand the meaning of the text in the contingent contemporaneity of the church's situation, but notably that contingent contemporaneity is not allowed simply to dominate the text: instead, the preacher and congregation should seek to listen carefully to the text, which is the basis of the explication of the word to the congregation.

There is much to commend in the increased attentiveness to hermeneutics in the current theological and ecclesial climate. However, for the Christian theologian, I wish to suggest (perhaps boldly, if you will forgive me) that an attentiveness to reading the text faithfully and hopefully is surely a way of reading the text which falls short of a fully Christian approach. After all, faith and hope belong to a triad in which they are surpassed by love. In the words of St Paul in 1 Cor 13:13: "faith, hope, and love

---

5. Cf. Anthony C. Thiselton, *Hermeneutics: An Introduction* (Grand Rapids: Eerdmans, 2009), 1-16.

6. Thiselton, *Hermeneutics: An Introduction*, 9. Clearly, not all hermeneutical theorists place emphasis on both aspects; Gadamer focuses only on the *Verstehen* aspect (see Anthony C. Thiselton, *The Hermeneutics of Doctrine* [Grand Rapids: Eerdmans, 2007], xix; cf. Thiselton, *Hermeneutics: An Introduction*, ch. 11).

abide, these three; and the greatest of these is love." If hermeneutics has a formative and communal nature, then for Christian biblical or theological hermeneutics, it would surely be advantageous to consider what it means not only to read a text faithfully and hopefully, but also to read a text lovingly.

The concern to read scripture in order to bring about love is one expressed by Augustine.[7] He considers that the building up of the love of God and of neighbour is essential to understanding and interpreting scripture appropriately. He writes: "Whoever, then, thinks that he understands the Holy Scriptures, or any part of them, but puts such an interpretation upon them as does not tend to build up this twofold love of God and our neighbor, does not yet understand them as he ought."[8] Indeed, Augustine considers a hermeneutic of love alongside the "precise meaning which the author whom he reads intended to express" (what I have termed the *faithful* aspect of hermeneutics), and "another meaning . . . of Scripture than the writer intended" (which might be considered close to what I have termed the *hopeful* aspect of reading).[9] For Augustine, reading a text faithfully and lovingly (and perhaps hopefully) is central to the correct interpretation of scripture.

My purpose in this chapter is to seek to outline (and nothing more; and in this the chapter is a bit of an experiment) what characterises a hermeneutics of love *(agape)* might have, and to suggest that the practice of reading the Bible with members of other faith communities might, for the Christian, be just one example of such a process of reading a text lovingly. I wish to conclude by suggesting that this process might allow one, furthermore, to understand and explain texts better in relation to the theme of an insider/outsider binary, and where we locate the self and the other in the ecclesial reading of a text.

What Does It Mean to Read Lovingly?
What Might the Hermeneutics of *Agape* Mean?

An obvious danger in seeking to express the need to read a text lovingly, as a key Christian identifier in hermeneutics, is the capacity for love to be-

---

7. I am grateful to Bill Danaher for reminding me of these passages in Augustine.
8. Augustine, *De Doctrina Christiana*, 1.36 (40).
9. Augustine, *De Doctrina Christiana*, 1.36 (41).

come a universalised and liberal principle binding on all of the particularities and difficulties of a text. We can elide all difficulty by removing any confrontational, judgemental or difficult texts, or we might fail to engage with them on the basis of their being "unloving." Any notion of self,[10] particularity or difference could be seen as a failure for love, and a retreat could all too easily be made to a form of lowest common denominator approaches to texts in the fear of their potential offensiveness. However, it is precisely here that the importance of the particularity of Christian love must be emphasised.[11] Not only is love a principle for reading which may only be meaningful for Christian readers (it is not my place to judge on its worth as a means of reading texts for non-Christians), but the love of which Paul speaks is also itself carefully defined and articulated. As soon as one suggests, therefore, that love might be a basis for reading texts, it is necessary to consider what is meant by this specifically Christian love, and to recognise its potential difference from other forms that love might take. The love which Paul speaks of, and which Christ reveals, is a particular form of love, made meaningful in the narrative of the New Testament. As Barth puts it:

> Christian love cannot in fact be equated with any other, or with any of the forms (even the highest and purest) of this other, just as this other love has obviously no desire to be confused with Christian. Nor can Christian love be fused with this other to form a higher synthesis. We cannot say of any other love that it is a kind of preparatory stage for Christian love. Nor can we commend Christian love by representing and portraying it as the purified form, the supreme climax, of this other love.[12]

To attend faithfully to the text of the New Testament requires that one attends (faithfully) to the particular and specific meaning of love in the text. This love is *agape,* and (as will be indicated) the word is used in such a way that the self is not consumed by the other, a type of love which marks — perhaps — the theologically liberal and universalised understanding of

---

10. In *De Doctrina Christiana,* 1.26, Augustine points to the fact that love of other does not exclude love of self. For Augustine, it is important that we love our neighbours *as ourselves.*

11. Cf. Anthony C. Thiselton, *The First Epistle to the Corinthians* (The New International Greek Commentary; Grand Rapids, Eerdmans, 2000), 1033-34.

12. Barth, *Church Dogmatics,* IV/2, 735.

the word, and which subjects all else to its love-principle (a version of love perhaps more akin to *eros* than to *agape*).[13] We cannot, therefore, presume that we know what it means for a Christian to read texts lovingly; instead, we need to attend to the particular form that Christian love is described as taking. In that way, our understanding must be *faithfully* loving, as well as hopefully loving: the triadic reading of faith, hope, and love must be held together, rather than any one (even love) coming to dominate at the expense of the others. While love is deemed in Christian theology to be "the greatest of these three," it is such in relation to the other two, rather than at the expense of the other two.

The relation between a faithfully appropriate reading of the text and a loving reading of the text is an issue to which Augustine directs his attention in his discussion of the interpretation of scripture and the engendering of love. He differentiates between a way of reading the text to bring about love, which might not be the most appropriate way of rendering the author's original meaning, and a way of reading the text which is a deliberate form of deception. While he thinks that the former is not culpable of deception, he is directly concerned with those who wilfully deceive regarding the nature of the text:

> there is involved in deception the intention to say what is false; and we find plenty of people who intend to deceive, but nobody who wishes to be deceived. Since, then, the man who knows practices deceit, and the ignorant man is practiced upon, it is quite clear that in any particular case the man who is deceived is a better man than he who deceives, seeing that it is better to suffer than to commit injustice. Now every man who lies commits an injustice; and if any man thinks that a lie is ever useful, he must think that injustice is sometimes useful. For no liar keeps faith in the matter about which he lies. He wishes, of course, that the man to whom he lies should place confidence in him; and yet he betrays his confidence by lying to him. Now every man who breaks faith is unjust. Either, then, injustice is sometimes useful (which is impossible), or a lie is never useful.[14]

For Augustine, there cannot be a direct desire to deceive in the interpretation of a text offered: this would be an act against faith. It is not pos-

---

13. Barth, *Church Dogmatics*, IV/2, 745. One must, however, be careful of demarcating too straightforwardly *eros* and *agape* (see below).

14. Augustine, *De Doctrina Christiana* 1.36 (40).

sible, therefore, to elide difference and particularity to a form of love principle which operates by rejecting the faithful claims of scripture, as this is an exercise in deceit. Even though Augustine's work has at times been interpreted in a more liberal way regarding his love hermeneutic, for him the bringing about of love cannot come at the expense of a faithful reading of the text. He is clear: "Whoever takes another meaning out of Scripture than the writer intended, goes astray."[15] Furthermore, even those who accidently misinterpret texts out of a desire to build up love, in doing this go astray and must be corrected (albeit this correction is to be gentle and loving, since it corrects an activity motivated by good reasons). He writes:

> Whoever takes another meaning out of Scripture than the writer intended, goes astray, but . . . if his mistaken interpretation tends to build up love, which is the end of the commandment, he goes astray in much the same way as a man who by mistake quits the high road, but yet reaches through the fields the same place to which the road leads. He is to be corrected, however, and to be shown how much better it is not to quit the straight road, lest, if he get into a habit of going astray, he may sometimes take cross roads, or even go in the wrong direction altogether.[16]

In the end, however, Augustine believes that such a well-motivated and loving approach may lead to loss of faith, and that both faith and love are required.[17] Love can never come at the expense of faith; the two are always bound together.

In direct relation to helping us to engage in a faithfully loving reading, St Paul offers tremendous help in his description of what comprises love:

> Love is patient; love is kind; love is not envious or boastful or arrogant or rude. It does not insist on its own way; it is not irritable or resentful; it does not rejoice in wrongdoing, but rejoices in the truth. It bears all things, believes all things, hopes all things, endures all things. Love never ends. (1 Cor 13:4-8)

The point of this is not simply that Paul says Christians should follow a form of love defined by *agape* (in contrast to, say, *eros*); whether one can en-

---

15. Augustine, *De Doctrina Christiana*, 1.36 (40).
16. Augustine, *De Doctrina Christiana*, 1.36 (41).
17. Augustine, *De Doctrina Christiana*, 1.37.

gage in such definitional approaches to words is always questionable.[18] The point is, rather, that Paul defines what is meant by love for the Christian through his description of what *agape* involves. In his majestic commentary on 1 Corinthians, Anthony Thiselton defines this love as follows:

> love *(agape)* denotes above all a *stance* or *attitude* which shows itself *in acts of will* as *regard, respect, and concern for the welfare of the other*. It is therefore profoundly *christological,* for *the cross* is the paradigm case of the act of *will* and *stance* which *places welfare of others above the interests of the self.* . . . **love does not seek its personal good** (13:5) but the welfare of *the other.*[19]

Such a process of removing the prioritisation of the interests of the self (but without wholly consuming the self) marks the central element of Christian love in its concern, respect and care for the other. This is not a form of love which does away, therefore, with otherness, but one which is based upon the otherness of the other to the self. Thus, if we are to apply the category of Christian love to the way in which Christians should read texts, such a love does not involve the removal of any difference or otherness (it is not about simply engaging with "warm and fuzzy" texts only), but seeks, grounded in the recognition of the other's otherness, to place the interests of the other above the interests of the self, regardless of who the other might be.[20]

It is the issue of who those others might be that leads us to consider what it means to read texts lovingly in the current age of religious pluralism. We now live in a globalised culture in which, if we do not have neigh-

---

18. To that degree, the sort of definition given by C. S. Lewis in *The Four Loves,* while perhaps theologically helpful, is hardly historically or linguistically accurate (C. S. Lewis, *The Four Loves* [Glasgow: Collins, 1960]). But equally, one might see the narrow definitional work of Margaret Mitchell in relation to the Corinthian letter as overly limiting in terms of the context of the letter: certainly, in terms of understanding the importance of the text now, the idea that love is simply a positive counter-point to Corinthian factionalism is unhelpful (see Margaret M. Mitchell, *Paul and the Rhetoric of Reconciliation: An Exegetical Investigation of the Language and Composition of 1 Corinthians* [Louisville: Westminster John Knox, 1991], 167).

19. Thiselton, *The First Epistle to the Corinthians,* 1035 (emphases original).

20. Cf. Thiselton: "Christians are to respect and care for those who may not seem attractive or like us in their culture, gender, race, or concerns, but are fellow believers or human beings on whom God has set his love." Anthony C. Thiselton, *I Corinthians: A Shorter Exegetical and Pastoral Commentary* (Grand Rapids: Eerdmans, 2006), 219-20.

Reading Scripture in a Pluralist World

bors of other faiths or none, we are more than aware of their presence through the instantaneous nature of the mass media. For all that such a situation may be referred to (with all due provisos) as post-modern, it is perhaps not so dissimilar to the *Sitz-im-Leben* of the First Epistle to the Corinthians from which the New Testament's teaching about love is taken: the commercial and pluralistic setting of Corinth has much that is common to the context of the twenty-first century,[21] and — after all — the issue of pluralism was a real one for the Corinthians who had to consider whether to eat meat sacrificed to "false gods" (1 Cor 8:1–11:1). It is in consideration of this context that it is possible to turn directly to the practice of Scriptural Reasoning and its potential for hermeneutics.

How Does Scriptural Reasoning Help Us Read This Way?

Scriptural Reasoning "is a practice before it is a theory. It properly can only be known in its performance."[22] Scriptural Reasoning involves Muslim, Jewish, and Christian people reading each other's texts together in small group study. It began with David Ford, Daniel Hardy, Peter Ochs, and Basit Koshul, and there are now various instances of the practice around the world. Scriptural Reasoning is difficult to describe for those who have not practised it, but might (crudely) be thought of as some form of inter-faith bible study.[23] It seems appropriate in suggesting that Scriptural Reasoning is a mode of engaging in a hermeneutics of *agape* to attempt to describe and narrate a discussion, which while singular, is in some ways exemplary of the sorts of interpretation of texts that sometimes happen in Scriptural Reasoning meetings. The context in which this discussion took place was a small group at the University of Cambridge who were undertaking an engagement with Surah 26:69-89, 102; 9:114 on Abraham. This had followed on from an early engagement with the difficult text in which Jesus commands us to hate our father and mother, wife and children, brothers and sisters (Luke 14:26), a text with which we had rightly struggled. Confronted with the difficulty of Jesus' words, as a Christian I had sought to say some-

21. Thiselton, *The First Epistle to the Corinthians*, 10.
22. Steven Kepnes, "A Handbook for Scriptural Reasoning," *Modern Theology* 22, no. 3 (2006): 370.
23. For further description of and reflection on Scriptural Reasoning, see David F. Ford, *Christian Wisdom: Desiring God and Learning in Love* (Cambridge: Cambridge University Press, 2007), chapter 8.

thing along the lines of: "Well, of course, Jesus didn't really mean that; it's about priorities." However, reading the Quran's teaching about Abraham and his disassociation from his father led one of our Jewish participants to talk about Abraham in the Torah — a man who thinks God's promise will be fulfilled through his wife's slave with whom he sleeps; who then sends his son and Hagar away; and who almost sacrifices his child. "Abraham hates his father and wife and sons; Jesus is telling us to be like Abraham!" was the excited cry from our Jewish friend. In the context of this setting, we read the Quran to receive a Midrash through Torah on Luke.

This occasion led me to reflect (uncomfortably) on what sorts of hermeneutics were being engaged in this. We were led from a problem with the Christian text (most especially for the Christians in the room, all of whom loved their families) to a Quranic text discussion. The two seemed unlinked. But from this discussion of the Quran we were taken to the Torah by a Jewish participant who wished to help us to understand the Christian text by a thought that the Quran raised for her. Her intertextual interpretation was such that it did not deproblematise the Christian text, but it did at least allow for a clearer sense of its not being a text that is so strange in the context of the narration of the strangeness and challenges of a scriptural life of faith. This was not a process which was self-beneficial for the Jewish and Muslim participants, but instead a process which arose out of what I might want to call, as a Christian, a hermeneutics of *agape* — and which I might describe (in a way the others would not) as a love for the other for the other's sake, arising from the love of God, as it is revealed to me in the self-sacrifice of Jesus Christ. During the reading of this text, there was a reading which was loving extended by a Jewish colleague, allowed by Muslim colleagues, and accepted by Christian colleagues.

Pointing towards the activities of non-Christians may well seem to suggest a return to the kind of liberal love principle about which I have already expressed nervousness. My desire here, however, is not to say that the non-Christian participants engaged in readings which were motivated by a wish to exemplify Christ's love, but simply to say that these kinds of moments in Scriptural Reasoning display, from a Christian perspective, a potential exemplification of what a hermeneutics of *agape* might be. When we look to the detailed unpacking by Paul of what love *(agape)* is like, several of the characteristics of that love are evident in such a reading. The activity was *patient*. Not only did it take time to come to such a reading, but the non-Christian participants were patient with a text which is difficult enough for Christians; and the Christians were patient in allowing members of other faith communities to read and interpret their texts. There was no blundering exclusivist impatience, but a willingness to wait patiently for God's timing.[24] The reading was also kind, seeking to offer a generous (another interpretation of the Greek word) reading of a text which was difficult for Christians; and it was received in generosity by Christians who did not forthrightly proclaim that it was a crucicentric text, or the likes. There was no bragging or envy involved, but also, notably, no inflated sense of self-importance. Not only was the reading offered as just one potential interpretation, but the text itself (difficult and jarring as it is for those for whom the family is central) was not dismissed; just as the reading was received without any sense that a member of another community could never read the text properly. The attempt to read the text without being rude is also a feature of the practice of Scriptural Reasoning: older readers should not interrupt younger ones; men should not interrupt women; no single voice should be allowed to dominate; and so on.[25] The very reading of scripture together with members of other Abrahamic communities is an enactment of a form of reading which does not insist on its own way: it is a form of hospitality to the other, who is allowed to join in the reading of the scripture which is sacred and holy to oneself. Furthermore, this invitation is waited for, and the reading "does not elbow its way into conversations."[26] This reading is not engaged in for the sake of proving the other wrong or the self right: in this way it is neither irritable nor resentful. As such, Scriptural Reasoning does not focus on the origins of Christianity in Judaism; or the origins of Islam in Christian and Jewish traditions.[27] It is not about a preoccupation with the self, and the interests of the self in relation to the other (in terms of supersession or antecedence of claim), but is rather about reading with the other for the sake of God and of the other. Provocative and irritating behaviour is checked in the setting of Scriptural Reasoning,[28] and patience and graciousness are required. Yet, there is no desire for the creation of unifying principles or the identification of conceptual unities in the Scriptural Reasoning. In this much, it embodies a love which rejoices in that which is true. This quest for the truth (in all its particularity and with all of its potential pain)[29] in

---

24. Thiselton, *The First Epistle to the Corinthians*, 1046-47 (cf. Heb 6:15).
25. This is checked by a chair who should be sensitive to these issues.
26. Thiselton, *The First Epistle to the Corinthians*, 1050.
27. See Kepnes, "A Handbook for Scriptural Reasoning."
28. Cf. Thiselton, *The First Epistle to the Corinthians*, 1052.
29. As I have put it elsewhere, we should not forget how "how uncomfortable those

no ways undermines a reading which seeks to adopt the hermeneutics of *agape*. After all, "[w]ould genuine love for the other seek premature closure of what troubles or challenges the other?"[30]

That love has an eschatological element, as that which never ends, and which exceeds faith and hope (things Calvin believed were no longer necessary after the *eschaton*), is also fitting as a descriptor of Scriptural Reasoning. In his "Handbook for Scriptural Reasoning," Steven Kepnes identifies the eschatological element to Scriptural Reasoning as follows:

> The eschatological dimension of SR practice recognizes that . . . in the SR "tent of meeting" people whose communities are otherwise at war with each other are sitting down in peaceful conversation. . . . [T]he liturgical aspect of SR can be seen in the belief that many SR members have that an ideal future time, a time of inter-religious peace, is anticipated, "glimpsed" and even "participated in" through SR practice.

Imagining SR practice as a glimpse of the end time is extremely powerful because, as with all eschatological thinking, it necessarily has implications for the present. The new eschatology of SR calls into question some of the exclusivist and triumphantalist aspects of the traditional eschatologies of Judaism, Christianity, and Islam in which one religion triumphs over the other two. One practical result of face-to-face SR readings of eschatological texts of the three monotheistic traditions is that it becomes harder to maintain eschatologies that expect to overcome the religious particularities of each tradition. This allows for the re-imagining of a new type of end-time in which universal peace is won through preserving the particularity of the other instead of obliterating it. Here, the end-time can function as the ideal that pulls the traditions along with it to a future time of human fulfillment, a reign of justice and

---

seats at the inter-faith table not only are but — if we are to be internally coherent and to be present as members of our own faiths — have to be. This is not to engage in something unloving; quite the opposite, it is to bear that discomfort out of love for the other. Surely such sacrificial love is an even greater virtue than that of tolerance: while tolerance pertains principally to ideas, love pertains to persons, and in sitting with those who believe different things than we do, we do not simply play with ideas but engage in love for the other." Tom Greggs, "Bringing Barth's Critique of Religion to the Inter-faith Table," *Journal of Religion* 88, no. 1 (2008): 83. For further discussion of this theme, see Tom Greggs, "Legitimizing and Necessitating Inter-faith Dialogue: The Dynamics of Inter-faith for Individual Faith Communities," *International Journal of Public Theology* 4, no. 2 (2010): 194-211.

30. Thiselton, *I Corinthians*, 227. Cf. here the discussion of Augustine and faithful readings of texts discussed above.

peace and communion with God. Reading scriptures together as a form of eschatological thinking also recalls past times of rich interaction between Jews, Christians, and Muslims and a beginning time of creation in which the world and the human was created as very good.[31]

The very activity of reading scriptures with members of other faith communities directs us towards the future time when many shall come from east and west to feast with Abraham, Isaac, and Jacob (Matt 8:11), and reminds the Christian reader that the Kingdom of God is always more than the limiting walls of the empirical *ecclesia*. Reading lovingly is an exercise in reading eschatologically, and we are helped to glimpse something of the vision of God's loving and peaceful kingdom through the simultaneous reading of scriptures together. This is not in a way which undermines the other's otherness, but in a way which traverses that otherness in the very otherness of God's love for us. Scriptural Reasoning may be just one of many ways of reading which aids the hermeneutics of *agape*.

However, it may not simply be the case that Scriptural Reasoning may be just an exemplification of a hermeneutics of *agape*, it may also help us to engage in deeper, and more loving readings, even in non–Scriptural Reasoning settings. The hermeneutical process of reading with Abrahamic others is humbling, as it is offered and received in tremendous generosity, but also because in it is found not just the pleasantness of being with those other children of Abraham for its own sake, but what I have come to think of as the necessity (for me as a Christian) of being with these other children of Abraham for my own sake — for the sake of my reading of my scripture, for the sake of my Christian faith, for the sake of my life before God.

What about the Self and the Other?

It is here that I wish to consider the effects of reading with members of other religious communities on the majority of my readings of scripture, which find their home in daily devotional and weekly liturgical acts. If Scriptural Reasoning is a practice that might be described as embodying a loving hermeneutics, how does the process of reading with others form a hermeneutics of *agape* which exists beyond the necessarily occasional

31. Kepnes, "A Handbook for Scriptural Reasoning," 381.

readings of scripture with members of different faith communities?[32] My concern here relates to the issue of reading with an awareness of one's propensity towards self-deception: as Ricoeur reminds us, we should examine the manner in which we read with a good degree of critical suspicion. In reading with members of other faith communities, we are confronted with the reality that in approaching scripture, in the words of Thiselton, "[i]t is all too easy to opt for convenient or self-affirming interpretations."[33] The very process of reading with others begins to undermine the capacity that one has, and occasional sleight of hand in which one engages, in terms of locating oneself in the text. Reading with members of other religious traditions raises issues for the all too easy self-identification with the insider. It also questions the identification of the other as the outsider, and it helps us to examine the all too simplified binaries which we tend to create in terms of our reading of our tradition in relation to the text.[34]

Christian readings of insiders and outsiders in the text of the New Testament are as slippery as they are confusing. It is perhaps wrong of me to point to a pastoral example to make this point, but the reduction of this argument to the absurd may nevertheless highlight tendencies many of us have.[35] The church to which I belong has a group of retired ladies who meet weekly (many of whom are in their 80s and all of whom are more pietistic Methodists than I am). I am deeply struck at their fellowship meetings by their capacity to read themselves as the insider at all points in the text. Thus, they are the moral insiders who obey the law (quite rightly, for they have lived good and godly lives), but they are also able to see themselves in contrast to the Pharisees as — in a way that always draws a smile from me — the prostitutes who will enter the Kingdom of God first; just as they also see themselves as the prodigal son, Zaccheus, etc. The point that I am making is

---

32. I use the term "necessarily occasional" here both to indicate the paucity of the practice in comparison to "normal" forms of scriptural reading with intra-religious communities and also because in order to remain genuinely particularist and genuinely inter-faith, there should be no suggestion that co-reading scripture with members of other communities should in some ways replace the faithful devotional and liturgical reading of scripture in which people of faith engage.

33. Thiselton, *Hermeneutics: An Introduction*, 5.

34. On binaries and how to overcome them, see the concluding chapter of Peter Ochs, *Peirce, Pragmatism and the Logic of Scripture* (Cambridge: Cambridge University Press, 2004).

35. I hope the reader will forgive my turning to a pastoral example. I do this in part to illustrate the point I am trying to make, but also in part in recognition of Anthony Thiselton's deep and continuous engagement with the church throughout his career.

this: in the reading of texts, there is an almost irresistible desire to self-identify (typologically perhaps in the case of Christian theology) with the "insider" or the hero, without once thinking about whether the other that one reads of in the text is someone who would be a repetition of one's self in the present, or whether that other in the text would be classed as the outsider in the contexts in which we find ourselves now.

The Gospel confronts this issue directly, and not simply in Jesus' engagement with the Pharisees.[36] A repeated theme of the New Testament is that those who consider themselves most on the inside are the ones who are likely to receive a rude awakening. The eschatological parable of the sheep and the goats makes this point. Not only do those who think that they are goats discover that they are sheep, but those who presume they are sheep also discover that they are goats (Matt 25:31-46). Furthermore, hero or insider status is often not related to being an insider to one's religious affiliation.[37] In the parable of the Good Samaritan, for example, the hero with whom as contemporary insiders most Christians identify is precisely the anti-hero outsider to the religious community to which this tale was narrated.[38]

Reading face to face with another, indeed with a member of another faith community, reading lovingly, confronts us with the need to engage texts with sensitivity when we read by ourselves. It challenges us to contemplate where we locate ourselves in texts, and crucially has the effect of deassuring us theologically of our insider status, our hubris and our self-created binary exclusivisms. The process of reading with religious others is not just a process which *displays* a loving reading, but it is one which *engenders* in a far more reaching way a reading which critically challenges the preoccupation with the self and the text, and points us towards the other, aiding us perhaps to understand something more of the ultimate otherness of God. As a Christian insider at the current juncture in the world's history, this should bring with it an awareness of Jesus' challenge not just (to employ earlier terms) *faithfully* to the insider status of the second temple Judaism (and notably not rabbinic Judaism) of which he was a part,

---

36. For a theological discussion of the Pharisees in the New Testament, see Dietrich Bonhoeffer, *Ethics* (trans. Reinhard Krauss, Charles C. West, and Douglas W. Stott; ed. Clifford J. Green; Minneapolis: Fortress Press, 2005), 309-15.

37. For a more detailed discussion of this passage, see Tom Greggs, "Beyond the Binary: Forming Evangelical Eschatology," in *New Perspectives for Evangelical Theology* (ed. Tom Greggs; Abingdon: Routledge, 2010), 153-67.

38. This is a theme I have discussed in "Preaching Inter-faith: Finding Hints about the Religious Other from the Good Samaritan," *Epworth Review* 36, no. 3 (2009): 60-70.

but *hopefully* back to the insider status of contemporary Christianity, in its institutionalised religious form. And since faith and hope are always exceeded by love, it will perhaps bring us to read our texts (even the painful and exclusivist ones) lovingly in relation to the contemporary Jewish and Muslim other in the world today.

Scripture and the Divided Church

Stephen Fowl

It is a great honor to be invited to contribute to a Festschrift for Anthony Thiselton. To appreciate the significance of Tony's work for the entire field of biblical studies it is worth contemplating the current academic landscape for a moment. Today one can simply assume that biblical scholars are methodologically self-reflective. Even if such self-reflection is not always clearly coherent, and even if one does not read widely in hermeneutics, one takes it for granted that hermeneutical questions are legitimate, important and worthy of attention. It is very easy to forget how utterly extraordinary it was in the late 1970s and early 1980s to combine serious biblical study and rigorous hermeneutical inquiry in the ways that Tony was doing. As I contemplated beginning a PhD in 1983 I found there was no program in the U.S. where one could do this. One either did a PhD in New Testament or a PhD in philosophy. Even in as methodologically self-reflective an environment as Sheffield's Department of Biblical Studies was at that time, Tony stood out for the breadth of his philosophical and hermeneutical learning. All of us today whose work trades on the presumption of the importance of hermeneutical rigor owe a great deal to Tony's pioneering work.

Although I do not recall ever speaking with Tony about this, I have always assumed that his very particular intellectual endeavors arose out of his concerns with the place of Scripture in the life of the church. His work with the Church of England's General Synod testifies to this. I share those concerns and as my contribution to this volume, I want to talk about Scripture and church division.

If you pay much attention to the way the commercial media cover Christianity it is clear that disagreements, arguments, and division among

Christians is newsworthy. My own denomination, the Episcopal Church, has split and its relationship to Anglicanism worldwide is in peril, too. I make no pretense to understand all of the fights within my own branch of the church and would never presume to understand those in other branches. Moreover, our current fights and divisions are not the first Christianity has witnessed. For over 500 years Christianity in the west has been fractured and continues to divide. Of course, before that, Eastern and Western branches of the church split. Division, then, is not something brand new to us as Christians.

I must confess at the outset that neither I nor Scripture has a recipe for ecclesiastical glue that will enable us to put the divided church back together. Even if I had such a recipe, I am not confident that I would know how best to use it. In part, this is because even though the church in the West has been divided for half a millennium, I think we are still in the position of learning how to understand our divided state and what it means for our engagements with Scripture.

It is tempting to think that differences over Scripture and its interpretation and embodiment lie at the very heart of church division in the West. Was it not, after all, Luther's insistence on Scripture alone — *sola scriptura* — which was the catalyst in his disputes with Rome? On at least two levels here, the answer must be, no.

I am neither a Luther scholar nor the son of a Luther scholar, but my outsider's view of this is that Luther's approach to Scripture and his interpretive practice were much more like than opposed to his late medieval and early modern contemporaries. He was certainly much more like them than he was like later Lutheran historical critics such as Rudolf Bultmann or Ernst Käsemann. Luther read the OT christologically, and he relied on figural interpretation. Although he spoke of the clarity of Scripture, he did not, therefore, assume that one could simply read Scripture apart from being formed to do so within the Church.

In addition, regardless of the rectitude of Luther's interpretations it is simply not possible to attribute the divisions within the post-Reformation church to Luther's deviation from a previously agreed upon approach to, and interpretation of, Scripture. Luther was not the first theologian to read Scripture in ways that differed from his contemporaries. From the moment Scripture was written down Christians, like Jews before them, have discussed, debated and disagreed with each other about how to interpret and embody Scripture in the various contexts in which they found themselves. Short of that time when we will know just as fully as we have been

Scripture and the Divided Church

known, and until God's law is written directly on our hearts, we Christians have been prone to and will continue to disagree, debate, and discuss matters of Scripture. Argument and debate over Scripture cannot in itself be at the heart of church division because argument and debate is an essential component of having Scripture in the first place.[1]

There are a variety of reasons for this. As followers of Christ we are called to a life-long engagement with Scripture. Learning, knowing, and embodying Scripture is not a one-time achievement, but a life's work. Moreover, the contexts in which Christians struggle to live Scripture are always changing. Hence, a faithful interpretation in one context may not suffice in a different context. For example, consider the following observation offered by Nicholas Lash with regard to ecclesiastical dress:

> If, in thirteenth century Italy, you wandered around in a coarse brown gown, with a cord round your middle, your 'social location' was clear: your dress said that you were one of the poor. If, in twentieth-century Cambridge, you wander around in a coarse brown gown with a cord round your middle, your social location is curious: your dress now says not that you are one of the poor, but that you are some kind of oddity in the business of 'religion.' Your dress now declares, not your solidarity with the poor, but your amiable eccentricity.[2]

Lash's point is not an attack on the Franciscans, but a logical observation about how temporal and cultural change necessitates ongoing interpretation.

Further, Scripture itself invites and sustains a chorus of interpretive voices. Luther was not the first Christian to have substantial disagreements with other Christians over Scriptural interpretation. Look at the letters between Augustine and Jerome, or Theodore of Mopsuestia's account of Origen just to name two famous examples. In a relatively few cases do Christians actually divide the body of Christ when they disagree with each other about Scripture.

Hence, I would like to suggest that when such divisiveness occurs in

---

1. The view that interpretive disagreement and debate are a constituent result of treating the Bible as Scripture was one of the central presumptions of my *Engaging Scripture* (Oxford: Blackwell, 1998). Given this, I argued that the central questions of theological interpretation of Scripture were closely connected to the ecclesial contexts within which those debates and arguments might be carried out.

2. Nicholas Lash, *Theology on the Way to Emmaus* (London: SPCK, 1986), 54.

debates over Scripture it is not so much an issue of Scriptural interpretation as it is the result of a separation of Scriptural interpretation from a variety of other different, yet related, practices. These are the practices needed to keep the body of Christ whole in the midst of the inevitable debate, discussion, and argument that is part of the Christian community's ongoing engagement with Scripture. I would like to look at some of these practices because they are crucial even in a divided church. Moreover, it may be the case that reinvigorating those practices will enhance the prospects that Christians' engagements with Scripture might play some role in healing ecclesial divisions.[3]

In addition, I would also like to look at several Scriptural passages which might help us understand and speak Christianly about the divided church. In this regard, my aim is to begin, but not conclude, a discussion of how we Christians in a divided church might proceed.

First, let me mention a few of the practices that need to be in good working order for Christians to engage in the discussions and debates about Scripture, which are integral components of their life in Christ prior to Christ's return, without tearing at Christ's body. These are not all of the relevant practices. I am not sure I know all of the relevant practices. These, however, seem to be rather important. Before I speak of practices, however, I must note that all of these practices presume and are held together by love, by the love Christ has for believers and which Christ commands believers to have for each other. All church division is fundamentally a failure of love. All division proceeds from believers assuming that they are better off apart from each other than together. Division is a contradiction of ecclesial love, especially love of our enemies within Christ's body. Doctrinal or Scriptural differences cannot divide the church unless there is this prior failure of love.[4]

Following from this, truth seeking and truth telling in Christ must be towards the top of any list of practices crucial to interpreting and embodying Scripture in the one body of Christ. On the one hand, this seems obvi-

---

3. James Andrews has noted that, at least for Augustine, Scripture has the capacity to heal division rather than to cause it. See Andrews, "Why Theological Hermeneutics Needs Rhetoric: Augustine's *De doctrina Christiana*," *International Journal for Systematic Theology* 12, no. 2 (2010): 184-200. I think this is true to the extent that other practices are already in place. That is, we do not have good reason to expect engagements with Scripture to have a therapeutic effect in the absence of these other practices.

4. This is a crucial point made by Ephraim Radner in *The End of the Church: A Pneumatology of Christian Division in the West* (Grand Rapids: Eerdmans, 1998), 230, 272.

Scripture and the Divided Church

ous. Debates, discussions and arguments about Scripture or anything else cannot be life-giving apart from issues of truthfulness. On the other hand, those of us who still bear the lacerations or scars from having had brothers or sisters "speak the truth to us in love" will recognize how awful and divisive such "truth telling" can be. This sort of truth telling is often a thin disguise for personal hostility. If truth telling is to be a practice essential to keeping the Christians' arguments about Scripture from being divisive, we will need to think of truth telling in Christological terms.

Here is a brief account of what that might mean. In a passage filled with military images, the apostle Paul commands us to bring every thought captive in obedience to Christ (2 Cor 10:5). It is not that Christ aims to obliterate all thoughts. Rather, the point of bringing every thought captive to Christ is so that our thoughts (as well as our feelings, dispositions and emotions) will be subjected to Christ's penetrating, healing gaze. Bringing all thoughts captive to Christ is a way of establishing or restoring their right relationship to the one who is the Truth (John 14:6).[5]

In fact, one can see this process narrated in the risen Christ's engagement with Peter around a charcoal fire in Galilee (John 21:1-19). Peter's deceit and betrayal is purged; he is restored in the course of being questioned by the resurrected one who is feeding him at the same time he interrogates him.[6] The truth about Peter is never glossed. Nevertheless, the resurrected Christ uses this truth to transform Peter.[7]

I mention truth telling first for two related reasons. The first reason is that truth is the first casualty of sin. This, of course, makes it much more difficult to recognize sin and our own sin, in particular. The second reason is that truth telling is the first component of the practices of forgiveness and reconciliation. I want to turn to these two practices as essential for engaging Scripture without dividing the body of Christ.

To engage in the communal discussion, argument, and debate which

---

5. In *Trinity and Truth* (Cambridge: Cambridge University Press, 2000), Bruce D. Marshall unpacks this Johannine notion in conversation with a wide range of contemporary philosophical discussions.

6. See Rowan Williams, *Resurrection* (New York: Pilgrim Press, 1982), 33-38.

7. Some may seek to make something of the alternation between Jesus' use of ἀγάπη in his question, "Do you love me?" and Peter's response using φιλέω. In John 5:20, speaking of the Father's love for the Son; in 11:3 speaking of Jesus' love for Lazarus; and in 16:27 speaking of God's love for the disciples, John uses φιλέω. This should make one very hesitant to draw too sharp a distinction between these two Greek terms both in the context of John 21 and elsewhere.

are crucial to faithful embodiment of Scripture without fracturing Christ's body, we must be capable of recognizing and naming sin, particularly our own sinfulness. This ability to recognize and name sin is not a one-time achievement, but an ongoing process of transformation and repentance.

The New Testament makes this point in many and various ways. For example, in Luke 11 Jesus notes that this process calls for habits of attentiveness and acuity; it requires the grace and capacity to keep one's eye "single" (ἁπλοῦς) as opposed to "unsound" or wicked (πονερός) (Luke 11:34-35).[8] Jesus offers this observation after he has been accused of casting out demons because he is in league with Satan (11:14-26). In response to this Jesus notes that a kingdom divided against itself cannot stand (11:17-18). The implication of this is that Jesus is casting out demons by "the finger of God." Hence, the appropriate response is to turn and follow him with a singularity of purpose. Just after this incident a woman in the crowd shouts out, "Blessed is the womb that bore you and the breasts which you sucked!" (11:27). Jesus corrects this assertion noting that the response he seeks is not admiration of himself (or his mother), but "keeping and doing the word of God." Again, there is an emphasis on the appropriate single-minded response Jesus demands. At this point Jesus addresses the crowd from which the woman in 11:27 shouted. He criticizes them for seeking a further sign from him. Because they have not perceived and responded to wisdom greater than Solomon's and calls for repentance greater than Jonah's they will be judged. The crowd suffers from a sort of blindness or deafness which renders them increasingly unable to understand and respond appropriately to Jesus as he marches to Jerusalem. The way to address this blindness is to keep one's eye ἁπλοῦς. Throughout Luke a variety of characters manifest this ability to see properly. These are the characters who respond well to Jesus when they encounter him. Think especially of Peter in Luke 5:1-11; the "woman who was a sinner" in Luke 7:36-50; and Zacchaeus in Luke 19:1-10. All of these characters who respond well to Jesus share the capacity to see themselves as sinners.[9]

Of course, Jesus does not simply meet sinners where he finds them in order to leave them that way. Rather, he offers forgiveness in a profligate manner, flagrantly disregarding the Temple and its sacrificial practices, unambiguously implying that the Messianic age has begun. Further, he invites such sinners to engage in life-giving and life-transforming patterns of

---

8. For a longer discussion of this point see my *Engaging Scripture*, 75-83.
9. For a fuller account of this phenomenon in Luke see my *Engaging Scripture*, 75-83.

repentance by becoming disciples and following him.[10] Without a community who are well practiced at asking for and offering forgiveness, and without a community committed to the penitential work of reconciliation, we have little reason to recognize, much less repent of our sin. If people think that sin is both the first *and last* word on their lives, then self-deception will always appear the easiest and best option.

When Christians' convictions about sin and their practices of forgiveness and reconciliation become distorted or inoperative, then Christians will also find that they cannot discuss, interpret, and embody Scripture in ways that will build up rather than tear apart the body of Christ. Rather than shaping and being shaped by faithful life and worship, Christians' debates around Scripture will tend to fragment them.

Alternatively, one should expect that a community whose common life is both marked by the truthfulness of Christ and regularly engaged in practices of forgiveness and reconciliation will be able to engage in the discussion, argument, and debate crucial to interpreting and embodying Scripture faithfully in ways that build up rather than tear apart the body of Christ. In the absence of these practices, however, one may well expect that Scriptural interpretation and its attendant debates will divide the body of Christ.

Before moving on I will mention just one more practice crucial to engaging Scripture without dividing Christ's body. This is patience. As a way of teasing out some issues around patience I want to focus on what I had often taken to be almost a throwaway line in Paul's letter to the Philippians. In 3:15 Paul wraps up a long plea to the Philippians to adopt a pattern of thinking, feeling, and acting that is focused around the patterns displayed to them by the crucified and resurrected Christ. This pattern of thinking, feeling, and acting will lead the Philippians to do certain things and avoid other things, all of which Paul lays out in some detail. In short, following Paul's admonitions will enhance the Philippians' prospects of attaining their true end in Christ. Paul then turns to himself. He does not claim that he has attained this end yet. Rather, he presses on to the finish line so that he might win the prize of the heavenly call of God in Christ Jesus. These are some of the most elevated lines in the entire New Testament. Instead of stopping there and moving on to something else, Paul adds, "If any of you are inclined to adopt a different pattern of thinking, feeling and

---

10. Recall that Luther began his 95 theses, "When our Lord and Master, Jesus Christ, said 'Repent,' he called for the entire life of believers to be one of repentance."

acting, God will reveal to you the proper mindset to adopt" (3:15).[11] After this impassioned plea, Paul seems willing to allow that others may think differently. This is not because Paul is a good liberal and thinks that in matters of faith people should be allowed their own opinions. Rather, he can display a certain detachment from his own argument because he is convinced that God is directing and enabling the advancement of the gospel (cf. Phil 1:6, 12). Paul does not have to coerce the Philippians into adopting his pattern of thinking, feeling and acting because he is confident that God will bring both him and the Philippians to their proper end in Christ. It is this steadfast conviction about God's providence that enables Paul to be patient when the result he seeks is not immediately achieved. It is just this sort of patience which keeps debates over Scripture from dividing the body of Christ. Further, this sort of patience can only be sustained in the light of convictions about God's providential care of the gospel and the church.

Thus far I have tried to make the following claims: first, as Christians and Christian communities seek to interpret and embody Scripture faithfully in the contexts in which they find themselves they can expect, and need, to engage in discussion, argument, and debate with each other. This is simply a feature of Christian life poised as ours is between the cross and resurrection, on the one hand, and the return of Christ, on the other hand. For the most part, these discussions and debates do not divide and have not divided the Church. Rather, when the body of Christ is fractured, it is because of a failure of love and a failure to maintain the practices I have mentioned above (as well as others) in good working order. I think the upshot of this is that Church division is, therefore, more likely the result of a failure to maintain a certain form of common life than irresolvable disputes over how to interpret this or that Scriptural text.

One response to the discussion of these practices is that as Christians, individually and corporately, participate in the lives of very particular local manifestations of the body of Christ they can properly direct their attention to those practices which are most likely to help "maintain the unity of the Spirit in the bond of peace." This is all to the good. It is crucial to recall, however, that all Christian gatherings in the present are shaped to some degree by the fact that the Church is already divided. It is, therefore, insufficient simply to note the importance and interconnected nature of a vari-

---

11. The translation here is taken from my *Philippians*, Two Horizons Commentary Series (Grand Rapids: Eerdmans, 2005), 159.

Scripture and the Divided Church

ety of ecclesial practices and Scriptural interpretation. Our current divisions have already shaped us. That division has shaped us believers is unarguable. It is not, however, always clear how ecclesial division does, can, or should shape Christians' engagements with Scripture. Moreover, to address this latter issue is already to presume we understand the nature of church division in the present. In this regard, it is striking to note how easy it is simply to present contemporary church division in terms taken from contemporary political life. It is quite common in ecclesial circles to hear terms like conservative, liberal, traditional, and progressive used to account for the various factions in ecclesial debates. Even when self-reflective people recognize that such labels do not move straightforwardly, and with any great precision, from partisan politics into ecclesial politics, they find it difficult to imagine and employ an alternative vocabulary.

Of course, it is not sufficient to resurrect the vocabulary current at the time of the initial division of the church in the West. Church division today is a very different issue for believers today than it was for Catholics, Lutherans, Calvinists, and others in the 16th century. At that point the issues were focused on where the true church was located and how to know this. Once the true church was found, all other options simply were not church. While Reformation polemics might provide a measure of entertainment to modern readers accustomed to various types of talk radio, the way the issues were framed at that time kept those involved from dealing with the issue of a divided church. One's opponents were not really part of the church in the first place. The problems of a divided church as we know it today are really the result of ecumenism. The more Catholics and non-Catholics, for example, recognize each other as true Christians, the greater the problem of their division, the sharper the pain of this fracture. Thus, there is a sense in which understanding the nature and consequences of a divided church are different tasks for Christians today, different and urgent.

In an underrecognized essay, Bruce Marshall seeks to argue why contemporary theology must treat church division as a matter of primary importance. In "The Disunity of the Church and the Credibility of the Gospel," Marshall makes his case by examining that part of Jesus' prayer for his followers related in John 17:20-26.[12] He argues that the prayer reveals at least three things about the unity of the church. The first thing that Marshall notes is that the unity Jesus asks the Father to grant to his disciples is a

---

12. *Theology Today* (April 1993): 78-89. Page references will be given parenthetically in the text.

visible unity. It is a unity that can be perceived by "the world" (17:21, 23). Upon seeing this unity the world is capable of believing that the Father has sent Jesus. Although John 17 says nothing directly about the nature of this visible unity among Jesus' followers, Marshall argues that one can infer some things from the rest of the New Testament. In particular Eph 4:1-6 would lead one to image that such unity consists in a unity of faith and worship, a unity of mutual love and service among believers, and a common baptism. Again, these are all public, visible practices that unite believers with one another and with the resurrected Christ and the Father who sent him (Marshall, 79). The single paradigmatic practice of this unity would be the common eucharistic meal in which the many are made one through sharing in the one bread (1 Cor 10:17). "Eucharistic fellowship is thus essential to the reality of the church, and, more than any other public practice, it gives the church that specific character by which the world comes to faith in the gospel, namely that of a visibly united body" (Marshall, 79).

The second element of unity revealed in Jesus' prayer is that the unity of believers is the unity that Jesus shares with the Father (17:22-23). Although there may be various ways of understanding the unity of the Father, Jesus (and the Spirit), the point seems to be that these are the same ties that bind believers to each other and to Christ.[13] At the very least, this idea is seconded by 2 Pet 1:4 where believers become participants in the divine nature.

The third, and most disturbing, observation is that Jesus seems to imply that the credibility of the gospel depends on the unity of the church. In 17:21 Jesus prays for the unity of his followers, "so that the world may believe that you have sent me." The unity of the church seems to be a necessary if not sufficient condition for holding that the Father sent Jesus.

Taking these three observations together Marshall comes to the following conclusion: "Thus the credibility of the gospel (holding it true) depends on the visibility in the world of the love that is the life of the triune God, that is, on the Eucharistic unity of that ongoing communal history that makes visible in the world what it is the gospel talks about, namely the missions of the Son and the Spirit from the Father, enacting that love in time" (Marshall, 83).

---

13. Marshall rightly notes that such a claim calls for an account of "how the triune God can be the same in the world as God is in God's own self" (80). Marshall notes that this is a complex question, but requires no special argument with regard to church unity and can in some sense be left to the side for the time being.

Scripture and the Divided Church

If these observations are accurate Marshall then notes that several conventional ways of addressing church division must be jettisoned. First, "the unity of the church cannot subsist 'invisibly' despite the historic, visible divisions of the Christian community — in particular the absence of eucharistic fellowship" (Marshall, 83). A second related point is that eucharistic unity cannot be treated as an optimal or salutary way of visibly manifesting a prior invisible unity (Marshall, 83). Third, "the gospel cannot be rendered credible (much modern theology to the contrary) either by showing that it meets some standard of truth the gospel does not itself provide (a putative universal reason, general *Wissenschaftslehre*, ineluctable human quest for authenticity, desire for liberation, or whatever), or by striving to get the content of the gospel right and assuming that the content will then secure its own credibility" (Marshall, 84). Finally, one cannot argue that the divided church is the result of the abiding sinfulness of humans which God does not yet will to remove. The point here is not to deny that church division is sin, but whether abiding sin can account for church division. In this respect Marshall notes that Christ calls sinners, not the righteous, into a united eucharistic fellowship where despite whatever residual or continuing sin they may manifest, they are made one by the Spirit. "The unity of the church is a unity among sinners; the continuing reality of sin in the lives of the church's members has no bearing on the church's unity" (Marshall, 85).

Given this state of affairs, Marshall notes that church division creates an *aporia* for believers. This can be seen in four propositions which can be distilled from his observations: (a) the gospel is true; (b) the gospel cannot be true if the church is eucharistically divided; (c) there are communities that are eucharistically divided from each other; (d) each of these communities are genuinely church. Although these four cannot all be true, there is no good, clear or easy way to discard any one of them. Marshall's argument pushes believers at a conceptual level to treat church division as a surd which has no adequate explanation (Marshall, 89). At a practical level Marshall's argument calls theologians of all stripes both to make church division and the task of finding dogmatic consensus a matter of extreme urgency and to reflect on whether theology and theologians have helped us to become anaesthetized to living in a divided church. If we, Christians, have become comfortable with our divided state it is likely that we have lost or muted our capacities to understand adequately our divided situation. As a way of helping address this last point, I would like to explore a variety of Scriptural texts which might help us think better about this situation.

In his very difficult and challenging book, *The End of the Church*, Ephraim Radner encourages Christians to read their current divided situation through the Scriptural image of divided Israel, when the Northern Kingdom of Israel broke from the Southern Kingdom of Judah. Radner argues that understanding contemporary division in these Scriptural terms may be a good place for Christians to begin to understand their divisions and the ways God views them. In this respect, Radner is inviting Christians into the practice of reading Scripture figurally in order that they might better comprehend and negotiate their way through their world.

In the rest of this essay I would like to argue that Christians should take Radner's invitation to figural reading very seriously. I then want specifically to take up Radner's invitation to understand current ecclesial divisions through the figure of divided Israel. In order to make the first part of this argument for figural reading, I will need to speak, all too briefly, about the "literal sense" of Scripture. For now, let me propose a working definition of the "literal sense" of Scripture. Others may want to challenge this, but this is an account that also would have a large number of supporters among theologians past and present.[14] Let us take the "literal sense" of a passage to be the meanings conventionally ascribed to a passage by faithful Christian communities and therefore presumed to be intended by God. Thus, the literal sense will be those meanings Christians conventionally ascribe to a passage in their ongoing struggles to live and worship faithfully before the triune God. Thus, the literal sense is primary, the basis and norm for all subsequent ways of interpreting a text. Take for example, the famous passage in Isa 7:14, "Behold a young woman (or virgin) will conceive and bear a child and you shall call him Immanuel." If this verse is read solely in the context of Isaiah, it appears that the child in question is the son born to Isaiah of Jerusalem as related in chapter 8. It is equally clear that Matthew and the Christian tradition generally take this verse to be a prophetic announcement of the birth of Jesus almost 750 years later. Christians can grant that both of these are the literal sense of Isa 7:14. This is because the God who inspires these words is perfectly able to make them refer to both of these characters. This is what Augustine and Aquinas

---

14. For a fuller account that situates this notion of the literal sense of Scripture more deeply into the history of theology see my *Engaging Scripture*, chapter 1; and, more recently, "The Importance of a Multivoiced Literal Sense of Scripture: The Example of Thomas Aquinas," in *Reading Scripture with the Church*, ed. A. K. M. Adam, Stephen Fowl, Kevin Vanhoozer, and Francis Watson (Grand Rapids: Baker Academic, 2006), 35-50.

Scripture and the Divided Church

both mean when they each speak of the possibility of there being many literal senses of the same passage.[15]

If this stands as a working definition of the literal sense, then figural interpretations will use a variety of interpretive techniques to extend the literal sense of Scripture in ways that enhance Christians' abilities to live and worship faithfully in the contexts in which they find themselves. Why is this important? A central and widely shared Christian conviction about Scripture is that God has providentially ordered Scripture so that, despite its manifest obscurities, Scripture provides Christians with a set of lenses through which to view and comprehend the world as they seek to negotiate their paths faithfully through it. If Christians are to use Scripture as the basis for ordering and comprehending the world, then they must also recognize that there will be times when the literal sense of Scripture may not offer a sharp enough vision to account for the world in which they find themselves. In those cases, Christians will need to read Scripture figuratively. Of course, these matters are hardly ever straightforward or clear. This is in part why if Christians are to engage Scripture as part of their ongoing struggles to live and worship faithfully before the triune God, they will inevitably find themselves discussing, arguing, and debating matters of Scriptural interpretation.

With regard to matters of ecclesial division, such figural reading will be essential to developing different, and better, ways of understanding and speaking about the divided state of the church. With the hope of doing this, I want to take up Radner's invitation to begin to read our situation of church division through lenses provided by biblical Israel and her divisions and then to go further by pulling in some New Testament texts.

Rather than seeing Israel's division into Northern and Southern kingdoms as a surprising event, passages like Psalm 106 and Jeremiah 3 lead one to view Israel's division as one of the results of Israel's persistent resistance to the Spirit of God. In the light of passages such as these, it appears that division is simply one manifestation of this resistance. Others include such things as grumbling against God and Moses in the wilderness, lapses into idolatry when Israel occupies the Promised Land, and the request for a human king. Interestingly, these manifestations of resistance tend to become a form of God's judgment on Israel.

Let me explain this a bit more. Take the example of Israel's request for a human king in 1 Samuel 8. Although Samuel takes this as a personal af-

---

15. See Augustine, *Confessions,* 12.31; and Thomas Aquinas, *Summa Theologiae,* 1a,1,10.

front, God makes it clear that it is simply part of a pattern of Israel's rejection of God's dominion which has carried on from the moment God led the Israelites out of Egypt. This rejection of God results in the request for a human king when the Israelites are faced with hostile neighbors, all of whom have human kings. The granting of this request becomes the form of God's judgment on Israel as her kings become both oppressively acquisitive and idolatrous (cf. 1 Sam 8:10-18; 12:16-25). Thus it becomes clear that one of the forms of God's judgment on the disordered desires of the people of God is giving us what we want.

If Christians treat division in this light it becomes clear that division is both a sign that we believers are willing to, and even desire to, live separate from our brothers and sisters in Christ; it is also God's judgment upon that desire. Christians' failure to love, especially to love our brothers and sisters with whom we are at odds, lies at the root of our willingness and desire for separation. This separation in the form of church division is God's judgment on believers' failure to love as Christ commands.

Further, one of the byproducts of Israel's resistance to God's Spirit is that their senses become dulled so that they are increasingly unable to perceive the workings of God's Spirit.[16] Isaiah makes this particularly clear in 6:10; 28:9; 29:9-13. As is often the case in the prophetic writings, this sort of stupefaction and blindness is a precursor to judgment. It also reflects a deep irony found throughout the prophets. At those times when Israel is most in need of hearing God's word and repenting, they have also rendered themselves least able to hear that word. Nevertheless, it is crucial to remember that in the prophets, God's judgment is a precursor to restoration. More specifically, it is restoration of a unified Israel as noted in passages such as Jer 3:15-18 and Ezek 39:21-29. This restored, unified Israel is so attractive and compelling that the nations are drawn to God because of what they see God doing for and with Israel (cf. Isa 2:1-4). This blessing of the nations fulfills God's purposes in initially calling Abraham out from among his own people (Gen 12:1-3).

This all too brief survey indicates that if we Christians understand the divided church in the light of biblical Israel and her division, then we face several conclusions regarding our current divisions. First, division is one particularly dramatic way of resisting the Spirit of God. Such resistance

---

16. I am less willing than Radner to speak in terms of the Spirit's "withdrawal." It would appear that human deafness and blindness rather than God's withdrawal of the Spirit is a more appropriate description.

Scripture and the Divided Church

further dulls our senses so that we are less able to discern the movements and promptings of God's Spirit. Thus, we become further crippled in, among other matters, reading God's word. Second, the response called for throughout the prophets to this phenomenon is repentance. Whether our senses are so dulled that we cannot discern the proper form of repentance, whether God's judgment is so close at hand that we cannot avoid it, one cannot say. Instead, we are called to repent and to hope in God's unfailing plan of restoration and redemption in Christ.[17]

The second set of scriptural texts one might look at with the aim of coming to see church division more Christianly are those New Testament passages which deal with unbelieving Israel. As much as church division in Corinth causes Paul pain, he is equally if not more disturbed by his fellow Jews' large-scale rejection of Jesus Christ as their Messiah. Romans 9–11 comes immediately to mind. It seems to me there are at least two ways to read the church's current divisions in the light of this passage. The wrong way is to devote time and energy to figuring out which part of the divided church is the natural vine, which parts are the grafted-in, and which are cut off. Instead, we should remember that the God who grafts in also can lop off. There is no place for presumption or complacency here. Instead, we should in our divisions try to provoke our divided brothers and sisters through ever greater works of love to return to the vine. Cardinal Ratzinger (now Benedict XVI) stated this well when he said, "Perhaps institutional separation has some share in the significance of salvation history which St. Paul attributes to the division between Israel and the Gentiles — namely that they should make 'each other envious,' vying with each other in coming closer to the Lord (Romans 11:11)."[18]

Both the OT texts noted above as well as Romans 9–11 present some of the consequences of church division for believers: Division is seen as a form of resistance to the Spirit of God. It dulls believers' abilities to hear and respond to both the Spirit and the word, which, in turn, generates further unrighteousness. Division provokes God's judgment and is not part of God's vision for the restoration of the people of God. While both presumption and complacency are real temptations, neither is an appropriate response to division. Rather, we are called to sustained forms of repen-

---

17. In one of the final chapters of *The End of the Church*, Radner raises the disturbing prospect that church division may render Christians incapable of being able to imagine the appropriate way to repent.

18. Cardinal Joseph Ratzinger, "Anglican-Catholic Dialogue: Its Problems and Hopes," in *Church Ecumenism and Politics* (San Francisco: Ignatius Press, 1987), 87.

tance, "vying with each other in coming closer to God" with the aim of drawing the other to God.[19]

In the final passage I want to examine, Christians are invited to look at the consequences of church division for the world. In this case I want to look at Ephesians. At the beginning of the epistle we are told that God's plan for the fullness of time is that all things shall be gathered together under Christ's lordship. Just as God's restoration of Israel brings a reunion of divided Israel and the infusion of Gentiles, so in Christ, God will bring all things together in their proper relationship to Christ. It is important to note that this includes those principalities and powers which are not yet under Christ's dominion (1:10).

For Paul's purposes, the paramount activity of Christ's gathering of all things is the unification of Jews and Gentiles in one body through the cross and resurrection. Ephesians 2 is focused on just this activity by which those near and those far off are brought together into one. This is and always has been God's providential plan for the redemption of the world. Paul calls this plan the "mystery which was made known to me by revelation" (3:3). It is, in short, the good news which Paul has been commissioned to proclaim. Then in 3:9-10 he makes a claim upon which I want to focus. Paul is reflecting on his commission to proclaim this gospel of the unification of Jew and Gentile in Christ. He claims that God has given him the charge "to make everyone see what is the plan of the mystery hidden for ages in God who created all things: so that through the church the riches of God's wisdom might be made known to the principalities and powers in the heavenlies." The church, by its very existence as a single body of Jews and Gentiles united in Christ, makes God's wisdom known to the principalities and powers. As it appears here in Ephesians the Church's witness to the principalities and powers is integrally connected to and may even depend upon its unity.

What does one make of this in the light of the current situation of division? The most extreme way of putting the matter is to say that the Church's witness to the principalities and powers is falsified or undermined by division. At the very least, one must say that the Church's witness to the principalities and powers is hindered and frustrated by division. Moreover, if a united body of Christ is God's means of witnessing to the principalities and powers, then a divided body of Christ would seem to imperil the larger mission of gathering up all things in Christ (1:10). In ei-

---

19. See also Radner, *The End of the Church*, 53.

ther case, it would appear that the consequences of division are not simply internal to the church and her life with God.

Here, then, are a variety of Scriptural passages which help believers to understand and speak theologically about Church division. Interpreting divided Israel and its resistance to the Spirit as a figure of the Church calls the divided Church to repentance. The reading of Romans 9–11 expands on this to provide some admonitions by way of analogy about how to live in a divided Church. Finally Ephesians implicitly warns of some of the consequences of division for the world at large, especially the principalities and powers.

In the course of this essay I have tried to address two different aspects of Scripture in the divided Church. The first begins from the recognition that all Christians are called faithfully to embody Scripture in word and deed in the particular contexts in which they find themselves. This will by nature involve communal discussion, argument and debate. This need not, however, lead to divisions within the church. Rather, it points to the need to have a variety of communal practices in good working order so that we can pursue the debates and discussions required to embody Scripture without fracturing Christ's body. This calls us to ever greater love and attentiveness when it comes to the common life of the local communities in which we find ourselves.

I have also looked at selected scriptural texts. Not surprisingly, Scripture does not directly address church divisions in the ways that we know it. Yes, Matthew 18 speaks of fraternal admonition and the importance of reconciliation among alienated Christians. In addition, Paul addresses divisions within, for example, the Corinthian and Galatian churches. But the New Testament does not, perhaps cannot, imagine Christ's body fractured in the ways it has been for almost 500 years. Hence, I am not trying to plumb Scripture's depths in order to see what Scripture "says" about Church division. Instead, the texts covered above, and other scriptural texts, can help believers begin to develop a scripturally shaped language and sets of categories for talking about divisions in the present, how to understand the consequences of division. Perhaps most importantly, understanding church divisions through a figural reading of a variety of scriptural texts invites believers to think about how God's judgment of contemporary divisions might result in a dulling of our abilities to hear and perceive the work of the Spirit among us, abilities which are central to our hopes of reading and embodying Scripture faithfully.

What Exactly Is Theological Interpretation of Scripture, and Is It Hermeneutically Robust Enough for the Task to Which It Has Been Appointed?

Stanley E. Porter

Introduction

The theological interpretation of Scripture has been widely heralded of late, continuing a movement that seems to have begun in earnest in the 1990s. There have been a variety of monographs and collections of essays published that attempt to define and promote some version of this form of interpretation,[1] and there have been a variety of works that attempt to demonstrate theological interpretation of Scripture — some of them retrospectively identifying such work[2] and others putting forward new efforts to exemplify this approach.[3] There is also a journal, the *Journal of Theolog-*

---

1. I cannot attempt to list them all. Examples include Francis Watson, *Text, Church, and World: Biblical Interpretation in Theological Perspective* (Grand Rapids: Eerdmans, 1994); idem, *Text and Truth: Redefining Biblical Theology* (Edinburgh: Clark, 1997); idem, *Paul and the Hermeneutics of Faith* (London: Clark, 2004); Ellen F. Davis and Richard B. Hays, eds., *The Art of Reading Scripture* (Grand Rapids: Eerdmans, 2003); A. K. M. Adam, Stephen E. Fowl, Kevin J. Vanhoozer, and Francis Watson, *Reading Scripture with the Church: Toward a Hermeneutic for Theological Interpretation* (Grand Rapids: Baker, 2006); and several volumes in the Scripture and Hermeneutics series, especially Craig Bartholomew, Colin Greene, and Karl Möller, eds., *Renewing Biblical Interpretation* (Carlisle: Paternoster, 2000), and Craig Bartholomew, Mary Healy, Karl Möller, and Robin Parry, eds., *Out of Egypt: Biblical Theology and Biblical Interpretation* (Milton Keynes: Paternoster, 2004).

2. For example, Stephen E. Fowl, *Engaging Scripture: A Model for Theological Interpretation* (Oxford: Blackwell, 1998); and Joel B. Green and Max Turner, eds., *Between Two Horizons: Spanning New Testament Studies and Systematic Theology* (Grand Rapids: Eerdmans, 2000).

3. I have selected five such recent treatments for discussion below.

What Exactly Is Theological Interpretation of Scripture?

ical Interpretation,[4] that is explicitly devoted to the theological interpretation of Scripture and related ideas. The status of the enterprise — at least so far as publishers are concerned — is shown by the fact that these publishers are now promoting a variety of second-generation definitional works of the field. These include reference works that attempt to synthesize and encapsulate the efforts that have been made in the area of the theological interpretation of Scripture,[5] monograph series encompassing this approach,[6] commentary series that claim to demonstrate the interpretive rewards of such an approach,[7] and even historically based works that attempt to gather evidence from previous voices that are often drawn into the discussion directly or indirectly.[8] The recipient of this *Festschrift*, Professor Anthony Thiselton, has been identified with this method in several regards as well. In one recent work, he has been identified as one of the hermeneutical innovators of what is called theological hermeneutics.[9] The authors, of whom I am one, have thus identified him as one of the major figures in developing a hermeneutics with specifically theological interests, and that brings to bear other hermeneutical thought, such as that found in philosophical hermeneutics, upon theology broadly defined, including both biblical interpretation and dogmatic theology.[10] However, this raises

---

4. Now apparently with its own supplement series as well.

5. Kevin J. Vanhoozer, ed., *Dictionary for Theological Interpretation of the Bible* (Grand Rapids: Baker, 2005); and the series Evangelical Ressourcement: Ancient Sources for the Church's Future (Baker).

6. Studies in Theological Interpretation published by Baker.

7. These include: Brazos Theological Commentary on the Bible (Baker), the Two Horizons New Testament Commentary (Eerdmans), the Two Horizons Old Testament Commentary (Eerdmans), The Church's Bible Commentary Series (Eerdmans), Ancient Christian Commentary on Scripture (InterVarsity Press), and Reformation Commentary on Scripture (InterVarsity Press). Never underestimate the determination of publishers, even in lean times, to capitalize on an opportunity to sell books.

8. Stephen E. Fowl, ed., *The Theological Interpretation of Scripture: Classic and Contemporary Readings* (Oxford: Blackwell, 1997). I cannot help observing that some included in this volume would, at least it seems to me, be surprised to be reprinted here.

9. Stanley E. Porter and Jason C. Robinson, *Hermeneutics: An Introduction to Interpretive Theory* (Grand Rapids: Eerdmans, 2011), 246-57. The other is Kevin J. Vanhoozer. See especially his *Is There a Meaning in This Text? The Bible, the Reader, and the Morality of Literary Knowledge* (Grand Rapids: Zondervan, 1998); *First Theology: God, Scripture, and Hermeneutics* (Downers Grove, IL: InterVarsity Press, 2002); and *The Drama of Doctrine: A Canonical-Linguistic Approach to Christian Theology* (Louisville: Westminster John Knox, 2005).

10. Major works on this topic include: Anthony C. Thiselton, *The Two Horizons: New*

the question of what the relationship is between the theological interpretation of Scripture and theological hermeneutics. There are those who have been identified with both, to the point of the two notions being treated as synonyms. As a token of esteem for my former supervisor and continuing conversation partner in hermeneutics, I wish to explore the underpinnings of the theological interpretation of Scripture, with the goal of determining whether it is in fact a hermeneutic, or whether it is instead something else, less a conscious hermeneutic than a set of assumptions or a perspective.

The Tenets of Theological Interpretation of Scripture

As mentioned above, there have been several recent treatments that attempt to define and exemplify the theological interpretation of Scripture. I have recently come across five such ventures that — rather than retrospectively — are designed to explicate the method, by either precept or example, or both.[11] I will analyze them briefly here to get a sense of the nature of what is called theological interpretation of Scripture.

In 2007, Joel Green published *Seized by Truth: Reading the Bible as Scripture*, a book woven around a number of previously published papers. Green begins by differentiating reading the Bible from reading Scripture, endorsing the latter against the former, which reflects modern historical-critical concerns. Although he recognizes the challenges of language, Green believes that the Bible is meant to be read as spiritually formative, shaping the mind of the believer. To do this, both the Old and New Testaments must be read as Scripture by those who have been "converted," that is, are open to having their minds "autobiographically re-

---

Testament Hermeneutics and Philosophical Description with Special Reference to Heidegger, Bultmann, Gadamer, and Wittgenstein (Grand Rapids: Eerdmans, 1980); *New Horizons in Hermeneutics: The Theory and Practice of Transforming Biblical Reading* (Grand Rapids: Zondervan, 1992); *The Hermeneutics of Doctrine* (Grand Rapids: Eerdmans, 2007); and his collected essays, *Thiselton on Hermeneutics: Collected Works with New Essays* (Grand Rapids: Eerdmans, 2006).

11. The five are: Joel B. Green, *Seized by Truth: Reading the Bible as Scripture* (Nashville: Abingdon, 2007); Daniel J. Treier, *Introducing Theological Interpretation of Scripture: Recovering a Christian Practice* (Grand Rapids: Eerdmans, 2008); Stephen E. Fowl, *Theological Interpretation of Scripture* (Eugene, OR: Cascade, 2009); J. Todd Billings, *The Word of God for the People of God: An Entryway to the Theological Interpretation of Scripture* (Grand Rapids: Eerdmans, 2010); and Joel B. Green, *Practicing Theological Interpretation: Engaging Biblical Texts for Faith and Formation* (Grand Rapids: Baker, 2011).

What Exactly Is Theological Interpretation of Scripture?

constructed."[12] We must become Model Readers,[13] who read the text with the same care and concerns as the author wrote it. Such reading must be located within the Church, shaped by theology, critically engaged with various reading partners, and imbued by the Holy Spirit. So far as methods are concerned, Green notes that scholarship has looked behind the text to historical matters, in the text itself, and in front of the text to its various readers. He argues for a text-centered approach (influenced by discourse analysis), beginning with the text, but also attentive to the cotext, context, and intertext.[14] Rejecting the notion that meaning is a phenomenon of the past, he concludes that interpretations cannot be evaluated as right or wrong but more or less valid. He concludes the book with a discussion of the authority of Scripture in the light of crises of its function, relevance, and authority. He instead asserts biblical authority as comprising several elements: an intrinsic quality, a feature of its narrative, as an invitation and as a bestowal of grace.

Daniel Treier, in his *Introducing Theological Interpretation of Scripture: Recovering a Christian Practice*, offers probably the most comprehensive introduction to theological interpretation. He begins the history of the endeavor with Karl Barth's commentary on Romans,[15] and briefly traces the work of evangelicals and Roman Catholics as particularly interested in the discipline, especially in this "postmodern" era that emphasizes the role of communities in interpretation. Treier's first section of substantive chapters focuses on consensus issues of theological interpretation. These include the role of premodern interpretation, in which scriptural reading is seen as being an act of piety, about Christ, and within the parameters of the early church's fourfold sense of Scripture. He next explores the role of the *regula fidei* or rule of faith, using the examples of David Yeago on Philippians 2:6-11 and *homoousion*, Francis Watson on

---

12. Green, *Seized by Truth*, 48, drawing upon Peter L. Berger and Thomas Luckmann, *The Social Construction of Reality: A Treatise in the Sociology of Knowledge* (New York: Doubleday, 1966), 160.

13. Green consciously draws upon Umberto Eco, *The Role of the Reader: Explorations in the Semiotics of Texts* (Bloomington: Indiana University Press, 1979), 7-11. For a critique of Eco, see Thiselton, *New Horizons in Hermeneutics*, 524-29, which raises questions whether Green has rightly understood or employed Eco and fully grasped the implications of the notion of a Model Reader for his approach to theological interpretation.

14. Green's view of discourse analysis is summarized by a chart on pp. 127-28 of *Seized by Truth*, which he calls a means of "close reading."

15. Treier, *Introducing Theological Interpretation*, 14-21. For a very different opinion of Barth, see Porter and Robinson, *Hermeneutics*, 214-26.

how to read Scripture as illuminated by doctrine, and the Brazos Theological Commentary by Jaroslav Pelikan on Acts.[16] In the third consensus chapter, Treier emphasizes the importance of interpreting Scripture in community or within the church. Seeing George Lindbeck and Stanley Hauerwas as predecessors,[17] he focuses upon Stephen Fowl's work, *Engaging Scripture*, in which he differentiates "determinate," "antideterminate," and "underdetermined" interpretations.[18] According to Treier, Fowl concludes (against Watson who is determinate) for underdetermined meanings without a general interpretive theory but with practice of the "virtues" of communal, ecclesial reading. In the second part of the book, Treier addresses continuing challenges for theological interpretation. These include, first, the relationship of theological interpretation to biblical theology, as well as to canonical approaches to Scripture. The second challenge is the relationship of theological interpretation to general hermeneutics. Seeing the rise of human "being," the work of Hans Georg Gadamer, and responses to Gadamer as important for theological interpretation,[19] Treier surveys a number of responses by those who either accept or reject a relationship with general hermeneutics, such as Werner Jeanrond and Anthony Thiselton and his use of speech-act theory,[20] as

---

16. See David S. Yeago, "The New Testament and the Nicene Dogma: A Contribution to the Recovery of Theological Exegesis," in *Theological Interpretation of Scripture*, ed. Fowl, 87-100; Watson, *Text, Church, and World* and *Text and Truth;* Jarislov Pelikan, *Acts* (Brazos Theological Commentary on the Bible; Grand Rapids: Baker, 2005).

17. George A. Lindbeck, *The Nature of Doctrine: Religion and Theology in a Postliberal Age* (Philadelphia: Westminster, 1984); Stanley Hauerwas, *A Community of Character: Toward a Constructive Christian Social Ethic* (Notre Dame, IN: University of Notre Dame Press, 1981).

18. Fowl, *Engaging Scripture*, passim.

19. Hans-Georg Gadamer, *Truth and Method* (trans. Joel Weinsheimer and Donald G. Marshall; 2nd ed; New York: Continuum, 1989), and opponents such as Jürgen Habermas, *The Theory of Communicative Action* (2 vols.; trans. Thomas McCarthy; Boston: Beacon, 1984, 1987); Paul Ricoeur, *Essays on Biblical Interpretation* (ed. Lewis S. Mudge; Philadelphia: Fortress, 1980); idem, *Figuring the Sacred: Religion, Narrative, and Imagination* (trans. David Pellauer; ed. Mark I. Wallace; Minneapolis: Fortress, 1995); E. D. Hirsch, Jr., *Validity in Interpretation* (New Haven: Yale University Press, 1967); and the relevance theory of Dan Sperber and Deirdre Wilson, *Relevance: Communication and Cognition* (2nd ed.; Oxford: Blackwell, 1995). For further discussion of most of these figures, see Porter and Robinson, *Hermeneutics*, 74-153.

20. Werner Jeanrond, *Theological Hermeneutics: Development and Significance* (New York: Crossroad, 1991); Thiselton, *Two Horizons* and *New Horizons;* and responses of Stephen Fowl in *Reading Scripture with the Church*, 35-50. Speech-act theory is presented in J. L.

What Exactly Is Theological Interpretation of Scripture?

well as further reactions. He also studies attempts to link general and special hermeneutics by Kevin Vanhoozer and Jens Zimmermann.[21] Finally, Treier notes the issue of globalization, in an attempt to break theological interpretation out of its distinctively western location and place it in relation to postcolonialism and various other forms of Christianity globally situated.

The third volume, Stephen Fowl's *Theological Interpretation of Scripture*, is the shortest and the most concise. His first chapter addresses the question of the nature and place of Scripture, that is, how theology and Scripture relate to each other. Explicitly rejecting the Christological analogy as an attempt to interpret Scripture (because it is modern, or because it is not used in the same way by all?), and the biblical theology movement's attempt to find timeless truths within contingent events, Fowl accepts John Webster's claim that one must begin the interpretive task with the triune God.[22] For Fowl, this provides the framework for reading Scripture as God's revelation, reflecting his providence, and involving his Spirit. Secondly, Fowl compares theological interpretation with other "concerns." The first is historical criticism, with its attempt to control confessional positions, establish historical reliability, and view history as autonomous. The second is biblical theology. Noting the contrastive nature of biblical theology, Fowl argues instead for the role of the rule of faith to bring unity to the diversity. The third concern is the Old Testament as Scripture. Fowl recognizes the problem of seeing Christ as a hidden sub-text of the Old Testament, and instead argues for the notion that

---

Austin, *How to Do Things with Words* (Oxford: Oxford University Press, 1962); John R. Searle, *Speech Acts: An Essay in the Philosophy of Language* (Cambridge: Cambridge University Press, 1969); Nicholas Wolterstorff, *Divine Discourse: Philosophical Reflections on the Claim That God Speaks* (Cambridge: Cambridge University Press, 1995); and Richard S. Briggs, *Words in Action: Speech Act Theory and Biblical Interpretation* (Edinburgh: T&T Clark, 2001). For critical commentary upon speech-act theory in biblical and theological studies, see Stanley E. Porter, "Hermeneutics, Biblical Interpretation, and Theology: Hunch, Holy Spirit, or Hard Work?" in I. Howard Marshall, *Beyond the Bible: From Scripture to Theology* (Grand Rapids: Baker, 2004), 97-127, esp. 112-18, where objections are raised that have not been addressed by speech act practitioners.

21. Vanhoozer, *Is There a Meaning in This Text?*; idem, *The Drama of Doctrine*; Jens Zimmermann, *Recovering Theological Hermeneutics: An Incarnational-Trinitarian Theory of Interpretation* (Grand Rapids: Baker, 2004). On proponents of theological hermeneutics, see Porter and Robinson, *Hermeneutics*, 245-73.

22. John Webster, *Holy Scripture: A Dogmatic Sketch* (Cambridge: Cambridge University Press, 2003), 5-41.

Christ is the end and the goal of the Old Testament and the goal of the life of believers. The fourth concern is the relationship to philosophical hermeneutics. Fowl wishes to distance theological interpretation from any general hermeneutic so as to avoid making theological interpretation an exercise in that hermeneutic. A fifth concern is various theories of meaning. Fowl, well-known for his distinctions here, wishes to dispense with the use of the notion of "meaning" (because there is no way to adjudicate between competing assertions of meanings) and recognize various interpretive aims. A final concern is the role of the human and divine authors. Here, following Mark Brett,[23] Fowl wishes to distinguish between authorial motives and communicative intentions, with the former undeterminable and the latter discussable. Fowl also recognizes how speech-act theory is similar to determining communicative intentions. However, he wishes to differentiate between what he calls therapeutic speech-act theory as a means of clarifying philosophical issues, and its use as a philosophy of language, the former of which he endorses and the latter of which he rejects. He concludes by noting the presence of human sinfulness, and seeing not hermeneutics but Christian communities as the regulator of interpretation. In the last substantive chapter, Fowl outlines the practices of theological interpretation. These include learning the methods of pre-critical interpretation, engaging in figural rather than literal reading, and reflecting the ecclesial practices of truth-telling, restoration and reconciliation, and patience.

The fourth treatment is Todd Billings' *The Word of God for the People of God: An Entryway to the Theological Interpretation of Scripture*. In many ways the most substantive of the treatments, it is also the most difficult to identify with what is actually entailed in theological interpretation. Billings contrasts theological interpretation with what he calls a "blueprint" and a "smorgasbord" approach, seeing theological interpretation as finding a way between prescription and complete freedom (perhaps something like Fowl's underdetermined meaning). Instead, it sees the reading of Scripture as part of the economy of salvation and follows the "rule of faith," which is a compendium of the Church's belief about the fundamental story of the Christian faith. However, Billings adds to this by noting the presupposition that there is a relationship between the Old Testament and the New, and that traditions were handed down in the Church. He sees the

---

23. Mark G. Brett, "Motives and Intentions in Genesis 1," *Journal of Theological Studies* 42 (1991): 1-16.

What Exactly Is Theological Interpretation of Scripture?

rule of faith as broadening the scope of scriptural interpretation, although he also wishes to maintain a sense of mystery. In order to engage in such reading, one must be selective in using the principles of general hermeneutics, and instead embrace preunderstandings and tradition, along with a modified form of historical criticism that endorses critical naiveté indebted to Joel Green.[24] Drawing on Kierkegaard,[25] Billings wants to ensure the right reading of Scripture by affirming that revelation is grounded in God's particular acts in relation to Israel and Jesus Christ, and that Scripture must be received as part of a Trinitarian hermeneutic, involving both inspiration and a theological view of canon. The work of the Holy Spirit is to overcome issues of relativism or hegemony in interpretation by indigenizing Scripture so that it is read by God's people in various contexts and serves as a critique of culture. Discerning the Spirit's work is seen to occur in community, that is, as the church, not on the basis of individual experience. Pre-modern interpretation is important for theological hermeneutics because it reflects the results of a spiritual and christologically-centered interpretation of Scripture. Even the so-called four senses of Scripture used by pre-modern exegetes, rather than proving an insuperable difficulty, in many ways reflect the concerns of modern interpreters over issues of history. Billings believes that pre-modern interpretation, even if not always accepted, illustrates how theological interpretation can be done by those who believe in God's revelatory activity, take Scripture as a unity, appreciate interpretive difficulties, and admit the limits of contextual interpretation. Billings concludes with an approach to reading Scripture as a participant in what he calls the Trinitarian drama of salvation. In this drama, we do not discover information about God but read Scripture as revelatory of God's action. Such interpretation should, Billings believes, become a spiritual discipline, determine the nature of ministry, and establish its mission.

The final work is a second attempt by Joel Green, entitled *Practicing Theological Interpretation: Engaging Biblical Texts for Faith and Formation*. Green admits that theological interpretation is not a specific interpretive method, but is a form of "'interested' exegesis"[26] along with Latino/a and African ideological approaches, its distinctive being that it is ecclesially lo-

---

24. Green, *Seized by Truth*, 126-36.
25. Søren Kierkegaard, *Philosophical Fragments, Johannes Climacus* (ed. Howard V. Hong and Edna H. Hong; Princeton: Princeton University Press, 1985).
26. Green, *Practicing Theological Interpretation*, 2.

cated. This volume focuses upon four major issues in theological interpretation. The first concerns the readers of Scripture. Green defines the reader of Scripture by again invoking Eco's category of the model reader,[27] the reader who reads the text in the way that the author wrote the text. Along the way, he invokes cognitive linguistics and its frame theory to account for the narrative structure of Scripture, that is, its grand narrative.[28] The second issue is history and historical criticism. Green defines three senses of historical criticism: reconstructing the past (with which theological interpretation is not concerned), explaining the move from tradition to text (of interest only for rhetorical purposes), and studying the historical situation (with which he is primarily concerned and which theological interpretation needs). Green, drawing on the work of Hayden White, defines history as "narrative representation of historical events,"[29] and believes that we must recognize the choices, mimetic qualities, cultural embeddedness, and effects of history writing. The third issue is the rule of faith and interpretation. The rule of faith emphasizes the role of theology in interpreting Scripture. For Green, the rule of faith helps set the parameters for Christian readings of texts, which are capable of a plurality of meanings (though not an infinitive number). The rule of faith does not determine the meaning, nor does it preside over Scripture or simply summarize Scripture. Instead, it helps to provide the overall structure for scriptural interpretation and the parameters in which theological interpretation should occur. As an example of how to use the rule of faith, Green cites the example of his view of the human as being a soul, not possessing a soul (anthropological monism), on the basis of the neurosciences.[30] He sees his view in harmony with the underlying kerygma of the major creeds, even if in tension with standard understandings of them. As an example of pre-modern interpretation, Green cites John Wesley, whom he sees as illustrating recognition of the need for

---

27. See also Wolfgang Iser, *The Implied Reader: Patterns of Communication in Prose Fiction from Bunyan to Beckett* (Baltimore: Johns Hopkins University Press, 1974).

28. Green, *Practicing Theological Interpretation*, 24-29, with special reference to Mark Turner, *The Literary Mind: The Origins of Thought and Language* (Oxford: Oxford University Press, 1996); Hayden White, *The Content of the Form: Narrative Discourses and Historical Representation* (Baltimore: Johns Hopkins University Press, 1987); and Berger and Luckmann, *Social Construction of Reality*.

29. Green, *Practicing Theological Interpretation*, 50, drawing on White, *Narrative Discourses*.

30. Green, *Practicing Theological Interpretation*, 81-95, drawing on his *Body, Soul, and Human Life: The Nature of Humanity in the Bible* (Grand Rapids: Baker, 2008).

What Exactly Is Theological Interpretation of Scripture?

scriptural interpretation, the role of context, and the Bible's ability to speak to an original and contemporary situation.

As a result of this brief survey of these significant and explicit introductions to theological interpretation of Scripture, there are several recurring ideas that are worth noting. The first is the general dissatisfaction with so-called historical criticism — even though historical criticism keeps recurring in various treatments, as I will note below. A second is the usually positive, though sometimes qualified, view of pre-modern (or pre-critical) interpretation, especially as represented and encapsulated in the rule of faith. A third is the significant role of the interpretive community, especially identified as the Christian church. A fourth is the ambiguous role, though not always clearly stated, of the Holy Spirit in the interpretive process. A fifth is the relationship of theological interpretation to general and special hermeneutics, where there is a difference of opinion on this relationship. A sixth and final idea that finds its way regularly into the discussion is the question of whether theological interpretation is a method or not. On this point, the representative authors above seem to be divided. I will return to this issue below as well.

Preliminary Evaluation of Representative Attempts

Before engaging in a more focused discussion of particular elements of theological interpretation of Scripture as phenomena in their own right, I wish to make some comments upon the individual treatments summarized immediately above. These comments are not meant as thorough assessments of these particular works, but a series of particular comments that bring to the fore some of the major issues found within each. I discuss them in the same order in which I presented them above.

As a relatively early attempt to capture the essence of theological interpretation of Scripture, Green has clearly identified a number of issues, such as the divide between theological and critical reading of the Bible. He also clearly articulates that theological interpretation is to occur ecclesially, is to be theological, and is to be the work of the Holy Spirit. However, his attempt to incorporate both psychology (neuroscience) and psycholinguistics along with discourse analysis,[31] as well as moderate forms of

---

31. Joel Green has recently made several attempts to practice his version of discourse analysis, similar to the one defined in *Seized by Truth*. See his "Discourse Analysis and New

reader-response criticism found in Eco, and his post-foundationalist conclusion endorsing validity over correctness in interpretation, certainly arouse interest if not serious questions. These questions concern the functionality of his interpretive method[32] to address the questions he raises, the possible generalization of his approach, and its relationship to what presents itself as his major even if unstated goal of theological interpretation — that is, the production of a robust and valid description of the meaning of a scriptural text.

Treier captures several of the same issues identified by Green, including the role of pre-modern interpretation, the role of theology, and the place of communities of interpretation. Even within these three areas, however, there are apparent differences of opinion among theological interpreters. Treier emphasizes the role of pre-modern interpretation but does not say much about forms of historical criticism, even though he attempts to provide a continuous example regarding the image of God (referred to as the *imago Dei*, no doubt because use of Latin adds gravitas to the discussion). Even the role of doctrine is seen to be differently conceived, when it is claimed by Treier that Fowl labels Watson as determinate regarding meaning, when Fowl endorses an underdetermined view (and Trier probably also a determinate view).[33] The same problems are seen in the major contentious issues, as one might expect. The relation to the biblical theology movement is problematic, again with Watson advocating a position much more positively disposed toward it than Treier seems to

---

Testament Interpretation," in *Hearing the New Testament: Strategies for Interpretation* (ed. Joel B. Green; Grand Rapids: Eerdmans, 1995), 175-96 (essentially the same in the second edition of 2010), and his *The Gospel of Luke* (NICNT; Grand Rapids: Eerdmans, 1997). While it is pleasing to see discourse analysis being used in mainstream commentaries and other works (especially as a response to traditional historical criticisms), there are some major problems with this attempt at discourse analysis, not least its virtually complete failure to recognize major efforts already made by other New Testament scholars, and his odd mix of terminology. Green's model appears to be a relatively unstructured hodgepodge of linguistics, literary criticism, translation theory, narratology, and philosophical hermeneutics — not all compatible with his stated intention of analyzing language in use. In *Seized by Truth*, there are also some linguistically naïve comments made regarding language itself, lexical ambiguity, and linguistic analysis that show that his comments are perhaps addressed to readers technically ill-equipped even for the method he proceeds to describe (*Seized by Truth*, 7-10).

32. He distances himself from the notion of method, although this is what it clearly is (Green, *Practicing Theological Interpretation*, 138-40).

33. Treier, *Introducing Theological Interpretation*, 85-87.

What Exactly Is Theological Interpretation of Scripture?

be.[34] The hermeneutical debate clearly divides the house, with such people as Jeanrond, Thiselton, Fowl, Vanhoozer, and others taking different positions regarding general and special hermeneutics. Treier's discussion of social locations appears to be forced (a chapter required by the publisher?), as the idea of social location — though it could have been introduced at any number of places in the previous discussion — is seen primarily in relation to global Christianity. Christianity has always been global, with its eastern roots and early spread to Africa, Asia Minor, Europe, and finally to the Americas.

No doubt because of the brevity of his treatment, Fowl cannot engage in more than briefly introducing the ideas that he discusses, and surely there would be more substantive argument if space allowed.[35] However, the impression that one receives is of assertions simply being matched with counter-assertions, the very thing that Fowl claims to wish to avoid — simply making other assertions or changing the terms of the discussion does not alleviate the issues. There is no substantive defense of the triune God as a hermeneutical key over christological claims, and the bald differentiation of theological interpretation from other concerns is problematic, especially in light of the discussions of other advocates of theological interpretation who are more inclusive. Does Fowl really eliminate the problems of historical criticism by claiming to have other interests than historical reliability? Does the rule of faith genuinely resolve problems of biblical theology? Does engaging in forced exegesis make the Old Testament more understandable as Christian Scripture? Is it possible not to have a theory of interpretation, even a general one (or is that one?)? Can the problem of meaning be solved by what appears to be linguistic legerdemain, and do "aims" satisfy when one wants to know the import of a text? Unfortunately, one must answer "no" to each of these questions. The practices of theological hermeneutics endorsed by Fowl look an awful lot like a method or an attempt at a hermeneutic, even if an underdeveloped one.

Billings treats many of the same topics as already extensively noted, although in a manner and order that is less clear as to its purpose. As a result, he wishes to chart a middle course in the use of the Bible, in which the rule of faith guides interpretation. He sees a christological focus as uniting the

---

34. I believe that Watson is grasping at intellectually indefensible straws in his attempts in *Text and Truth*, 18-26, to salvage the biblical theology movement from the criticisms of James Barr, *The Semantics of Biblical Language* (Oxford: Oxford University Press, 1961).

35. As is provided, for example, at places in his *Engaging Scripture*.

Testaments, and invokes three common ideas — pre-modern interpretation, the role of the church in interpretation, and the role of the Holy Spirit. However, when it comes to finding a means by which this might happen, Billings shies away from adopting what the pre-modern exegetes would do in practice, and invokes a number of modern critical stances, including Green's regarding various contexts (his close reading model), Vanhoozer's regarding the Trinitarian drama of Scripture, and speech-act theory as a means of establishing the thrust of the Bible as related to God's action, rather than information. As already indicated, each of these is itself questionable.

In several respects, Green's second treatment is both a conspectus of theological interpretation — with its emphasis upon the relation to historical criticism, the role of the rule of faith, and the place of pre-modern interpretation — and a defense and redefinition of his own approach to theological interpretation. This approach clearly wishes to distance theological interpretation of Scripture from being any kind of a method in a definable and specific sense. At least as importantly, it seems, Green's treatment wishes to provide an apologetic for his own approach. This involves the incorporation (again) of Eco-ian reader-response criticism and several key insights from cognitive and neuroscientific thought. In fact, it appears that cognitive and neuroscientific thought is given equal or prior status in relation to the other elements, when Green, for example, fully embraces frame theory and monist anthropology — in the latter engaging in an extended (and ultimately unconvincing, because he neglects key biblical texts) defense. This raises the question of what it means to call something theological interpretation of Scripture, if theology is trumped by, if not explicitly historical criticism, other forms of contemporary criticism — no doubt subject to the same kinds of critique that have been brought by Green and others against historical criticism. In fact, Green's distinction of three types of historical criticism is itself problematic, because he clearly uses historical criticism to perform all of the tasks that he is demonstrating, including engaging in a form of reconstructing the past. This is despite his claim — one that he seems to contradict in his own interpretive examples — that he is not concerned with reconstructing the past, at the same time as he is engaged in reconstructing the meaning of a text, such as Acts or James.

Without going into further detail, it is clear — simply on the basis of what various advocates of theological interpretation themselves state — that theological interpretation cannot be seen simply as a unified approach to the interpretation of Scripture. More could be said about these

What Exactly Is Theological Interpretation of Scripture?

internal difficulties, and even contradictions, among the various advocates. However, discovering their difficulties with one another is not the purpose of this essay — even if these difficulties do make it very difficult to conceive of theological interpretation as anything more than an underdefined and varying set of tendencies or interests, with some overlap between proponents.

Is Theological Interpretation a Hermeneutic, and If So, What Kind?

This brings us to the evaluation of whether theological interpretation of Scripture is a hermeneutic, and, if a hermeneutic, what kind of hermeneutic it is. Theological interpretation of Scripture is, indeed, a hermeneutic — if by hermeneutic we mean nothing more than a reasonably (to varying degrees) coherent stance toward understanding. In that sense, theological hermeneutics is a hermeneutic, much as virtually every approach to understanding is a hermeneutic. However, advocates of theological interpretation of Scripture appear to mean more than this broad definition by their invocation of the common descriptive label for what they are attempting to do. Their efforts at self-definition, their appealing to sometimes common and overlapping viewpoints — even if used in various ways — and their stance in distinction from, if not outright opposition to, forms of historical criticism, indicate, at least to me, that they mean much more than merely that theirs is one approach along with myriads of others. In this section, I wish to tackle, even if only briefly, several of the defining ideas noted above, to assess more carefully the nature of this supposed hermeneutic.

Historical Criticism and Theological Interpretation

Let me begin by saying that I am very much in sympathy with many of the statements made by advocates of theological interpretation in their opposition to or their questioning of the domination of forms of historical criticism. Can there be doubt (apart possibly from some deeply-entrenched German scholars?) that historical criticism in its various forms has been a part of or a major contributor to a disconnectedness in biblical scholarship from the theological interests of the church? Peering behind the text has neglected the text itself in the interpretive process — in fact, its claims to be able to see what others previously have not or cannot, by examination of the same textual evidence as used by others, strikes me as an exercise in often groundless assertion or even a flight of imaginative (though critically condoned) fantasy. Even if one had confidence that traditionally-conceived forms of historical criticism could perform the tasks that they are sometimes said to achieve, there remains the major issue of the pertinence and applicability of their results to the church and Christian believers who wish to gain more from reading the Bible than simply the (often questionable) historical backdrop against which significant events occurred. Traditional historical criticism, whether unitarily conceived or multifarious, has not been able to forge a significant interpretive bridge between the then and the now. As a result, I can readily understand efforts to dismiss or bracket out as theologically irrelevant and even unproductive most, if not virtually all, results of such historical criticism. The theological interpretation of Scripture attempts to capture this sentiment.

Or does it? There seems to be a palpable ambiguity regarding various forms of historical criticism in virtually all summative descriptions of theological interpretation of Scripture. For example, Treier is probably the most dismissive of historical criticism. While recognizing its plurivocity,[36] he stereotypes it in opposition to theological interpretation. Fowl makes a more explicit distinction.[37] Green appreciates the possible sterility of reading the Bible (he differentiates this from reading Scripture),[38] but is ambivalent toward non-theological ways of reading the Bible. On the one hand, they may be dry, but they can be drawn upon when they become components of certain types of reading strategies (such as his form of discourse analysis),[39] or, even more so, they can be essential to theological interpretation when they help to reconstruct the biblical historical situation.[40] So, for Green, historical criticism is very much a part of theological interpretation, even if one still advocates for a theological dimension or reconstrues theological interpretation within a so-called "linguistic turn" (which, as Roy Harris has pointed out, is not very linguistic at all) in historical studies that distance interpretation from events.[41] Billings does not

36. Treier, *Introducing Theological Interpretation*, 201.
37. Fowl, *Theological Interpretation*, 15-24.
38. Green, *Seized by Truth*, 3.
39. Green, *Seized by Truth*, 128.
40. Green, *Practicing Theological Interpretation*, 45.
41. See Roy Harris, *The Linguistics of History* (Edinburgh: Edinburgh University Press, 2004), passim, especially criticizing those such as Hayden White.

What Exactly Is Theological Interpretation of Scripture?

even bother to make such distinctions, but says that theological interpretation of an ancient text is dependent upon historical criticism.[42] I find it interesting, and somewhat troubling, how there can be such a range of disagreement regarding the relationship of theological interpretation to historical criticism. For some, theological interpretation is completely "other" than historical criticism; for some, the two are clearly compatible; and for still others, the former is dependent on the latter. If this range of views is the case, then it is difficult to define theological interpretation as a hermeneutic distinct from historical criticism, and it makes it virtually impossible to understand the kinds of criticism often thrown at historical criticism when it can be rehabilitated so easily by undifferentiated incorporation. There must be more to theological interpretation than its simply being theological as opposed to historical.

Along with this varied approach to historical criticism, there is the further issue of why it is that so many other types of not inherently theological interpretation are often incorporated within it. These interpretive methods may not be typically defined as historical criticisms, but they are certainly modern, non-theological critical approaches to interpretation. These include reader-response criticism, as found in Eco and Iser (see especially Green); types of discourse analysis, including socio-culturally based analysis (Green again); neuroscience and cognitive theory (Green still again); and speech-act theory (both Treier and Billings). Fowl is the one author who seems to steer clear of these approaches, but not all such approaches. Fowl appropriates the philosophical pragmatism of Jeffrey Stout and Richard Rorty, when he consciously avoids questions of meaning and opts instead for interpretive interests.[43] Each of these modern interpretive approaches, although not historical-critical in the traditional sense, is still non-theological in virtually every way and, if truth be told, at least a form of historically positioned criticism, that is, a form of criticism responding to historical (even if textual) situations and with historical interests.

Each of these interpretive approaches can be and has rightly been ana-

42. Billings, *Word of God*, 55.
43. Fowl, *Theological Interpretation*, 48, citing Jeffrey Stout, "What Is the Meaning of a Text?" *New Literary History* 14 (1982): 1-12, and Richard Rorty, *Philosophy and the Mirror of Nature* (Oxford: Blackwell, 1980), esp. ch. 6, discussed in more detail in Fowl, "The Role of Authorial Intention in the Theological Interpretation of Scripture," in *Between Two Horizons*, ed. Green and Turner, 71-87; and "The Ethics of Interpretation or What's Left Over after the Elimination of Meaning," in *The Bible in Three Dimensions* (ed. D. J. A. Clines, Stephen E. Fowl, and Stanley E. Porter; Sheffield: JSOT Press, 1990), 379-98.

lyzed and criticized. Here is not the place to enter into such discussion in any detail. Suffice it to say that forms of reader-response theory vary, and their incorporation is bound to shift the center of interpretive authority from author and text to reader. Perhaps some theological interpreters desire this, as we have already seen above in some of the statements made by major proponents in their views of author and intention, text, and reader and community (see also below). But such reader-oriented approaches can also be criticized as being either preservationist, that is, legitimizing the place not of the actual reader but of a reader constructed by the author or circumscribed by the text, or uncontrolled, that is, positing a reader not simply as determiner of meaning but as its very creator.[44] As already mentioned above, discourse analysis as defined here by Green (or elsewhere by him) is not sufficiently robust or linguistically rigorous to serve as the basis of an interpretive method, even if combined with theology. I find it intriguing that cognitive linguistics and the supposed findings of neuroscience are apparently treated as authoritatively equivalent to the biblical text,[45] an inconsistent position for what purports to be a theological hermeneutic. As noted above, speech-act theory has been associated with a number of hermeneuts and consequently adopted by some theological interpreters, such as Treier and Billings, and rejected by others, such as Fowl. I agree with Fowl, though for different reasons, that speech-act theory is not the way forward as an interpretive tool and especially as a philosophy of language.[46] It addresses a correct notion — that language is functional in nature — but does so with an artificially limited concept of language that is unable to formulate linguistic criteria for determination of illocutionary force.[47] Finally, Rortian pragmatism would appear to be antithetical to any notion of normative or authoritative theological interpretation of Scripture.[48]

The uses of historical criticism by most theological interpreters — Fowl being the exception to a degree — make it difficult to understand the basis of strong opposition to historical criticism, especially when forms of historical criticism and other types of contemporary criticism are readily integrated into theological interpretation.

---

44. See Thiselton, *New Horizons*, 515-55.
45. Green, *Practicing Theological Interpretation*, 81-85.
46. Fowl, *Theological Interpretation*, 48-49.
47. See Geoffrey Leech and Jenny Thomas, "Language, Meaning and Context," in *An Encyclopaedia of Language* (ed. N. E. Collinge; London: Routledge, 1990), 173-206, esp. 196. Cf. Porter and Robinson, *Hermeneutics*, 267.
48. See Thiselton, *New Horizons*, 393-405.

What Exactly Is Theological Interpretation of Scripture?

Pre-Modern Interpretation and the Rule of Faith

Pre-modern interpretation is often hailed by theological interpreters of Scripture as the effective antidote to historical criticism and as the means of doing theological interpretation. For example, Fowl, as noted above, draws a strong distinction between pre-modern interpretation and historical criticism, and when he turns to the practices and habits of theological interpretation, he immediately begins with pre-modern interpretation.[49] But what exactly is pre-modern interpretation? At this point, the situation becomes much more ill-defined. For Treier, although recognizing its lack of unity, he boils pre-modern interpretation down to a pious reading that is christological and typological and shares the same concerns as are found in the fourfold interpretation of Scripture. For Fowl, pre-modern interpretation is distinctly theological and even figural, a desired quality. Billings similarly sees pre-modern interpretation as concerned with the theological meaning of Scripture, hence his endorsement of the different senses of Scripture (the fourfold interpretation) and the reading of the Old Testament as Christian Scripture. In good Methodist form, Green extends the notion of pre-modern to include John Wesley. All of the proponents of theological interpretation noted here are hovering around a set of common, if admittedly vague, notions regarding what pre-modern interpretation entails.

Most who invoke the importance of pre-modern interpretation recognize a number of possible objections to it. They note, for example, that many perceive of pre-modern interpretation as naïve or ignorant, others that it is primitive or ahistorical, others that it is esoteric or irrelevant.[50] In other words, they admit and acknowledge that there are elements of pre-modern interpretation that are potentially troublesome for modern interpreters. However, they also believe that these shortcomings can be overcome by recognizing the common set of beliefs that the pre-moderns enjoyed and adopting the theological perspective that they had. What is clearly missing is acknowledgment of some of the explicit problems of pre-modern interpretation. For example, the pre-moderns, including Christians, often had contradictory views, even over such things as Scripture and its interpretation. We know, for example, that many of the early

---

49. Fowl, *Theological Interpretation*, 54.
50. See, for example, Fowl, *Theological Interpretation*, 15-18; Billings, *Word of God*, 151-55.

church disputes, which often resulted in councils, were focused upon debates over the divine and human nature of Christ, the transmission of sin, or the beings of the Trinity.[51] This does not even raise more highly problematic issues for the pre-moderns, such as beliefs regarding the nature of women and their relationship to men within the church and in society as a whole.[52] Those involved in such theological disputes — and they certainly were theological disputes — shared the same Christian worldview, in which God was the one who created and maintained the world of dependent human existence. Those involved in the disputes also appealed to the same body of biblical evidence when arguing for their respective positions, and they basically engaged in similar forms of biblical interpretation, whether they were so-called Alexandrians or Antiochenes.[53] Those involved were also seeking theological resolution, especially if such resolution also entailed theological vindication. In the end, disagreement remained, sometimes lengthy and protracted disagreement, among the varying factions. One might well argue that in some instances the dispute was resolved (if it was) not along evidential, logical, or even theological lines so much as on the basis of the personalities and even ecclesial politics involved.

One can possibly account for the vagueness in discussing pre-modern interpretation by proponents of theological interpretation because of the recognition of its highly problematic nature. In other words, one of the unspoken factors in the discussion is that in many ways the pre-modern church, especially in the early centuries surrounding the formulation of the creeds, was often divided, either temporarily or even more lastingly, along various theological lines — whether regarding the nature of Jesus Christ or of the godhead or something else. As a result, a number of theological interpreters appeal more specifically or additionally to the "rule of faith." The

---

51. Most decent church histories recount the controversies in sufficient detail to make the point. For more specialized treatments, see, for example, the still very valuable Adolf von Harnack, *History of Dogma* (trans. Neil Buchanan et al.; 7 vols.; repr. New York: Russell and Russell, 1958), esp. vols. 3-5; J. N. D. Kelly, *Early Christian Doctrines* (rev. ed.; New York: Harper & Row, 1978); and the lighter, more popular exposition, Luke Timothy Johnson, *The Creed: What Christians Believe and Why It Matters* (New York: Doubleday, 2003).

52. See Rosemary Radford Ruether, "Misogynism and Virginal Feminism in the Fathers of the Church," in *Religion and Sexism: Images of Woman in the Jewish and Christian Traditions* (ed. Rosemary Radford Ruether; New York: Simon and Schuster, 1974), 150-83.

53. See James L. Kugel and Rowan A. Greer, *Early Biblical Interpretation* (Philadelphia: Westminster, 1986), 177-99 (by Greer).

rule of faith, using terminology that goes back to the early church fathers and referring to the conspectus of agreed upon beliefs of the early church, is seen to be encapsulated in the major creeds, especially the Apostles' Creed or Nicene Creed. At first blush, this appears to bring some interpretive stability, until one thinks further on the matter. The creeds were not permanent resolutions of disputes, but contextually-based negotiated settlements regarding a particular set of theological issues — issues that often left some early Christian leaders satisfied with the outcome and others disappointed — and even banished or excommunicated.[54] As important as the Apostles' Creed, Nicene Creed, and Constantinopolitan Creed have been, none was sufficient to resolve all of the major theological issues of pre-modern Christianity, as none forestalled many subsequent councils and their creeds as attempts to resolve doctrinal and theological disputes. History indicates that such unresolved issues continued, with resulting splits between eastern and western churches, the Roman Catholic church and various forms of Protestantism, Calvinists and Arminians, various forms of Protestantism, Anabaptists and others, and the list could go on — all within the pre-modern interpretive period.[55]

Thus, the invocation of pre-modern interpretation, as appealing as it may be when it is vaguely defined, is highly problematic when one considers more specific events within the pre-modern church. This tension is not resolved by appeal to the rule of faith, which is itself embedded within an interpretive and contextual situation that resulted in the formulation of many creeds and on-going theological disputes.

The Interpretive Community, or the Role of the Church or Ecclesia

The notion of meaning is problematic within theological interpretive circles. Most theological interpreters wish to distance themselves from the

---

54. A still useful source regarding the development of the major creeds, including their various versions, is Philip Schaff, *The Greek and Latin Creeds, with Translations* (London: Hodder and Stoughton, 1878). See also A. E. Burn, *An Introduction to the Creeds and to the Te Deum* (London: Methuen, 1899), and J. N. D. Kelly, *Early Christian Creeds* (2nd ed.; London: Longman, 1960).

55. There are many church histories that capture these movements and disputes. I have found helpful Kenneth Scott Latourette, *A History of Christianity* (New York: Harper & Row, 1953), and Williston Walker, *A History of the Christian Church* (rev. Cyril C. Richardson et al.; New York: Scribner's, 1959). There are no doubt others as well.

popular intentionalism represented by Hirsch in his *Validity in Interpretation*.⁵⁶ This does not mean, however, that they all have a common conception of meaning. There are some who appeal to theological interpretation because they wish to close the gap between then and now and find a hermeneutic that bridges such a divide with a unified theory of meaning.⁵⁷ Green, on the other hand, believes that any given text may have multiple, though not infinite, numbers of meanings. He is concerned not to discover a single correct meaning, something he attributes to the grammatical-historical method, but only to find those that are valid "good readings" (this notion remains vague, as it is unclear for what it is valid).⁵⁸ There are still others, however, who are less convinced by the concept of meaning altogether. Fowl, as noted above, wishes to eliminate discussion or talk of meaning and speak instead of interests.⁵⁹ There is clearly a difference of opinion among theological interpreters of Scripture regarding such a concept as meaning. In many ways, this serves to undermine the entire theological interpretive agenda, as it, at least in several instances, appears to be heading in the same direction as the dreaded historical criticism to which it is so vocally opposed — an unclear and imprecise notion of meaning that does not allow for the kinds of theological and dogmatic results that theological interpreters seem to desire or the approach seems to demand.

One of the ways that this difference of opinion has been addressed is through the notion of the role of the interpretive community or church. All of the proponents of theological interpretation of Scripture noted above have a role for the church or ecclesial community. Green puts reading Scripture within an ecclesial setting as part of a community of interpreters who share a similar reading stance of subordination to Scripture.⁶⁰ Treier argues for the importance of the church as one of the three essentials of theological interpretation. He draws heavily upon Fowl's argument for biblical interpretation within the church being underdetermined, that is, not needing any general theory of meaning but rather being dependent upon practical reason.⁶¹ In his later treatment, Fowl argues that reading

---

56. See, for example, Green, *Seized by Truth*, 51; Treier, *Introducing Theological Interpretation*, 134; Fowl, *Theological Interpretation*, 40-43.

57. See, for example, Green, *Seized by Truth*, 51; Billings, *Word of God*, 169-88.

58. Green, *Practicing Theological Interpretation*, 74 and n. 3. See also *Seized by Truth*, 137-38.

59. See Fowl, *Theological Interpretation*, 40-43.

60. Green, *Seized by Truth*, 66.

61. Treier, *Introducing Theological Interpretation*, 87, citing Fowl, *Engaging Scripture*,

What Exactly Is Theological Interpretation of Scripture?

Scripture ecclesially is a source of unity, not division (as one might first imagine), if it is done with regard for other essential practices, such as truth seeking/telling, repentance and reconciliation, and patience.[62] Billings ties the work of the Holy Spirit to the church, seeing the Spirit as "converting" the church and the church as the location where Scripture is read under the Spirit's influence.[63] Green's later work summarizes the way that the church functions in theological interpretation when he says: "If the church is one, . . . if there is only one church through the centuries and across the globe, then this letter [he is dealing with James] has our names written on it."[64] In other words, the church bridges the gap from the then to the now in understanding. There is no doubt that the church has been a central place for theological interpretation through the ages, and, as especially Green has emphasized, should constitute the place of theological and spiritual formation. However, the question is whether ecclesial reading provides the necessary parameters for interpretation, or serves as a useful control on interpretive practices.

There are two major issues here. One is the church itself, and the other is the notion of interpretive communities in the larger sense. The picture drawn of the church by theological interpreters of Scripture is a highly suspect one, especially when it comes to serving as a guide to theological interpretation in any meaningful and generalizable sense. There may be one church of Jesus Christ, but there are lots of different manifestations of that church, with varying beliefs and practices, some of them incidental no doubt, but many of them fundamental to the point of causing schism and division. The history of Christianity is one of constant and recurring division, often around major theological issues (even if we would prefer that it be around incidentals). It is one thing to say that Luther read the Bible

---

passim, and Stephen E. Fowl and L. Gregory Jones, *Reading in Communion: Scripture and Ethics in Christian Life* (Grand Rapids: Eerdmans, 1991), passim. Practical reason, based on the work of Alasdair MacIntyre, *After Virtue: A Study in Moral Theory* (2nd ed.; Notre Dame, IN: University of Notre Dame Press, 1984), is a fundamental notion for Fowl, found not only in *Engaging Scripture* and *Theological Interpretation*, but also in *Philippians* (THNTC; Grand Rapids: Eerdmans, 2005), 6, 28-29. However, it is not entirely clear what the concept entails, and Fowl may be unloading an awful lot of freight on this one word (i.e., engaging in the lexical fallacy of illegitimate totality transfer) in his understanding of the term in Philippians.

62. Fowl, *Theological Interpretation*, 64-70.
63. Billings, *Word of God*, 122-26.
64. Green, *Practicing Theological Interpretation*, 17-18.

figurally and in ways similar to the medieval Catholic Church, as Fowl says (and is no doubt correct),[65] but there were key areas where they differed, to the point of major theological controversies and divisions over fundamental issues, many of them related to Scripture, its interpretation, and resulting practices (meant here in the same sense as used by Fowl and others).[66] The contemporary church is certainly no better. Not only do we have major divisions between eastern and western churches, but within the west we have major divisions between what are often characterized as mainline and evangelical churches, and any number of other types of divisions. Major differences in interpretation of Scripture are seen to be at the heart of continual disputes both over traditional theological areas of difference, such as the nature of the resurrection and meaning and basis of baptism and the Lord's Supper, and over more contemporary issues, related to such matters as gender roles and function, church order and authority, and even (dreaded) eschatology.[67] It would appear, or at least it seems to me, that invoking the notion of ecclesial reading may mean one of a small number of things to theological interpreters of Scripture. One is that they are arguing that we should invoke an incredibly broad notion of the church or ecclesial community, one that can encompass the diversity within the church through the centuries. If this is the case, then there is a question of how useful such a community is for theological or scriptural interpretation, when it cannot even resolve major issues that have plagued it through the years. There is little to no hope of agreement on anything substantive, including possibly the meaning of the death and resurrection of Jesus Christ.[68] A second sense of church would be the ecclesial community that

---

65. Fowl, *Theological Interpretation*, 64.

66. Fowl, *Theological Interpretation*, 64-70.

67. Some may wish to dismiss these issues as not being fundamental, or as not reflecting the kind of unifying belief found in the creeds or indicative of the rule of faith. That may be true in a narrow sense. However, I believe it can be argued that the less central beliefs reflect prior decisions regarding central beliefs. There is also the issue of how one decides which issues are fundamental and how one adjudicates among interpretations of them. Cf. Stephen E. Fowl, "Theological and Ideological Strategies of Biblical Interpretation," in *Scripture: An Ecumenical Introduction to the Bible and Its Interpretation* (Peabody, MA: Hendrickson, 2005), 163-75, esp. 173.

68. Recent disputes over the nature and significance of the death of Jesus are a case in point. There are major disputes over what is meant by the atonement and justification, with the positions appealing to church history, theology, and Scripture. For treatments of some of the issues, see Charles E. Hill and Frank A. James III, eds., *The Glory of the Atonement* (Downers Grove, IL: InterVarsity Press, 2004); and Mark Husbands and Daniel J. Treier, eds.,

What Exactly Is Theological Interpretation of Scripture?

most satisfactorily includes my interpretations of Scripture. In other words, I agree to associate with those who have similar views on Scripture and its interpretation. This may well be what most theological interpretation of Scripture entails. For example, Green refers many times to Wesleyan distinctives (e.g. the Wesleyan quadrilateral) and uses John Wesley as an example in his writings.[69] It seems to me that he means something very different about an ecclesial community than do non-Wesleyans. Where this leaves those who do not hold similar beliefs, I am not sure. A third use of the concept of church is simply as an abstraction to be invoked in opposition to other types of interpretation, especially historical criticism. However, just as the notion of historical criticism is an abstraction that encompasses many different types of criticism, the church in this sense encompasses far more than can be usefully harmonized into a means of control on theological interpretation.

Such concepts of the church have similarities to other notions regarding interpretive communities.[70] The idea of interpretive communities has been associated with kinds of pragmatic criticism that have noted that definitive interpretation has proved elusive, and that interpreters tend to associate with communities of interpreters who hold to similar strategies for interpretation or arrive at similar interpretive conclusions. Even here, however, the concept of interpretive community is difficult to define. Does it serve as a way of lumping together, or of drawing a boundary around, those who arrive at similar interpretations of a text, such as the Bible, or does it set the parameters of legitimate interpretive procedure within which those in the community end up interpreting, or even must interpret? In other words, does interpretation take place first, and then we congregate and associate on the basis of common understandings, or do our associations and affinities set the parameters of our interpretation? Is an interpretive community descriptive or is it prescriptive? These are very different and potentially conflicting views of community. In the first, the boundaries of community are fluid and constantly changing, as we inter-

---

Justification: What's at Stake in the Current Debate (Downers Grove, IL: InterVarsity Press, 2004).

69. For example, Green, *Seized by Truth*, 85-88, and *Practicing Theological Interpretation*, 99-121.

70. The major figure is Stanley Fish, *Is There a Text in This Class? The Authority of Interpretive Communities* (Cambridge, MA: Harvard University Press, 1980), esp. 14. I note that Fish is not referred to by Stanley J. Grenz, "Community, Interpretive," in *Dictionary for Theological Interpretation*, ed. Vanhoozer, 128-29.

pret texts differently and shift our interpretive allegiances as a result. In the second, the boundaries of community are more fixed and constant, and determine the limits of what is legitimate interpretation.

The major question here is whether either is acceptable for theological interpretation of Scripture. My reading of the proponents of the method indicates that they would be unhappy with the first definition for several reasons. One is that the church or ecclesial community is apparently conceived by them as preceding interpretation, and in some way as setting the interpretive agenda. The second is that they make the claim that interpretation itself is to emerge from the community, and not be a means of classification. However, I am not sure that I can envision proponents of theological interpretation being entirely satisfied with the second view of an interpretive community either, and this for several reasons as well. One is that their notion of the church or ecclesial interpretation seems far broader and more widely encompassing than the one offered by this definition of interpretive community. This second definition also seems to be too exclusivistic (even if communities are multiple), with some inside and some outside the pale of the interpretive community. A third is that their vague descriptions and invocation of ecclesial community, as well as their hesitancy to define meaning in a univocal way, would seem to argue against such a narrow construal of the effect of an interpretive community on reading.

In other words, it is unclear to me how the notion of an ecclesial or other type of reading community helps to define what is meant by theological interpretation of Scripture.

Holy Spirit

The role of the Holy Spirit in interpretation is invoked in a number of different ways by theological interpreters of Scripture, with there being some difficulties in defining what role the Spirit plays and how. As noted above, Fowl views the Spirit's role in the formation of Scripture rather than in its interpretation, while Treier associates the Spirit with the community, and Green treats the influence of the Holy Spirit as more of a collaborative influence that reminds us of our finitude and need for the interpretive other.[71] Billings has the most robust role for the Holy Spirit to play, but it

---

71. Fowl, *Theological Interpretation*, 1-12; Treier, *Introducing Theological Interpretation*, 79-100; Green, *Seized by Truth*, 94-100.

What Exactly Is Theological Interpretation of Scripture?

is focused mostly upon what he calls the indigenizing of the biblical message so that it is pertinent to all cultures.[72]

In light of what we have seen above regarding theological interpretation of Scripture, I don't think it is too surprising to find that the Holy Spirit is barely mentioned, even if part of the triune God. He is at worst virtually completely marginalized and at best constricted to a particular, even if ill-defined, function of indigenization. The prospect of the Holy Spirit actually entering into the interpretive process — a factor that some Christian traditions, obviously very different from most theological interpreters as here defined, welcome — is not something that those who are looking to the church fathers and pre-modern interpretation are probably going to be willing to accept or welcome. Such a factor would be too contemporary, too uncontrollable, and too potentially innovative and creative for such an approach to Scripture, where the emphasis is upon relatively static means of understanding, such as pre-modern interpretation, tradition, and a vague and idealized sense of the church.

General and Special Hermeneutics

Hermeneutics is at best a difficult notion to define, and theological interpreters of Scripture do no better (or for that matter, no worse) than others in addressing the issues. In discussion of the nature of theological interpretation of Scripture, it is understandable that various proponents attempt to position their conception of it in relation to general and special hermeneutics. After all, one of the major questions or points of contention — and one of the main focuses of this article — is the hermeneutical nature of what is called theological interpretation of Scripture. Many proponents of theological interpretation use the term "hermeneutics" in a variety of casual and, apparently (if such is possible in such a context), non-technical ways. Thus, Green refers to various hermeneutical issues throughout his two books, but without, so far as I can tell, defining hermeneutics in detail or coming down on the issue of his understanding of hermeneutics and theological interpretation in relation to the topics of general and special hermeneutics. The major point of dispute is found between Treier and Billings on the one hand and Fowl on the other. Both Treier and Billings, although in slightly different (and for our pur-

---

72. Billings, *Word of God*, 105-48.

poses insignificant) ways, argue that theological interpretation of Scripture needs to be sensitive to elements of both general and special hermeneutics, and in fact utilize elements of both.[73] In other words, just as the Bible is a written text like others, its interpretation requires that interpreters avail themselves of elements of general hermeneutics (a view with which Green would no doubt agree). However, the Bible is not simply a book like any other, and in order to fully comprehend and appropriate this work, one needs to approach it as a unique theological text, and thus special hermeneutics is necessary. Fowl strongly objects to such a position. He believes that an appeal to any type of hermeneutics, whether it is general or special, makes interpretation of Scripture subservient to another means of interpretation, that is, that understanding is determined through other means than the interpretation of Scripture.[74] In particular, he finds fault with two major areas of hermeneutical debate already recounted. The first is theories of meaning themselves, where he altogether rejects the technical use of the term "meaning." Fowl's contention is that disputes over meaning are not resolved simply by appealing to the concept of meaning, but that these differences reflect different "interpretive aims."[75] Of course, we could wish that resolving interpretive disputes were this easy — as it sometimes becomes clear that differences of interpretation reflect more than simply different interpretive interests or aims, but fundamental differences in understanding and their resulting meanings, meanings that must be discussed. The other is Fowl's rejection of speech-act theory as a theory of language, and with it a theory of authorial intention. He first wishes to differentiate intentions from motives (equating the latter with psychological impetus), but more than that he does not believe that speech-act theory, though widely used by a variety of theological interpreters, can provide a robust theory to adjudicate intentions of authors.[76]

The issue of the relationship of theological interpretation of Scripture to general and special hermeneutics is an intriguing one. Fowl wishes to distance himself from two major explicit issues that have become part

---

73. Treier, *Introducing Theological Hermeneutics*, 140-56, and Billings, *Word of God*, 32-38.

74. Fowl, *Theological Interpretation*, 37-40, esp. 39.

75. Fowl, *Theological Interpretation*, 40-43. See above on Fowl's reliance here on Stout and Rorty.

76. Fowl, *Theological Interpretation*, 44-49, esp. 48. See above on speech-act theory and Fowl's reliance on Brett.

of various forms of theological interpretation or theological hermeneutics, especially the forms found in the works of Thiselton and Vanhoozer and their followers. As noted above, he is no doubt correct that there are distinct limitations to speech-act theory, and that trying to build a general (or special) hermeneutic around speech-act theory, as some theological interpreters of Scripture have attempted, has serious shortcomings. Especially as used by Vanhoozer as a means of transferring intentionality from the earthly to the divine author,[77] the theory simply compounds its difficulties. Speech-act theory has been unable to provide linguistic criteria for delimiting illocutionary acts and hence intentionality, and transferring such intentions to God simply removes the prospect of testability one step further. Speech-act theory confines itself to the sentence level, whereas what is needed is a means of textual analysis that extends to larger units of meaning, including the discourse, and is able to find means of construing the semantic force of statements within definable and testable contexts. Speech-act theory has not been able to do this, and shows no prospects of being able to do this. Vanhoozer himself, after attempting a form of general hermeneutics in his *Is There a Meaning in This Text?*, has redirected his interpretive efforts to developing a special hermeneutics in his *The Drama of Doctrine*.[78] This does not appear to be moving in the right interpretive direction, as he appears simply to substitute a more complex metaphor for an underdeveloped theory of language. However, having said this, I am not convinced that the solution to the difficulty is, with Fowl, to distance oneself from either general or special hermeneutics. Fowl himself, even if he avows to be doing differently, has adopted one general hermeneutical model instead of another. In his indebtedness to Stout and Rorty, Fowl adopts a pragmatic hermeneutics, with its own shortcomings already noted above. Consistent with his disparagement of the concept of meaning and endorsement of interpretive aims, pragmatism is anti-foundationalist, advocating for interpretation that works, that is, that satisfies the needs of a given community or interpretive purpose (hence Fowl's ability to dismiss an argument simply by claiming that he does not find it persuasive).[79] Is this what most theological interpreters of Scripture are seeking when they look to such an approach? There is no indication of this in what they say.

77. Vanhoozer, *Is There a Meaning?* 201-65. Cf. Porter and Robinson, *Hermeneutics*, 261.
78. Porter and Robinson, *Hermeneutics*, 259, 262.
79. For example, Fowl, *Theological Interpretation*, 48.

STANLEY E. PORTER

Other Related Approaches

There are other methods that are sometimes brought into the discussion of theological interpretation. The two major ones are biblical theology and a canonical approach to Scripture. Treier notes the major disputes over the Biblical Theology Movement, including efforts by such people as Watson to revive the movement against Barr's criticism, and attempts to modify biblical theology so that it might become more theologically useful to the church in its interpretation of Scripture.[80] The three modifications that he notes are, first, the incorporation of progressive revelation in the manner suggested by D. A. Carson;[81] secondly, the canonical approach of Brevard Childs that derives its authority from the text;[82] and thirdly, redefining biblical theology in terms of systematic or dogmatic theology as proposed by Watson.[83] As this discussion occurs in the portion of the volume addressed to debates, rather than fundamental beliefs, within the theological interpretation movement, I take it that Treier holds out some hope that forms of biblical theology, and even a canonical approach to Scripture, can be incorporated into theological interpretation of Scripture — if they are not identified with each other already. Fowl, on the other hand, wishes to

---

80. Treier, *Introducing Theological Interpretation*, 104-19.

81. See D. A. Carson, "Unity and Diversity in the New Testament: The Possibility of Systematic Theology," in *Scripture and Truth* (ed. D. A. Carson and John D. Woodbridge; Grand Rapids: Baker, 1992), 65-95. There have been other discussions of biblical (especially New Testament) theology. See, for example, Scott J. Hafemann, ed., *Biblical Theology: Retrospect and Prospect* (Downers Grove, IL: InterVarsity Press, 2002); Peter Balla, *Challenges to New Testament Theology: An Attempt to Justify the Enterprise* (Peabody, MA: Hendrickson, 1997); A. K. M. Adam, *Making Sense of New Testament Theology: "Modern" Problems and Prospects* (Macon, GA: Mercer University Press, 1995); and Dan O. Via, *What Is New Testament Theology?* (Minneapolis: Fortress, 2002).

82. Treier does not cite the major works of Brevard Childs, which include, among others, *Introduction to the Old Testament as Scripture* (Philadelphia: Fortress, 1979); *The New Testament as Canon: An Introduction* (Philadelphia: Fortress, 1984); and *Biblical Theology of the Old and New Testaments* (Minneapolis: Fortress, 1994). A volume dedicated to Childs is Craig G. Bartholomew et al., eds., *Canon and Biblical Interpretation* (Scripture and Hermeneutics 7; Grand Rapids: Zondervan, 2006). Treier instead cites Childs's close follower, Christopher Seitz. See his *The Character of Christian Scripture: The Significance of a Two-Testament Bible* (Grand Rapids: Baker, 2011).

83. Watson, *Text and Truth*. Treier also cites Joel B. Green, "Scripture and Theology: Uniting the Two So Long Divided," in *Between Two Horizons*, ed. Green and Turner, 23-43; and Steve Motyer, "Two Testaments, One Biblical Theology," in *Between Two Horizons*, ed. Green and Turner, 143-64.

What Exactly Is Theological Interpretation of Scripture?

distance theological interpretation of Scripture from biblical theology. He characterizes biblical theology as fundamentally opposed to theological interpretation because of two factors: its historical orientation, and its conscious distancing of itself from theological concerns — both of which put it at odds with theological interpretation.[84] Fowl does not appear to hold out much hope that these distinct differences can be overcome. This is understandable in light of his other comments regarding hermeneutics noted above.

Conclusion

Where does this leave us? What kind of a hermeneutic is represented by theological interpretation of Scripture? Before returning to this question, I wish to say something about the relation of theological interpretation to the question of method. In other words, is theological interpretation a method for understanding Scripture? In one sense, all of the proponents of theological interpretation, by virtue of their discussing it in relation to other approaches and, one might dare say, methods of biblical interpretation, treat theological interpretation as some type of method. Their treatments of its characteristics and its distinctives all appear to have the ostensive purpose of positioning it in relation to other approaches to the interpretation of Scripture. However, the question of method is only raised explicitly and at length by Green. In both volumes, he disputes that theological interpretation is a method. In his earlier work, he concludes by characterizing theological interpretation as a set of "sensitivities and sensibilities,"[85] while in his later work, he begins by saying that theological interpretation of Scripture is "not a carefully defined 'method.'"[86] Instead, it is what he calls a form of "interested" exegesis that occurs within an "ecclesial location," with "no particular methodological commitments."[87] He also does not argue for singular meaning but a number of valid meanings, although what valid means when there is no ability to adjudicate meanings is left unclear. Green explicitly incorporates various critical methods into his view of theological interpretation, including literary analysis and his

---

84. Fowl, *Theological Interpretation*, 24-31.
85. Green, *Seized by Truth*, 140.
86. Green, *Practicing Theological Interpretation*, 2.
87. Green, *Practicing Theological Interpretation*, 2, 3.

form of discourse analysis and a restricted definition of historical criticism, literary criticism, and neuroscience. On that basis, it is very difficult to see Green's definition of theological interpretation of Scripture as anything other than an eclectic — even with some heightened theological sensibilities and sensitivities — form of contemporary criticism. As he seems to indicate, the overall aim of what he calls theological interpretation is more about preserving the authority of Scripture while retaining forms of modern criticism than it is about defining a specifically theological hermeneutic.

Perhaps Green is exceptional in this regard. What about the others? Fowl is an interpretive minimalist. He wishes to distance himself from many other interpretive methods and hermeneutics, including biblical theology, types of literary criticism that rely upon authorial intention, speech-act theory, general hermeneutics and special hermeneutics — all apparently because he wishes to practice a form of pragmatic interpretation with theological aims and interests. This is why he can endorse an underdetermined sense of meaning rather than determinate or antideterminate. However, this cannot be what is being propounded as a way forward in theological interpretation of Scripture, when this is simply pragmatism with theological interests, and no means by which to determine one reading as better than another apart from arguing that one has different aims than the other.

The proposals of Treier and Billings appear to be grappling most seriously with the question of theological interpretation of Scripture as a type of theological hermeneutic. However, it is unclear that either has actually proved his case. In one of his examples, Billings shows his approach at work. He presents the example of the problem of praying the curses of the Psalms. The problem is created because we as Christians are told to love our enemies. This involves him in a survey of several pre-modern interpreters who attempt to deal with this issue, before he concludes that "we should utter those psalms — even with their curses — because they are part of God's transformative word through Scripture."[88] They serve as reminders of God's care for us, express our sufferings, and express the anguish of God's people, recognizing the struggle of Christians this side of eternity.[89] This should arouse some questions among interpreters of the Bible, including those who are wishing to be responsible theological inter-

---

88. Billings, *Word of God*, 192.
89. Billings, *Word of God*, 192-93.

What Exactly Is Theological Interpretation of Scripture?

preters. First, Billings invokes an interpretive grid that prioritizes the canonical witness, with the standard being Jesus' statement regarding love of enemies. Secondly, I find it difficult to justify the interpretation of the curses of the Psalms, even in light of his exposition of theological interpretation. This seems to go much further than even the home–Bible study kind of interpretation that he seems to endorse earlier (but reflecting an early church father).[90] Thirdly, there is no clear means by which one can make the interpretive leap from the imprecations of the Psalms to this understanding, unless one has some previous interpretive framework in mind — one that I do not believe emerges from the framework that Billings proposes or that the pre-modern interpreters reveal. Instead, it appears to be an invocation of a politically correct reading of the Psalms in light of modern sensibilities — something that seems to run counter to much (but not all!) of the claim of theological interpretation of Scripture.

Treier indeed seems to wish for theological interpretation of Scripture to be seen as a hermeneutic. In his concluding section, he argues for such a position along two major lines. The first is that he endorses a modified form of nine theses given by Richard Hays and Ellen Davis regarding Scripture as a serviceable definition of theological interpretation.[91] However, as soon as he has cited them, he needs to qualify them, as they probably would not be sufficient for Roman Catholics or evangelicals, as they are primarily designed for mainline Protestants, as he notes. Besides this, there are some apparent internal inconsistencies, such as when principle one states that scriptural texts "do not have a single meaning limited to the intent of the original author" and that the four Gospels "narrate the truth about Jesus."[92] I suppose one could assert that the Gospels relate the truth about Jesus in texts that do not have singular meanings that express the authors' intentions, but on the other hand it seems more plausible to see the truth as emerging from the four Gospels as in some way reflecting the intentions of the authors (to convey history) and resulting in texts that have singular as opposed to multiple or undefinable meanings. The second major line of support is Treier's invocation of the metaphor of interpretive lens. I note that Treier — perhaps unlike at least some of the others who discuss theological interpretation — invokes the concept of "truth" as

---

90. Billings, *Word of God*, 151-55.
91. Treier, *Introducing Theological Interpretation*, 200, citing Davis and Hays, *Art of Reading*, 3-5.
92. Treier, *Introducing Theological Interpretation*, 200.

something that is "comprehensive" and "certain" in relation to God.[93] However, he also contends that human fallenness means that we perceive partially, and that we need a variety of lenses to have a chance at perceiving this truth. These include not only various types of biblical criticism, but features of theological criticism in order to bring these various partial views into a coherent account. This involves recognizing some perspectives as wrong and others as contradictory, but still others as complementary or multi-dimensional. But here Treier encounters a hurdle he is unable, or at least unwilling, to jump over. Debating the meaning of Rom 1:17 in relation to Luther's view and the views of modern scholars, he believes that, "at a certain level of detail," Luther's interpretation seems to be wrong[94] — in other words, when compared to modern scholarship with its differing views (as noted in a footnote). Here is where Treier falls back: "If understanding the text's basic theological message depends entirely on a technically precise construal of this phrase, then the church remains hamstrung, unable to reach such understanding."[95] Instead, "[w]hatever it means exactly"[96] (and Treier has said that one cannot arrive at such a meaning, even though there may be one), and Treier believes that Luther was wrong, nevertheless the mistaken interpretation led to progress in interpretation until today and God's Spirit used and blessed such activity. As a result, theological interpretation, according to Treier, is knowing God more fully through his divine activity.

I cannot help but think that there are at least two problematic elements to Treier's viewpoint, perhaps representative of a number of those who take a similar view of theological interpretation. Treier, on the one hand, wishes to maintain the notion of theological truth, but on the other hand appears to be afraid of contending for it or of engaging in the argumentative efforts to determine it. The solution to the problem of discerning the truth is not less engagement and the endorsement of incorrect interpretation but the admission of past errors, even if by pre-modern exegetes, and engaging in attempts to argue for interpretations that have more grounds for being correct. In this sense, the metaphor of the lenses is not an apt one for what Treier is trying to do. He does not use lenses to bring clarity, but is instead engaged in interpretive squinting. When things

---

93. Treier, *Introducing Theological Interpretation*, 202.
94. Treier, *Introducing Theological Interpretation*, 203.
95. Treier, *Introducing Theological Interpretation*, 203-4.
96. Treier, *Introducing Theological Interpretation*, 204.

What Exactly Is Theological Interpretation of Scripture?

appear to be too clear, then squinting helps to blur the images together so that the distinct lines fade, and the larger picture devoid of its particular outlines is more visually acceptable. The example of Luther's interpretive failure confirms that reliance upon pre-modern interpretation, rather than providing a way forward, acts as a means of justification for accepting and even putting forward a less precise interpretive position — perhaps borne out of frustration with historical criticism yet lacking the will to abandon it, or perhaps reflecting a desire to be interpretively au courant with contemporary and even post-modern interpretive notions even if at the expense of the ultimate truth so earnestly sought. The fact that Treier appeals to Karl Barth as the inaugural theological interpreter — a reference made by others[97] — no doubt helps to explain why some find this type of reading useful.[98]

I asked two questions in the title of this paper — what is theological interpretation of Scripture, and is it hermeneutically robust enough for the task to which it has been appointed? The answer to the first question is — it depends upon whom you ask. Theological interpretation of Scripture, even though it is often referred to as if it were a thing, is — at least according to several recent attempts at definition — less of a definable entity than many things, some in harmony and some in contradiction. The answer to the second question regarding its hermeneutical robustness is — no, it is not, at least as it has so far been defined. For some, theological hermeneutics remains simply an ancillary form of modern criticism. Even for those who wish to distinguish it especially from historical criticism, it is often heavily dependent upon other forms of modern critical interpretation. In all cases, it lacks a hermeneutical robustness that is appropriate for its self-proclaimed task of providing a means of theologically interpreting Scripture.

---

97. For example, Green, *Seized by the Truth*, 58-59; Fowl, *Theological Interpretation*, 3; Billings, *Word of God*, passim.
98. On Barth as a disappointing reader of Scripture, and hardly one I would want to emulate for theological or other purposes, see Porter and Robinson, *Hermeneutics*, 225-26.

"Let Us Cook You Your Tea, Vicar!" Church, Hermeneutics, and Postmodernity in the Work of Anthony Thiselton and Stanley Hauerwas

John B. Thomson

Some years ago local children from a pit village north of Doncaster approached the vicar and said, "Let us cook you your tea, vicar." As a result scores of youngsters, appropriately supervised, have been cooking tea for the vicar and his assistants twice a week for the past eight years, representing a distinctively holy communion. In an urban parish in Doncaster the congregation recently worked with local schools, a centre for adults with learning difficulties, uniformed organisations, and local businesses to produce a scarecrow "saints and Bible characters" trail, stations of the cross in the windows of local shops and community facilities, and carol singing in the local park and pubs. Some years ago a congregation in the inner city of Sheffield transformed its large Victorian building into a multiplex facility for the community and now acts as host to thousands of people every year in a public display of Christian hospitality. These, together with many other stories, contribute to a complex narrative embodying something of the living story of the Church in this part of England. Yet how are we to understand these narratives? Can hermeneutics expose the theological significance of such communities in a postmodern and post-secular society? How might this help us to see the surprise of Church in the practices of these ordinary congregations?

Anthony Thiselton and Stanley Hauerwas are both ecclesial people, who, though members of the academy, are rooted in Christian communities and whose work, I believe, is of significant service to these communities. In broad terms Thiselton's work on biblical and philosophical hermeneutics within the context of late/post modernity has flagged up the conditioning and generative role of the Church in theology. Hauerwas, as a theological ethicist, found that his concerns about Christian character,

"Let Us Cook You Your Tea, Vicar!"

agency, and virtue required an ecclesiological approach that could delineate a distinctive Christian witness in contemporary society. I am grateful to both since they have helped me see more clearly the surprising vocation of the Church in contemporary society.[1] My intention in this paper is to explore the way their respective projects help us to look at ordinary Christian communities in a new and hopeful theological light.

Thiselton, Hermeneutics, and the Church

Although much of Thiselton's work appears to engage with philosophical and biblical ideas, his early work displays insights about the role of the Church in his hermeneutics. In an article on "Truth" he follows Wittgenstein in arguing that the meaning of language is not just in an object but in the training and habits that enable us to "see it."[2] Training and habits presume a community within which people are formed and developed. This does not imply that truth is a community's construction, since a theological understanding of truth holds that truth depends upon God and can only be fully known at the eschaton. Consequently, in agreement with Pannenberg, Thiselton argues that the Bible's truth does not exist as a timeless abstraction but has to be proved again and again in each generation.[3] It is therefore encountered in history and is discerned through the wisdom of communal judgements. Such a view coheres with his critical advocacy of the philosophical hermeneutics of Gadamer. In *The Two Horizons*, Thiselton concurs with Gadamer's critique of method as a hermeneutical strategy since method represents a modernist approach which fails to take account of subjectivity, time and the situatedness of human existence. It also conflates the empirical methodology of the natural sciences and that of the human sciences by implying that interpretation involves an abstract spectator relationship to reality. Such a view misunderstands hermeneutics which are about encounter and disclosure rather than subjectivity or empiricism. Gadamer argues that practical wisdom (Greek phronesis), or the "sensus communis," enables understanding to

---

1. My PhD thesis on the work of Stanley Hauerwas, published as John B. Thomson, *The Ecclesiology of Stanley Hauerwas: A Christian Theology of Liberation* (Aldershot: Ashgate, 2003), was supervised by Anthony C. Thiselton and Vernon White.

2. Anthony C. Thiselton, "Truth," in *The New International Dictionary of New Testament Theology*, vol. 3 (ed. Colin Brown; Exeter: Paternoster, 1978), 894-95.

3. Thiselton, "Truth," 899-900.

take place when, for example, we encounter a work of art or engage in a game. In these cases we are drawn into the world of the work of art or the game and interpret it contingently from within this dynamic relationship. Practical wisdom is therefore an art rather than a technique. It recognises that interpretation is not an abstract activity but rather an embedded one reflecting our location within interpreting communities which have their own prejudices or pre-judgements. Neither the community nor its prejudices, or traditions, determine understanding, since in the event of interpretation the two horizons of "interpreter" and "text" engage with each other as the "text" is submitted to and new insight emerges.[4] However, the social character of both language and identity means that interpretation is a communal activity and, for Christians, one which necessarily includes the Church.

Thiselton is, however, aware that interpreters belong to many communities in different ways, which relativize each particular community. Hence, although recognising the primacy of the ecclesial community, as a scholar he is also part of the university community, albeit as an ordained rather than a lay scholar. Both university and Church represent different, though related, "games," each with their own rules. However, they do need "the transmission and testing of the knowledge that is mediated through *the community and the tradition of which the individual scholar is a part*," implying in this interaction that the insights Thiselton brings as an ecclesial person contribute to his work as a scholar.[5] For Thiselton, theology, though, is not ecclesiology in disguise but rather represents a discourse available to, and testable by, those beyond the Church since theology is a claim to universal truth. However, in so doing theology self-consciously pays attention to its tradition and narrative identity. For a Christian scholar, hermeneutics is about acknowledging the generative, though not determinative involvement of Christian identity in understanding.[6]

This subtle relationship and the threat to it by socio-pragmatism form the backcloth to Thiselton's exploration of the interpretation of texts in

---

4. Anthony C. Thiselton, *The Two Horizons: New Testament Hermeneutics and Philosophical Description with Special Reference to Heidegger, Bultmann, Gadamer, and Wittgenstein* (Exeter: Paternoster, 1980), 294-314.

5. Anthony C. Thiselton, "Academic Freedom, Religious Tradition and the Morality of Christian Scholarship," in *Approaches to Authority, Community, and the Unity of the Church* (ed. Mark Santer; London: SPCK, 1982), 30 (Thiselton's italics).

6. Thiselton, "Academic Freedom," 36.

"Let Us Cook You Your Tea, Vicar!"

New Horizons in Hermeneutics.[7] Thiselton is concerned that "in transforming theology into questions about the community (i.e. into ecclesiology), or knowledge into contextual practice (i.e. into social history) socio-pragmatic hermeneutics leaves no room for the creation as the work of grace in Christian theology, and no room for new horizons in hermeneutics."[8] Instead socio-pragmatic hermeneutics, ecclesial or otherwise, simply affirms a community's corporate self-interests and values by using the texts as pretexts for its pre-existing beliefs. Ironically socio-pragmatic hermeneutics, as a postmodern reaction to the singular spectator empiricism of modernity, is fundamentally conservative and closed; it does not listen to or dialogue with the text. Yet the very development of traditions which move under the impact of new questions and contexts, whilst retaining a degree of identifiable continuity within the public world, demonstrates their porous, open, and dialogical character. They are not hermetically sealed.[9] Communal traditions are soft systems which act as settings within which hermeneutics takes place and which inform the starting point of interpretation. They condition but do not construct the interpretation. Thus, for Christians, public worship represents such a setting, but it does not pre-determine the way the Bible will be listened to and understood on every occasion. Similarly the theology of the cross subverts any self-interested hermeneutic which might seduce the Church, since it decentres individual and corporate self-interest particularly within the Church.[10] Nevertheless embodied hermeneutics is at the heart of an incarnational faith, such as Christianity, since revelation operates through the interwovenness of word and deed and the action and witness of the community. The latter gives credibility and facilitates understanding of the word which is both spoken and read since "the text is more than a 'docetic' or 'disembodied' system of signifiers."[11] Likewise it is the language of this community as it is spoken or practiced in contemporary life, which draws its credibility from the public tradition of the community. Indeed since narratives create communities this also becomes the way in which the claims of particular communities are articulated.[12] Nevertheless narrative

---

7. Anthony C. Thiselton, *New Horizons in Hermeneutics: The Theory and Practice of Transforming Biblical Reading* (London: HarperCollins, 1992).
8. Thiselton, *New Horizons*, 7.
9. Thiselton, *New Horizons*, 9.
10. Thiselton, *New Horizons*, 28.
11. Thiselton, *New Horizons*, 75.
12. Thiselton, *New Horizons*, 354-55, 481.

can itself become a bid for power or simply a game of texts if there is no accountability beyond the narrator or narrating community.[13] Thus for the Church, narratives "activate the eschatological call of Christian pilgrimage, in the sense of beckoning onwards towards new future action."[14] The end acts as a check on temptations to convenient interpretation, whilst the promises present within them speak of extra-linguistic possibilities and decentre the present as an immutable or fixed point of reference.[15]

Hermeneutics is therefore fundamentally the practice of listening rather than the act of viewing. It is about paying attention to the particular questions that human living raises rather than generating abstract theories about humanity. As such it involves understanding, love and respect for the "other." It is also a communal activity, since listening is dependent upon a shared language, and generates practical wisdom or phronesis, the wisdom which grows through a timeful engagement with the particulars of human life. Questions about truth are therefore ones which test the coherence of this wisdom, rather than trying to make it correspond with an abstract ideal.[16] Hermeneutics is particularly important to the Church since its doctrine does not emerge from abstract thinking but from the contingent, communal practices and performance of worship.[17] Doctrine reflects a hermeneutical response to questions which arise from ecclesially situated existence.[18] Christology, for example, is not an abstract study about the identity of Jesus of Nazareth, but a way of forming disciples into the sort of life which his story displays. Christology is therefore a practical activity rather than a theoretical one and is about transformation of life rather than simply intellectual interest.[19] It is a drama of self-involving speech-acts rather than the detached thinking of a spectator and thereby exposes the character of Christian identity and its claims to represent truthful theology.[20] Consequently believing is always embodied in habits,

13. Thiselton, *New Horizons*, 485-506.
14. Thiselton, *New Horizons*, 569. See also Anthony C. Thiselton, "Human Being, Relationality, and Time in Hebrews, 1 Corinthians, and Western Traditions," *Ex Auditu* 13 (1997): 76-95.
15. Thiselton, *New Horizons*, 606-7.
16. Anthony C. Thiselton, *The Hermeneutics of Doctrine* (Grand Rapids: Eerdmans, 2007), xvi-xix.
17. Thiselton, *The Hermeneutics of Doctrine*, 5.
18. Thiselton, *The Hermeneutics of Doctrine*, 3.
19. Thiselton, *The Hermeneutics of Doctrine*, 7.
20. Thiselton, *The Hermeneutics of Doctrine*, 9. See also Thiselton, *New Horizons*, 324-25.

"Let Us Cook You Your Tea, Vicar!"

commitments, and action within the context of a communal life which is located and contingent. These generate a distinctively Christian character as disciples are trained in the shared language, practices, and traditions of the community.[21] Belief is about habits rather than clear thinking. It is a way of life rather than a package of ideas.[22] Doctrine is the communal endorsement and transmission of these habits as expressed and embedded in the life, worship, and action of the Christian community.[23] To understand doctrine therefore requires participation in the life of this community since doctrine is a language or conversation that emerges from within a form of life rather than representing an abstract form of human thought.[24]

Consequently the Church's teaching is always provisional since new questions will arise which require a review of existing tradition if the questions are to be listened to. The Church's doctrinal language is therefore constructive rather than simply conservative, allowing new insights to be gained which cohere with the existing narrative of God's dealings with the world.[25] This entails ecclesial formation, education, and training whose primary locus is worship and whose practical wisdom is open to discovering more of the truth. Furthermore this formation and training develop a distinctive character which displays patience, tolerance, respect for the other, and a disposition to listening, a "hermeneutics of altereity."[26] Tradition and performance are therefore mutually enriching, enabling the Church to improvise in new situations in ways faithful to its identity and generative classical texts.[27] This dialectic expands understanding and enables a faithful transcending of past perspectives. It displays theology as a reflective practice rather than an ideology. As a result there will be some tension between the contingencies of context and readership relative to claims for truth. To some extent, the multiplicity of little discipleship narratives contributes to the ongoing grand narrative of God in the world, just as the canon of Scripture functions as a coherent plurality which generates Christian tradition and doctrine.[28] As mentioned above Thiselton resists the reduction of the truth claims of theology to ecclesiology or ethno-

21. Thiselton, *The Hermeneutics of Doctrine*, 19-23.
22. Thiselton, *The Hermeneutics of Doctrine*, 28.
23. Thiselton, *The Hermeneutics of Doctrine*, 34.
24. Thiselton, *The Hermeneutics of Doctrine*, 55-59.
25. Thiselton, *The Hermeneutics of Doctrine*, 74.
26. Thiselton, *The Hermeneutics of Doctrine*, 86-88, 101.
27. Thiselton, *The Hermeneutics of Doctrine*, 88-90.
28. Thiselton, *The Hermeneutics of Doctrine*, 127-36.

centric consensus. Truth remains the telos beyond the limits of contingent communal reasoning and understanding and is rooted in the object of inquiry that exists in its own right.[29] Christian doctrine is symphonic but not ethnographic. It is substantial but not finished and its classic texts reflect a choir of polyphonic voices which together have a formative effect on new generations of Christians living in different and varied situations.[30] Doctrine therefore represents truth on the way rather than an abstract certitude outside of time and place.

Stanley Hauerwas, Theological Ethics and Church

Stanley Hauerwas's work on ethics took him unexpectedly back to church.[31] Indeed his theological ethics as a whole represent an attempt to articulate a distinctively Christian ethic whose character necessitates the Church. This is not simply about recognising the corporate character of Christian discipleship but is about recognising the hermeneutical implications of ecclesial identity. How we see or interpret the world is relative to the communities we are formed by. There is no abstract spectator perspective divorced from the contingencies of time and place. Consequently the effect of participating within the Christian community is to understand God, the Scriptures, the Christian story, and the world in a distinctive manner. Hauerwas's understanding of the place of the Church in Christian living emerges most clearly in his 1981 collection of essays entitled *A Community of Character*. In these essays he sought "to reassert the social significance of the church as a distinctive society with an integrity peculiar to itself . . . the truth of whose convictions cannot be divorced from the sort of community the Church is and should be."[32] He thereby attempted to generate a specific politics of the Church by asking "what kind of community the church must be to rightly tell the stories of God."[33] *A Community of Character* begins with ten theses which Hauerwas uses to articulate the architecture of his theology. Immediately evident in each thesis is the social

29. Thiselton, *The Hermeneutics of Doctrine*, 128-29.
30. Thiselton, *The Hermeneutics of Doctrine*, 144.
31. Stanley Hauerwas, *Hannah's Child: A Theologian's Memoir* (London: SCM, 2010), 13-14.
32. Stanley Hauerwas, *A Community of Character: Towards a Constructive Christian Social Ethic*, 4th ed. (Notre Dame: University of Notre Dame Press, 1981), 1.
33. Hauerwas, *A Community of Character*, 4.

"Let Us Cook You Your Tea, Vicar!"

and narrative character of Christian ethics consequent upon its fundamentally ecclesial nature. The primary vocation of the Church is to live its story as a people on a journey convinced of the lordship of God in the world and serving the world on the terms implied by this cross-informed story. Jesus is known today through this social ethic, and the Scriptures are interpreted within the politics of the church.[34] Furthermore the canon of Scripture is those stories which express the forgiving life of God experienced by God's people, and the tradition called Church is an ongoing argument about the way these should be interpreted.[35] Appealing to Scripture for Hauerwas is appealing not to texts but to a narrative community called church.[36]

Hauerwas's hermeneutics flags up the importance of tradition and community in the Christian story. The Church is a school of virtue rooted in an apprentice model of education, whose authorities, the saints, are those who have more fully appropriated and displayed the faith and are thereby able to educate other disciples in living and dying in ways appropriate to the story. The truthfulness of the Christian tradition is witnessed to in its capacity to sustain hope and patience in the face of the tragic, since tragedy subverts the possibility of self-deception.[37] Yet it is definitively established by the peaceable performance of the Church as the contemporary story of the peaceable Christ.[38] In his work on Bonhoeffer he argues that there is a necessary connection between peaceableness, non-violence, and the quest for a truthful politics.[39] Peaceableness, therefore, is not an abstract ideal which judges the Church but a hermeneutical way of living in which the Church continues to embody the way of Jesus witnessed to in the cross.[40] It is a form of life which challenges the liberal pragmatism of

---

34. Hauerwas, *A Community of Character*, 37.

35. Stanley Hauerwas, "Forgiveness and Political Community," *Worldview* 23, nos. 1-2 (January-February 1980): 15-16.

36. Stanley Hauerwas, *In Good Company: The Church as Polis* (Notre Dame: University of Notre Dame Press, 1995), 9, 20 n. 4.

37. Hauerwas, *A Community of Character*, 60, 91; and Stanley Hauerwas, "The Church's One Foundation Is Jesus Christ Her Lord," in *Theology without Foundations: Religious Practice and the Future of Theological Truth* (ed. Stanley Hauerwas, Nancey Murphy, and Mark Nation; Nashville: Abingdon, 1994), 143-62.

38. Stanley Hauerwas, *The Peaceable Kingdom: A Primer in Christian Ethics*, 3rd ed. (Notre Dame: University of Notre Dame Press, 1986).

39. Stanley Hauerwas, *Performing the Faith: Bonhoeffer and the Practice of Nonviolence* (London: SPCK, 2004), 19.

40. Hauerwas, *Performing the Faith*, 16.

Reinhold Niebuhr and is indebted to the Anabaptist tradition of John Howard Yoder. It is this awareness of the significance of the history of Jesus for Christology that Hauerwas believes to be at the core of a recovery of a church of integrity. This is in contrast to other accounts which in their concentration upon the teaching of the Kingdom lost sight of the whole of Jesus' life as a resource for imitation by the Church. For Hauerwas, Jesus' life was a recapitulation of God's way with Israel, which discloses the sort of God Christians and Jews worship. For Christians the cross is the supreme illustration of this peaceful trust in the ways of God, whose virtues are renunciation, humility, and service. Hence his ecclesiology is intrinsically eschatological, since the victory of Christ witnessed to in the resurrection gives the Church the confidence to risk living peaceably in a world as yet uncommitted to peaceful living since this is to live with the grain of the universe.[41] This is what living the kingdom means for it reflects what Jesus showed, namely that this sort of peaceable life is possible now since God is sovereign. Friendship of the outcast, peaceful resistance to the evil one, forgiveness all illustrate kingdom living informed by this eschatology.

Ecclesial formation, character and virtue therefore dispose Christians to inhabit the world in a distinctive way thereby enabling them to "gain the experience to negotiate and make positive contributions to whatever society we may find ourselves in."[42] In particular this will enable Christians in America to recognise that liberalism forms them to interpret the world in a manner that conflicts with the Christian story, particularly in the latter's assumptions about the right to life and happiness, individualism and freedom of choice. Indeed "the story that liberalism teaches us is that we have no story and as a result we fail to notice how deeply that story determines our lives."[43] The Church therefore serves the world by being a contrast community and thereby supplies the world with a truthful story about its own identity. It acts as a hermeneutic for the world as well as for itself since the world has no integrating narrative that makes sense of its constituent parts without the story of God witnessed to in the Church. Yet at the same time Hauerwas believes that ethical demands

---

41. Stanley Hauerwas, *With the Grain of the Universe: The Church's Witness and Natural Theology* (London: SCM, 2001).

42. Hauerwas, *A Community of Character*, 74.

43. Hauerwas, *A Community of Character*, 84. This is particularly evident in the modern university. See Hauerwas, *With the Grain of the Universe*, 231; and Stanley M. Hauerwas, *The State of the University: Academic Knowledges and the Knowledge of God* (Oxford: Blackwell, 2007), 3-8.

such as the Decalogue are community-specific and contextual. They cannot be understood apart from the story of God's covenant with Israel. Rather than abstracting them and setting them up as transcendent universals, such stories supply the Church with a tradition and history through which to see how the same God works at different times and in different places and thereby suggest how the Church might rightly envision God's ways with the world in the present context. Likewise there is a plurality of discipleship stories which are embraced in God's story. Indeed part of the Church's character is to be able to listen to the "otherness" of these stories with respect and attentiveness.

Hauerwas does not equate the Church with the kingdom. Instead the life of the kingdom is broader than the Church. For "the Church does not possess Christ; his presence is not confined to the Church. Rather it is in the Church that we learn to recognise Christ's presence outside the Church."[44] The Church is therefore a foretaste of this kingdom, a community whose training enables it to identify the presence of the kingdom beyond itself and whose presence also identifies the world as that community that as yet does not believe. The Church therefore "tries to develop the resources to stand within the world witnessing to the peaceable kingdom and thus rightly understanding the world."[45] The virtues required for this involve trust, hope, and love and as an empirical reality, the marks of this Church, which represent the social witness of this Church, are the resources of its sacraments, preaching, and distinctive living.

In stressing the communal character of hermeneutics, Hauerwas is not implying that there is only one horizon within the interpretive dynamic. Agreeing with Iris Murdoch's criticism of the narcissistic implications of Cartesian thinking and her work on attention and art, Hauerwas believes that we need to be trained to see the "other" as beyond our own self-consciousness.[46] Indeed the "other" is to be regarded as a gift and someone to be befriended.[47] Christians need to be formed and trained to see life and its challenges in a way analogous to "an artist engaged in his work rather than a critic making a judgment about a finished product."[48] Since no-one is an abstract spectator, such training involves inhabiting

---

44. Hauerwas, *The Peaceable Kingdom*, 97.
45. Hauerwas, *The Peaceable Kingdom*, 102.
46. Stanley Hauerwas, *Vision and Virtue: Essays in Christian Ethical Reflection* (Notre Dame: University of Notre Dame Press, 1981), 34.
47. Hauerwas, *The State of the University*, 64-70.
48. Hauerwas, *Vision and Virtue*, 14, 30-36.

and employing the wisdom of the Christian community. Such communal wisdom provides a distinctively Christian way of "seeing" or describing issues such as abortion, the care of children and the elderly, euthanasia, and disability. For example, Christians believe that a good death *(euthanasia)* is one which leaves a good memory, and they trustfully locate that death in the ongoing story of the grace of God embodied in the church. In liberal ethics autonomy disconnects people from this communal story, subverts any sense of history, and undermines the capacity of a community to celebrate the lives of the elderly by caring for them. Furthermore caring for children, the disabled, and the elderly reflects the Christian commitment to welcome the new and strange which self-centred liberal ethics finds increasingly conflictual with its autonomous convictions. Hauerwas is therefore particularly concerned to focus upon the character of the Church, the "who," in order to make possible a faithful and truthful Christian hermeneutical engagement with the "what" or "other." His concern is that the post-Enlightenment liberal tradition has ignored the social and communal character of human identity in its epistemology and in the process fails to recognise that this "other" is "seen" by different communities in different ways relative to the languages they speak. Indeed he regards the Church itself as God's new language, a community whose way of life not only speaks of God but interprets life from within the divine story its life narrates.[49] In this he rejects the notion of the spectator, since all are embedded in embodied communities, whether this is a conscious belonging or one unreflectively taken for granted. He is also concerned that the Church has been colonised by the subtle subversion of liberal thinking and capitalist consumerism which combine to strip Christians of the resources to interpret the world as Christians. In taking this stand he represents part of a wider debate about the legacy of the Enlightenment with its confidence in the singular and abstract subject able to grasp the meaning of the world as a sort of spectator. For Hauerwas the thinking subject is always embedded in contexts and communities which both dispose and form that subject to interpret the world and human living within it in ways related to that embeddedness. Consequently since there is no neutrality in human thought, Hauerwas argues that Christians ought to articulate their own distinctive vision of human living without embarrassment in public discussion. They should not be reduced to si-

---

49. Stanley Hauerwas, *Christian Existence Today: Essays on Church, World, and Living in Between* (Durham, NC: The Labyrinth Press, 1988), 47-65.

"Let Us Cook You Your Tea, Vicar!"

lence by a self-deceptively confident way of thinking rooted in a false notion of spectator objectivity.

Given Hauerwas's commitment to Christian formation and truthful interpretation, the role of liturgy emerges as central to his thinking. Worship happens when the Church gathers to be exposed as a community to the transforming grace of God. This is necessarily a corporate activity and consciously situates the Church within the narrative of God's salvation. It is akin to a training session in which Christians are equipped to perform their faith in the world. Consequently Hauerwas teaches ethics through liturgy and also focuses his attention upon particular churches, such as Broadway Methodist Church, as resources for seeing the effect of training upon performance.[50] Worship also situates biblical hermeneutics since it ensures that the texts of the Bible are recognised as Scripture by locating them within the community which "knows its life depends on faithful remembering of God's care of his creation through the calling of Israel and the life of Jesus."[51] Such a political reading of Scripture has been hidden in liberal hermeneutics with the consequence that Scripture has lost its authority and revelatory power. Hauerwas notes that theologians rarely learn their texts in a liturgical context which properly contextualises them, so there is no connection made between the politics of the community which identifies these texts as their Scriptures and the work of most theologians.[52] This leaves the Scriptures prey to deconstruction by those who seek to understand them principally by fitting them into alien patterns of thought. For Hauerwas, such a failure to fit our world into the world the Scriptures open up represents an apolitical reading of these Scriptures.[53] Hermeneutics is therefore fundamentally a political and temporal process and has linguistic and social dimensions that distinguish the church from the world. Hence Hauerwas applauds the strangeness evident in William Stringfellow's determination to practise the language of apocalyptic rather than feeling obliged to translate this into the deceptive language of liberalism.[54] Through keeping Christian language pure a truthful reading of life can be had. He also sees martyrdom is a partic-

---

50. Stanley Hauerwas, *In Good Company: The Church as Polis* (Notre Dame: University of Notre Dame Press, 1995), 153-63. On Broadway Methodist Church see Hauerwas, *Christian Existence Today*, 111-31.

51. Hauerwas, *A Community of Character*, 53.

52. Hauerwas, *A Community of Character*, 56 n. 9.

53. Hauerwas, *A Community of Character*, 55.

54. Stanley Hauerwas, *Dispatches from the Front: Theological Engagements with the Secular* (Durham, NC: Duke University Press, 1994), 107-13.

ular hermeneutical challenge to the world since martyrdom trusts the true interpretation of its meaning to God.[55]

All this gives new meaning to local Christian practice. For example sermons emerge as the contingent ongoing interpretation of the divine ethos for a particular Christian community. They are the *parole* of theology rather than the *langue* or the way a community articulates its faith in time. Hauerwas's sermons reflect his conviction that Christian hermeneutics requires the Church if it is to avoid a narcissistic concentration upon texts.[56] Discussing the thought of Hans Frei, he argues that "realistic narrative" must reflect the authority of a community's tradition rather than being seen simply in terms of literary intelligibility. This is why liturgy is so important to Hauerwas as mentioned above since the "plain sense" of the story is illuminated through the corporate life of the Christian community. The Church itself is both the subject and agent of the narrative and hence it is the people, rather than the words or sentences, that exhibit these narratives.[57] The sermon is therefore a communal action of the Church articulated through the office of the preacher which seeks to be faithful to Scripture and to attend to the revelation which follows upon the existent tradition.[58] As he comments, "our stories become part of the story of the kingdom" making "Jesus' story a many-sided tale."[59]

Thiselton and Hauerwas: Hermeneutics and the Surprise of Church in Postmodernity

Both Thiselton and Hauerwas seek to understand the vocation and character of the Church within the context of postmodernity. Postmodernity represents a mood as much as a movement, an approach to understanding characterised by suspicion and anxieties about power.[60] The "postmoderns" are particularly hostile to any sense that the "other's" particular-

---

55. Stanley Hauerwas, *Against the Nations: War and Survival in a Liberal Society* (Notre Dame: University of Notre Dame Press, 1992), 62-90, 91-108.
56. Garrett Green, *Theology, Hermeneutics, and Imagination: The Crisis of Interpretation at the End of Modernity* (Cambridge: Cambridge University Press, 2000), 187.
57. Green, *Theology, Hermeneutics, and Imagination*, 192.
58. Green, *Theology, Hermeneutics, and Imagination*, 193.
59. Green, *Theology, Hermeneutics, and Imagination*, 51-52.
60. Jean-François Lyotard, *The Postmodern Condition: A Report on Knowledge*, trans. G. Bennington and B. Massumi (Minneapolis: University of Minnesota Press, 1984), xxiii.

"Let Us Cook You Your Tea, Vicar!"

ity and consequent irreducibility should be compromised. The present is all, the subject is unstable and all teleology and humanism are deceptive. The effect of postmodernity has been to contest meta-narratives and mega-solutions with a consequent "shattering of innocent confidence in the capacity of the self to control its destiny."[61] The outcome is that truth is reduced to rhetoric and claims to truth seen as manipulative bids for power.[62] For Thiselton and Hauerwas these challenges demand a fresh understanding of the Church and, more importantly, of faithful performance.[63] For both this led them to establish and demonstrate the importance of a substantive communal tradition or culture whose claims to plausibility can be observed in a form of life.[64] This interpersonal enfleshed tradition stabilizes the social self and prevents it disappearing into an arbitrary flux of rhetorical signs. It also ensures the preservation and subversive influence of memory which Hauerwas believes both modernism and postmodernism actively subvert in the service of the economic drives of capitalism.[65] Indeed Hauerwas regards the university as "the great institution of legitimization in modernity" whose fundamental drive is no longer truth seeking but money making and which promotes an abstract rather than contextual interpretation of knowledge.[66]

Furthermore in challenging sceptical postmodernity Thiselton argues that truth proves itself in relationships and the trust expressed in the respect accorded to the other, whether this be another person or a literary text.[67] Within the Christian narrative he regards the cross as the exhibition and promise of God's non-manipulative respectful power whilst for Hauerwas the life and passion of Christ display God's peaceableness. If the self and truth are found in this divine narrative, then the Church becomes pivotal as the community which explicitly lives in this story, especially at the local level where is it public, visible and accountable. Indeed for Hauerwas, the Christian self is no longer the abstract stable subject of modernity or the fluid instability of postmodernity, but rather the baptised

---

61. Anthony C. Thiselton, *Interpreting God and the Postmodern Self: On Meaning, Manipulation, and Promise* (Edinburgh: T&T Clark, 1995), 11.
62. Thiselton, *Interpreting God and the Postmodern Self*, 11-16.
63. Thiselton, *Interpreting God and the Postmodern Self*, 34-38.
64. Stanley Hauerwas, *A Better Hope: Resources for a Church Confronting Capitalism, Democracy, and Postmodernity* (Grand Rapids: Brazos, 2000), 17.
65. Hauerwas, *A Better Hope*, 146-48.
66. Hauerwas, *The State of the University*, 5-8.
67. Hauerwas, *The State of the University*, 47-50.

self, whose identity is rooted in the Christian community and its embodiment through time.[68] Consequently the communal character of the Church and the materiality of spirituality re-emerge surprisingly as fundamental to witness through the performance of local Christian communities, such as Broadway and Aldersgate Methodist Churches.[69] These act as embodied embryonic signs of the truthfulness of the Christian story and prevent it from dissolving into ideas or rhetoric.[70] Here Christians are formed through the liturgy to display practices such as forgiveness, peacemaking, praise, enduring friendship, and caring for the sick and dying which offer a text for wider society to interpret and an ecclesial hermeneutic about God.[71] Yet these particular instantiations of Christian performance are located within the greater story of the Church and Israel whose significance is carried in the theological memory of the whole Church. The local Church is always part of the catholic Church and ensures that the latter does not become an abstraction.

The Church as tradition and embodied communities is therefore central to both Thiselton's and Hauerwas's projects within the ethos of postmodernity. The tangibility of the Church, expressed in its embodiment, practices and performance, communal identity, training and formation, language, tradition, contingency, embeddedness, practical wisdom, narrative, attention, discipleship as an ethic rather than an idea, worship, and character, contests the instabilities and fluidities of postmodern thinking. They thereby flag up the remarkable value and significant witness of mundane congregations whose life exhibits these practical and material realities. This is not to say that their projects are identical. Thiselton's work has emerged through engagement with the challenges of biblical interpretation and conversations with philosophy. It began with texts but increasingly attends to ecclesial embodiment as the context for understanding these texts. Testimony becomes enfleshed. Hauerwas's project sought for a distinctive Christian ethic or way of life, which rapidly implied an exploration of the Church and how Christians embody the story of God in the world. Thiselton's hermeneutics focus more upon the theology that has emerged through the Church's interpretation of its core texts and history, whereas Hauerwas is increasingly engaged by the interpretive significance

---

68. Stanley Hauerwas, *Sanctify Them in the Truth: Holiness Exemplified* (Edinburgh: T&T Clark, 1998), 78.
69. Hauerwas, *Sanctify Them*, xi.
70. Hauerwas, *With the Grain of the Universe*, 217-18.
71. Hauerwas, *A Better Hope*, 18.

of the life of the Church as it practices and performs its life in contemporary North Atlantic societies. Thiselton is committed to a transcendent notion of truth, truth that acts as a universal telos to all inquiries and is a goal beyond the constraints of particular traditions. It is this commitment to transcendent truth which is to orientate and condition the truth seeking of the Church. For Thiselton, Hauerwas's approach runs the danger of equating theology with ecclesiology or theology with ethnography, and thereby becoming effectively a form of socio-pragmatism. This could lead to a Durkheimian view of the Church and strip it of any transcendental "other," as Nigel Biggar once asserted.[72] I have argued elsewhere that Hauerwas regards his work as theology rather than simply ethnography.[73] However, as Hauerwas comments, "I have steadfastly tried to let my own so-called doctrine of God emerge from within my presentation of issues as basic as why we continue to have children or how we are to account for our care of the mentally handicapped."[74] In this way Hauerwas argues that training and habits condition the Church to perform its faith in ways which display its claims that this is the way God acts in the world.

Certainly Hauerwas's theological ethics, with his interest in the character and contemporary performance of Christian living, appear more confident about the influence of Christian pragmatics upon doctrine and its interpretation than Thiselton. Thiselton's reserve about the capacity of the Church to embody a substantially virtuous and peaceable form of life may reflect his reading of the long and ambivalent historical performance of the Church, particularly in Europe. In ways which evoke Reinhold Niebuhr, Thiselton's stress upon grace and transcendence implies a degree of scepticism about the capacity of the Church to represent sufficiently the conditions for truthful apprehension. Sin corrupts communities as well as individuals, and consequently habits and virtues cannot be trusted to deliver the sort of community whose behaviour is an unambiguous revelation of God. The human condition easily becomes narcissistic. Only the subversion of the cross and the surprising character of the story it represents can act as a check and challenge to such self-preoccupation. This story is not recapitulated by the Church but witnessed to by it and its Scriptures. The very objectivity of these texts helps to keep the Church attentive to the disturbing

---

72. Hauerwas, *Sanctify Them*, 37.

73. John B. Thomson, *Living Holiness: Stanley Hauerwas and the Church* (London: Epworth, 2010), 75-76.

74. Stanley M. Hauerwas, "Many Hands Working: A Response to Charles Mathewes," *Anglican Theological Review* 82, no. 2 (Spring 2000): 362.

truth which they convey. By implication Thiselton is questioning Hauerwas's anthropology and over-realized eschatology in the light of the fall, the cross and the historical performance of the Church. In contrast Hauerwas's worry is that the Church can easily become an abstract Church, an idea of Church rather than a flesh and blood baptised community. This was his critique even of his mentor, Karl Barth. Barth, for all his stress on the witness of the Church, still felt able in the *Dogmatics* to represent the significance and ethos of the Church in a way that was not intrinsically bound up with the performance of the Church.[75] Thus, for Hauerwas, the embodiment of the Church in its micro performances is even more integral to his theological project than for Thiselton. This is where sanctification is visible, a redeemed baptismal anthropology which acts as the primary witness of the pilgrim Church. Theology is therefore displayed through the "texts" of trained Church living rather than imagined through reflection simply upon literary texts. Thus, as Brad Kallenberg has argued, Hauerwas's theology involves interpreting the embodied apologetic of the Church rather than articulating a rhetorical apologetic for God in the world.[76] For Hauerwas such ecclesial forms of life act as a language making claims to truth about God and the world which is not self-contained or watertight but is inhabited by God and therefore open to change.[77] It is a language of peaceable friendship which attends to those beyond its community in ways which cohere with this ethos. Indeed, "God's dominion is not limited or confined to the Church . . . rather . . . its 'origin,' its most concentrated expression is there displayed." The Church is not a closed language.[78] Indeed the Church is to be a Church for the world.[79]

Conclusion

"Let us cook you your tea, vicar!" reflects a set of assumptions, traditions, and understandings of the vocation of the Church in the society of a South

---

75. Hauerwas, *With the Grain of the Universe*, 34-53. See also Hauerwas's interpretation of Bonhoeffer's political theology as reclaiming the visibility of the Church as the necessary condition for the proclamation of the gospel in Hauerwas, *Performing the Faith*, 34.

76. Brad J. Kallenberg, *Ethics as Grammar: Changing the Postmodern Subject* (Notre Dame: University of Notre Dame Press, 2001), 156.

77. Hauerwas, *Christian Existence Today*, 10.

78. Stanley Hauerwas, *Wilderness Wanderings: Probing Twentieth-Century Theology and Philosophy* (Boulder, CO: Westview, 1997), 6.

79. Hauerwas, *A Better Hope*, 157. See also Hauerwas, *The State of the University*, 55-56.

"Let Us Cook You Your Tea, Vicar!"

Yorkshire pit village. Superficially it seems an innocuous request, but it has surprising theological significance. The work of Anthony Thiselton and of Stanley Hauerwas shed light on the surprising theological importance of the Church within contemporary postmodern society. Through their respective projects we see how Church as tangible contingent communities of disciples is vital to how we interpret the faith. These congregations of the Church are part of that catholic community, contemporary and past, performing contemporary improvisations of the divine story as embodied apologetics of the Gospel. Both Thiselton and Hauerwas challenge the suspicious deconstruction of postmodernity by pointing us to embodied communities of attention and practice which, in conversation with the texts of Scripture, are dramatic witnesses to the story of God today. This ecclesial hermeneutics renarrates the significance of the apparently impotent and marginal Christian communities in many areas covered by the Diocese of Sheffield. It portrays their micro-practices as contributing to the resources we have for theological understanding in contemporary life. Their embodiment, witness, story, habits, character, hospitality, friendship, memory, and improvised performances on the Scriptural script are substantial contributors to the plausibility of the Gospel. Theology, therefore, interprets the story of God embodied in the Scriptures witnessed to in the ambiguous performances of the Church, past and present. Congregations are not simply reservoirs for Christian activists, but instantiations of graced life, webbed into a greater story which gives theological significance to their ecclesial practices. As Martyn Percy comments, "the belief that God is Father, Son and Holy Spirit is not an arid set of directives, but rather a faith that is embedded in a community of praxis that makes beliefs work."[80] In consequence "the theological programme . . . invites theologians to take more notice of local contextual ecclesial and operant pastoral practice as primary theological material, rather than such praxis merely being seen as the outcome of discerning and interpreting formal theological or denominational propositions."[81] This is the surprise of the Church which the hermeneutical projects of Thiselton and Hauerwas flag up in their distinctive ways, a surprise which gives hope to the Church in postmodernity.

---

80. Martyn Percy, *Shaping the Church: The Promise of Implicit Theology* (Farnham: Ashgate, 2010), 4.
81. Percy, *Shaping the Church*, 14.

Index of Modern Authors

Achtemeier, P. J., 76
Adam, A. K. M., 228, 234, 262
Alexander, T. D., 10
Allen, R., 149
Almond, P. C., 58
Anderson, P. N., 120, 123
Andrews, J., 220
Apel, K.-O., 51
Atkinson, J., 1, 2, 9
Aune, D. E., 74
Austin, J. L., 239

Babbit, F. C., 161
Balentine, S. E., 28
Balla, P., 262
Barr, J., 9, 28, 96, 245, 262
Barrett, C. K., 47, 50
Barth, K., 9, 10, 35-37, 41, 44, 46-48, 201, 202, 205, 206, 237, 267, 284
Bartholomew, C. G., 4, 6, 10, 11, 234, 262
Barton, J., 10, 28
Barton, S., 11
Bartsch, H.-W., 34
Bassler, J. M., 66
Bauckham, R. J., 54, 122
Baur, F. C., 34, 184
Beale, G. K., 62
Beisser, F., 190
Beker, J. C., 55, 66
Bell, R. H., xiii, 192, 193

Bellis, A. O., 106
Bennington, G., 280
Berger, P. L., 237, 242
Bernandez, E., 80
Best, E., 84, 85
Betz, O., 184
Beutler, J., 124
Bienaimé, G., 105
Biggar, N., 283
Billings, J. T., 236, 240, 241, 249-51, 254, 255, 259, 264, 265
Black, C. C., 108
Blackman, E. C., 183
Blakeslee, M., 150
Blakeslee, S., 150
Blatz, B., 144
Bonhoeffer, D., x, 188, 215
Brett, M. G., 240
Briggs, R. S., xii, 115, 239
Broadhead, E. K., 122
Brown, C., 8, 269
Brown, R. E., 125, 134, 140
Brown, S. C., 11
Broyles, C. C., 28, 29
Bultmann, R., ix, xi, 2, 6, 11, 32-48, 50, 52, 67, 92, 121, 136, 140, 188, 218, 236, 270
Burn, A. E., 253
Byrne, B., 63

Index of Modern Authors

Calvin, J., 191
Cameron, R., 127, 145
Campbell, B. L., 87
Campbell, D., 55
Caragounis, C. C., 122
Carson, D. A., 262
Catchpole, D. R., 64
Caygill, H., 194
Chan, M. L. Y., xi, 53
Childs, B., 95, 100, 101, 109, 111, 115, 262
Ciampa, R. E., 99
Clements, R. E., 28
Clines, D. J. A., 9, 182, 249
Coggins, R. J., 9
Collier, G., 99
Collinge, N. E., 250
Collins, J. J., 106
Conzelmann, H., 184
Coulson, S., 170
Craig, E., 10
Cranfield, C. E. B., 179
Cross, F. M., 189
Cullmann, O., 37
Culpepper, R. A., 123
Cuyckens, H., 150

Danker, F., 168
Davids, P. H., 88
Davies, J. G., 8
Davis, E. F., 112, 234, 265
Dawson, A., 172
DeConick, A. D., 125, 138, 144, 146
Delcor, M., 181
Delitzsch, F., 24
Dilthey, W., 32, 34, 37, 51
Dirven, R., 80
Dodd, C. H., 122, 124
Donaldson, T. L., 57, 59, 60
Donfried, K. P., 89
Donner, H., 109
Driver, D., 101
Driver, G. R., 181
Dunderburg, I., 125
Dunn, J. D. G., xii, 11, 53, 56, 58, 121-23, 132, 135
Durkheim, E., 283

Eco, U., 237, 244, 245, 249
Einstein, A., 196
Elliger, K., 181-83, 195
Elliott, N., 59
Ellis, E. E., 64, 78, 184
Enns, P., 103
Eriksson, A., 64, 88
Evans, C. A., 28, 29, 61, 133
Evans, V., 171

Fauconnier, G., 150, 152
Fee, G. D., 53, 60
Feldheimer, R., 88
Ferguson, S. B., 8-10
Fillmore, C., 155
Fischer, J., 190
Fish, S., 114, 257
Fitzmyer, J. A., 77
Foes, A., 155
Ford, D. F., 11, 209
Fortna, R. T., 122-24, 134
Fowl, S., xiv, 9, 54, 91, 219, 222, 224, 228, 234-36, 238-40, 244, 245, 248-51, 254-56, 258-64
Frank, R. M., 80
Frei, H. W., 108, 109, 280
Frey, J., 138, 142
Funk, R. W., 128
Furnish, V. P., 70

Gadamer, H.-G., ix, 2, 6, 32, 33, 51-53, 67, 93, 114, 236, 238, 269, 270
Geeraerts, D., 150, 155
Gerhardsson, B., 75
Gibbs, R., 170
Gifford, P., 11
Gill, C., 71
Gitay, Y., 29
Godet, F., 184
Goldingay, J., x, 23
Goppelt, L., 107
Grady, J. E., 150, 154, 170
Graham, A., 9
Green, C. J., 10, 215
Green, G., 110, 280
Green, J. B., 6, 9, 10, 11, 234, 236, 237,

287

INDEX OF MODERN AUTHORS

241, 242, 243-45, 248, 250, 251, 254, 255,
257, 258, 262-64, 267
Green-McCreight, K. E., 108
Greene, C., 4
Greer, R. A., 252
Greggs, T., xiii, xiv, 212, 215
Grenz, S. J., 257
Grieb, A. K., 65
Gunkel, H., 184

Habermas, J., 238
Hafemann, S. J., 262
Hagner, D. A., 58
Hanhart, R., 109
Hanson, A. T., 176-78, 191
Hardy, D., 209
Harnack, A. von, 252
Harris, M. J., 53
Harris, R., 248
Hart, T. A., 10
Haskell, H. J., 159
Hauerwas, S., 238, 268, 269, 274-82, 284, 285
Hawthorne, G., 184
Hayes, J., 165
Hays, R. B., 54, 62, 63, 65, 94, 95, 234, 265
Healy, M., 234
Heckel, U., 189
Heidegger, M., ix, 2, 6, 27, 32-35, 51, 52, 153, 155, 235, 270
Hengel, M., 63
Herrmann, U., 34, 35, 37
Hill, C. E., 256
Hirsch, E. D., 238, 254
Hodgson, L., 192, 193
Hofius, O., 190
Hong, E. H., 241
Hong, H. V., 241
Hooker, M. D., 62
Hoover, R. W., 128
Horrell, D. G., 64
Houlden, J. L., 9
Howard, W. F., 176
Hübner, H., 134, 176, 178, 180, 188
Hunsinger, G., 109

Hunter, R. J., 9
Hurtado, L., 53, 54, 56, 58, 64, 74, 75, 77, 78
Husbands, M., 256

Iogia, T., 125
Iser, W., 114, 242, 249

James, F. A., 256
Janaway, C., 195
Jauss, H. R., 12, 90
Jeanrod, W., 114, 238, 245
Jeremias, J., 132
Johnson, L. T., 58, 252
Johnson, M., 149, 150, 156, 163, 166
Johnson, R., 34
Jones, G., 255
Jones, W. H. S., 156
Jüngel, E., 190

Kähler, M., 120
Kallenberg, B. J., 284
Kaminsky, J. S., 106
Kant, I., 9, 194, 195
Käsemann, E., xi, 36, 37, 40-42, 45, 47, 49, 92, 179, 218
Kee, H. C., 163, 165
Kelly, J. N. D., 252, 253
Kennedy, G. A., 74, 75
Kepnes, S., 209, 211, 213
Kermode, F., 111
Kierkegaard, S., 37, 241
Kim, S., 55, 61, 63
Klapproth, D. M., 79, 80
Knox, W. L., 185, 191
Koch, D.-A., 176
Koester, C. R., 140, 144
Koester, H., 127, 128
Kolenkow, A. B., 159
Konrad, F., 71, 72
Koshul, B., 209
Krasovec, J., 10
Krauss, R., 215
Kugel, J. L., 16, 103, 252

Labahn, M., 134

Index of Modern Authors

Lakey, M., 50
Lakoff, G., 149, 150, 156, 163, 166
Lampe, P., 69, 88
Lang, F., 180, 186, 188
Langer, B., 24
Lash, N., 219
Latourette, K. S., 253
Lau, W., 25
Leech, G., 250
Leithart, P. J., 96
Levenson, J. D., 106
Levering, M., 112
Lewis, C. S., 208
Lincoln, A. T., 71, 85
Lindbeck, G. A., 238
Linge, D. E., 114
Locke, J., 194
Longenecker, B. W., 11, 54
Longenecker, R. N., 53, 64, 94
Luckmann, T., 237, 242
Lüdemann, H., 35
Lundin, R., 2, 6
Luther, M., 10, 35, 37, 41, 42, 45, 188, 218, 223, 266, 267
Luzzato, S. D., 104
Lyotard, J.-F., 280

MacDonald, N., 113
MacIntyre, A., 255
Macquarrie, J., 188
Magee, B., 196
Malcolm, I. G., 79
Malcolm, M., xi
Marjanen, A., 142, 145
Marshall, B. D., 221, 225-27
Marshall, D. G., 52, 94, 238
Marshall, I. H., 7-9, 12, 50, 239
Massumi, B., 280
Mathewes, C., 283
McCarthy, T., 238
McConnell, F., 111
McGrath, A. E., 9
McGrath, J. F., 133-35
McKim, D. K., 8
McNeill, D., 172
McNeill, J. T., 192

Melanchthon, P., 187
Merklein, H., 184, 191
Metzger, B. M., 9
Meyer, B. F., 93
Michel, O., 183
Miles, S. H., 156
Milgrom, J., 104
Miller, M., 165
Miller, P. D., 27, 28
Mitchell, M. M., 82, 208
Moberly, W., 111
Möller, K., 4, 10, 234
Moltmann, J., 47
Moo, D. J., 53, 63
Moores, J. D., 64
Morgan, R., xi, 9
Motyer, S., 262
Moule, C. F. D., 63
Moulton, J. H., 176
Murdoch, I., 277
Murphy, N., 275

Nation, M., 275
Neusner, J., 165
Newmann, C. C., 56
Niebuhr, R., 276, 283
Niehbuhr, K.-W., 82
Nineham, D., 33
Nolland, J., 76, 77, 157, 158, 161, 163

Oakley, T., 170
O'Brien, P. T., 56, 87
Ochs, P., 103, 209, 214
Odeberg, H., 133
Ogden, S., 34
Olbricht, T., 88
Olson, D. T., 100
Otto, R., 37

Palmer, G. B., 79
Pannenberg, W., xii, 47, 269
Parris, D., xii, 153, 155
Parry, R., 234
Paton, W. R., 155
Patterson, S. J., 120
Pauck, W., 187

289

INDEX OF MODERN AUTHORS

Pelikan, J., 238
Pellauer, D., 238
Percy, M., 285
Petersen, N. R., 54
Pilch, J. J., 156, 167
Placher, W. C., 109
Plummer, A., 176
Popkes, E. E., 142, 145
Popper, K., 196
Porter, S. E., xiv, 6, 11, 61, 235, 237-39, 249, 250, 261, 267
Price, H. H., 52, 67

Radner, E., 220, 228-32
Ratzinger, J., 231
Richardson, A., 11
Richardson, C. C., 253
Richardson, N., 56, 60
Richmond, J., 188
Ricoeur, P., 20, 32, 148-51, 161, 238
Ringe, S. H., 134
Robbins, V. K., 74
Robertson, A., 176
Robinson, H. W., 189
Robinson, J. A. T., 124
Robinson, J. C., 235, 237, 238, 250, 261, 267
Robinson, J. M., 33, 144
Rogerson, J., 2, 11
Römer, T., 100
Rorty, R., 249, 261
Rosenmüller, E. F. C., 24
Rosner, B. S., 10, 99
Rowe, C. K., 65, 95, 106
Ruether, R. R., 252
Russell, N., 194

Sakenfeld, K. D., 11
Sampley, J. P., 69
Sanders, E. P., 65
Sanders, J. A., 61
Santer, M., 8, 270
Sarot, M., 10
Satterthwaite, P., 9
Schaff, P., 253

Schleiermacher, F. D. E., xi, 11, 32, 35, 37, 51, 188
Schmithals, W., 40
Schnackenburg, R., 124
Schneemelcher, W., 144
Schopenhauer, A., 195, 196
Schrage, W., 177-79, 185, 194
Schröter, J., 138
Schulz, S., 42
Scott, I. W., 63
Scott, J. M. C., 134
Searle, J. R., 154, 155, 239
Seitz, C. R., 112, 262
Sell, A., 11
Sellin, G., 183, 186
Sharifan, F., 79, 80
Sharpe, E. J., 75
Sherwood, S. K., 104
Shuckburgh, E., 160
Skinner, D. J., 181
Smend, R., 109
Smith, N. K., 194
Smyth, H. W., 158
Sperber, D., 238
Stander, H. F., 113
Stanley, C. D., 61
Stanton, G. N., 11
Steen, G., 170
Steinmetz, D., 92
Stendahl, K., 56
Stenning, J. F., 181
Stephens, W. P., 10
Stott, D. W., 215
Stout, J., 249, 261
Stuhlmacher, P., 184
Suggs, M. J., 135
Swain, S., 71, 73

Thatcher, T., 122-24, 134
Thielman, F., 62
Thiselton, A. C., ix-xiii, xv, 1-12, 15, 33-36, 38-41, 43, 46-48, 50-52, 60, 65, 67-69, 76, 81, 90-94, 98, 102, 107, 148, 175, 176, 183, 184, 203-5, 208, 211, 212, 214, 217, 235-38, 245, 250, 261, 268-74, 280-85

Index of Modern Authors

Thomas, J., 250
Thomson, J. B., xiv, 269, 283
Tillich, P., 9
Torrance, J., 2
Treier, D. J., 91, 236-38, 244, 248-51, 254, 256, 258-60, 262, 264-66
Tuckett, C. M., 64, 122
Turner, M., 9, 150-53, 157, 164, 171, 234, 242

Uro, R., 120, 125, 143, 145

Vanhoozer, K. J., 11, 228, 234, 235, 239, 245, 257, 261
Vermeylen, J., 24
Via, D. O., 262

Wagner, J. R., 62, 65
Walhout, C., 2, 6
Walker, W., 253
Wallace, M. I., 238
Walters, S. D., 113
Wansbrough, H., 122
Watson, D., 88
Watson, F., 62, 63, 95-97, 101, 228, 234, 237, 244, 245, 262
Webster, J. B., 190, 239
Weinsheimer, J., 52, 94, 238
Weiß, J., 185-87, 192
Wendland, H.-D., 183
Wenham, J., 1
Wesley, J., 251, 257
West, C. C., 215
Westermann, C., 24, 181
White, H., 242, 248

White, J. L., 83
White, V., 269
Whitehouse, O. C., 19
Whybray, R. N., 181, 182, 189
Wilckens, U., 188, 194
Wilk, F., 62
Wilken, R. L., 112, 113, 115
Willett, M. E., 134
Williams, C. H., 134
Williams, M. A., 145
Williams, R., 221
Willis, W., 186, 187
Wilson, D., 238
Wink, W., 131
Witherington, B., 54, 66, 67, 85, 134
Wittgenstein, L., ix, 2, 6, 9, 32, 33, 53, 196, 236, 270
Wolterstorff, N., 10, 171, 239
Woodbridge, J. D., 262
Wrede, W., 40
Wright, D. F., 9
Wright, E. G., 189
Wright, N. T., 54, 61, 62
Wyrick, J. D., 15

Yeago, D. S., 237, 238
Yeo, K.-K., 69
Yoder, J. H., 276
Young, F., 107, 108

Zeller, D., 193
Ziemke, T., 80
Zimmermann, J., 239
Zöller, G., 195

Index of Ancient Sources

OLD TESTAMENT		1	100	32:18	104
		5:11-31	113	34	103
Genesis		10:5-11	105		
1:26-27	142	11	99, 101	Joshua	
2:7	142	11:4	99	5:12	103
12:1-3	230	11:6	99		
12:2	61	11:34	99	1 Samuel	
12:3	65	14:4	103	8	229
17:2	61	16:24	103	8:10	230
22:16	61	20:1	103	12:16-25	230
22:18	65	20:2	103, 104	14:27	24
34	59	20:11	104	14:29	24
		20:12	104		
Exodus		20:24-29	103	1 Kings	
3:14	134	21:3-4	105	3:7	20
15:26	164	21:4	105	8:50	20
17:1	104	21:4-7	99	18–19	59
17:6	104	21:16	104		
20:1-3	71	25:1	99	1 Chronicles	
20:32	182	25:7-13	59	28:12	182
23:21	138	25:11	59		
31:3	182	26	100	Job	
32:6	98, 99			6:15	20
35:31	182	Deuteronomy		11:11-20	167
		13:1-5	169	11:14-15	167
Leviticus		18:9-22	169	12:11	181, 182
19:2	71	21:22-23	57	13:3-4	166
26:16	165	28:22	165	13:7	167
		32	104	13:9	167
Numbers		32:4	104	28:12-28	134
1–10	101, 102	32:15	104	33:16	181

292

34:3	181, 182	41:22	182	Jeremiah	
41:3	179	42:1-4	22	2:23	20
		42:18-25	22	3	229
Psalms		43:10	134	3:6	20
78	99	43:25	134	3:7	20
106	99, 229	45:18-19	134	3:8	20
143:10	182	46:4	134	3:10	20
		47:3	18	3:11	20
Proverbs		49:8	18	3:12	20
3:17	134	51:12	134	3:15-18	230
3:18	134	52:6	134	3:21	20
3:19	133	54:14	24	3:22	20
8	134	55–66	15, 17, 20, 22	3:25	20
8:7	134	56–66	22, 23, 28, 29, 31	5:11	20
8:23	133	56	22	5:22	20
8:27	133	56:1	17	5:25	20
8:30	133	56:9-11	30	8:14	20
8:32	134	56:9–57:13	30	9:2	20
8:34-35	134	56:9–59:8	22	9:5	20
8:35	133, 134	57	30	11:10	20
9:5	134	57:15	17	12:1	20
		58:1	19, 20	12:6	20
Isaiah		58:2	17	14:7	20
1–12	22	59:4	17	17:9	193
2:1-4	230	59:9	17	28:16-17	27
6:10	230	59:12a	20	34:18	20
7:14	228	59:14	17		
9:1	24	59:16	17	Ezekiel	
10:7	182	59:17	17	14:13	20
10:12	182	60–62	27	20:27	20
13–23	22	60	22, 27, 28	39:21-29	230
28:9	230	60:1	24	40–48	27
29:9-13	230	60:1-3	23		
30:19-26	28	60:1–62:12	22	Daniel	
38:21	164	60:4-22	25	2	180
40–55	22, 23, 27, 29	61	169		
40	181	61:2	18, 19, 170	Hosea	
40:1-8	188	61:10	17	9:7	19
40:12	177, 181	62:1	17		
40:13	175-77, 179, 180, 182, 185	63:1	17	Joel	
		63:4	18	2:32 [MT 3:5]	177
40:14	185	65:1–66:17	22		
40:15	185	66:22-23	15	Amos	
40:16	185	66:22-24	15	5:18-20	18
41:4	134	66:24	15		
41:8-10	22				

INDEX OF ANCIENT SOURCES

Micah		9:9	133	6:19-20	126
5:1-3 [ET 2-4]	28	9:10	134	6:22-23	136
		9:14-17	180	6:25-30	126
		9:17-18	134, 177	7:3-5	126, 129
OLD TESTAMENT		9:18	177	7:6	127, 129
APOCRYPHA				7:7	124, 130
				7:7-8	127
Baruch		OLD TESTAMENT		7:16	126
3:12	134	PSEUDEPIGRAPHA		8:10	121
3:14-15	134			8:11	213
3:29	134	*1 Enoch*		8:17	141
3:37	134	90	61	8:20	127
4:2	133	93:11-14	177	9:37-38	126
				10:6	123
Judith		*4 Ezra*		10:16	126
9:2-4	59	3	61	10:17	124
				10:21-22	124
1 Maccabees		*Jubilees*		10:24	124
2:26	59	2:23	61	10:24-25	123
2:54	59	30:18	59	10:26	126
2:58	59			10:27	126, 136
		Liber Antiquitatum		10:34	126
4 Maccabees		*Biblicarum*		10:35-36	126
18:12	59	20:8	103	10:37-38	126, 129
				10:40	124
Sirach		*Testament of Levi*		11:5	136
6:26	134	6:3	59	11:7-8	127
15:3	134			11:19	135
24	134	*Testament of Reuben*		11:25-27	135
24:8	134	1–2	73	11:27	123
24:17	134			11:27-30	135
24:19	134			12:29	126
24:21	134	NEW TESTAMENT		12:31-32	126
24:30-31	134			12:34-35	126
36:19	182	Matthew		13:24-30	126
38:13-14	165	1:28-30	127	13:33	127
45:23-24	59	2:1-12	27	13:45-46	126
48:1-2	59	3:8	140	15:14	126
		4:16	136	15:24	123, 133
Tobit		5:3	126	15:28	121
2:9-10	166	5:6	126	17:20	121
		5:10-11	126	18	233
Wisdom		5:14	141	18:3	122, 129
6:22	134	5:14-16	136	18:12-13	123, 127, 129
7:26	134	5:15	126	22:2-10	126
8:13	134	5:16	24	23:25-26	127

Index of Ancient Sources

23:34	135	12:1-9	126	5:1-11	222
23:37-38	135	12:6	133	6:20	126
24:14	141	12:13-17	127	6:22	126
24:43	126	12:14b	136	6:39	126
25:31-46	215	12:24	123	6:40	124
25:46	122	12:28	124	6:41-42	126, 129
		12:28-31	124	6:44-45	126
Mark		12:32	136	7:9	121
1:4	140	13:9	124	7:22	136
2:5	121	13:11	123	7:24-25	127
2:10	126	13:12-13	124	7:35	135
2:19-20	123, 129	13:13	124	7:36-50	222
2:21	126	14:9	141	7:50	121
2:22	126	14:22	123	8:16	126, 136
3	132	14:22-25	78	8:17	126
3:27	126	14:27	124	8:19-21	127
3:28-30	126	14:58	126, 129	9:58	127
3:31-35	127	14:61	131	10:2	126
3:35	124	15:29	129	10:16	124, 133
4:3-8	126, 129	15:32	131	10:21-22	135
4:9	126	21:10	127	10:22	123
4:11-12	29			11:9	124, 130
4:19	141	**Luke**		11:9-10	127
4:21	126	1:2	135	11:14-26	222
4:22	126	1:26-38	173	11:21-22	126
4:25	126	1:46-55	173	11:27	222
4:29	126	2:29-32	173	11:27-28	127
4:30-32	126, 129	3:2-6	173	11:33	126
4:40	121	3:8	140	11:33-35	136
5:25-26	166	3:16-17	173	11:34-35	222
5:34	121	3:22	173	11:39-40	127
6	172	3:23	173	11:52	126
6:4	126, 129	4:3	173	12:3	126, 136
6:21	126	4:9	173	12:10	126
6:34	123	4:16-21	169	12:16-21	126
6:50	123, 135	4:16-30	169	12:22	126
7:15	126	4:18	133	12:27-30	126
8:27-30	130	4:21	168, 170	12:32	123
8:29	131, 137	4:22	168, 169	12:33	126
8:35	123	4:23	154, 158, 164, 168, 169, 174	12:39	126
9:37	133			12:51	126
10:15	129	4:23a	169	12:52-53	126
10:30	122	4:23b	169	13:20-21	127
10:31	126	4:23-24	126, 129	14:16-24	126
10:52	121	4:24-27	168, 169	14:26	209
11:23-24	124	4:28-30	169	14:26-27	126, 129

295

INDEX OF ANCIENT SOURCES

15:4-7	123, 127, 129	3:5	122, 123	5:38	132
17:5	121	3:11	123	5:39	122
17:6	121	3:13	133, 134	5:40	140
17:19	121	3:15	139, 140	5:46	130
18:7-8	18	3:15-16	122	6:20	123, 135
18:8	121	3:16	132, 139, 140	6:26-58	123
21:22	19	3:16-17	134	6:27	122, 139
22:32	121	3:17	132, 140	6:29	122, 132, 140
22:56	136	3:18	122, 132	6:30-58	134
23:13	126	3:19	140	6:33	133, 141, 149
23:29	127	3:19-21	136	6:35	121, 122, 139
24:25-26	76	3:21	122	6:37	140
		3:26	131	6:38	132
John		3:28	131	6:38-42	133
1:1	132	3:29	123, 124, 129	6:39	132
1:1-18	133	3:30	131	6:40	122, 139, 140
1:3	133	3:31	131	6:41	121, 130
1:4	133, 136	3:34	132	6:44	132, 140
1:4-9	136	3:35	132	6:44-45	140
1:5	133	3:36	122, 139, 140	6:47	122, 139, 140
1:6-7	131	4:10	134, 139	6:48	121, 139
1:6-8	131	4:14	122, 134, 139	6:50-51	133
1:7	140	4:25	131	6:51	121, 140, 141
1:7-8	131	4:25-26	130, 131	6:53	139, 140
1:9	140	4:31-38	124	6:54	122, 139
1:11	134	4:34	132	6:57	132
1:14	132, 134, 136	4:36	122	6:58	133
1:15	131	4:39	122	6:62	133
1:17	136	4:42	140	6:65	140
1:18	132, 134	4:44	129	6:68	122
1:19	131	4:53	140	6:69	130
1:20	131	5:18	138	7	132
1:29	141	5:19	123, 132	7:16	132
1:30	131	5:19-21	124	7:18	132
1:31	131	5:19-30	123	7:21	132
1:32	131	5:20	221	7:25-36	134
1:34	131, 132	5:22	132	7:26	132
1:41	131	5:23	132	7:26-27	132
1:49	130, 132	5:24	122, 123, 132, 140	7:29	132
1:51	123	5:25	123	7:31	132, 140
2:11	122, 140	5:26	132	7:41-42	132
2:19	129	5:27	132	8:12	121, 130, 136, 141
2:23	140	5:30	132	8:23	141
2:28	131	5:33-34	131	8:24	121
3:3	123	5:36	131, 132	8:28	121
3:3-15	122	5:37	132	8:31-32	136

Index of Ancient Sources

8:35	124	13:16	124	20:31	131, 132
8:42	132	13:19	121	21:1-19	221
8:51-52	139	13:20	124, 132	22:1-3	129
8:58	130	13:34-35	124	22:4-7	130
9	136	14:6	121, 136, 139, 221		
9:4	132	14:9	138	**Acts**	
9:5	141	14:11-12	140	2:41	135
9:22	132	14:16-17	123	4:4	135
10:1-5	124	14:17	136	4:29	135
10:1-18	129	14:24	132	4:31	135
10:7	121	14:30	140	9:1	59
10:9	121	15:1	121	9:1-28	55
10:10	139	15:5	121	9:15	60
10:11	121	15:14-15	124	13:24	140
10:14	121	15:16	124	19:4	140
10:24	132	15:18-19	140	22:1-21	55
10:28	122	15:18-21	124	26:4-23	55
10:30	138	15:21	132		
10:36	132	15:26	136	**Romans**	
10:38	140	15:26-27	123	1–8	49
10:41-42	140	16:1-4	124	1:2	61
11:2	140	16:4-15	123	1:3-4	55
11:3	221	16:5	132	1:6	56
11:9-10	124	16:11	140	1:18-32	54
11:25	121, 139	16:12-15	136	1:24-32	82
11:25-26	140	16:12-24	130	3:21	61
11:27	132	16:13	136	3:21-26	54
11:42	132	16:21	124	3:31	61
11:45	140	16:23-24	124	4:3	62
12:11	140	16:27	221	4:17	190
12:20-26	124	16:32	124	4:25	54
12:24	124	16:33	140	5:6-11	88
12:25	122	17	226	6:1-4	77
12:31	140	17:2-3	122	6:3-4	77
12:34	132	17:3	132, 136, 139	6:4	56
12:42	140	17:8	132	6:5	54
12:44	132	17:11	138	8:3	188
12:45	132	17:14	140	8:28	56
12:46	141	17:16	141	8:30	56
12:47	140	17:18	132	9–11	49, 178, 230, 233
12:49	132	17:20-26	225	9:1-5	88
12:50	122	17:21	225	9:5	53
13–17	124	17:23	132, 225	9:17	62
13:1-13	123	18:36	141	9:24	56
13:1-20	124	18:37	136	10:4	61, 62
13:13-16	123	20:21	132	10:8	190

297

INDEX OF ANCIENT SOURCES

10:11	62	3:18	55	10:16-22	192
10:13	177	4:4	54	10:17	83
11:11	230	5–14	82	10:21	54
11:25-27	179	5–7	82, 83	11:12-16	50
11:33	179	5–6	83	11:23-26	77
11:33-36	178, 179	5:1	83	11:24	83
11:34	175, 176, 184	5:3	83	11:27	83
12:2	74	5:7	83	12:12	83, 190
		5:9	83	12:12-31	192
1 Corinthians		5:10	83	12:13	83, 189
1–4	81	5:11	83	12:14	83
1:2	56	5:11-21	55	12:15	83
1:4-5	192	6:9	83	12:16	83
1:5	99	6:10	83	12:17	83
1:9	56	6:13	83	12:18	83
1:10	186	6:15	83	12:19	83
1:10-11	191	6:16	83	12:20	83
1:10-17	191	6:18	83	12:20-21	82
1:17	194	6:20	83	12:22	83
1:18	189, 190	7:2	83	12:23	83
1:18-31	177	7:4	83	12:24	83
1:19	179	7:14	83	12:25	83
1:20	55	7:15	56	12:27	83
1:21-23	190	7:34	83	13:1	83
1:23	57	8–14	82, 83	13:2	83
1:23-24	194	8–10	98	13:3	83
1:24	56	8:1	83	13:4	83
1:30	191, 194	8:1–11:1	209	13:4-8	207
2:2	54, 57, 194	8:6	53, 63	13:5	208
2:6	177	9:1	55, 56	13:13	203
2:6-8	55	9:27	83	14:1	83
2:6-16	177-80, 188, 192	10	97, 99, 100	14:14	183
2:7	177	10:1	99	15	45, 55, 81, 82
2:8	56	10:1-4	99, 105	15:3	54, 64
2:10	178	10:1-11	98	15:3-4	62, 64
2:10-12	191	10:1-13	100	15:3-5	76
2:11	54	10:2-13	177	15:8-9	55
2:12	178, 191	10:4	102, 103	15:8-10	55
2:13-15	180	10:6	99, 102	15:20-58	192
2:14	177, 180	10:6-11	99	15:45	61
2:16	xii, 175, 176, 183, 186, 187, 191, 194, 197	10:7-10	102	16:22	74
		10:8	83		
		10:9	102	**2 Corinthians**	
2:17-18	177	10:11	99, 102	5:16	63
3	97	10:14	100	5:17	55
3:8	83	10:16	83	10:5	221

Index of Ancient Sources

Galatians		2:1-11	187	Revelation	
1:13-14	59	2:5-11	64	21	27
1:13-17	55	2:6-11	237, 238		
1:15	56, 63	2:7	63		
1:15-16	55-57	2:11	56	NEW TESTAMENT	
3:6-9	95	3:4-11	55	APOCRYPHA	
3:7-9	65	3:6	59		
3:8	62	3:15	224	Acts of Thomas	
3:13	57			47	138
3:14a	95	Colossians		133	138
3:22	62	3–4	82		
4	112			Gospel of Thomas	
4:4	54	1 Thessalonians		2	127, 130, 146
5	82	2:1-16	12	3:1-3	128
5:13	56	4	82	3:3-4	141
6:15	55	4:7	56	3:5	142
				4:1-3	126
Ephesians		1 Timothy		4:2-3	126
1–3	84, 85	5:23	164	4:2-4	144
1:3-14	84			5	127, 146
1:10	232	Hebrews		6:3	127
1:15-23	84	1:1-2	110	6:4-5	126
2	232	2:22	142	7:2	127
2:1-10	84			8:1-3	128
2:11-22	84	1 Peter		8:4	126
2:16	86	1–2a	86	9	128, 129
3:1-13	84	1:1-2	86	9:1-5	126
3:3	232	1:1-12	87	10	28, 127
3:9-10	232	1:3	71	11:3-4	143
3:14-21	84	1:3-12	86	13	138
3:17	194	1:10-11	76	14:4	128
4–6	84	1:12–2:3	87	14:5	126
4:2-16	84	1:13	74, 86	15	138
4:2–6:9	85	1:14–2:3	71, 86	16	127
4:13	194	2b–5	86	16:1-2	126
4:25–5:2	84	2:4-10	86, 87	16:3	126
5	112	2:11-12	86, 87	16:4	144
5:3-18	84	2:13–3:7	87	17	127
5:18–6:9	85	3:8–4:11	87	18	141
5:31-32	112	3:18	78	19:1	141
6:10-17	85	3:18-22	78	20	128
6:18-20	85	3:22	78	20:1-4	126, 129
		4:1-6	87	21	127
Philippians		4:1-11	87	21:1-4	144
1:6	224	4:7-11	87	21:5	126, 127
1:12	224	4:12–5:11	87	21:10	126

299

21:11	126	64:1-11	126, 127	105	144
22:4-7	143	65:1-7	126	106:1	143
23:2	124, 144	65:8	126	107:1-3	127, 129
24:3	127	66	126	108	137
26:1-2	126, 129	67	141	109:1-3	128
28	142	68	127	111	137
29	142	68:1	126, 127	111:2-3	141
30:3-4	137	69	127	112	142
31	129	69:2	126, 127	113:1-4	128
31:1-2	126	70	142	114	143
32	128	71	126, 129		
33:1	126, 127	72:1-3	128		
33:2-3	126, 127	73	126, 127	**EARLY CHRISTIAN**	
34	126, 127	75	144	**AND MEDIEVAL**	
35:1-2	126	76	146	**LITERATURE**	
36:1-3	126, 127	76:1-2	126, 128		
37	137, 144	76:3	126, 127	Augustine	
39	146	77	137	*Confessions*	
39:1-2	126, 127	78:1-3	127	12.31	229
39:3	126, 128	79:1	127	*De Doctrina*	
40:1-2	128	79:1-3	127, 128	1.26	205
41	128	80	142	1.36	204, 206, 207
41:1-2	126	82	137	1.37	207
43	127	83	141, 142		
44	127	84	142	*2 Clement*	
45:1-4	126, 127	85	142	12:2	143
46:1-2	127	86	137, 146	16	89
47:3-4	126	86:1-2	127		
47:5	126	87–89	127	Clement of Alexandria	
47:54	127	87	142	*Stromateis*	
49	141	89:1-2	127	3.13.92	143
50	142	90:1-2	127, 128		
52	137	91:1-2	127	Eusebius	
52:1	137	92	146	*Praeparatio Evangelica*	
54	126	92:1-2	127	13.12.10	133
55:1-2	126, 127, 129	93:1-2	127-29		
56	142	94:1-2	127	Gregory Nazianzen	
57:1-4	126, 128	95	127	*Orations*	
59	137	95:1-2	128	10.13	163
61	127	96:1-2	127		
61:1	127	96:3	126	John Chrysostom	
61:2-5	138	99:1-3	127	*Homilies on Matthew*	
61:3	127	100:1-4	127	16.5	163
62:2	128	101:1	126, 128		
63:1-3	126, 128	103	127		
63:4	126	104:2	129		

Index of Ancient Sources

Origen
On First Principles
4.2.9 — 115

Theodoret of Cyrrhus
Commentaire sur Isaïa
3.268-69 — 19

Thomas Aquinas
Summa Theologica
1a,1,10 — 229

HELLENISTIC JEWISH AUTHORS

Josephus
Jewish Wars
1:656-58 — 165

RABBINIC LITERATURE

Babylonian Talmud
b. Berakot.
34a — 166
34b — 165

b. Gittin.
67b — 165
70a — 165

70b — 165

b. Nedarim.
41a — 165

b. Šabbat.
66b — 165

Mishna
Ta'anit
3:8 — 166

Targum
Targum Neofiti
21:1 — 103

Targum of Isaiah
40:13 — 177

DEAD SEA SCROLLS

11QT^a
64:15-20 — 57

GRECO-ROMAN LITERATURE

Cicero
Letters to His Friends
4.5.5 — 160

Hippocrates
The Physician
142.2 — 156

Martial
Epigrams
1.47 — 155

Plato
Charmides
164D3-165A7 — 193

Protagoras
343A1-B3 — 193

Plutarch
Life of Sertorius
1.5 — 72
1.6 — 72
3.3 — 72
10.4 — 73
22.3 — 72
23.1 — 72
27.3 — 72

QURAN

Surah
9:114 — 209
26:69-89 — 209
26:102 — 209

www.ingramcontent.com/pod-product-compliance
Lightning Source LLC
Chambersburg PA
CBHW021847300426
44115CB00005B/41